SO-ABK-821

JAMES E. MILLER, JR.
Professor of English, University of Chicago. Fulbright Lecturer in Naples and
Rome, 1958–59, and in Kyoto, Japan, 1968. President of the National Council of
Teachers of English, 1970. Awarded a Guggenheim fellowship, 1969–70. Recent
books: *Quests Surd and Absurd: Essays in American Literature; Theory of Fiction:
Henry James;* and *Word, Self, Reality: The Rhetoric of Imagination.*

MYRTLE J. JONES
Assistant Professor of English, Floyd Junior College, Rome, Georgia. John Hay
Fellow, Colorado College, 1964. Formerly teacher of English, East Rome High
School.

HELEN McDONNELL
Chairman, English Department, Ocean Township High School, Oakhurst, New
Jersey. Chairman, Committee on Comparative and World Literature, National
Council of Teachers of English. Reviewer of books in English and English education
for *Scholastic Teacher* and contributor of articles on education to magazines and
books.

THREE CENTURIES
OF ENGLISH LITERATURE
1625 / 1900

SCOTT, FORESMAN AND COMPANY • Glenview, Illinois
Dallas, Tex. • Oakland, N.J. • Palo Alto, Cal. • Tucker, Ga. • Brighton, England

i

This volume consists of chapters four through eight of
England in Literature, a part of the America Reads
Series. The first three chapters are also available in
a softbound edition entitled *The Early Development of*
English Literature.

Cover: "Woodpecker" tapestry by
William Morris, made in 1885–87.
William Morris Gallery and Brangwyn
Gift, London.

ISBN: 0-673-10217-3

Copyright © 1976, 1973
Scott, Foresman and Company.
All Rights Reserved.
Printed in the United States of America.

2345678910-RRC-858483828180797877

CONTENTS

chapter four
THE SEVENTEENTH CENTURY
PAGE 234

chapter five

THE EIGHTEENTH CENTURY

PAGE 276

THE ROMANTICS

PAGE 340

chapter seven
THE VICTORIANS
PAGE 386

chapter eight
ALICE IN WONDERLAND
PAGE 439

ALICE IN WONDERLAND by Lewis Carroll

SPECIAL FEATURES AND SHORT ARTICLES

THREE

CENTURIES

OF

ENGLISH

LITERATURE

(OVERLEAF) MAP CIRCA 1646. BAYTON-WILLIAMS, 18 LOWNDES STREET, BELGRAVIA, LONDON, S.W. 1.

THE
Suderland
KINGDOME
Assyn Shire

OF THE SCOTS

Skye

Loquabria

Mula
Breadalbayn Strathern
Lorna
Knapdail Argadi
Lennos

MARE
Ila Cantyre
Arran
KINGDOM OF THE PICTS
Cuningham

Coyl
Nidisdale

Carict

The Mulle of Canty

HIBER-

HIBER-

MAN

NIÆ

NJCVM;

PARS,

THE

Vulgo

Dublin

PART OF

IRISH

Waterford

IRELAND.

SEA.

WALES.

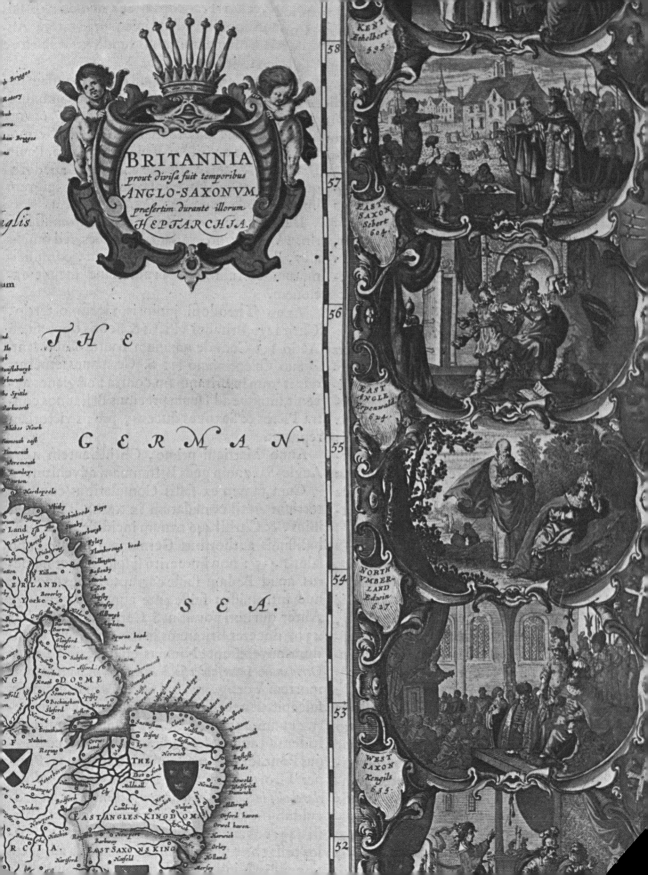

I. THE METAPHYSICAL POETS

Dr. Samuel Johnson, the great eighteenth-century literary figure, following a suggestion by John Dryden, labeled a school of poets of the early seventeenth century the *metaphysical* poets, because of their emphasis on the intellect or wit as against feeling and emotion. (See the article on page 271.) Johnson was not alone in believing these poets defective. But contemporary poets, particularly T. S. Eliot, have praised and imitated the metaphysical poets, and their reputations (especially that of John Donne) are much higher now than they were before the twentieth century.

Metaphysical poetry has come to be defined by its style rather than its content. The emphasis is on paradox: as Dr. Johnson put it, "The most heterogeneous ideas are yoked by violence together." The method of development is frequently the ingenious, often witty, elaboration of a *conceit* (a metaphor or analogy carried to great lengths). Other characteristics are the use of puns, the use of surprising comparisons, and the use of learned or scientific allusions. The total effect of a metaphysical poem at its best is to startle the reader into seeing and knowing what he has not *really* noticed or thought about before.

John Donne   1572 / 1631

SONG

Go and catch a falling star,
　Get with child a mandrake root,[1]
Tell me where all past years are,
　Or who cleft the devil's foot;
5　Teach me to hear mermaids singing,
Or to keep off envy's stinging,
　　And find
　　What wind
Serves to advance an honest mind.

10　If thou be'st born to strange sights,
　Things invisible to see,
Ride ten thousand days and nights,
　Till Age snow white hairs on thee;
Thou, when thou return'st, will tell me
15　All strange wonders that befell thee,
　　And swear
　　No where
Lives a woman true, and fair.

If thou find'st one, let me know;
20　Such a pilgrimage were sweet.
Yet do not; I would not go,
　Though at next door we might meet.
Though she were true, when you met her,
And last, till you write your letter,
25　　Yet she
　　Will be
False, ere I come, to two or three.

---

1. *Get . . . mandrake root.* Mandrake is a European herb with a forked root, fancied to resemble the figure of a man. Recognizing the resemblance but the impossibility of a plant's reproducing as humans do, Donne includes this in his catalogue of impossibilities.

**OF CRITICAL
INTEREST**

ON DONNE'S POETRY

by Samuel T. Coleridge

With Donne, whose muse on dromedary trots,
Wreathe from pokers into truelove knots;
Rhyme's sturdy cripple, fancy's maze and clue,
Wit's forge and fire-blast, meaning's press and screw.

1836

THE BAIT

Come live with me, and be my love,
And we will some new pleasures prove
Of golden sands, and crystal brooks,
With silken lines, and silver hooks.

5   There will the river whispering run
Warmed by thy eyes, more than the sun.
And there th' enamoured fish will stay,
Begging themselves they may betray.

When thou wilt swim in that live bath,
10 Each fish, which every channel hath,
Will amorously to thee swim,
Gladder to catch thee, than thou him.

If thou, to be so seen, be'st loath,
By sun, or moon, thou darkenest both,
15 And if myself have leave to see,
I need not their light, having thee.

Let others freeze with angling reeds,
And cut their legs, with shells and weeds,
Or treacherously poor fish beset,
20 With strangling snare, or windowy net:

Let coarse bold hands, from slimy nest
The bedded fish in banks out-wrest,
Or curious traitors, sleave silk flies
Bewitch poor fishes' wandering eyes.

25 For thee, thou need'st no such deceit,
For thou thyself art thine own bait;
That fish, that is not catched thereby,
Alas, is wiser far than I.

THE INDIFFERENT

I can love both fair and brown,
Her whom abundance melts, and her whom want
    betrays,
Her who loves loneness best, and her who masks and
    plays,[1]
Her whom the country formed, and whom the town,
5   Her who believes, and her who tries,
Her who still weeps with spongy eyes,
And her who is dry cork, and never cries;
I can love her, and her, and you, and you,
I can love any, so she be not true.

10 Will no other vice content you?
Will it not serve your turn to do as did your mothers?
Or have you all old vices spent, and now would find
        out others?
Or doth a fear that men are true torment you?
O we are not, be not you so;
15 Let me, and do you, twenty know.
Rob me, but bind me not, and let me go.
Must I, who came to travail[2] thorough[3] you
Grow your fixed subject, because you are true?

Venus heard me sigh this song,
20 And by love's sweetest part, variety, she swore
She heard not this till now; and that it should be so
        no more.
She went, examined, and returned ere long,
And said, "Alas, some two or three
Poor heretics in love there be,
25 Which think to 'stablish dangerous constancy.
But I have told them, 'Since you will be true,
You shall be true to them who are false to you.'"

---

1. *masks and plays*, i.e., loves social pleasures.
2. *travail.* In the 17th century our words *travel* and *travail* ("pain
and trouble; labor") were spelled the same; either spelling was
used for either meaning.
3. *thorough*, through.

THE CANONIZATION[1]

For God's sake, hold your tongue, and let me love,
   Or chide my palsy, or my gout,
My five gray hairs, or ruined fortune flout,
   With wealth your state, your mind with arts
      improve,
5   Take you a course,[2] get you a place,[3]
     Observe his Honor, or his Grace,[4]
Or the King's real, or his stampèd face[5]
   Contèmplate; what you will, approve,[6]
     So you will let me love.

10 Alas, alas, who's injured by my love?
   What merchant's ships have my sighs drowned?
Who says my tears have overflowed his ground?
   When did my colds a forward spring remove?[7]
     When did the heats which my veins fill
15   Add one more to the plaguy bill?[8]
Soldiers find wars, and lawyers find out still
   Litigious men, which quarrels move,
    Though she and I do love.

Call us what you will, we are made such by love;
20   Call her one, me another fly,
We are tapers too, and at our own cost die,[9]
   And we in us find the eagle and the dove,[10]
     The phoenix riddle[11] hath more wit[12]
     By us; we two being one, are it.
25 So to one neutral thing both sexes fit.
   We die and rise the same, and prove
    Mysterious by this love.[13]

We can die by it, if not live by love,
   And if unfit for tombs and hearse
30 Our legend be, it will be fit for verse;
   And if no piece of chronicle we prove,
     We'll build in sonnets pretty rooms;
     As well a well-wrought urn becomes
The greatest ashes, as half-acre tombs,
35   And by these hymns, all shall approve
    Us canonized for love:

And thus invoke us; "You whom reverend love
   Made one another's hermitage;[14]
You, to whom love was peace, that now is rage;
40   Who did the whole world's soul contract, and
     drove
     Into the glasses of your eyes
     (So made such mirrors and such spies,
That they did all to you epitomize)
    Countries, towns, courts: beg from above
45   A pattern of your love!"[15]

---

1. *Canonization,* declaring a deceased person to be a saint; also, to make something divine.
2. *Take you a course,* follow some way of advancing yourself.
3. *place,* position at Court.
4. *Observe . . . Grace,* cultivate some lord or bishop.
5. *stampèd face,* the face of the king stamped on coins.
6. *approve,* try out.
7. *a forward spring remove,* hold back an early spring.
8. *plaguy bill,* list of plague victims, published weekly.

9. *at our . . . die.* Dying was a widely-used metaphor for the consummation of physical love. The expression refers to the popular belief that each indulgence in sexual relations shortened one's life by a day.
10. *eagle . . . dove.* The eagle symbolized strength or the masculine quality; the dove, gentleness or the feminine element.
11. *phoenix riddle,* the mystery of the legendary bird which was said to burn itself to death every five hundred years and then rise again from its own ashes. It is used as a symbol both of immortality and of desire rising from its own exhaustion.
12. *hath more wit,* makes more sense.
13. *We die . . . this love.* Because physical consummation does not change or diminish our love, we are different from ordinary humans (as saints are).
14. *hermitage,* refuge from the world.
15. *beg . . . love.* The poet and his mistress, having died and become saints, are implored by the world to beg from Heaven a pattern of their love, so that later lovers may model their loves on this one.

A VALEDICTION: FORBIDDING MOURNING

As virtuous men pass mildly away,
   And whisper to their souls to go,
Whilst some of their sad friends do say
   The breath goes now, and some say, No:

5 So let us melt, and make no noise,
   No tear-floods, nor sigh-tempests move,
'Twere profanation of our joys
   To tell the laity our love.

Moving of th' earth brings harms and fears,
10   Men reckon what it did and meant,
But trepidation of the spheres,
   Though greater far, is innocent.[1]

Dull sublunary[2] lovers' love
   (Whose soul is sense) cannot admit
15 Absence, because it doth remove
   Those things which elemented[3] it.

But we by a love so much refined
   That our selves know not what it is,
Inter-assurèd of the mind,
20   Care less, eyes, lips, and hands to miss.

Our two souls therefore, which are one,
   Though I must go, endure not yet
A breach, but an expansion,
   Like gold to aery thinness beat.

25 If they be two, they are two so
   As stiff twin compasses[4] are two;
Thy soul, the fixed foot, makes no show
   To move, but doth, if th' other do.

And though it in the centre sit,
30   Yet when the other far doth roam,
It leans and hearkens after it,
   And grows erect, as that comes home.

Such wilt thou be to me, who must
   Like th' other foot, obliquely run;
35 Thy firmness makes my circle[5] just,
   And makes me end where I begun.

---

1. *trepidation . . . innocent*. Movements (trepidation) of the heavenly spheres, though greater than those of an earthquake, provoke no fears in (nor danger to) man.
2. *sublunary*, beneath the moon; i.e., earthly and subject to change.
3. *elemented*, composed.

4. *compasses*. The image is of the instrument used for describing a circle. One branch or leg of the compass is held steady, as a pivot, while the other leg is rotated to draw the circle.
5. *circle*. The circle was a symbol of perfection.

DISCUSSION

1. *"Song"*:
  (a) Why are so many images and orders crowded into the first stanza?
  (b) What is the state of mind of the speaker of the poem, and what do you think has happened to him?

2. *"The Indifferent"*:
  (a) What is startling about the attitude of the speaker in this poem?
  (b) What role does Venus play in the poem, and why?

  (c) Do you see any similarity between this poem and Shakespeare's Sonnet 130 (page 146)?

3. *"The Canonization"*:
  (a) Reconstruct the conversation that has led the speaker of the poem to say what he does.
  (b) Explain the title of the poem.

4. *"The Bait"*:
  (a) Compare this poem with the poem by Christopher Marlowe which

opens with the same line (page 143).
  (b) Explain line 26: "For thou thyself art thine own bait."

5. *"A Valediction: Forbidding Mourning"*:
  (a) How do the lovers of this poem differ from the "dull sublunary lovers" of stanza 4?
  (b) Explain the next-to-last line of the poem: "Thy firmness makes my circle just."

From HOLY SONNETS

6

This is my play's last scene; here heavens appoint
My pilgrimage's last mile; and my race
Idly yet quickly run, hath this last pace,
My span's last inch, my minute's latest point;
5 And gluttonous death will instantly unjoint
My body and my soul, and I shall sleep a space;
But my ever-waking part shall see that face
Whose fear already shakes my every joint;
Then as my soul to heaven, her first seat, takes
        flight,
10 And earth-born body in the earth shall dwell,
So fall my sins, that all may have their right,
To where they are bred, and would press me—
        to Hell.
Impute me righteous,[1] thus purged of evil,
For thus I leave the world, the flesh, and devil.

---

1. *Impute me righteous.* According to Christian doctrine, even after a man's soul has been purged (through repentance) of sins he himself has committed, he still is burdened with the original sin of Adam and has to be saved ("imputed righteous") by the merit of Christ.

10

Death, be not proud, though some have callèd thee
Mighty and dreadful, for thou art not so;
For those whom thou think'st thou dost overthrow
Die not, poor Death, nor yet canst thou kill me.
5 From rest and sleep, which but thy pictures be,
Much pleasure; then from thee much more must
        flow,
And soonest our best men with thee do go,
Rest of their bones, and soul's delivery.
Thou art slave to fate, chance, kings, and
        desperate men,
10 And dost with poison, war, and sickness dwell,
And poppy[1] or charms can make us sleep as well
And better than thy stroke; why swell'st[2] thou then?
One short sleep past, we wake eternally,
And death shall be no more; Death, thou shalt die.

---

1. *poppy,* the source of various narcotic drugs.
2. *swell'st,* puff up with pride.

7

At the round earth's imagined corners, blow
Your trumpets, angels; and arise, arise
From death, you numberless infinities
Of souls, and to your scattered bodies go;
5 All whom the flood did, and fire shall, o'erthrow,
All whom war, dearth, age, agues, tyrannies,
Despair, law, chance, hath slain, and you whose
        eyes
Shall behold God, and never taste death's woe.[1]
But let them sleep, Lord, and me mourn a space;
10 For, if above all these, my sins abound,
'Tis late to ask abundance of Thy grace
When we are there. Here on this lowly ground,
Teach me how to repent; for that's as good
As if Thou hadst sealed my pardon with Thy blood.

---

1. *and you . . . woe,* those still alive at the Last Judgment and the end of the world, who will be judged without having experienced death.

14

Batter my heart, three-personed God; for You
As yet but knock, breathe, shine, and seek to mend;
That I may rise and stand, o'erthrow me, and bend
Your force to break, blow, burn, and make me new.
5 I, like an usurped town, to another due,
Labour to admit You, but O, to no end;
Reason, Your viceroy in me, me should defend,
But is captived, and proves weak or untrue.
Yet dearly I love You, and would be lovèd fain,
10 But am betrothed unto Your enemy.
Divorce me, untie or break that knot again;
Take me to You, imprison me, for I,
Except You enthral me, never shall be free,
Nor ever chaste, except You ravish me.

MEDITATION 17

Nunc lento sonitu dicunt, morieris.
(Now this bell tolling softly for another, says to me,
Thou must die.)

PERCHANCE he for whom this bell tolls may be so ill as that he knows not it tolls for him; and perchance I may think myself so much better than I am, as that they who are about me and see my state may have caused it to toll for me, and I know not that. The church is catholic, universal, so are all her actions; all that she does belongs to all. When she baptizes a child, that action concerns me; for that child is thereby connected to that head which is my head too, and ingrafted into that body whereof I am a member.[1] And when she buries a man, that action concerns me: all mankind is of one author and is one volume; when one man dies, one chapter is not torn out of the book, but translated into a better language; and every chapter must be so translated. God employs several translators; some pieces are translated by age, some by sickness, some by war, some by justice; but God's hand is in every translation, and his hand shall bind up all our scattered leaves again for that library where every book shall lie open to one another. As therefore the bell that rings to a sermon calls not upon the preacher only, but upon the congregation to come, so this bell calls us all; but how much more me, who am brought so near the door by this sickness.

There was a contention as far as a suit[2] (in which piety and dignity, religion and estimation,[3] were mingled) which of the religious orders should ring to prayers first in the morning; and it was determined that they should ring first that rose earliest. If we understand aright the dignity of this bell that tolls for our evening prayer, we would be glad to make it ours by rising early, in that application, that it might be ours as well as his whose indeed it is. The bell doth toll for him that thinks it doth; and though it intermit again, yet from that minute that that occasion wrought upon him, he is united to God. Who casts not up his eye to the sun when it rises? but who takes off his eye from a comet when that breaks out? Who bends not his ear to any bell which upon any occasion rings? but who can remove it from that bell which is passing a piece of himself out of this world? No man is an island, entire of itself; every man is a piece of the continent, a part of the main. If a clod be washed away by the sea, Europe is the less, as well as if a promontory were, as well as if a manor of thy friend's or of thine own were. Any man's death diminishes me because I am involved in mankind, and therefore never send to know for whom the bell tolls; it tolls for thee. . . .

---

1. *head . . . member.* That is, the Christian church is the head of all men, as well as a body made up of its members.

2. *contention . . . suit,* a controversy that went as far as a lawsuit.
3. *estimation,* self-esteem.

DISCUSSION

1. *Holy Sonnet 6:*
Explain how the speaker "distributes" himself after death.

2. *Holy Sonnet 7:*
What is the reversal introduced in line 9, beginning with "But let them sleep . . ."?

3. *Holy Sonnet 10:*
(a) Is this sonnet somewhat like whistling in the dark, or is there some truth to the main argument?
(b) In what sense will death ever die?

4. *Holy Sonnet 14:*
Explain the striking paradoxes of the last two lines—enthrallment leading to freedom, ravishing to chastity.

5. *Meditation 17:*
Discuss the meaning and effectiveness of the two main metaphors: (a) man as a chapter in a book; (b) man as a piece of a continent.

TO HIS COY MISTRESS

by Andrew Marvell

Had we but world enough, and time,
This coyness, lady, were no crime.
We would sit down, and think which way
To walk, and pass our long love's day.
5 Thou by the Indian Ganges' side
Shouldst rubies find: I by the tide
Of Humber[1] would complain[2] I would
Love you ten years before the flood,[3]
And you should, if you please, refuse
10 Till the conversion of the Jews;[4]
My vegetable love should grow
Vaster than empires and more slow;
An hundred years should go to praise
Thine eyes, and on thy forehead gaze;
15 Two hundred to adore each breast,
But thirty thousand to the rest;
An age at least to every part,
And the last age should show your heart.
For, lady, you deserve this state;[5]
20 Nor would I love at lower rate.

But at my back I always hear
Time's wingèd chariot hurrying near;
And yonder all before us lie
Deserts of vast eternity.
25 Thy beauty shall no more be found,
Nor in thy marble vault shall sound
My echoing song; then worms shall try
That long preserved virginity;
And your quaint[6] honor turn to dust,
30 And into ashes all my lust:
The grave's a fine and private place,
But none, I think, do there embrace.

Now therefore, while the youthful hue
Sits on thy skin like morning dew,

35 And while thy willing soul transpires[7]
At every pore with instant fires,
Now let us sport us while we may,
And now, like amorous birds of prey,
Rather at once our time devour
40 Than languish in his slow-chapped[8] power,
Let us roll all our strength and all
Our sweetness up into one ball,
And tear our pleasures with rough strife
Thorough the iron gates of life:
45 Thus, though we cannot make our sun
Stand still, yet we will make him run.

---

7. *transpires*, breathes out.
8. *slow-chapped*, slow-jawed.

---

1. *Humber,* a river that flows through Marvell's home town of Hull.
2. *complain,* i.e., sing plaintive love songs.
3. *flood,* the Biblical flood.
4. *conversion of the Jews.* It was a popular belief that this would occur just before the Last Judgment and the end of the world.
5. *state,* dignity.
6. *quaint,* fastidious; out-of-fashion.

OF HUMAN INTEREST

Andrew Marvell

"He was of middling stature, pretty strong sett, roundish faced, cherry cheek't, hazell eie, browne haire. He was in his conversation very modest, and of very few words: and though he loved wine he would never drinke hard in company, and was wont to say that, he would not play the goodfellow in any man's company in whose hands he would not trust his life. He had not a generall acquaintance. . . .

"He kept bottles of wine at his lodgeing, and many times he would drinke liberally by himselfe to refresh his spirits, and exalt his Muse. . . .

"Obiit Londini, Aug. 18, 1678; and is buried in St. Giles church in-the-fields about the middle of the south aisle. Some suspect that he was poysoned by the Jesuits, but I cannot be positive."

From *Aubrey's Brief Lives* (1690), edited by Oliver Lawson Dick. Copyright 1949 by Oliver Lawson Dick. Reprinted by permission of the publishers, Martin Secker & Warburg Limited and The University of Michigan Press. [First published in 1690.]

EXTENSION

Contemporary writers have found Marvell's "To His Coy Mistress" a fascinating poem—not so much about love as about time. (For example, there is a reference to it in Part III of T. S. Eliot's *The Waste Land,* and in the title of Robert Penn Warren's novel *World Enough and Time.*) The contemporary American poet Archibald MacLeish was moved to write a poem directly to Marvell.

YOU, ANDREW MARVELL

by Archibald MacLeish

And here face down beneath the sun
And here upon earth's noonward height
To feel the always coming on
The always rising of the night:

5 To feel creep up the curving east
The earthy chill of dusk and slow
Upon those under lands the vast
And ever climbing shadow grow

And strange at Ecbatan[1] the trees
10 Take leaf by leaf the evening strange
The flooding dark about their knees
The mountains over Persia change

And now at Kermanshah[2] the gate
Dark empty and the withered grass
15 And through the twilight now the late
Few travelers in the westward pass

And Baghdad[3] darken and the bridge
Across the silent river gone
And through Arabia the edge
20 Of evening widen and steal on

And deepen on Palmyra's[4] street
The wheel rut in the ruined stone
And Lebanon fade out and Crete[5]
High through the clouds and overblown

25 And over Sicily the air
Still flashing with the landward gulls
And loom and slowly disappear
The sails above the shadowy hulls

And Spain go under and the shore
30 Of Africa the gilded sand
And evening vanish and no more
The low pale light across that land

Nor now the long light on the sea:

And here face downward in the sun
35 To feel how swift how secretly
The shadow of the night comes on . . .

---

4. *Palmyra,* ancient city of central Syria.
5. *Crete,* an island of Greece, in the Mediterranean.

From *Collected Poems 1917–1952* by Archibald MacLeish. Reprinted by permission of the publisher, Houghton Mifflin Company.
1. *Ecbatan,* city in old Persia, now in modern Iran. (Note that MacLeish names cities from east to west, just as the sun seems to move and the shadow of dusk moves.)
2. *Kermanshah,* ancient province and town in Iran.
3. *Baghdad,* most important city in Mesopotamia, now the capital of Iraq.

DISCUSSION

1. Lines 21–22 of "To His Coy Mistress" are two of the most famous lines of English poetry: "But at my back I always hear/Time's wingèd chariot hurrying near."

   (a) Discuss the meaning and effect of the lines.

   (b) How do they relate to Archibald MacLeish's poem?

2. Explain the meaning of the last two lines of "To His Coy Mistress" ("Thus, though we cannot make our sun/Stand still, yet we will make him run") and relate them to the rest of the poem.

3. Why does the MacLeish poem seem to begin in the middle of something, opening with the conjunction *And,* and to break off without actually concluding?

EASTER WINGS

by George Herbert

Lord, who createdst man in wealth and store,[1]
    Though foolishly he lost the same,
        Decaying more and more
           Till he became
5   Most poor:
             With thee
          O let me rise
        As larks, harmoniously,
    And sing this day thy victories:
10 Then shall the fall further the flight in me.

My tender age in sorrow did begin;
    And still with sicknesses and shame
        Thou didst so punish sin,
           That I became
15   Most thin.
             With thee
          Let me combine,
      And feel this day thy victory;
    For, if I imp[2] my wing on thine,
20 Affliction shall advance the flight in me.

---

1. *store*, abundance.
2. *imp*, a technical term used in falconry. Additional feathers were grafted (imped) onto a falcon's wings to improve its ability to fly.

DRINKING

by Abraham Cowley

From some copies of verses translated paraphrastically out of Anacreon[1]

The thirsty earth soaks up the rain,
And drinks, and gapes for drink again.
The plants suck in the earth, and are
With constant drinking fresh and fair.
5 The sea itself, which one would think
Should have but little need of drink,
Drinks ten thousand rivers up,
So filled that they o'erflow the cup.
The busy sun—and one would guess
10 By's drunken, fiery face no less—
Drinks up the sea, and when he's done,
The moon and stars drink up the sun.
They drink and dance by their own light;
They drink and revel all the night.
15 Nothing in nature's sober found,
But an eternal health goes round.
Fill up the bowl, then, fill it high,
Fill all the glasses there, for why
Should every creature drink but I?
20 Why, man of morals, tell me why?

---

1. *Anacreon*, Greek lyric poet (c. 563–478 B.C.) whose poems praised love and wine. Cowley's poem is a paraphrase of the original Latin.

DISCUSSION

1. Explore the ways in which George Herbert makes the physical shape of his poem reflect its content, and vice versa.

2. (a) What progression do you find in the series of images in Abraham Cowley's "Drinking"?

(b) Would you say that Samuel Johnson's remarks about metaphysical wit (page 271) apply in any way to this poem?

II. SONGS AND LYRICS—
CLASSICAL, CAVALIER, CAREFREE

The two major sides in the religious struggle which divided England in the seventeenth century differed markedly in their life-styles. The somber Puritans came to be known as Roundheads because they habitually wore their hair short. The Anglicans of the established church, supporters of the Stuart kings, were more dashing and brightly attired and were known as Cavaliers (because of their resemblance to the courtiers of the King's cavalry). The Cavalier Poets flourished during the reign of Charles I (1625–1649). Ben Jonson was an earlier poet, of course, and not one of their group, but his poetry inspired both their admiration and their imitation. Prominent among them were Sir John Suckling, Richard Lovelace, Robert Herrick, and George Wither. Their poetry tended to follow classical models of elegance, and was written in support of wine, women, and the carefree life. If metaphysical poetry emphasized intellect and wit, Cavalier poetry stressed grace and charm.

COME, MY CELIA

by Ben Jonson

Come, my Celia, let us prove,[1]
While we can, the sports of love;
Time will not be ours forever;
He at length our good will sever.
5 Spend not then his gifts in vain.
Suns that set may rise again;
But if once we lose this light,
'Tis with us perpetual night.
Why should we defer our joys?
10 Fame and rumor are but toys.
Cannot we delude the eyes
Of a few poor household spies,
Or his easier ears beguile,
So removèd by our wile?
15 'Tis no sin love's fruit to steal;
But the sweet thefts to reveal,
To be taken, to be seen,
These have crimes accounted been.

From the play *Volpone.* Volpone is attempting to seduce Celia, whose husband he has temporarily gotten out of the way.
1. *prove,* experience.

IT IS NOT GROWING LIKE A TREE

by Ben Jonson

It is not growing like a tree
In bulk, doth make men better be;
Or standing long an oak, three hundred year,
To fall a log at last, dry, bald, and sear:
5   A lily of a day
   Is fairer far in May;
 Although it fall and die that night,
 It was the plant and flower of light.
In small proportions we just beauties see,
And in short measures life may perfect be.

THE CONSTANT LOVER

by Sir John Suckling

Out upon it! I have loved
 Three whole days together;
And am like to love three more,
 If it prove fair weather.

5 Time shall molt away his wings
 Ere he shall discover,
In the whole wide world again,
 Such a constant lover.

But the spite on't is, no praise
10 Is due at all to me:
Love with me had made no stays
 Had it any been but she.

Had it any been but she,
 And that very face,
15 There had been at least ere this
 A dozen dozen in her place.

WHAT CARE I?

by George Wither

Shall I, wasting in despair,
Die because a woman's fair?
Or my cheeks make pale with care
'Cause another's rosy are?
5 Be she fairer than the day
Or the flowery meads in May—
    If she be not so to me,
    What care I how fair she be?

Shall my foolish heart be pined
10 'Cause I see a woman kind?
Or a well disposèd nature
Joinèd with a lovely feature?
Be she meeker, kinder, than
Turtle-dove or pelican,
15   If she be not so to me,
    What care I how kind she be?

Shall a woman's virtues move
Me to perish for her love?
Or her merits' value known
20 Make me quite forget mine own?
Be she with that goodness blest
Which may gain her name of Best;
    If she seem not such to me,
    What care I how good she be?

25 'Cause her fortune seems too high,
Shall I play the fool and die?
Those that bear a noble mind
Where they want of riches find,
Think what with them they would do
30 Who without them dare to woo;
    And unless that mind I see,
    What care I how great she be?

Great or good, or kind or fair,
I will ne'er the more despair;
35 If she love me, this believe,
I will die ere she shall grieve;
If she slight me when I woo,
I can scorn and let her go.
    For if she be not for me,
40   What care I for whom she be?

TO ALTHEA, FROM PRISON

by Richard Lovelace

When Love with unconfinèd wings
    Hovers within my gates,
And my divine Althea brings
    To whisper at the grates;
5 When I lie tangled in her hair
    And fettered to her eye,
The birds that wanton in the air
    Know no such liberty.

When flowing cups run swiftly round
10   With no allaying Thames,[1]
Our careless heads with roses bound,
    Our hearts with loyal flames;
When thirsty grief in wine we steep,
    When healths and drafts go free,
15 Fishes that tipple in the deep
    Know no such liberty.

When, like committed linnets, I
    With shriller throat will sing
The sweetness, mercy, majesty,
20   And glories of my King;
When I shall voice aloud how good
    He is, how great should be,
Enlargèd winds, that curl the flood,
    Know no such liberty.

25 Stone walls do not a prison make,
    Nor iron bars a cage;
Minds innocent and quiet take
    That for an hermitage;
If I have freedom in my love
30   And in my soul am free,
Angels alone, that soar above,
    Enjoy such liberty.

---

1. *no allaying Thames,* no diluting water from the Thames River.

TO LUCASTA,
ON GOING TO THE WARS

by Richard Lovelace

Tell me not, sweet, I am unkind,
  That from the nunnery
Of thy chaste breast and quiet mind
  To war and arms I fly.

5 True, a new mistress now I chase,
  The first foe in the field;
And with a stronger faith embrace
  A sword, a horse, a shield.

Yet this inconstancy is such
10 As thou too shalt adore;
I could not love thee, dear, so much
  Loved I not honor more.

UPON JULIA'S CLOTHES

by Robert Herrick

Whenas in silks my Julia goes,
Then, then, methinks, how sweetly flows
That liquefaction of her clothes.

Next, when I cast mine eyes, and see
That brave[1] vibration, each way free,
O, how that glittering taketh me!

---

1. *brave*, splendid.

TO THE VIRGINS,
TO MAKE MUCH OF TIME

by Robert Herrick

Gather ye rosebuds while ye may,
  Old time is still a-flying;
And this same flower that smiles today
  Tomorrow will be dying.

5 The glorious lamp of heaven, the sun,
  The higher he's a-getting
The sooner will his race be run,
  And nearer he's to setting.

That age is best which is the first,
10 When youth and blood are warmer;
But being spent, the worse, and worst
  Times still succeed the former.

Then be not coy, but use your time,
  And, while ye may, go marry;
15 For, having lost but once your prime,
  You may forever tarry.

DISCUSSION

1. *Ben Jonson:*
(a) Explore the truth of the last line of "It Is Not Growing Like a Tree": "And in short measures life may perfect be."
(b) Discuss the morality or justness of the last four lines of "Come, My Celia."

2. *George Wither:*
Discuss the state of mind of the speaker in "What Care I?" Does he seem to protest too much?

3. *Sir John Suckling:*
In "The Constant Lover," a reversal of sentiment seems to begin in stanza 3. What is it, and how genuine is it?

4. *Richard Lovelace:*
(a) In "To Lucasta," why does the speaker say that his beloved will "adore" his "inconstancy"?

(b) Each stanza of "To Althea" ends with a different image—birds, fishes, winds, angels. Explain their function in the poem.

5. *Robert Herrick:*
(a) In "Upon Julia's Clothes," discuss the effect of the word *liquefaction*.
(b) Compare "To the Virgins" with Marvell's "To His Coy Mistress," especially in the handling of the theme of time's swift passage.

III. JOHN MILTON   1608 / 1674

ON HIS HAVING ARRIVED AT THE AGE OF TWENTY-THREE

How soon hath Time, the subtle thief of youth
Stolen on his wing my three and twentieth year!
My hasting days fly on with full career,
But my late spring no bud or blossom shew'th.[1]
5 Perhaps my semblance[2] might deceive the truth
That I to manhood am arrived so near;
And inward ripeness doth much less appear,
That some more timely-happy spirits endu'th.[3]
Yet be it less or more, or soon or slow,
10 It shall be still in strictest measure even[4]
To that same lot, however mean or high,
Toward which Time leads me, and the will of
     Heaven;
All is, if I have grace to use it so,
As ever in my great Task-Master's eye.

1. *shew'th*, shows.
2. *semblance*, youthful appearance.
3. *endu'th*, endows.
4. *even*, adequate; i.e., his "inward ripeness" or inner readiness will be adequate to whatever destiny Time and Heaven are leading him.

ON HIS BLINDNESS

When I consider how my light is spent
Ere half my days in this dark world and wide,
And that one talent[1] which is death to hide
Lodged with me useless, though my soul more
     bent
5 To serve therewith my Maker, and present
My true account, lest He returning chide;
"Doth God exact day-labor, light denied?"
I fondly[2] ask. But Patience, to prevent
That murmur, soon replies, "God doth not need
10 Either man's work or His own gifts. Who best
Bear His mild yoke, they serve Him best. His state
Is kingly: thousands at His bidding speed,
And post o'er land and ocean without rest;
They also serve who only stand and wait."

1. *talent,* the gift of writing. This refers to Jesus' parable of the talents, or coins, which tells of the "unprofitable servant" who was condemned for hiding his one talent in the earth instead of spending it. (Mathew 25: 15–30)
2. *fondly,* foolishly.

OF LITERARY INTEREST

Milton's sonnets

Although Milton wrote only twenty-three sonnets during a period of approximately thirty years, he was an expert in the use of this literary form. "On His Having Arrived at the Age of Twenty-Three" was found among his Cambridge manuscripts. He had inserted it in a letter to a friend who had apparently remonstrated with him upon his aimless student life. In reply, Milton wrote: "That you may see that I am something suspicious of myself, or do take notice of a certain belatedness in me, I am the bolder to send you some of my nightward thoughts some little while ago, made up in a Petrarchan stanza which I told you of."

Milton became completely blind at the age of forty-five. "On His Blindness" was written shortly after this personal catastrophe.

DISCUSSION

1. In "On His Having Arrived at the Age of Twenty-Three," how does Milton reconcile himself to his meager accomplishments?
2. Compare "On His Blindness" with the sonnet written at the age of twenty-three (more than two decades earlier), both of which are concerned with Milton's achievements.

PARADISE LOST

FROM BOOK I—INVOCATION

Of man's first disobedience, and the fruit
Of that forbidden tree, whose mortal taste
Brought death into the world, and all our woe,
With loss of Eden, till one greater man[1]
5 Restore us, and regain the blissful seat,
Sing heavenly muse,[2] that on the secret top
Of Oreb, or of Sinai, didst inspire
That shepherd,[3] who first taught the chosen seed,
In the beginning how the heavens and earth
10 Rose out of chaos: Or if Sion hill[4]
Delight thee more, and Siloa's brook[4] that flowed
Fast by the oracle of God; I thence
Invoke thy aid to my adventurous song,
That with no middle flight intends to soar
15 Above the Aonian mount,[5] while it pursues
Things unattempted yet in prose or rhyme.
And chiefly thou, O spirit,[6] that dost prefer
Before all temples the upright heart and pure,
Instruct me, for thou knowest; thou from the first
20 Wast present, and, with mighty wings outspread
Dove-like satest brooding on the vast abyss
And madest it pregnant: What in me is dark
Illumine, what is low raise and support;
That to the height of this great argument
25 I may assert eternal providence,
And justify the ways of God to men.

The action of Paradise Lost *begins in medias res
(in the midst of things), after Satan's rebellion and
after he and his legions are driven from Heaven and
thrown into Chaos. The opening episodes show the
fallen angels "rolling in the fiery gulf" until Satan
rises and addresses his companions.*

PORTRAIT OF MILTON COURTESY PRINCETON UNIVERSITY LIBRARY.

"... Farewell happy fields
250 Where joy forever dwells: Hail horrors, hail
Infernal world, and thou profoundest Hell
Receive thy new possessor: One who brings
A mind not to be changed by place or time.
The mind is its own place, and in itself
255 Can make a heaven of Hell, a hell of Heaven.
What matter where, if I be still the same,
And what I should be, all but less than[7] he
Whom thunder hath made greater? Here at least
We shall be free; the Almighty hath not built
260 Here for his envy, will not drive us hence:
Here we may reign secure, and in my choice
To reign is worth ambition though in Hell:
Better to reign in Hell, than serve in Heaven."

*Satan rallies his legions and they build their kingdom
in Hell. Bent on revenge, Satan searches throughout
Chaos to find man and his world. He learns that God
has forbidden Adam and Eve to eat of the fruit of
the Tree of Knowledge, and decides that he will
lure them into disobedience. He slips into the Garden
of Eden, enters the body of the serpent, and finds
Eve alone. He approaches her, rendering himself
"pleasing" in shape and "lovely," with the purpose
of flattering and thus tricking her.*

FROM BOOK IX

Oft he bowed
525 His turret crest, and sleek enameled neck,
Fawning, and licked the ground whereon she trod.
His gentle dumb expression turned at length

---

1. *greater man,* Christ.
2. *heavenly muse,* the spirit that spoke to Moses on Mount Sinai and Mount Horeb (Oreb) in the wilderness.
3. *that shepherd,* Moses.
4. *Sion hill, Siloa's brook,* sacred places in Jerusalem.
5. *Aonian mount,* Mount Helicon in Greece, home of the Muses.
6. *spirit,* the Holy Spirit, the third person of the Holy Trinity, or God.

---

7. *all but less than,* less only than.

The eye of Eve to mark his play; he glad
Of her attention gained, with serpent tongue
530 Organic, or impulse of vocal air,
His fraudulent temptation thus began.
SATAN:
"Wonder not, sovereign mistress, if perhaps
Thou canst, who art sole wonder, much less arm
Thy looks, the heaven of mildness, with disdain,
535 Displeased that I approach thee thus, and gaze
Insatiate, I thus single, nor have feared
Thy awful brow, more awful thus retired.
Fairest resemblance of thy maker fair,
Thee all things living gaze on, all things thine
540 By gift, and thy celestial beauty adore
With ravishment beheld, there best beheld
Where universally admired; but here
In this enclosure wild, these beasts among,
Beholders rude, and shallow to discern
545 Half what in thee is fair, one man except,
Who sees thee? (and what is one?) who shouldst
            be seen
A goddess among gods, adored and served
By angels numberless, thy daily train."
    So glozed[8] the tempter, and his proem[9] tuned;
550 Into the heart of Eve his words made way,
Though at the voice much marveling; at length
Not unamazed she thus in answer spake.
EVE:
"What may this mean? Language of man pronounced
By tongue of brute, and human sense expressed?
555 The first at least of these I thought denied
To beasts, whom God on their creation-day
Created mute to all articulate sound;
The latter I demur,[10] for in their looks
Much reason, and in their actions oft appears.
560 Thee, serpent, subtlest beast of all the field
I knew, but not with human voice endued;
Redouble then this miracle, and say,
How camest thou speakable of mute, and how
To me so friendly grown above the rest
565 Of brutal kind, that daily are in sight?
Say, for such wonder claims attention due."
    To whom the guileful tempter thus replied.
SATAN:
"Empress of this fair world, resplendent Eve,

Easy to me it is to tell thee all
570 What thou commandest, and right thou shouldst
            be obeyed:
I was at first as other beasts that graze
The trodden herb, of abject thoughts and low,
As was my food, nor aught but food discerned
Or sex, and apprehended nothing high:
575 Till on a day roving the field, I chanced
A goodly tree far distant to behold
Laden with fruit of fairest colors mixed,
Ruddy and gold: I nearer drew to gaze;
When from the boughs a savory odor blown,
580 Grateful to appetite, more pleased my sense
Than smell of sweetest fennel or the teats
Of ewe or goat dropping with milk at even,
Unsucked of lamb or kid, that tend their play
To satisfy the sharp desire I had
585 Of tasting those fair apples, I resolved
Not to defer; hunger and thirst at once,
Powerful persuaders, quickened at the scent
Of that alluring fruit, urged me so keen.
About the mossy trunk I wound me soon,
590 For high from ground the branches would require
Thy utmost reach or Adam's: Round the tree
All other beasts that saw, with like desire
Longing and envying stood, but could not reach.
Amid the tree now got, where plenty hung
595 Tempting so nigh, to pluck and eat my fill
I spared not, for such pleasure till that hour
At feed or fountain never had I found.
Sated at length, erelong I might perceive
Strange alteration in me, to degree
600 Of reason in my inward powers, and speech
Wanted not long, though to this shape retained.
Thenceforth to speculations high or deep
I turned my thoughts, and with capacious mind
Considered all things visible in heaven,
605 Or Earth, or Middle,[11] all things fair and good;
But all that fair and good in thy divine
Semblance, and in thy beauty's heavenly ray
United I beheld; no fair[12] to thine
Equivalent or second, which compelled
610 Me thus, though importune perhaps, to come
And gaze, and worship thee of right declared
Sovereign of creatures, universal dame."
    So talked the spirited[13] sly snake; and Eve

---

8. *glozed,* flattered.
9. *proem,* prologue.
10. *demur,* question; i.e., I doubt that rational sense was denied
to animals.

11. *Middle,* the air.
12. *fair,* beauty.
13. *spirited,* possessed by a spirit.

Yet more amazed unwary thus replied.

EVE:

615 "Serpent, thy overpraising leaves in doubt
The virtue of that fruit, in thee first proved:
But say, where grows the tree, from hence how far?
For many are the trees of God that grow
In Paradise, and various, yet unknown
620 To us, in such abundance lies our choice,
As leaves a greater store of fruit untouched,
Still hanging incorruptible, till men
Grow up to their provision, and more hands
Help to disburden nature of her birth."
625   To whom the wily adder, blithe and glad.

SATAN:

"Empress, the way is ready, and not long,
Beyond a row of myrtles, on a flat,
Fast by a fountain, one small thicket past
Of blowing[14] myrrh and balm; if thou accept
630 My conduct, I can bring thee thither soon."
    "Lead then," said Eve. He leading swiftly rolled
In tangles, and made intricate seem straight,
To mischief swift. Hope elevates, and joy
Brightens his crest, as when a wandering fire,
635 Compact of unctuous vapor,[15] which the night
Condenses, and the cold environs round,
Kindled through agitation to a flame,
Which oft, they say, some evil spirit attends
Hovering and blazing with delusive light,
640 Misleads the amazed night-wanderer from his way
To bogs and mires, and oft through pond or pool,
There swallowed up and lost, from succor far.
So glistered the dire snake, and into fraud
Led Eve our credulous mother, to the tree
645 Of prohibition,[16] root of all our woe;
Which when she saw, thus to her guide she spake.

EVE:

    "Serpent, we might have spared our coming
        hither,
Fruitless to me, though fruit be here to excess,
The credit of whose virtue rest with thee,
650 Wondrous indeed, if cause of such effects.
But of this tree we may not taste nor touch;
God so commanded, and left that command
Sole daughter of his voice:[17] the rest, we live
Law to ourselves, our reason is our law."

---

14. *blowing*, blooming.
15. *Compact . . . vapor*, made of oily mist.
16. *tree/Of prohibition*, forbidden tree.
17. *Sole . . . voice*, his only command.

OF HUMAN INTEREST

John Milton

"His harmonicall and ingeniose Soul did lodge in a beauti-full and well proportioned body. He was a spare man. He was scarce so tall as I am (*quaere*, quot feet I am high: *resp.*, of middle stature).

"He had abroun hayre. His complexion exceeding faire—he was so faire that they called him *the Lady of Christ's College*. Ovall face. His eie a darke gray.

"He was very healthy and free from all diseases: seldome tooke any physique (only sometimes he tooke manna): only towards his latter end he was visited with the Gowte, Spring and Fall.

"He had a delicate tuneable Voice, and had good skill. His father instructed him. He had an Organ in his howse; he played on that most. Of a very cheerfull humour. He would be chearfull even in his Gowte fitts, and sing.

"He had a very good Memorie; but I believe that his excellent Method of thinking and disposing did much to helpe his Memorie."

From *Aubrey's Brief Lives* (1690), edited by Oliver Lawson Dick. Copyright 1949 by Oliver Lawson Dick. Reprinted by permission of the publishers, Martin Secker & Warburg Limited and The University of Michigan Press. [First published in 1690.]

655   To whom the tempter guilefully replied.

SATAN:

    "Indeed? hath God then said that of the fruit
Of all these garden trees ye shall not eat,
Yet lords declared of all in earth or air?"
    To whom thus Eve yet sinless.

EVE:

                                    "Of the fruit
660 Of each tree in the garden we may eat,
But of the fruit of this fair tree amidst
The garden, God hath said, 'Ye shall not eat
Thereof, nor shall ye touch it, lest ye die.'"
    She scarce had said, though brief, when now
        more bold
665 The tempter, but with show of zeal and love
To man, and indignation at his wrong,
New part puts on,[18] and as to passion moved,
Fluctuates disturbed, yet comely and in act
Raised,[19] as of some great matter to begin.
670 As when of old some orator renowned
In Athens or free Rome, where eloquence

---

18. *New part puts on*, assumes a new role.
19. *in act raised*, poised in stance.

Flourished, since mute, to some great cause
    addressed,
Stood in himself collected, while each part,
Motion, each act won audience ere the tongue,
675 Sometimes in height began, as no delay
Of preface brooking through his zeal of right.[20]
So standing, moving, or to height upgrown
The tempter all impassioned thus began.
SATAN:
    "O sacred, wise, and wisdom-giving plant,
680 Mother of science,[21] now I feel thy power
Within me clear, not only to discern
Things in their causes, but to trace the ways
Of highest agents, deemed however wise.
Queen of this universe, do not believe
685 Those rigid threats of death; ye shall not die:
How should ye? by the fruit? it gives you life
To knowledge. By the threatener, look on me,
Me who have touched and tasted, yet both live,
And life more perfect have attained than fate
690 Meant me, by venturing higher than my lot.
Shall that be shut to man, which to the beast
Is open? or will God incense his ire
For such a petty trespass, and not praise
Rather your dauntless virtue, whom the pain
695 Of death denounced,[22] whatever thing death be,
Deterred not from achieving what might lead
To happier life, knowledge of good and evil;
Of good, how just? of evil, if what is evil
Be real, why not known, since easier shunned?
700 God therefore cannot hurt ye, and be just;
Not just, not God;[23] not feared then, nor obeyed:
Your fear itself of death removes the fear.
Why then was this forbid? Why but to awe,
Why but to keep ye low and ignorant,
705 His worshipers; he knows that in the day
Ye eat thereof, your eyes that seem so clear,
Yet are but dim, shall perfectly be then
Opened and cleared, and ye shall be as gods,
Knowing both good and evil as they know.
710 That ye should be as gods, since I as man,
Internal man,[24] is but proportion meet,

I of brute human, ye of human gods.
So ye shall die perhaps, by putting off
Human, to put on gods, death to be wished,
715 Though threatened, which no worse than this can
    bring.
And what are gods that man may not become
As they, participating[25] godlike food?
The gods are first, and that advantage use
On our belief, that all from them proceeds;
720 I question it, for this fair earth I see,
Warmed by the sun, producing every kind,
Them nothing: If they all things, who enclosed
Knowledge of good and evil in this tree,
That whoso eats thereof, forthwith attains
725 Wisdom without their leave? and wherein lies
The offense, that man should thus attain to know?
What can your knowledge hurt him, or this tree
Impart against his will if all be his?
Or is it envy, and can envy dwell
730 In heavenly breasts? these, these and many more
Causes import[26] your need of this fair fruit.
Goddess humane, reach then, and freely taste."
    He ended, and his words replete with guile
Into her heart too easy entrance won:
735 Fixed on the fruit she gazed, which to behold
Might tempt alone, and in her ears the sound
Yet rung of his persuasive words, impregned[27]
With reason, to her seeming, and with truth;
Meanwhile the hour of noon drew on, and waked
740 An eager appetite, raised by the smell
So savory of that fruit, which with desire,
Inclinable now grown to touch or taste,
Solicited her longing eye; yet first
Pausing a while, thus to herself she mused.
EVE:
745   "Great are thy virtues, doubtless, best of fruits,
Though kept from man, and worthy to be admired,
Whose taste, too long forborne, at first assay[28]
Gave elocution to the mute, and taught
The tongue not made for speech to speak thy
    praise:
750 Thy praise he also who forbids thy use,
Conceals not from us, naming thee the tree
Of knowledge, knowledge both of good and evil;
Forbids us then to taste, but his forbidding

---

20. *Sometimes in height . . . right.* As if too agitated to begin
at the beginning, the speaker burst into the middle of his speech.
21. *science,* knowledge.
22. *denounced,* threatened.
23. *God therefore . . . God.* The serpent reasons that for God to
punish Eve with death would be unjust, and if God were unjust He
would not be God.
24. *Internal man,* like man inside (intellectually) but not in
appearance.

25. *participating,* sharing.
26. *import,* prove.
27. *impregned,* impregnated.
28. *assay,* try.

"GOD JUDGING ADAM," BY WILLIAM BLAKE, 1795. THE TATE GALLERY, LONDON.

Commends thee more, while it infers the good
755 By thee communicated, and our want:
For good unknown, sure is not had, or had
And yet unknown, is as not had at all.
In plain then, what forbids he but to know,
Forbids us good, forbids us to be wise?
760 Such prohibitions bind not. But if death
Bind us with after-bands, what profits then
Our inward freedom? In the day we eat
Of this fair fruit, our doom is, we shall die.
How dies the serpent? he hath eaten and lives,
765 And knows, and speaks, and reasons, and discerns,
Irrational till then. For us alone
Was death invented? or to us denied
This intellectual food, for beasts reserved?
For beasts it seems: yet that one beast which first
770 Hath tasted, envies not, but brings with joy
The good befallen him, author unsuspect,[29]
Friendly to man, far from deceit or guile.
What fear I then, rather what know to fear
Under this ignorance of good and evil,
775 Of God or death, of law or penalty?
Here grows the cure of all, this fruit divine,
Fair to the eye, inviting to the taste,
Of virtue to make wise: what hinders then
To reach, and feed at once both body and mind?''

780   So saying, her rash hand in evil hour
Forth reaching to the fruit, she plucked, she eat:
Earth felt the wound, and nature from her seat
Sighing through all her works gave signs of woe,
That all was lost. Back to the thicket slunk
785 The guilty serpent, and well might, for Eve
Intent now wholly on her taste, naught else
Regarded, such delight till then, as seemed,
In fruit she never tasted, whether true
Or fancied so, through expectation high
790 Of knowledge, nor was godhead from her thought.
Greedily she engorged without restraint,
And knew not eating death . . . .

*Eve offers the fruit to Adam, who eats out of love
for her. They immediately fall to accusing each other.
Sin and death enter the world. God orders Adam and
Eve expelled from Eden, and sends the Angel Michael
to execute His will. Michael shows the future to
Adam, and then Adam goes to wake Eve and depart
from Paradise.*

FROM BOOK XII

Descended, Adam to the bower where Eve
Lay sleeping ran before, but found her waked;
And thus with words not sad she him received.
610   "Whence thou returnest, and whither wentest, I
          know;
For God is also in sleep, and dreams advise,
Which he hath sent propitious, some great good
Presaging, since with sorrow and heart's distress
Wearied I fell asleep: but now lead on;
615 In me is no delay; with thee to go,
Is to stay here; without thee here to stay,
Is to go hence unwilling; thou to me
Art all things under heaven, all places thou,
Who for my willful crime art banished hence.
620 This further consolation yet secure
I carry hence; though all by me is lost,
Such favor I unworthy am vouchsafed,
By me the promised seed shall all restore.''
     So spake our mother Eve, and Adam heard
625 Well pleased, but answered not; for now too nigh
The archangel stood, and from the other hill
To their fixed station, all in bright array
The cherubim descended; on the ground
Gliding meteorous, as evening mist
630 Risen from a river o'er the marish[30] glides,
And gathers ground fast at the laborer's heel
Homeward returning. High in front advanced,
The brandished sword of God before them blazed
Fierce as a comet; which with torrid heat,
635 And vapor as the Libyan air adust,[31]
Began to parch that temperate clime; whereat
In either hand the hastening angel caught
Our lingering parents, and to the eastern gate
Led them direct, and down the cliff as fast
640 To the subjected plain; then disappeared.
They looking back, all the eastern side beheld
Of Paradise, so late their happy seat,
Waved over by that flaming brand, the gate
With dreadful faces thronged and fiery arms:
645 Some natural tears they dropped, but wiped them
          soon;
The world was all before them, where to choose
Their place of rest, and providence their guide:
They hand in hand with wandering steps and slow,
Through Eden took their solitary way.   □

---

29. *author unsuspect,* a reliable authority.

30. *marish,* marsh.
31. *Libyan air adust,* hot desert winds of Libya.

EXTENSION

It is perhaps a paradox that the fall of man should ever be called "fortunate," but there is a long tradition in which the original sin of Adam and Eve is seen as proving ultimately beneficial for mankind: only through the fall was man enabled to win God's grace. (See, for example, "Adam Lay in Bondage" in the Medieval section.) In Book XII of *Paradise Lost*, lines 469–478, Adam reflects on the idea of the fortunate fall in a speech he makes to the Archangel Michael:

> O goodness infinite, goodness immense!
> That all this good of evil shall produce,
> And evil turn to good; more wonderful
> Then that which by creation first brought forth
> Light out of darkness! full of doubt I stand,
> Whether I should repent me now of sin
> By me done and occasioned, or rejoice
> Much more, that much more good thereof shall spring,
> To God more glory, more good will to men
> From God, and over wrath grace shall abound.

A contemporary British poet has written his own version of this idea:

THE FORTUNATE FALL

by A. Alvarez

Perhaps Eve in the garden knew the sun
With her whole flesh; and pruned the rose's soul—
The thing was thornless, pliable, like Eve—
And she the garden whence all flowers sprung.

5 But Adam knew her as the fruit he stole,
The apple, sleeping, God made him conceive.
His side and eyes were opened. They were bare,
The tree despoiled and knowledge risen whole.

Before she even fumbled with the leaves
10 Adam was finished. Of course, she had a flair
For fumbling that was folly to oppose,
Tricky, pleading, knowing. Why should he grieve?

So he chose for her, chose his own despair.
Her hair, like rain, closed on the thorny rose.

(1953)

From *Penguin Modern Poets* No. 18. Copyright © Penguin Books Ltd., 1970. Reprinted by permission of Curtis Brown Ltd.

DISCUSSION

1. In the Invocation, Milton asserts that his purpose in *Paradise Lost* is to "justify the ways of God to men." Does he accomplish this purpose in the parts you have read?

2. Explain and explore these famous quotations:

"The mind is its own place, and in itself / Can make a heaven of Hell, a hell of Heaven."

"Better to reign in Hell, than serve in Heaven."

3. How does Satan lure Eve into eating the forbidden fruit?

4. Just before Eve eats the fruit, she meditates and persuades herself that she should go ahead and eat. Examine the lines (745–779) and discuss the plausibility of her reasoning.

5. What consolation does Eve have in the closing lines of the poem?

6. How does Milton's version of the story differ from the King James Version in the Bible (pages 223–225 in this text)?

READER'S THEATER

Assign the parts of Eve, Satan, and the narrator, and do a dramatic reading of the temptation scene. How would you design the tree and the fruit for today's theater?

WRITING

Check over the King James Version and the Milton presentation of the temptation scene, and rewrite it in modern language; or simply improvise the scene and see how it all comes out.

IV. John Dryden   1631 / 1700

A SONG FOR ST. CECILIA'S DAY

From harmony, from heavenly harmony,
    This universal frame began:
    When Nature underneath a heap
    Of jarring atoms lay,
5   And could not heave her head,
The tuneful voice was heard from high:
    "Arise, ye more than dead."

Then cold and hot and moist and dry[1]
    In order to their stations leap,
10   And Music's power obey.
From harmony, from heavenly harmony,
    This universal frame began:
    From harmony to harmony
Through all the compass of the notes it ran,
15 The diapason closing full in Man.

What passion cannot Music raise and quell!
    When Jubal struck the chorded shell,[2]
    His listening brethren stood around,
    And wondering, on their faces fell
20   To worship that celestial sound.
Less than a god they thought there could not dwell
    Within the hollow of that shell
    That spoke so sweetly and so well.
What passion cannot Music raise and quell!

25   The trumpet's loud clangor
    Excites us to arms
    With shrill note of anger
    And mortal alarms.
    The double, double, double beat
30   Of the thundering drum
    Cries: "Hark! the foes come;
Charge, charge, 'tis too late to retreat!"

    The soft complaining flute
    In dying notes discovers[3]
35   The woes of hopeless lovers
Whose dirge is whispered by the warbling lute.
    Sharp violins proclaim
    Their jealous pangs and desperation,
    Fury, frantic indignation,
40   Depth of pain, and height of passion
    For the fair, disdainful dame.

    But oh! what art can teach,
    What human voice can reach
        The sacred organ's praise?
45   Notes inspiring holy love,
    Notes that wing their heavenly ways
    To mend the choirs above.
Orpheus[4] could lead the savage race;
    And trees unrooted left their place,
50   Sequacious[5] of the lyre;
But bright Cecilia raised the wonder higher:
    When to her organ vocal breath was given,
    An angel heard, and straight appeared,
    Mistaking earth for heaven.

GRAND CHORUS

55   As from the power of sacred lays
    The spheres began to move,[6]
And sung the great Creator's praise
    To all the blessed above;
So when the last and dreadful hour
60   This crumbling pageant shall devour,
The trumpet shall be heard on high,
The dead shall live, the living die,
And Music shall untune the sky.

1. *cold . . . dry*, air, fire, water, and earth, which were the four elements of the universe according to classical and medieval natural philosophy.
2. *Jubal . . . shell*. Jubal is referred to in the Bible as "the father of all such as handle the harp and pipe." (Genesis 4:21). Dryden pictures Jubal's lyre as made of a tortoise shell.

3. *discovers*, reveals; expresses.
4. *Orpheus*. In Greek mythology, Orpheus was such a wonderful musician that animals and even inanimate objects followed him when he played on his lyre.
5. *Sequacious*, following after.
6. *spheres . . . move*. It was believed that the stars made music as they revolved in their spheres.

OF LITERARY INTEREST

St. Cecilia and her praise

St. Cecilia, a Christian martyr of the third century, is the patron saint of music and by tradition the inventor of the pipe organ. At an annual London music festival held on St. Cecilia's Day (November 22), it was customary to present an original ode set to music. Dryden, in his ode, tried to translate the effects of various instruments into poetry.

Alexander Pope, Dryden's disciple, also wrote an ode to St. Cecilia, and a number of modern poets, including W. H. Auden, have likewise done so. George Barker has recently written an "Ode Against St. Cecilia's Day," a bitter antiwar poem invoking silence and grief rather than joyful music.

The ode

An ode (for example, "A Song for St. Cecilia's Day") is an exalted, often rapturous, lyric poem on a lofty subject, with complex or irregular stanzas. The form of the ode grew out of Greek drama, in which the chorus, accompanied by music, chanted a strophe when moving to the left on the stage, an antistrophe when moving to the right, and an epode when standing still. The Greek poet Pindar established the regular pattern for the ode, with fixed forms for the various parts. However, the English ode has tended almost always to be irregular, with stanzaic structure shifting readily to accommodate shifts of thought and mood. Some odes tend to be primarily eulogistic, others meditative. Most odes are written to praise someone or to commemorate some event. An ode may also be inspired by an object or creature; see, for example, Shelley's "Ode to the West Wind" or Keats's "Ode to a Nightingale."

OF HUMAN INTEREST

Dryden's marriage

In his early thirties, Dryden married Lady Elizabeth Howard, somewhat older than himself. The marriage was not a happy one, and Dryden almost never mentioned the subject of marriage without attacking it. He wrote this epitaph even before his wife died:

> Here lies my wife: here let her lie!
> Now she's at rest. And so am I.

COURTESY OF THE TRUSTEES OF THE BRITISH MUSEUM.

DISCUSSION

1. (a) What does Dryden mean by "universal frame" in line 2?

(b) What idea does he develop in the first two stanzas of the poem?

(c) Explain lines 14-15.

2. (a) What idea is developed in the third stanza?

(b) How are stanzas 4-6 related to this idea?

(c) What comparison of pagan and Christian music does Dryden make in stanza 6?

(d) What is the concluding idea of the poem?

V. THE DIARY OF SAMUEL PEPYS

Samuel Pepys (1633–1703), from the vantage point of his post in the Naval Office in London, was able to observe society, government, and mankind during an exciting period of English history—the Restoration of the monarchy beginning in 1660. He kept a diary in a secret code from 1660 to 1669, revealing as much about himself as about his times. He apparently wrote for himself, without intending to publish his work. It was not until 1825 that the diary was examined and the code deciphered. His diary (along with John Evelyn's covering the same period) has served ever since to give glimpses and insights into the intimate and domestic, as well as the public and official, life of the period.

At the time he was writing the entries that are excerpted below, Pepys was thirty years old. Since June 1660 he had been a Commissioner and a Principal Officer of the Navy Board as Clerk of the Acts, a position gained through the influence of the Earl of Sandwich, his cousin by marriage. Pepys, along with fellow members of the Board, lived in official Navy housing adjacent to their office.

NATIONAL PORTRAIT GALLERY, LONDON

APRIL 1663

Sat. 18th. Up betimes and to my office, where all the morning. At noon to dinner. With us Mr. Creed,[1] who has been deeply engaged at the office this day about the ending of his accounts, wherein he is most unhappy to have to do with a company of fools who after they have signed his accounts and made bills upon them yet dare not boldly assert to the Treasurer that they are satisfied with his accounts. Hereupon all dinner, and walking in the garden the afternoon, he and I talking of the ill management of our office, which God knows is very ill for the King's advantage. I would I could make it better. In the evening to my office, and at night home to supper and bed.

Sun. 19th (Easter day). Up and this day put on my close-kneed coloured suit, which, with new stockings of the colour, with belt, and new gilt-handled sword, is very handsome. To church alone, and so to dinner, where my father and brother Tom dined with us, and after dinner to church again, my father sitting below in the chancel. After church done, where the young Scotchman preaching I slept all the while, my father and I to see my uncle and aunt

Wight, and after a stay of an hour there my father to my brother's and I home to supper, and after supper fell in discourse of dancing, and I find that Ashwell[2] hath a very fine carriage, which makes my wife almost ashamed of herself to see herself so outdone, but to-morrow she begins to learn to dance for a month or two. So to prayers and to bed.

Mon. 20th. Up betimes as I use to do, and in my chamber begun to look over my father's accounts, which he brought out of the country with him by my desire, whereby I may see what he has received and spent, and I find that he is not anything extravagant, and yet it do so far outdo his estate that he must either think of lessening his charge, or I must be forced to spare money out of my purse to help him through, which I would willing do as far as £20 goes. . . .

After dinner, it raining very hard, by coach to Whitehall, where, after Sir G. Carteret, Sir J. Minnes, Mr. Coventry[3] and I had been with the Duke,[4] we to the Committee of Tangier and did matters there, and so broke up. With Sir G. Carteret and Sir John Minnes by coach to my Lord Treasurer's, thinking to have spoken about getting money for paying the Yards; but we found him with some ladies at cards: and so,

---

1. *Creed,* John Creed, Deputy-Treasurer of the Fleet.

2. *Ashwell,* Mary Ashwell, recently hired as maid-companion to Mrs. Pepys.
3. *Carteret, Minnes, Coventry,* older members of the Navy Board.
4. *Duke,* the Duke of York, the king's brother, and Lord Admiral of the Navy. He later became King James II.

it being a bad time to speak, we parted, and Sir J. Minnes and I home, and after walking with my wife in the garden late, to supper and to bed, being somewhat troubled at Ashwell's desiring and insisting over eagerly upon her going to a ball to meet some of her old companions at a dancing school here in town next Friday, but I am resolved she shall not go. So to bed. . . .

Wed. 22nd. Up betimes and to my office very busy all the morning there. . . . So to my uncle Wight's, by invitation, whither my father, wife, and Ashwell came, where we had but a poor dinner, and not well dressed,[5] besides, the very sight of my aunt's hands and greasy manner of carving, did almost turn my stomach. After dinner by coach to the King's Playhouse, where we saw but part of "Witt without money," which I do not like much, but coming late put me out of tune, and it costing me four halfcrowns for myself and company. So, the play done, home, and I to my office a while and so home, where my father (who is so very melancholy) and we played at cards, and so to supper and to bed.

Thurs. 23rd. St. George's day and Coronacion, the King and Court being at Windsor, at the installing of the King of Denmark by proxy and the Duke of Monmouth. I up betimes, and with my father, having a fire made in my wife's new closet[6] above, it being a wet and cold day, we sat there all the morning looking over his country accounts. . . . We resolve upon sending for Will Stankes[7] up to town to give us a right understanding in all that we have in Brampton, and before my father goes to settle every thing so as to resolve how to find a living for my father and to pay debts and legacies. . . .

At cards till late, and being at supper, my boy being sent for some mustard to a neat's tongue, the rogue staid half an hour in the streets, it seems at a bonfire, at which I was very angry, and resolve to beat him to-morrow.

Fri. 24th. Up betimes, and with my salt eel[8] went down in the parler and there got my boy and did beat him till I was fain to take breath two or three times, yet for all I am afeard it will make the boy never the better, he is grown so hardened in his tricks, which I am sorry for, he being capable of making a brave man, and is a boy that I and my wife love very well.

So made me ready, and to my office, where all the morning, and at noon home, whither came Captain Holland, who is lately come home from sea, and has been much harassed in law about the ship which he has bought, so that it seems in a despair he endeavoured to cut his own throat, but is recovered it; and it seems—whether by that or any other persuasion (his wife's mother being a great zealot) he is turned almost a Quaker, his discourse being nothing but holy, and that impertinent, that I was weary of him. At last pretending to go to the Change[9] we walked thither together, and there I left him and home to dinner, sending my boy by the way to enquire after two dancing masters at our end of the town for my wife to learn, of whose names the boy brought word.

After dinner all the afternoon fiddling upon my viallin (which I have not done many a day) while Ashwell danced above in my upper best chamber, which is a rare room for musique, expecting this afternoon my wife to bring my cozen Scott and Stradwick, but they came not, and so in the evening we by ourselves to Half-way house to walk, but did not go in there, but only a walk and so home again and to supper, my father with us, and had a good lobster intended for part of our entertainment to these people to-day, and so to cards, and then to bed, being the first day that I have spent so much to my pleasure a great while.

Sat. 25th. Up betimes and to my vyall and song book a pretty while, and so to my office, and there we sat all the morning. . . .

At noon we rose, Sir W. Batten[10] ashamed and vexed [because of a dispute with Pepys], and so home to dinner, and after dinner walked to the old Exchange and so all along to Westminster Hall, White Hall, my Lord Sandwich's lodgings, and going by water back to the Temple did pay my debts in several places in order to my examining my accounts to-morrow to my great content. So in the evening home, and after supper (my father at my brother's) and merrily practising to dance, which my wife hath begun to learn this day of Mr. Pembleton, but I fear

---

5. *dressed,* prepared; cooked.
6. *closet,* small private room. Pepys had recently added an upper story to his house.
7. *Will Stankes,* manager of a family property in the country from which Pepys' father received income.
8. *salt eel,* piece of rope used as a whip.

9. *Change,* the Royal Exchange, a building where merchants assembled to transact business.
10. *Sir W. Batten,* an older colleague on the Navy Board, and a neighbor. Pepys disliked him and considered him dishonest.

will hardly do any great good at it, because she is conceited that she do well already, though I think no such thing. So to bed. . . .

Lastly I did hear that the Queen is much grieved of late at the King's neglecting her, he having not supped once with her this quarter of a year, and almost every night with my Lady Castlemaine; who hath been with him this St. George's feast at Windsor, and came home with him last night; and, which is more, they say is removed as to her bed from her own home to a chamber in White Hall, next to the King's own; which I am sorry to hear, though I love her much.

Sun. 26th (Lord's-day). Lay pretty long in bed talking with my wife, and then up and set to the making up of my monthly accounts, but Tom[11] coming, with whom I was angry for botching my camlott[12] coat, to tell me that my father and he would dine with me, and that my father was at our church, I got me ready and had a very good sermon of a country minister upon "How blessed a thing it is for brethren to live together in unity!" So home and all to dinner, and then would have gone by coach to have seen my Lord Sandwich at Chelsey if the man would have taken us, but he denying it we staid at home, and I all the afternoon upon my accounts, and find myself worth full £700, for which I bless God, it being the most I was ever yet worth in money.

In the evening (my father being gone to my brother's to lie to-night) my wife, Ashwell, and the boy and I, and the dogg, over the water and walked to Half-way house, and beyond into the fields, gathering of cowslipps, and so to Half-way house, with some cold lamb we carried with us, and there supped, and had a most pleasant walk back again, Ashwell all along telling us some parts of their mask at Chelsey School, which was very pretty, and I find she hath a most prodigious memory, remembering so much of things acted six or seven years ago. So home, and after reading my vows, being sleepy, without prayers to bed, for which God forgive me!

Mon. 27th. Up betimes and to my office, where doing business alone a good while till people came about business to me. Will Griffin tells me this morning that Captain Browne, Sir W. Batten's brother-in-law, is dead of a blow given him two days ago by a seaman, a servant of his, being drunk, with a stone striking him on the forehead, for which I am sorry, he having a good woman and several small children. . . . Home by coach, where I found Mary[13] gone from my wife, she being too high for her, though a very good servant, and my boy too will be going in a few days, for he is not for my family, he is grown so out of order and not to be ruled, and do himself, against his brother's counsel, desire to be gone, which I am sorry for, because I love the boy and would be glad to bring him to good. At home with my wife and Ashwell talking of her going into the country this year, wherein we had like to have fallen out, she thinking that I have a design to have her go, which I have not, and to let her stay here I perceive will not be convenient, for she expects more pleasure than I can give her here, and I fear I have done very ill in letting her begin to learn to dance. . . .

Tues. 28th. Up betimes and to my office, and there all the morning, only stepped up to see my wife and her dancing master at it, and I think after all she will do pretty well at it. . . .

Thurs. 30th. [Will Stankes had arrived the previous day from the country.] Lord! what a stir Stankes makes with his being crowded in the streets and wearied in walking in London, and would not be wooed by my wife and Ashwell to go to a play, nor to White Hall, or to see the lyons,[14] though he was carried in a coach. I never could have thought there had been upon earth a man so little curious in the world as he is. . . .

MAY 1663

Fri. May 1st. Up betimes and my father with me, and he and I all the morning and Will Stankes private, in my wife's closet above, settling our matters concerning our Brampton estate, &c., and I find that there will be, after all debts paid within £100, £50 per annum clear coming towards my father's maintenance, besides £25 per annum annuities to my Uncle Thomas and Aunt Perkins. Of which, though I was in my mind glad, yet thought it not fit to let my father know it thoroughly, but after he had gone out to visit my uncle Thomas and brought him to dinner with him, and after dinner I got my father, brother Tom, and myself together, I did make the

---

11. *Tom*, his brother, who had recently taken over their father's tailoring business.
12. *camlott*, expensive imported fabric made of camel's hair.

13. *Mary*, not Mary Ashwell, but a previous servant.
14. *lyons* (lions), in the menagerie at the Tower of London, one of the chief sights of the city.

business worse to them, and did promise £20 out of my own purse to make it £50 a year to my father, propounding that Stortlow may be sold to pay £200 for his satisfaction therein and the rest to go towards payment of debts and legacies. The truth is I am fearful lest my father should die before debts are paid, and then the land goes to Tom and the burden of paying all debts will fall upon the rest of the land. Not that I would do my brother any real hurt. I advised my father to good husbandry and to living within the compass of £50 a year, and all in such kind words, as not only made them but myself to weep, and I hope it will have a good effect.

That being done, and all things agreed on, we went down, and after a glass of wine we all took horse, and I, upon a horse hired of Mr. Game, saw him out of London, at the end of Bishopsgate Street, and so I turned and rode, with some trouble, through the fields towards Hide Park, whither all the world, I think, are going; and in my going, met W. Howe[15] coming galloping upon a little crop black nag; it seems one that was taken in some ground of my Lord's, by some mischance being left by his master, a thief; this horse being found with black cloth ears on, and a false mayne, having none of his own. . . .

By and by, about seven or eight o'clock, homeward. . . . In my way, in Leadenhall Street, there was morris-dancing which I have not seen a great while. So set my horse up at Game's, paying 5s. for him. And so home to see Sir J. Minnes, who is well again, and after staying talking with him awhile, I took leave and went to hear Mrs. Turner's daughter, at whose house Sir J. Minnes lies, play on the harpsicon;[16] but, Lord! it was enough to make any man sick to hear her; yet I was forced to commend her highly. So home to supper and to bed, Ashwell playing upon the tryangle[17] very well before I went to bed. . . .

Sat. 2nd. Being weary last night, I slept till almost seven o'clock, a thing I have not done many a day. So up and to my office (being come to some angry words with my wife about neglecting the keeping of the house clean, I calling her beggar, and she me pricklouse, which vexed me) and there all the morning. So to the Exchange and then home to dinner, and very merry and well pleased with my wife, and so to the office again, where we met extraordinary upon drawing up the debts of the Navy to my Lord Treasurer. So rose and up to Sir W. Pen[18] to drink a glass of bad syder in his new far low dining room, which is very noble, and so home, where Captain Ferrers and his lady are come to see my wife. . . .

Sun. 3rd (Lord's day). Up before 5 o'clock and alone at setting my Brampton papers to rights according to my father's and my computation . . . . So made myself ready and to church, where Sir W. Pen showed me the young lady which young Dawes, that sits in the new corner-pew in the church, hath stole away from Sir Andrew Rickard, her guardian, worth £1,000 per annum present, good land, and some money, and a very well-bred and handsome lady: he, I doubt, but a simple fellow. However, he got this good luck to get her, which methinks I could envy him with all my heart.

Home to dinner with my wife, who not being very well did not dress herself but staid at home all day, and so I to church in the afternoon and so home again, and up to teach Ashwell the grounds of time and other things on the tryangle, and made her take out a Psalm very well, she having a good ear and hand. And so a while to my office, and then home to supper and prayers, to bed, my wife and I having a little falling out because I would not leave my discourse below with her and Ashwell to go up and talk with her alone upon something she has to say. She reproached me but I had rather talk with any body than her, by which I find I think she is jealous of my freedom with Ashwell, which I must avoid giving occasion of.

Mon. 4th. Up betimes and to setting my Brampton papers in order and looking over my wardrobe against summer, and laying things in order to send to my brother to alter. By and by took boat intending to have gone down to Woolwich,[19] but seeing I could not get back time enough to dinner, I returned and home. Whither by and by the dancing-master came, whom standing by, seeing him instructing my wife, when he had done with her, he would needs have me try the steps of a coranto, and what with his desire and my wife's importunity, I did begin, and then was obliged to give him entry-money 10s., and am become his scholler. The truth

15. *W. Howe,* also in the service of Pepys' cousin and patron, the Earl of Sandwich.
16. *harpsicon,* harpsichord.
17. *tryangle,* probably a triangular spinet.
18. *Sir W. Pen* (Penn), a neighbor and fellow member of the Navy Board. His son was William Penn who founded Pennsylvania.
19. *Woolwich,* an important naval dockyard.

is, I think it a thing very useful for a gentleman, and sometimes I may have occasion of using it, and though it cost me what I am heartily sorry it should, besides that I must by my oath[20] give half as much more to the poor. . . .

Tues. 5th. Up betimes and to my office, and there busy all the morning, among other things walked a good while up and down with Sir J. Minnes, he telling many old stories of the Navy, and of the state of the Navy at the beginning of the late troubles,[21] and I am troubled at my heart to think, and shall hereafter cease to wonder, at the bad success of the King's cause, when such a knave as he (if it be true what he says) had the whole management of the fleet. . . .

Wed. 6th. Up betimes and to my office a good while at my new rulers, then to business, and towards noon to the Exchange with Creed, where we met with Sir J. Minnes coming in his coach from Westminster, who tells us, in great heat, that, by God, the Parliament will make mad work; that they will render all men incapable of any military or civil employment that have borne arms in the late troubles against the King, excepting some persons; which,

if it be so, as I hope it is not, will give great cause of discontent, and I doubt will have but bad effects. I left them at the Exchange and walked to Paul's Churchyard to look upon a book or two, and so back, and thence to the Trinity House, and there dined, where among other discourse worth hearing among the old seamen, they tell us that they have catched often in Greenland in fishing whales with the iron grapnells that had formerly been struck into their bodies covered over with fat; that they have had eleven hogsheads of oyle out of the tongue of a whale.

Thence after dinner home to my office, and there busy till the evening. Then home and to supper, and while at supper comes Mr. Pembleton, and after supper we up to our dancing room and there danced three or four country dances, and after that a practice of my coranto I began with him the other day, and I begin to think that I shall be able to do something at it in time. Late and merry at it, and so weary to bed.

Sat. 9th. Up betimes and to my office, whither sooner than ordinary comes Mr. Hater[22] desiring to speak a word to me alone, which I was from the disorder of his countenance amused at, and so the poor man began telling me [that he was in difficulties

---

20. *oath.* Pepys was trying to cure himself of too much devotion to pleasure through a system of self-imposed fines.
21. *late troubles,* the execution of King Charles I and the establishment of the Puritan Commonwealth under Cromwell.

22. *Mr. Hater,* Tom Hater, Pepys' chief clerk.

with the authorities for attending a Quaker meeting, which was then illegal. Pepys promised to intercede for him with Mr. Coventry, an influential member of the Board.] At noon dined at home with a heavy heart for the poor man, and after dinner went out to my brother's, and thence to Westminster, where at Mr. Jervas's, my old barber, I did try two or three borders and perriwiggs, meaning to wear one; and yet I have no stomach [for it,] but that the pains of keeping my hair clean is so great. He trimmed me, and at last I parted, but my mind was almost altered from my first purpose, from the trouble that I foresee will be in wearing them also. Thence by water home and to the office, where busy late, and so home to supper and bed, with my mind much troubled about T. Hater.

Mon. 11th. Up betimes, and by water to Woolwich on board the Royall James, to see in what dispatch she is to be carried about to Chatham. So to the yard a little, and thence on foot to Greenwich, where going I was set upon by a great dogg, who got hold of my garters, and might have done me hurt; but, Lord, to see in what a maze I was, that, having a sword about me, I never thought of it, or had the heart to make use of it, but might, for want of that courage, have been worried. . . .

Fri. 15th. [Pepys first details extensive items of gossip about the Court and members of the nobility, all illustrating "the unhappy posture of things at this time."]

Sir Thomas [Crew] showed me his picture and Sir Anthony Vandike's, in crayon in little, done exceedingly well. Having thus freely talked with him, and of many more things, I took leave . . . and so well pleased home, where I found it almost night, and my wife and the dancing-master alone above, not dancing but talking. Now so deadly full of jealousy I am that my heart and head did so cast about and fret that I could not do any business possibly, but went out to my office, and anon late home again and ready to chide at every thing, and then suddenly to bed and could hardly sleep, yet durst not say any thing, but was forced to say that I had bad news from the Duke concerning Tom Hater as an excuse to my wife, who by my folly has too much opportunity given her with the man, who is a pretty neat black man,[23] but married. But it is a deadly folly and plague that I bring upon myself to be so jealous and by giving myself such an occasion more than my wife desired of giving her another month's dancing. Which however shall be ended as soon as I can possibly. . . .

Sat. 16th. Up with my mind disturbed and with my last night's doubts upon me, for which I deserve to be

---

23. *black man,* dark-haired man.

SEVENTEENTH-CENTURY LONDON. COURTESY OF THE TRUSTEES OF THE BRITISH MUSEUM.

beaten if not really served as I am fearful of being, especially since God knows that I do not find honesty enough in my own mind but that upon a small temptation I could be false to her, and therefore ought not to expect more justice from her, but God pardon both my sin and my folly herein. To my office and there sitting all the morning, and at noon dined at home. After dinner comes Pembleton, and I being out of humour would not see him, pretending business, but, Lord! with what jealousy did I walk up and down my chamber listening to hear whether they danced or no, which they did, notwithstanding I afterwards knew and did then believe that Ashwell was with them. So to my office awhile, and, my jealousy still reigning, I went in and, not out of any pleasure but from that only reason, did go up to them to practice, and did make an end of "La Duchesse," which I think I should, with a little pains, do very well. So broke up and saw him gone. . . .

Sun. 17th (Lord's day). Up and in my chamber all the morning, preparing my great letters to my father, stating to him the perfect condition of our estate. My wife and Ashwell to church, and after dinner they to church again, and I all the afternoon making an end of my morning's work, which I did about evening, and then to talk with my wife till after supper, and so to bed having another small falling out and myself vexed with my old fit of jealousy about her dancing-master. But I am a fool for doing it. So to bed by daylight, I having a very great cold, so as I doubt whether I shall be able to speak to-morrow at our attending the Duke, being now so hoarse.

Wed. 20th. Up and to my office, and anon home and to see my wife dancing with Pembleton about noon, and I to the Trinity House to dinner and after dinner home, and there met Pembleton, who I perceive has dined with my wife, which she takes no notice of, but whether that proceeds out of design, or fear to displease me I know not, but it put me into a great disorder again. . . .

Thurs. 21st. Up, but cannot get up so early as I was wont, nor my mind to business as it should be and used to be before this dancing. However, to my office, where most of the morning talking of Captain Cox of Chatham about his and the whole yard's difference against Mr. Barrow the storekeeper. . . . After much good advice and other talk I home and danced with Pembleton, and then the barber trimmed me, and so to dinner, my wife and I having high words about her dancing to that degree

that I did enter and make a vow to myself not to oppose her or say anything to dispraise or correct her therein as long as her month lasts, in pain of 2s. 6d. for every time, which, if God pleases, I will observe, for this roguish business has brought us more disquiett than anything [that] has happened a great while. After dinner to my office, where late, and then home; and Pembleton being there again, we fell to dance a country dance or two, and so to supper and bed. But being at supper my wife did say something that caused me to oppose her in, she used the word devil, which vexed me, and among other things I said I would not have her to use that word, upon which she took me up most scornfully, which, before Ashwell and the rest of the world, I know not now-a-days how to check, as I would heretofore, for less than that would have made me strike her. So that I fear without great discretion I shall go near to lose too my command over her, and nothing do it more than giving her this occasion of dancing and other pleasures, whereby her mind is taken up from her business and finds other sweets besides pleasing of me, and so makes her that she begins not at all to take pleasure in me or study to please me as heretofore. . . .

Fri. 22nd. Up pretty betimes, and shall, I hope, come to myself and business again, after a small playing the truant, for I find that my interest and profit do grow daily, for which God be praised and keep me to my duty. To my office, and anon one tells me that Rundall, the house-carpenter of Deptford, hath sent me a fine blackbird, which I went to see. He tells me he was offered 20s. for him as he came along, he do so whistle. So to my office, and busy all the morning, among other things, learning to understand the course of the tides, and I think I do now do it. At noon Mr. Creed comes to me, and he and I to the Exchange, where I had much discourse with several merchants, and so home with him to dinner, and then by water to Greenwich, and calling at the little alehouse at the end of the town to wrap a rag about my little left toe, being new sore with walking, we walked pleasantly to Woolwich, in our way hearing the nightingales sing. . . .

Sat. 23rd. Waked this morning between four and five by my blackbird, which whistles as well as ever I heard any; only it is the beginning of many tunes very well, but there leaves them, and goes no further. So up and to my office, where we sat, and among other things I had a fray with Sir J. Minnes in defence of my Will[24] in a business where the old coxcomb would have put a foot upon him, which was only in Jack Davis and in him a downright piece of knavery in procuring a double ticket and getting the wrong one paid as well as the second was to the true party. But it appeared clear enough to the board that Will was true in it. . . .

Sun. 24th (Lord's day). . . . forebore going to church this morning, but staid at home looking over my papers about Tom Trice's business, and so at noon dined, and my wife telling me that there was a pretty lady come to church with Peg Pen to-day, I against my intention had a mind to go to church to see her, and did so, and she is pretty handsome. But over against our gallery I espied Pembleton, and saw him leer upon my wife all the sermon, I taking no notice of him, and my wife upon him, and I observed she made a curtsey to him at coming out without taking notice to me at all of it, which with the consideration of her being desirous these two last Lord's days to go to church both forenoon and afternoon do really make me suspect something more than ordinary, though I am loth to think the worst, but yet it put and do still keep me at a great loss in my mind, and makes me curse the time that I consented to her dancing. . . . But I must have patience and get her into the country, or at least to make an end of her learning to dance as soon as I can.

After sermon to Sir W. Pen's, with Sir J. Minnes to do a little business to answer Mr. Coventry to-night. And so home and with my wife and Ashwell into the garden walking a great while, discoursing what this pretty wench should be by her garb and deportment; with respect to Mrs. Pen she may be her woman, but only that she sat in the pew with her, which I believe he would not let her do. So home, and read to my wife a fable or two in Ogleby's Æsop, and so to supper, and then to prayers and to bed. My wife this evening discoursing of making clothes for the country, which I seem against, pleading lack of money, but I am glad of it in some respects because of getting her out of the way from this fellow, and my own liberty to look after my business more than of late I have done. So to prayers and to bed. . . .

Mon. 25th. I staid within most of the morning, and by and by the barber came and Sarah Kite my cozen, poor woman, came to see me and borrow 40s. of me, telling me she will pay it at Michaelmas again to me.

I was glad it was no more, being indifferent whether she pays it me or no, but it will be a good excuse to lend her nor give her any more. So I did freely at first word do it, and give her a crown more freely to buy her child something, she being a good-natured and painful wretch, and one that I would do good for as far as I can that I might not be burdened. . . .

Ashwell did by and by come to me with an errand from her mistress to desire money to buy a country suit for her against she goes as we talked last night, and so I did give her £4, and believe it will cost me the best part of 4 more to fit her out, but with peace and honour I am willing to spare anything so as to be able to keep all ends together, and my power over her undisturbed. So to my office and by and by home, where my wife and her master were dancing, and so I staid in my chamber till they had done, and sat down myself to try a little upon the Lyra viall,[25] my hand being almost out, but easily brought to again.

Tues. 26th. Lay long in bed talking with my wife. So up and to my office a while and then home, where I found Pembleton, and by many circumstances I am led to conclude that there is something more than ordinary between my wife and him, which do so trouble me that I know not at this very minute that I now write this almost what either I write or am doing, nor how to carry myself to my wife in it, being unwilling to speak of it to her for making of any breach and other inconveniences, nor let it pass for fear of her continuing to offend me and the matter grow worse thereby. So that I am grieved at the very heart, but I am very unwise in being so.

There dined with me Mr. Creed and Captain Grove, and before dinner I had much discourse in my chamber with Mr. Deane, the builder of Woolwich, about building of ships. But nothing could get the business out of my head, I fearing that this afternoon by my wife's sending every [one] abroad and knowing that I must be at the office she has appointed him to come. This Is my devilish jealousy, which I pray God may be false, but it makes a very hell in my mind, which the God of heaven remove, or I shall be very unhappy. So to the office, where we sat awhile. By and by my mind being in great trouble I went home to see how things were, and there I found as I doubted Mr. Pembleton with my wife, and nobody else in the house, which made me almost mad, and going up to my chamber after a turn or

---

24. *Will* (Hewer), Pepys' chief clerk.

25. *Lyra viall* (viol), a stringed musical instrument.

two I went out again and called somebody on pretence of business and left him in my little room at the door (it was the Dutchman, commander of the King's pleasure boats, who having been beat by one of his men sadly, was come to the office to-day to complain) telling him I would come again to him to speak with him about his business. So in great trouble and doubt to the office, and Mr. Coventry nor Sir G. Carteret being there I made a quick end of our business and desired leave to be gone, pretending to go to the Temple, but it was home, and so up to my chamber, and as I think if they had any intention of hurt I did prevent doing anything at that time, but I continued in my chamber vexed and angry till he went away, pretending aloud, that I might hear, that he could not stay, and Mrs. Ashwell not being within they could not dance. And, Lord! to see how my jealousy wrought so far that I went softly up to see whether any of the beds were out of order or no, which I found not, but that did not content me, but I staid all the evening walking, and though anon my wife came up to me and would have spoke of business to me, yet I construed it to be but impudence, and though my heart full yet I did say nothing, being in a great doubt what to do. So at night, suffered them to go all to bed, and late put myself to bed in great discontent, and so to sleep.

Wed. 27th. So I waked by 3 o'clock, my mind being troubled, and after having lain till past 4 o'clock seemed going to rise, though I did it only to see what my wife would do, and so going out of the bed she took hold of me and would know what ailed me, and after many kind and some cross words I began to tax her discretion in yesterday's business, but she quickly told me my own, knowing well enough that it was my old disease of jealousy, which I denied, but to no purpose. After an hour's discourse, sometimes high and sometimes kind, I found very good reason to think that her freedom with him is very great and more than was convenient, but with no evil intent, and so after awhile I caressed her and parted seeming friends, but she crying in a great discontent. So I up and by water to the Temple, and thence with Commissioner Pett to St. James's. . . .

This day there was great thronging to Banstead Downs, upon a great horse-race and foot-race. I am sorry I could not go thither. So home back as I came, to London Bridge, and so home, where I find my wife in a musty humour, and tells me before Ashwell that Pembleton had been there, and she would not have him come in unless I was there, which I was ashamed of; but however, I had rather it should be so than the other way. So to my office, to put things in order there, and by and by comes Pembleton, and word is brought me from my wife thereof that I might come home. So I sent word that I would have her go dance, and I would come presently. So being at a great loss whether I should appear to Pembleton or no, and what would most proclaim my jealousy to him, I at last resolved to go home, and took Tom Hater with me, and staid a good while in my chamber, and there took occasion to tell him how I hear that Parliament is putting an act out against all sorts of conventicles,[26] and did give him good counsel, not only in his own behalf, but my own, that if he did hear or know anything that could be said to my prejudice, that he would tell me, for in this wicked age . . . a man ought to be prepared to answer for himself in all things that can be inquired concerning him. After much discourse of this nature to him I sent him away, and then went up, and there we danced country dances, and single, my wife and I; and my wife paid him off for this month also, and so he is cleared. After dancing we took him down to supper, and were very merry, and I made myself so, and kind to him as much as I could, to prevent his discourse, though I perceive to my trouble that he knows all, and may do me the disgrace to publish it as much as he can. Which I take very ill, and if too much provoked shall witness it to her. After supper and he gone we to bed.

Thurs. 28th. . . . after dinner by water to the Royall Theatre; but that was so full they told us we could have no room. And so to the Duke's House; and there saw ''Hamlett'' done, giving us fresh reason never to think enough of Betterton.[27] Who should we see come upon the stage but Gosnell, my wife's maid? but neither spoke, danced, nor sung; which I was sorry for. But she becomes the stage very well. . . .

Fri. 29th. This day is kept strictly as a holy-day, being the King's Coronation. We lay long in bed, and it rained very hard, rain and hail, almost all the morning. By and by Creed and I abroad, and called

---

26. *conventicles,* unlawful religious assemblies (as of the Quakers) where worship was conducted not according to the rites of the Church of England.

27. *Betterton,* Thomas Betterton, famous Shakespearean actor. He was especially noted for his portrayal of Hamlet, a role he played for over 50 years.

at several churches; and it is a wonder to see, and by that to guess the ill temper of the City at this time, either to religion in general, or to the King, that in some churches there was hardly ten people in the whole church, and those poor people. So to a coffee-house, and there in discourse hear the King of France is likely to be well again. So home to dinner, and out by water to the Royall Theatre, but they not acting to-day, then to the Duke's house, and there saw ''The Slighted Mayde,'' wherein Gosnell acted Pyramena, a great part, and did it very well, and I believe will do it better and better, and prove a good actor. I to my brother's, and thence to my uncle Fenner's to have seen my aunt James (who has been long in town and goes away to-morrow and I not seen her), but did find none of them within, which I was glad of, and so back to my brother's to speak with him, and so home, and in my way did take two turns forwards and backwards through the Fleete Ally to see a couple of pretty [strumpets] that stood off the doors there, and God forgive me I could scarce stay myself from going into their houses with them, so apt is my nature to evil after once, as I have these two days, set upon pleasure again. . . .

Sun. 31st (Lord's day). Lay long in bed talking with my wife, and do plainly see that her distaste (which is beginning now in her again) against Ashwell arises from her jealousy of me and her, and my neglect of herself, which indeed is true, and I to blame; but for the time to come I will take care to remedy all. So up and to church, where I think I did see Pembleton, whatever the reason is I did not perceive him to look up towards my wife, nor she much towards him; however, I could hardly keep myself from being troubled that he was there, which is a madness not to be excused now that his coming to my house is past, and I hope all likelyhood of her having occasion to converse with him again. Home to dinner, and after dinner up and read part of the new play of ''The Five Houres' Adventures,'' which though I have seen it twice, yet I never did admire or understand it enough, it being a play of the greatest plot that ever I expect to see, and of great vigour quite through the whole play, from beginning to the end. To church again after dinner (my wife finding herself ill . . . did not go), and there the Scot preaching I slept most of the sermon. This day Sir W. Batten's son's child is christened in the country, whither Sir J. Minnes, and Sir W. Batten, and Sir W. Pen are all gone. I wonder, and take it highly ill that I am not invited by the father, though I know his father and mother, with whom I am never likely to have much kindness, but rather I study the contrary, are the cause of it, and in that respect I am glad of it.

Being come from church, I to make up my month's accounts, and find myself clear worth £726, for which God be praised, but yet I might have been better by £20 almost had I forborne some layings out in dancing and other things upon my wife, and going to plays and other things merely to ease my mind as to the business of the dancing-master, which I bless God is now over. . . .

This month the greatest news is, the height and heat that the Parliament is in, in enquiring into the revenue, which displeases the Court, and their backwardness to give the King any money. Their enquiring into the selling of places do trouble a great many; among the chief, my Lord Chancellor (against whom particularly it is carried), and Mr. Coventry; for which I am sorry. The King of France was given out to be poisoned and dead; but it proves to be the measles: and he is well, or likely to be soon well again. I find myself growing in the esteem and credit that I have in the office, and I hope falling to my business again will confirm me in it, and the saving of money, which God grant! So to supper, prayers, and bed.   □

DISCUSSION

1. What aspect of Pepys' diary do you find interesting? What seemed boring? trivial? shameful?

2. Discuss Pepys' relationship with his wife:

(a) How would you characterize his feelings about his wife?

(b) How well did he understand his own feelings?

(c) How does his own behavior compare with his wife's?

3. More than any other kind of writing, a diary reveals the character of the man who writes it. Point out passages that reveal aspects of Pepys' character. Was he a good man, a bad man, or simply human?

4. What insights does Pepys' diary offer into the society of his day? Point out passages that reveal social customs or structures different from those prevailing today.

WRITING

1. Use your imagination and write a day's entry for Pepys' diary, perhaps a day on which he discovered his wife in the arms of another man, or a day on which she discovered him giving way to temptation.

2. Write a day's entry for your own diary, choosing the most interesting day of the past week. Be as honest as you can in describing your feelings about events and people.

3. Keep a diary for a week, modeling it after Pepys', and see what you can discover about yourself in the process of close examination of your life and yourself.

THE GREAT FIRE OF 1666. COURTESY OF THE MASTER AND COURT OF THE WORSHIPFUL COMPANY OF GOLDSMITHS OF LONDON.

VI. BACKGROUND

The Seventeenth Century

WITH Queen Elizabeth's death in 1603, the uneasy peace which she had imposed on the contentious religious factions of the realm began to dissolve. James I, Elizabeth's successor to the throne, lacked both her quick political touch and her flexibility; he was a stubborn Anglican who was determined to make both Catholic and Puritan "conform" to the official religion of the state—a policy which,

as continued by Charles I, his son, was to prove disastrous. The general belief in an ordered universe and the shared feelings of national unity and destiny, which had provided domestic peace and social stability during Elizabeth's long reign, also began to crumble. The history of the seventeenth century was consequently one of violence and upheaval. By the end of the century England had witnessed seven years of bloody civil war which terminated in the beheading of King Charles I in 1649, the overthrow of the monarchy and the establishment of a totalitarian Puritan Commonwealth (1649–1660), the restoration of the monarchy (Charles II, 1660–1685), the deposing of another king (James II, 1685–1688), and the establishment on the throne of a foreign monarch (William III, who reigned with his wife, Mary, 1689–1702).

If the conflict between Anglicans and Puritans—Cavalier elegance and decadence on the one side arrayed against Puritan sobriety and fanaticism on the other—dominates the age, there were other forces at work which were of equal importance. The religious conflicts gave birth to new modes of worship, producing a multiplicity of religious sects and forcing men to rely on their own moral and religious intuitions. The old, static order of social station and duty was disrupted, not only by the armed conflicts which swept the land, but also by the spiritual trauma which followed the execution of Charles I, whom many viewed as God's true representative on earth (although the Puritans obviously dissented). Men were forced, amid a welter of arguments and counterarguments, to decide for themselves what direction their lives should take. The cruel conflicts and persecutions of the age forced the growth of individualism.

Contributing to the development of individualism and to the decay of the old hierarchical order were a number of scientific developments. The astronomer Galileo conducted experiments in Italy which confirmed the Copernican theory that the earth was not, as the Elizabethans believed, the center of the universe, but was, in fact, only one of the planets that revolved around the sun. Other scientific experiments and discoveries—principally those of William Harvey on the circulation of the blood, and of Sir Isaac Newton on the theory of gravity—radically changed the ways men looked at themselves and their world.

The development of a strong and prosperous middle class also challenged the old views and ways. Tradesmen flourished, and by the end of the century had become competitive with members of the Court as leaders of society. The rise of the middle class and its growing representation in Parliament no doubt helped transform the government into the constitutional monarchy it was by the end of the century.

Other events contributed to the passing of the old order. In 1665, shortly after the restoration of Charles II, a ferocious outbreak of bubonic plague killed a quarter of the population of London. In the following year the Great Fire destroyed whole sections of the city, leaving more than thirteen thousand buildings and many public monuments in ashes. The rebuilding of the capital city represents only one aspect of the vast restructuring and slow healing that the nation was to undergo in the last half of the century.

Much of seventeenth-century literature was born of the uncertainties and intense questioning of the time. Donne's famous religious sonnet, "Batter my heart, three-person'd God," for instance, has about it a fierce intensity, a sort of barely controlled violence, which must in some manner portray the personal force behind contemporary religious issues. In general the poets of the seventeenth century seem to be engaged in an earnest search for the essential elements of man's relationship with the world and his fellow men; there is in much of their writing a sense of urgency, a startling impatience with the constrictions of time and circumstance, a strenuous arguing against the inglorious facts of the human condition, particularly against the ultimate curb on all human striving, death. The poetry of the Cavaliers is on the lighter and more elegant side of these concerns; and the poetry of Puritan Milton more solemn and somber-hued, but the urgency and argument are there (Milton's argument "to justify the ways of God to man" perhaps the most ambitious of all). Pepys' orientation is more worldly, his concerns as a man on the make in Restoration London more pedestrian; but the earnestness is there, and no detail of the contemporary scene is too trivial or too personal for his record.

Beneath the chaotic surface of the seventeenth century vital changes in individual outlook, religious attitudes, and governmental policies took place. The image of the age is one of difficult and painful change, of prejudices, hostilities, abrupt reversals in fortune, and finally of deep-rooted tensions and uncertainties not unlike those of our own time. □

METAPHYSICAL WIT

by Samuel Johnson

WIT, like all other things subject by their nature to the choice of man, has its changes and fashions, and at different times takes different forms. About the beginning of the seventeenth century appeared a race of writers that may be termed the metaphysical poets. . . .

The metaphysical poets were men of learning, and to show their learning was their whole endeavor; but, unluckily resolving to show it in rhyme, instead of writing poetry they only wrote verses, and very often such verses as stood the trial of the finger better than of the ear; for the modulation was so imperfect that they were only found to be verses by counting the syllables. . . .

If wit be well described by Pope as being "that which has been often thought, but was never before so well expressed,"[1] they certainly never attained nor ever sought it, for they endeavored to be singular in their thoughts, and were careless of their diction. But Pope's account of wit is undoubtedly erroneous; he depresses it below its natural dignity, and reduces it from strength of thought to happiness of language.

If by a more noble and more adequate conception that be considered as wit which is at once natural and new, that which though not obvious is, upon its first production, acknowledged to be just;[2] if it be that which he that never found it, wonders how he missed; to wit of this kind the metaphysical poets have seldom risen. Their thoughts are often new, but seldom natural; they are not obvious, but neither are they just; and the reader, far from wondering that he missed them, wonders more frequently by what perverseness of industry they were ever found.

But wit, abstracted from its effects upon the hearer, may be more rigorously and philosophically considered as a kind of *discordia concors*,[3] a combination of dissimilar images, or discovery of occult resemblances in things apparently unlike. Of wit, thus defined, they have more than enough. The most heterogeneous ideas are yoked by violence together: nature and art are ransacked for illustrations, comparisons, and allusions; their learning instructs, and their subtlety surprises; but the reader commonly thinks his improvement dearly bought, and, though he sometimes admires, is seldom pleased.

From this account of their compositions it will be readily inferred that they were not successful in representing or moving the affections. As they were wholly employed on something unexpected and surprising, they had no regard to that uniformity of sentiment which enables us to conceive and to excite the pains and the pleasure of other minds. . . . Their wish was only to say what they hoped had been never said before.

. . . Those writers who lay on the watch for novelty could have little hope of greatness; for great things cannot have escaped former observation. Their attempts were always analytic: they broke every image into fragments, and could no more represent by their slender conceits and labored particularities the prospects of nature or the scenes of life, than he who dissects a sunbeam with a prism can exhibit the wide effulgence of a summer noon. . . .

Yet great labor directed by great abilities is never wholly lost: if they frequently threw away their wit upon false conceits, they likewise sometimes struck out unexpected truth: if their conceits were far-fetched, they were often worth the carriage. To write on their plan it was at least necessary to read and think. . . .

From "Cowley," in *The Lives of the English Poets* by Samuel Johnson (1779).

1. From Alexander Pope's *Essay on Criticism*. Excerpts appear in the section on the Eighteenth Century.
2. *just*, exact; proper.

3. *discordia concors*, literally, "a harmonious discord."

The
Changing
English Language

THE desire for order and certainty which emerged amidst the turmoil of the seventeenth century was reflected in the development of the language. Particularly in the latter half of the century, Englishmen, reacting against the novelties and unregulated spontaneity which characterized Elizabethan expression, began to call for an ordered, rational language.

English was discovered to have no body of grammatical rules that could serve as a systematic and unfailing guide to "correct" expression, and therefore Latin models were turned to once more. John Dryden, who was one of the loudest in his outcries against the unruly language of his predecessors ("we . . . have not so much as a tolerable dictionary, or a grammar, so that our language is in a manner barbarous," he wrote) is said at one point in his career to have translated his thoughts first into Latin to discover their most proper form of expression in English.

The Royal Society, founded in 1660 by a group of learned man and scientists, objected to the Eliza-

bethan love of verbal gymnastics on the ground that it was unscientific, and demanded of its members instead "a close, naked, natural way of speaking; positive expressions, clear senses, a native easiness, bringing as near the mathematical plainness as they can." The scientists were supported in this matter by the Puritans, who objected to display of any kind, whether in matters of religion, dress, or language.

As Englishmen expanded their interests abroad in the seventeenth century, their language continued to absorb foreign words. Increased commercial rivalry with the Dutch brought in such terms as *bowsprit, brandy, cruise, freight, keel, smack*, and *sloop*. From the American colonies came such words as *canoe, maize, papoose*, and *squaw*. The popularity of Italian music in the latter half of the century gave rise to terms such as *aria, allegro, contralto, cantata, opera, oratorio, piano, soprano*, and *trombone*. The main change, however, was the growing emphasis on ease and clearness of expression, which came to full bloom in attempts to standardize, refine, and give permanent order and status to English in the eighteenth century.

Cavalier (left) from Battles of the English Civil War, by Austin Woolrych, B. T. Botsford, London. Roundhead (right) by courtesy of the Trustees of The London Museum.

BIOGRAPHIES

Abraham Cowley   1618 / 1667

During his lifetime Cowley was most admired for long and learned poems embroidered with bold conceits. He published his first book of poetry at fifteen, and the bulk of his later work was in imitation of classical poets, both Greek and Roman.

A royalist, Cowley served as secretary to the exiled Queen during the Civil Wars, coding and decoding her correspondence. He was probably a spy, and he journeyed about the continent and England on royal missions.

Returning to England after the Restoration, he became one of the charter members of the Royal Society, and finally retired to his country estate to write.

John Donne   1572 / 1631

The dichotomy of flesh and spirit found in Donne's work reflects the sequence of styles in his own life. He came from a prosperous Catholic family, studied at both Oxford and Cambridge, and began to read law. As a young man his main interests seem to have been the theater, women, and the writing of bawdy and cynical verse. In 1596 he joined a military campaign and journeyed to Cadiz; the following year he went on another campaign to the Azores. In 1598 he was appointed secretary to one of the Queen's ministers, but he eloped with the minister's niece three years later and lost favor and his position.

Among the various means by which Donne tried to support his growing family (he eventually fathered twelve children) was pamphlet writing, and some of his tracts were in support of the Anglican Church. In 1607 King James, impressed by these works, urged Donne to take holy orders. (Donne had converted to the established Church before 1600.) Since the King refused to grant him any other position, Donne finally joined the clergy in 1615.

Donne preached regularly before members of the court and London's wealthy merchant class, and the literary and dramatic flair of his sermons made him widely admired. In 1621 he was appointed Dean of St. Paul's Cathedral, and he was in line for a bishopric when he died.

During his later years, Donne became obsessed with the idea of death. He is said to have preached his own funeral oration several weeks before his death, and he posed, wrapped in a shroud, for the effigy on his own tomb.

John Dryden   1631 / 1700

Dryden lived in a time of political and religious turmoil, and his own beliefs seemed to shift with the times. Coming from a family with Puritan and anti-Royalist leanings, he began his literary career in 1659 with a poem in praise of Cromwell. After the Restoration the next year, he came out in favor of the Anglican Church and the monarchy by publishing a poem in praise of Charles II. When the Crown became Catholic with the accession of James II in 1685, Dryden became a convert to Catholicism. One of his most celebrated poems, *The Hind and the Panther,* was a defense of the Catholic religion. He remained a Catholic after the Protestants William and Mary came to power three years later, even at the cost of the royal pensions and offices he had held. From then on, he had to depend entirely upon his pen for a living.

Dryden wrote poetry, verse satire, prose prefaces, and literary criticism, but his chief source of income was the stage. One of the most prolific dramatists of the Restoration, he turned out comedies, tragedies, and heroic plays for the newly opened theaters. His best play was *All for Love,* a version of the story of Antony and Cleopatra. He also translated Vergil, revised Chaucer, collaborated on an adaptation of Shakespeare's *The Tempest,* and made *Paradise Lost* into an opera.

Dryden was one of the first writers to break away from the extravagant style of the late metaphysical poets and to write in a more restrained and natural style. The heroic couplet he used in many of his satires and plays became the dominant poetic style for a century.

George Herbert   1593 / 1633

Herbert was a member of an ancient and distinguished Welsh family. He was an outstanding scholar at Cambridge, and in 1619 was made orator of the university, a post which required him to express, in florid Latin, the sentiments of the university on public occasions. The post also required him to spend much time at court. However, it did not lead to the political advancement he had hoped for, and in 1630 he followed the practice of many younger sons from highly connected families and took holy orders. He accepted appointment as a country priest. Unlike many others, however, he actually did the work of a priest, preaching and praying, visiting the poor and sick, and rebuilt his church out of his own pocket. He died of consumption after a ministry of only three years. A collection of the religious poetry for which he is known was published after his death.

Robert Herrick   1591 / 1674

Like Donne and Herbert, Herrick turned from a worldly life to holy orders. He loved London and the society of poets and wits like Ben Jonson, and when in 1629 he was appointed to a country parish in Devonshire, he considered it a bitter exile. Gradually, though, he came to delight in the life and customs of the West Country. As a Royalist, he lost his post during the Puritan upheaval and returned to London in 1647. The next year he published his only book, a collection of 1200 poems. Because the times were tempestuous (the country was obsessed with the trial and execution of King Charles I), Herrick's book was soon lost to public view. After the Restoration, Herrick was reinstated in his parish and resumed his quiet country life. His poetry was rediscovered only in the 19th century.

Ben Jonson   1572 / 1637

Jonson was a charismatic person who fascinated his contemporaries. His work was scholarly, the result, perhaps, of several years of classical schooling he received as a boy and many years of self-tutelage in later life. He never went to university (though both Oxford and Cambridge later awarded him honorary degrees). Instead he took up his stepfather's trade, bricklaying, and then entered the army. During service in Flanders he killed a Spaniard in single-handed combat as both English and Spanish armies looked on.

On his return to London in 1595 he became an actor and a playwright. He produced his first successful play, *Every Man in His Humour*, in 1598 (Shakespeare, a friend, acted in it). Shortly after this, Jonson, always hot-headed, was imprisoned and nearly executed for killing a fellow actor in a duel. Once released, he continued his career in the theater, gained the favor of James I, and became a writer of court masques—elaborate spectacles which involved music, dancing, and pageantry. During this period he also wrote a number of satiric comedies, two of which—*Volpone* and *The Alchemist*—are still considered among the supreme satiric achievements of the English stage.

After the death of James I, Jonson was neglected by both the public and the court, for Charles I patronized painters rather than writers. Nevertheless, he became the center of a circle of young poets who dubbed themselves "The

Tribe of Ben" and regularly joined him at the Mermaid Tavern for feasts of wine and wit. At his death Jonson was widely mourned as the last of the great Elizabethans. He lies buried in Westminster Abbey under the inscription "O Rare Ben Jonson."

Richard Lovelace   1618 / 1658

Handsome and clever, the eldest son of a wealthy family, Richard Lovelace was very much the courtly Cavalier poet. When King Charles and his queen visited Oxford in 1636, they were so favorably impressed by undergraduate Lovelace's demeanor that they commanded he be given an M.A. on the spot. However, his allegiance to King Charles during the Civil Wars caused him several stays in prison (during the first of which he wrote "To Althea").

His periods of imprisonment and his adventures in the French campaign against the Spanish, during which he was wounded, exhausted his inheritance. He spent the last years of his life impoverished and depressed, and died at the age of 39 in a London slum.

Andrew Marvell   1621 / 1678

Marvell was a quiet and sensible man with Puritan leanings who became devoted to Cromwell's cause. Yet he was so extremely tolerant of others' opinions that as a student at Cambridge he allowed a Jesuit to persuade him to quit his studies. (The senior Marvell, an Anglican minister, found his son in a London bookshop and convinced him to return to the university.) After earning his degree, he traveled abroad for several years and then became a tutor to the daughter of Sir Thomas Fairfax, Lord-General of the Parliamentary Forces.

In 1657 Marvell was appointed assistant to Milton, who was then Latin Secretary. Two years later Marvell was elected to the House of Commons, where he served his constituents conscientiously, refusing all bribes and writing frequent newsletters. These newsletters, together with some satires and religious tracts, made up most of the writings for which he was known during his lifetime. Three years after his death a volume of his poetry was published by a woman who claimed to be his widow, but who later turned out to be his housekeeper.

John Milton   1608 / 1674

In his parents' cultured Puritan home, Milton began to write poetry at the age of ten. After finishing his formal education with an M.A. from Cambridge, he returned to his family's country home at Horton to study under his own direction. There he read almost everything available in Latin, Greek, Italian, and English, and wrote the elegy *Lycidas* and the masque *Comus*. After five years at Horton, Milton embarked on a two-year tour of Europe, where he found his literary reputation had already begun to spread. With the outbreak of the Civil Wars, he returned to England, where he tutored and wrote pamphlets. When his first marriage went awry, he became an early and vehement advocate of divorce on the grounds of incompatibility, a cause which he championed in his pamphlets and which many people in Puritan England found reprehensible. (Milton was married three times, widowed twice.)

Under the new Commonwealth, Milton was appointed Latin Secretary (a post comparable to Secretary of Foreign Affairs). While he held this office, eyestrain from years of reading late into the night caused him to become totally blind.

Despite a brief imprisonment, the seizure of most of his property, and the destruction of some of his pamphlets, Milton survived the Restoration essentially unharmed. He and his daughters retired to a quiet life. Accounts tell of tension between the stern and dictatorial Milton and his unsympathetic daughters, who resented having to read aloud in languages they did not understand and take dictation for hours on end, but the final years of Milton's life were productive, if not completely peaceful. During his last decade he wrote (through dictation) *Paradise Lost*, *Paradise Regained*, and *Samson Agonistes*.

Samuel Pepys   1633 / 1703

In his *Diary*, Pepys probably revealed more about himself and his society than any biographer or historian has done. He had the knack of being at the center of important events: as a schoolboy he was an eyewitness to the beheading of Charles I; years later, he was with the fleet that brought Charles II back to England to restore the monarchy. A shrewd observer and a meticulous businessman, he noted in his *Diary* everything from daily trivia and personal intimacies to the most dramatic of public events—the Plague of 1665 and the Fire of London in 1666. He was a conscientious public servant who eventually achieved, through deft use of social influence and incessant politicking, the high office of Secretary to the Navy in 1673.

Though his years in high office were not uneventful (he was imprisoned twice, and released both times due largely to the influence of powerful friends), his public career ended with the Glorious Revolution of 1688. He spent the rest of his years in retirement at Clapham, publishing in 1690 his *Memoirs of the Navy*, the only work other than his official reports which he ever intended the public or posterity to read.

Sir John Suckling   1609 / 1642

Suckling, like Lovelace, was a graceful and carefree Cavalier dandy. Living mainly off a sizable inheritance, he cut a dashing figure at court. He preferred women, music, and gambling to the refinements of wit and intellect. During the Civil Wars he raised a gaudily outfitted company of "gentlemen" for a campaign against the Scots, but the whole company withdrew swiftly if not graciously on first contact with the enemy.

In 1641 Suckling, a Loyalist, became involved in a plot to free one of the King's imprisoned ministers. The plot was discovered; Suckling was accused of conspiracy to overthrow Parliament. Realizing that the King could no longer provide protection, he fled to France. There he died in poverty the following year, possibly by his own hand.

George Wither   1588 / 1667

Wither first made his reputation as a poet and satirist. His satires were considered libelous and several times landed him in prison. He was in London during the plague of 1625 and wrote a lengthy poem about it. During the Civil Wars he served as a military commander, first on the side of King Charles I, later on the side of the Puritans. In 1642 he sold his estate to raise a troop of horse and was placed in charge of Farnham Castle. A few days later he set off for London, leaving the castle undefended, and was captured by Royalists. He would have been hanged except for the intervention of Sir John Denham, who said that so long as Wither lived, he himself would not be the worst poet in England.

As a convinced Puritan, Wither wrote many hymns and religious tracts. After the Restoration he spent another three years in jail, but passed the last years of his life quietly in London.

276

WILLIAM HOGARTH, "THE BENCH" (1758). COURTESY OF THE TRUSTEES OF THE BRITISH MUSEUM.

Jonathan Swift
1667 / 1745

The eighteenth century—at least the first half of it—was the Age of Reason, for it had rigid rules for everything from the "taming" of Shakespeare to the pruning of gardens and the way people should conduct themselves. Men of the age looked upon their forefathers as rude barbarians and themselves as the first civilized Englishmen.

Yet to some it was painfully clear that, actually, their society was still as irrational and crude as ever. And thus, in literature, satire became the dominant form; it varied with the temperaments of the men producing it—from the mild and smiling admonitions of Joseph Addison to the bitterly disillusioned condemnations of Jonathan Swift.

A MODEST PROPOSAL

For Preventing the Children of
Poor People in Ireland from Being a Burden to
Their Parents or Country, and for Making
Them Beneficial to the Public

It is a melancholy object to those who walk through this great town,[1] or travel in the country, when they see the streets, the roads, and cabin doors crowded with beggars of the female sex, followed by three, four, or six children, all in rags and importuning every passenger for an alms. These mothers, instead of being able to work for their honest livelihood, are forced to employ all their time in strolling to beg sustenance for their helpless infants; who as they grow up either turn thieves, for want of work, or leave their dear native country to fight for the pretender[2] in Spain, or sell themselves to the Barbados.[3]

I think it is agreed by all parties that this prodigious number of children in the arms, or on the backs, or at the heels of their mothers, and frequently of their fathers, is, in the present deplorable state of the kingdom, a very great additional grievance; and therefore whoever could find out a fair, cheap, and easy method of making these children sound, useful members of the commonwealth would deserve so well of the public as to have his statue set up for a preserver of the nation.

But my intention is very far from being confined to provide only for the children of professed beggars: it is of a much greater extent and shall take in the whole number of infants at a certain age who are born of parents in effect as little able to support them as those who demand our charity in the streets.

As to my own part, having turned my thoughts for many years upon this important subject and maturely weighed the several schemes of our projectors, I have always found them grossly mistaken in their computation. It is true, a child just dropped from its dam may be supported by her milk for a solar year, with little other nourishment: at most not above the value of two shillings which the mother may certainly get, or the value in scraps, by her lawful occupation of begging; and it is exactly at one year old that I propose to provide for them in such a manner, as, instead of being a charge upon their parents or the parish, or wanting food and raiment for the rest of their lives, they shall, on the contrary, contribute to the feeding and partly to the clothing of many thousands.

There is likewise another great advantage in my scheme, that it will prevent those voluntary abortions and that horrid practice of women murdering their bastard children, alas! too frequent among us, sacrificing the poor innocent babes, I doubt more to avoid the expense than the shame, which would move tears and pity in the most savage and inhuman breast.

The number of souls in this kingdom being usually reckoned one million and a half, of these I calculate there may be about two hundred thousand couple, whose wives are breeders; from which number I subtract thirty thousand couple, who are able to maintain their own children (although I apprehend there cannot be so many, under the present distresses of the kingdom), but this being granted, there will remain an hundred and seventy thousand breeders.

---

1. *this great town,* Dublin.
2. *the pretender,* James Stuart (1688–1766), son of King James II, "pretender" or claimant to the throne which his father had lost in the Revolution of 1688. He was Catholic, and Ireland was loyal to him.
3. *sell . . . Barbados.* Because of extreme poverty, many of the Irish bound or "sold" themselves to obtain passage to the West Indies or other British possessions in North America. They agreed to work for their new masters, usually planters, for a specified number of years.

I again subtract fifty thousand for those women who miscarry, or whose children die by accident or disease within the year. There only remains one hundred and twenty thousand children of poor parents annually born. The question therefore is, How this number shall be reared and provided for? which, as I have already said, under the present situation of affairs, is utterly impossible by all the methods hitherto proposed. For we can neither employ them in handicraft or agriculture; we neither build houses (I mean in the country) nor cultivate land: they can very seldom pick up a livelihood by stealing till they arrive at six years old, except where they are of towardly[4] parts; although I confess they learn the rudiments much earlier; during which time they can, however, be properly looked upon only as probationers; as I have been informed by a principal gentleman in the county of Cavan, who protested to me that he never knew above one or two instances under the age of six, even in a part of the kingdom so renowned for the quickest proficiency in that art.

I am assured by our merchants that a boy or a girl before twelve years old is no salable commodity; and even when they come to this age they will not yield above three pounds, or three pounds and half a crown at most, on the exchange; which cannot turn to account either to the parents or kingdom, the charge of nutriment and rags having been at least four times that value.

I shall now therefore humbly propose my own thoughts, which I hope will not be liable to the least objection.

I have been assured by a very knowing American of my acquaintance in London that a young healthy child well nursed is at a year old a most delicious, nourishing, and wholesome food, whether stewed, roasted, baked, or boiled; and I make no doubt that it will equally serve in a fricassee or a ragout.[5]

I do therefore humbly offer it to public consideration that of the hundred and twenty thousand children already computed, twenty thousand may be reserved for breed, whereof only one-fourth part to be males; which is more than we allow to sheep, black cattle, or swine; and my reason is that these children are seldom the fruits of marriage, a circumstance not much regarded by our savages; therefore one male will be sufficient to serve four females. That the remaining hundred thousand may, at a

year old, be offered in sale to the persons of quality and fortune through the kingdom; always advising the mother to let them suck plentifully in the last month, so as to render them plump and fat for a good table. A child will make two dishes at an entertainment for friends; and when the family dines alone, the fore or hind quarter will make a reasonable dish, and seasoned with a little pepper or salt will be very good boiled on the fourth day, especially in winter.

I have reckoned upon a medium that a child just born will weigh twelve pounds, and in a solar year, if tolerably nursed, will increase to twenty-eight pounds.

I grant this food will be somewhat dear, and therefore very proper for landlords, who, as they have already devoured most of the parents, seem to have the best title to the children.

Infant's flesh will be in season throughout the year, but more plentifully in March, and a little before and after: for we are told by a grave author, an eminent French physician,[6] that fish being a prolific diet, there are more children born in Roman Catholic countries about nine months after Lent than at any other season; therefore, reckoning a year after Lent, the markets will be more glutted than usual, because the number of popish infants is at least three to one in this kingdom: and therefore it will have one other collateral advantage, by lessening the number of papists among us.

I have already computed the charge of nursing a beggar's child (in which list I reckon all cottagers, laborers, and four-fifths of the farmers) to be about two shillings per annum, rags included; and I believe no gentleman would repine to give ten shillings for the carcass of a good fat child, which, as I have said, will make four dishes of excellent nutritive meat, when he has only some particular friend or his own family to dine with him. Thus the squire will learn to be a good landlord and grow popular among his tenants; the mother will have eight shillings net profit and be fit for work till she produces another child.

Those who are more thrifty (as I must confess the times require) may flay the carcass; the skin of which artificially[7] dressed will make admirable gloves for ladies and summer boots for fine gentlemen.

---

4. *towardly*, dutiful; easily managed.
5. *ragout*, a highly seasoned meat stew.

6. *grave author . . . physician*, François Rabelais (c.1494–1553), who was anything but a "grave author."
7. *artificially*, artfully; skillfully.

As to our city of Dublin, shambles[8] may be appointed for this purpose in the most convenient parts of it, and butchers we may be assured will not be wanting; although I rather recommend buying the children alive and dressing them hot from the knife as we do roasting pigs.

A very worthy person, a true lover of his country, and whose virtues I highly esteem, was lately pleased, in discoursing on this matter, to offer a refinement upon my scheme. He said that many gentlemen of this kingdom, having of late destroyed their deer, he conceived that the want of venison might be well supplied by the bodies of young lads and maidens, not exceeding fourteen years of age nor under twelve; so great a number of both sexes in every country being now ready to starve for want of work and service; and these to be disposed of by their parents, if alive, or otherwise by their nearest relations. But with due deference to so excellent a friend and so deserving a patriot, I cannot be altogether in his sentiments; for as to the males, my American acquaintance assured me from frequent experience that their flesh was generally tough and lean, like that of our schoolboys, by continual exercise, and their taste disagreeable; and to fatten them would not answer the charge. Then as to the females, it would, I think, with humble submission be a loss to the public, because they soon would become breeders themselves: and besides, it is not improbable that some scrupulous people might be apt to censure such a practice (although indeed very unjustly), as a little bordering upon cruelty; which, I confess, has always been with me the strongest objection against any project, however so well intended.

But in order to justify my friend, he confessed that this expedient was put into his head by the famous Psalmanazar,[9] a native of the island Formosa, who came from thence to London above twenty years ago: and in conversation told my friend that in his country when any young person happened to be put to death, the executioner sold the carcass to persons of quality as a prime dainty; and that in his time the body of a plump girl of fifteen, who was crucified for an attempt to poison the emperor, was

---

8. *shambles*, slaughterhouses.
9. *Psalmanazar*, the imposter George Psalmanazar (c.1679–1763), a Frenchman who passed himself off in England as a Formosan, and wrote a totally fictional "true" account of Formosa, in which he described cannibalism.

OF HUMAN INTEREST

Was Swift a misanthrope?

Swift was often accused of being a hater of mankind. Here is his own statement, from a letter to Alexander Pope: ". . . when you think of the world, give it one lash the more at my Request. I have ever hated all Nations, Professions, and Communities; and all my love is towards Individuals; for instance, I hate the Tribe of Lawyers, Physicians . . . Soldiers, English, Scotch, French, and the rest. But principally I hate and detest that animal called Man, although I heartily love John, Peter, Thomas, and so forth. . . ."

---

sold to his imperial majesty's prime minister of state, and other great mandarins of the court, in joints from the gibbet, at four hundred crowns. Neither indeed can I deny that if the same use were made of several plump girls in this town, who, without one single groat to their fortunes, cannot stir abroad without a chair, and appear at a playhouse and assemblies in foreign fineries which they never will pay for, the kingdom would not be the worse.

Some persons of a desponding spirit are in great concern about that vast number of poor people, who are aged, diseased, or maimed; and I have been desired to employ my thoughts, what course may be taken to ease the nation of so grievous an incumbrance. But I am not in the least pain upon that matter, because it is very well known that they are every day dying and rotting, by cold and famine, and filth and vermin, as fast as can be reasonably expected. And as to the young laborers, they are now in almost as hopeful a condition: they cannot get work, and consequently pine away for want of nourishment to a degree that if at any time they are accidentally hired to common labor, they have not strength to perform it; and thus the country and themselves are happily delivered from the evils to come.

I have too long digressed and therefore shall return to my subject. I think the advantages, by the proposal which I have made, are obvious and many, as well as of the highest importance.

For first, as I have already observed, it would greatly lessen the number of papists, with whom we are yearly overrun, being the principal breeders of the nation, as well as our most dangerous enemies;

and who stay at home on purpose to deliver the kingdom to the pretender, hoping to take their advantage by the absence of so many good protestants, who have chosen rather to leave their country than stay at home and pay tithes against their conscience to an episcopal curate.[10]

Secondly, the poorer tenants will have something valuable of their own, which by law may be made liable to distress,[11] and help to pay their landlord's rent; their corn and cattle being already seized, and money a thing unknown.

Thirdly, whereas the maintenance of a hundred thousand children, from two years old and upwards, cannot be computed at less than ten shillings a piece per annum, the nation's stock will be thereby increased fifty thousand pounds per annum, beside the profit of a new dish introduced to the tables of all gentlemen of fortune in the kingdom, who have any refinement in taste. And the money will circulate among ourselves, the goods being entirely of our own growth and manufacture.

Fourthly, the constant breeders, beside the gain of eight shillings sterling per annum by the sale of their children, will be rid of the charge of maintaining them after the first year.

Fifthly, this food would likewise bring great custom to taverns: where the vintners will certainly be so prudent as to procure the best receipts for dressing it to perfection, and consequently have their houses frequented by all the fine gentlemen, who justly value themselves upon their knowledge in good eating: and a skilful cook, who understands how to oblige his guests, will contrive to make it as expensive as they please.

Sixthly, this would be a great inducement to marriage, which all wise nations have either encouraged by rewards or enforced by laws and penalties. It would increase the care and tenderness of mothers toward their children, when they were sure of a settlement for life to the poor babes, provided in some sort by the public, to their annual profit instead of expense. We should see an honest emulation among the married women, which of them could bring the fattest child to the market. Men would become as fond of their wives during the time of their pregnancy as they are now of their mares in foal, their cows in calf, or sows when they are ready to farrow; nor offer to beat or kick them (as is too frequent a practice) for fear of a miscarriage.

Many other advantages might be enumerated. For instance, the addition of some thousand carcasses in our exportation of barreled beef, the propagation of swine's flesh, and improvement in the art of making good bacon, so much wanted among us by the great destruction of pigs, too frequent at our tables; which are no way comparable in taste or magnificence to a well-grown, fat, yearling child, which roasted whole will make a considerable figure at a lord mayor's feast, or any other public entertainment. But this and many others I omit, being studious of brevity.

Supposing that one thousand families in this city would be constant customers for infants' flesh, besides others who might have it at merry-meetings, particularly weddings and christenings, I compute that Dublin would take off annually about twenty thousand carcasses; and the rest of the kingdom (where probably they will be sold somewhat cheaper) the remaining eighty thousand.

I can think of no one objection that will possibly be raised against this proposal, unless it should be urged that the number of people will be thereby much lessened in the kingdom. This I freely own, and it was indeed one principal design in offering it to the world. I desire the reader will observe that I calculate my remedy for this one individual kingdom of Ireland, and for no other that ever was, is, or, I think, ever can be upon earth. Therefore let no man talk to me of other expedients: of taxing our absentees at five shillings a pound: of using neither clothes nor household furniture, except what is of our own growth and manufacture: of utterly rejecting the materials and instruments that promote foreign luxury: of curing the expensiveness of pride, vanity, idleness, and gaming in our women: of introducing a vein of parsimony, prudence, and temperance: of learning to love our country in the want of which we differ even from LAPLANDERS and the inhabitants of TOPINAMBOO:[12] of quitting our animosities and factions, nor acting any longer like the Jews, who were murdering one another at the very moment their city was taken:[13] of being a little cautious not to sell our country and conscience for nothing: of teaching landlords to have at least one

---

10. *protestants . . . curate.* Swift is here attacking the absentee landlords.
11. *distress,* distraint, the legal seizure of property for payment of debts.

12. *Topinamboo,* a savage area of Brazil.
13. *city was taken.* While the Roman Emperor Titus was besieging Jerusalem, which he took and destroyed in A.D. 70, within the city factions of fanatics were waging bloody warfare.

degree of mercy toward their tenants: lastly, of putting a spirit of honesty, industry, and skill into our shop-keepers; who, if a resolution could now be taken to buy only our native goods, would immediately unite to cheat and exact upon us in the price, the measure, and the goodness, nor could ever yet be brought to make one fair proposal of just dealing, though often and earnestly invited to it.[14]

Therefore, I repeat, let no man talk to me of these and the like expedients, till he has at least some glimpse of hope that there will be ever some hearty and sincere attempt to put them in practice.

But as to myself, having been wearied out for many years with offering vain, idle, visionary thoughts, and at length utterly despairing of success, I fortunately fell upon this proposal; which, as it is wholly new, so it has something solid and real, of no expense and little trouble, full in our own power, and whereby we can incur no danger in disobliging ENGLAND. For this kind of commodity will not bear exportation, the flesh being of too tender a consistence to admit a long continuance in salt, although perhaps I could name a country which would be glad to eat up our whole nation without it.[15]

After all, I am not so violently bent upon my own opinion as to reject any offer proposed by wise men, which shall be found equally innocent, cheap, easy, and effectual. But before something of that kind shall be advanced in contradiction to my scheme, and offering a better, I desire the author or authors will be pleased maturely to consider two points. First, as things now stand, how they will be able to find food and raiment for an hundred thousand useless mouths and backs. And secondly, there being a round million of creatures in human figure throughout this kingdom, whose whole subsistence put into a common stock would leave them in debt two millions of pounds sterling, adding those who are beggars by profession to the bulk of farmers, cottagers, and laborers, with their wives and children, who are beggars in effect; I desire those politicians, who dislike my overture, and may perhaps be so bold as to attempt an answer, that they will first ask the parents of these mortals, whether they would not at this day think it a great happiness to have been sold for food at a year old in the manner I prescribe, and thereby have avoided such a perpetual scene of misfortunes as they have since gone through by the oppression of landlords, the impossibility of paying rent without money or trade, the want of common sustenance, with neither house nor clothes to cover them from the inclemencies of the weather, and the most inevitable prospect of entailing the like or greater miseries upon their breed for ever.

I profess, in the sincerity of my heart, that I have not the least personal interest in endeavoring to promote this necessary work, having no other motive than the public good of my country, by advancing our trade, providing for infants, relieving the poor, and giving some pleasure to the rich. I have no children by which I can propose to get a single penny; the youngest being nine years old, and my wife past child-bearing.   (1729)

---

14. *invited to it.* Swift had already made all these proposals in various pamphlets.

15. *a country . . . without it.* England; this is another way of saying, "The British are devouring the Irish."

DISCUSSION

1. (a) At what point did you first realize that Swift was "putting you on"? What was your reaction?

(b) Why might Swift have used the word "Modest" in his title?

2. Paragraph 4 refers to "a child just dropped from the dam." The essay contains other examples of terms usually applied only to animals. Why does Swift use this device?

3. (a) List some of the shocking details of life in Ireland that the essay casually reveals.

(b) What is their cumulative effect?

4. (a) Who are the major targets of this satire?

(b) Does Swift suggest that the Irish themselves are in a way responsible for their plight? Explain.

5. (a) What sort of man would write an essay like this?

(b) What in today's world might such a man be moved to write about?

WRITING

1. Select a modern abuse and write a short satirical essay about it.

2. Assume that you are either (a) an Anglo-Irish absentee landlord, or (b) a literate native Irishman, and write Swift a letter expressing your opinion of his essay.

3. Prepare a dialogue in which two or three of Swift's contemporaries discuss his essay.

READERS' THEATER

Select key sections of "A Modest Proposal" for reading aloud by one or more students while another student, who holds a book in front of him, pantomimes a reader's reaction.

Daniel Defoe   1659 / 1731

ENGRAVINGS BY JOHN DUNSTALL SHOWING SCENES OF THE GREAT PLAGUE OF LONDON, 1665, FROM A CONTEMPORARY BROADSHEET. BY COURTESY OF THE TRUSTEES OF THE LONDON MUSEUM.

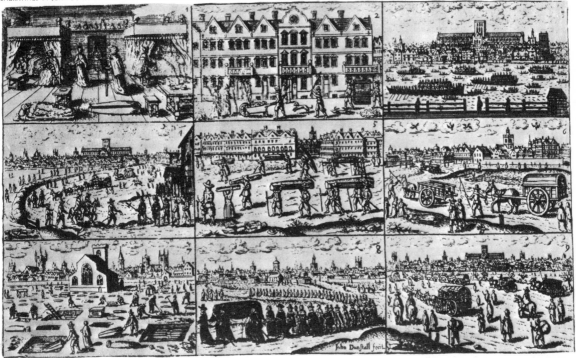

From JOURNAL OF THE PLAGUE YEAR

I

. . . IT pleased God that I was still spared, and very hearty and sound in health, but very impatient of being pent up within doors without air, as I have been for fourteen days or thereabouts, and I could not restrain myself, but I would go to carry a letter for my brother to the post-house. Then it was indeed that I observed a profound silence in the streets. When I came to the post-house, as I went to put in my letter, I saw a man stand in one corner of the yard and talking to another at a window, and a third had opened a door belonging to the office. In the middle of the yard lay a small leather purse with two keys hanging at it, with money in it, but nobody would meddle with it. I asked how long it had lain there; the man at the window said it had lain almost an hour, but that they had not meddled with it, because they did not know but the person who dropped it might come back to look for it. I had no such need of money, nor was the sum so big that I had any inclination to meddle with it, or to get the money at the hazard it might be attended with; so I seemed to go away, when the man who had opened the door said he would take it up, but so that if the right owner came for it he should be sure to have it. So he went in and fetched a pail of water, and set it down hard by the purse, then went again and fetched some gunpowder, and cast a good deal of powder upon the purse, and then made a train from that which he had thrown loose upon the purse. The train reached about two yards. After this he goes in a third time and fetches out a pair of tongs red hot, and which he had prepared, I suppose, on purpose, and first setting fire to the train of powder, that singed the purse, and also smoked the air sufficiently. But he was not content with that, but he then takes up the purse with the tongs, holding it so long till the tongs burnt through the purse, and then he shook the money out into the pail of water, so he carried it in. The money, as I remember, was about thirteen shillings and some smooth groats and brass farthings.

There might perhaps have been several poor people as I have observed above, that would have been hardy enough to have ventured for the sake of the money; but you may easily see by what I have observed that the few people who were spared were very careful of themselves at that time when the distress was so exceeding great. . . .

II

Passing through Tokenhouse Yard, in Lothbury, of a sudden a casement violently opened just over my head, and a woman gave three frightful screeches, and then cried, "Oh! death, death, death!" in a most inimitable tone, and which struck me with horror and a chillness in my very blood. There was nobody to be seen in the whole street, neither did any other window open, for people had no curiosity now in any case, nor could anybody help one another, so I went on to pass into Bell Alley.

Just in Bell Alley, on the right hand of the passage, there was a more terrible cry than that, though it was not so directed out at the window; but the whole family was in a terrible fright, and I could hear women and children run screaming about the rooms like distracted, when a garret-window opened, and somebody from a window on the other side the alley called and asked, "What is the matter?" upon which, from the first window it was answered, "O Lord, my old master has hanged himself!" The other asked again, "Is he quite dead?" and the first answered, "Ay, ay, quite dead; quite dead and cold!" This person was a merchant and a deputy alderman, and very rich. I care not to mention the name, though I knew his name too, but that would be an hardship to the family, which is now flourishing again.

But this is but one; it is scarce credible what dreadful cases happened in particular families every day. People in the rage of the distemper, or in the torment of their swellings, which was indeed intolerable, running out of their own government, raving and distracted, and oftentimes laying violent hands upon themselves, throwing themselves out at their windows, shooting themselves, &c.; mothers murdering their own children in their lunacy, some dying of mere grief as a passion, some of mere fright and surprise without any infection at all, others frighted into idiotism and foolish distractions, some into despair and lunacy, others into melancholy madness. . . .

III

. . . here I must observe also that the plague, as I suppose all distempers do, operated in a different manner on differing constitutions; some were immediately overwhelmed with it, and it came to violent fevers, vomitings, insufferable headaches, pains in the back, and so up to ravings and ragings with those pains; others with swellings and tumours in the neck or groin, or armpits, which till they could be broke put them into insufferable agonies and torment; while others, as I have observed, were silently infected, the fever preying upon their spirits insensibly, and they seeing little of it till they fell into swooning, and faintings, and death without pain.

I am not physician enough to enter into the particular reasons and manner of these differing effects of one and the same distemper. . . . I am only relating what I know, or have heard, or believe of the particular cases, and what fell within the compass of my view; but this may be added too, that though the former sort of those cases, namely, those openly visited, were the worst for themselves as to pain . . . yet the latter had the worst state of the disease; for in the former they frequently recovered, especially if the swellings broke, but the latter was inevitable death; no cure, no help could be possible, nothing could follow but death. . . .

IV

. . . the shutting up of houses, so as to confine those that were well with those that were sick, had very great inconveniences in it, and some that were very tragical. . . . But it was authorised by a law, it had the public good in view as the end chiefly aimed at, and all the private injuries that were done by the putting it in execution must be put to the account of the public benefit.

It is doubtful to this day whether, in the whole, it contributed anything to the stop of the infection. . . . Certain it is that if all the infected persons were effectually shut in, no sound person could have been infected by them, because they could not have come near them. But the case was this, and I shall only touch it here, namely, that the infection was propagated insensibly, and by such persons as were not visibly infected, who neither knew whom they infected or who they were infected by.

A house in Whitechapel was shut up for the sake of one infected maid, who had only spots, not the tokens come out upon her, and recovered; yet these people obtained no liberty to stir, neither for air or exercise forty days. Want of breath, fear, anger, vexation, and all the other griefs attending such an injurious treatment cast the mistress of the family into a fever, and visitors came into the house and said it was the plague, though the physicians declared it was not. However, the family were obliged to begin their quarantine anew on the report of the visitor or examiner, though their former quarantine wanted but a few days of being finished. This oppressed them so with anger and grief, and, as before, straitened them also so much as to room, and for want of breathing and free air, that most of the family fell sick, one of one distemper, one of another, chiefly *scorbutic*[1] ailments; only one a violent colic; till, after several prolongings of their confinement, some or other of those that came in with the visitors to inspect the persons that were ill, in hopes of releasing them, brought the distemper with them and infected the whole house, and all or most of them died, not of the plague as really upon them before, but of the plague that those people brought them, who should have been careful to have protected them from it. And this was a thing which frequently happened, and was, indeed, one of the worst consequences of shutting houses up. . . .

V

. . . the common people, who, ignorant and stupid in their reflections, as they were brutishly wicked and thoughtless before, were now led by their fright to extremes of folly; and, as I have said before that they ran to conjurers and witches, and all sorts of deceivers, to know what should become of them (who fed their fears, and kept them always alarmed and awake on purpose to delude them and pick their pockets), so they were as mad upon their running after quacks and mountebanks, and every practising old woman, for medicines and remedies; storing themselves with

such multitudes of pills, potions, and preservatives, as they were called, that they not only spent their money, but even poisoned themselves beforehand, for fear of the poison of the infection, and prepared their bodies for the plague, instead of preserving them against it. On the other hand, it is incredible, and scarce to be imagined, how the posts of houses and corners of streets were plastered over with doctors' bills and papers of ignorant fellows, quacking and tampering in physic, and inviting the people to come to them for remedies, which was generally set off with such flourishes as these, viz.: "Infallible preventive pills against the plague." "Never-failing preservatives against the infection." "Sovereign cordials against the corruption of the air." "Exact regulations for the conduct of the body in case of an infection." "Anti-pestilential pills." "Incomparable drink against the plague, never found out before." "An universal remedy for the plague." "The only true plague water." "The royal antidote against all kinds of infection"; and such a number more that I cannot reckon up; and if I could, would fill a book of themselves to set them down.

Others set up bills to summon people to their lodgings for directions and advice in the case of infection. These had specious titles also, such as these:—

"An eminent High Dutch physician, newly come over from Holland, where he resided during all the time of the great plague last year in Amsterdam, and cured multitudes of people that actually had the plague upon them."

"An Italian gentlewoman just arrived from Naples, having a choice secret to prevent infection, which she found out by her great experience, and did wonderful cures with it in the late plague there, wherein there died 20,000 in one day."

"An ancient gentlewoman, having practised with great success in the late plague in this city, anno 1636, gives her advice only to the female sex. To be spoke with," &c.

"An experienced physician, who has long studied the doctrine of antidotes against all sorts of poison and infection, has, after forty years' practice, arrived to such skill as may, with God's blessing, direct persons how to prevent their being touched by any contagious distemper whatsoever. He directs the poor gratis."

I take notice of these by way of specimen. I could give you two or three dozen of the like and yet have abundance left behind. 'T is sufficient from these to apprise any one of the humour of those times, and how a set of thieves and pickpockets not only robbed

---

1. *scorbutic*, related to scurvy.

and cheated the poor people of their money, but poisoned their bodies with odious and fatal preparations; some with mercury, and some with other things as bad, perfectly remote from the thing pretended to, and rather hurtful than serviceable to the body in case an infection followed. . . .

VI

It is here to be observed that after the funerals became so many that people could not toll the bell, mourn or weep, or wear black for one another, as they did before; no, nor so much as make coffins for those that died; so after a while the fury of the infection appeared to be so increased that, in short, they shut up no houses at all. It seemed enough that all the remedies of that kind had been used till they were found fruitless, and that the plague spread itself with an irresistible fury; so that as the fire the succeeding year spread itself, and burned with such violence that the citizens, in despair, gave over their endeavours to extinguish it, so in the plague it came at last to such violence that the people sat still looking at one another, and seemed quite abandoned to despair; whole streets seemed to be desolated, and not to be shut up only, but to be emptied of their inhabitants; doors were left open, windows stood shattering with the wind in empty houses for want of people to shut them. In a word, people began to give up themselves to their fears, and to think that all regulations and

methods were in vain, and that there was nothing to be hoped for but an universal desolation. . . .

VII

In the middle of their distress, when the condition of the city of London was so truly calamitous, just then it pleased God, as it were, by His immediate hand to disarm this enemy; the poison was taken out of the sting. It was wonderful; even the physicians themselves were surprised at it. Wherever they visited they found their patients better; either they had sweated kindly, or the tumours were broke, or the carbuncles went down, and the inflammations round them changed colour, or the fever was gone, or the violent headache was assuaged, or some good symptom was in the case; so that in a few days everybody was recovering, whole families that were infected and down, that had ministers praying with them, and expected death every hour, were revived and healed, and none died at all out of them.

Nor was this by any new medicine found out, or new method of cure discovered, or by any experience in the operation which the physicians or surgeons attained to; but it was evidently from the secret invisible hand of Him that had at first sent this disease as a judgment upon us; and let the atheistic part of mankind call my saying what they please, it is no enthusiasm; it was acknowledged at that time by all mankind. □

DISCUSSION

1. Defoe is regarded as a master of verisimilitude—the art of piling detail upon detail so that his fictional accounts have the authenticity of real life. From the *Journal*, select several examples of verisimilitude and show how Defoe's technique operates.
2. Does Defoe seem more concerned with the physical horrors of the plague, or with the psychological? Explain.
3. Why does Defoe's *Journal* ring more true than the usual account in a history book would?
4. Compare Defoe's style in the *Journal* with that of Samuel Pepys in his

Diary, considering such factors as the following: Which seems more personal? more informal? designed more for a reading audience rather than for the author's own eyes?

WRITING

Choosing with care details that will establish a verisimilitude similar to Defoe's, write a brief fictional description of some event outside your immediate experience, such as the air raids of World War II, being trapped in a hijacked aircraft, or something similar.

Joseph Addison   1672 / 1719

NED SOFTLY THE POET

The Tatler, No. 163
Will's Coffee-house, April 24, 1710

I yesterday came hither about two hours before the company generally make their appearance, with a design to read over all the newspapers; but upon my sitting down, I was accosted by Ned Softly, who saw me from a corner in the other end of the room, where I found he had been writing something. "Mr. Bicker-staff," says he, "I observe by a late paper of yours that you and I are just of a humor; for you must know, of all impertinences, there is nothing which I so much hate as news. I never read a Gazette in my life, and never trouble my head about our armies, whether they win or lose, or in what part of the world they lie encamped." Without giving me time to reply, he drew a paper of verses out of his pocket, telling me that he had something which would entertain me more agreeably, and that he would desire my judgment upon every line, for that we had time enough before us till the company came in.

Ned Softly is a very pretty poet, and a great admirer of easy lines. Waller is his favorite; and as that admirable writer has the best and worst verses of any among our great English poets, Ned Softly has got all the bad ones without book, which he repeats upon occasion, to show his reading and garnish his conversation. Ned is indeed a true English reader, incapable of relishing the great and masterly strokes of this art, but wonderfully pleased with the little Gothic ornaments of epigrammatical conceits, turns, points, and quibbles, which are so frequent in the most admired of our English poets, and practised by those who want genius and strength to represent, after the manner of the ancients, simplicity in its natural beauty and perfection.

Finding myself unavoidably engaged in such a conversation, I was resolved to turn my pain into a pleasure, and to divert myself as well as I could with so very odd a fellow. "You must understand," says Ned, "that the sonnet I am going to read to you was written upon a lady, who showed me some verses of her own making, and is, perhaps, the best poet of our age. But you shall hear it."

Upon which he began to read as follows:

TO MIRA ON HER INCOMPARABLE POEMS

When dressed in laurel wreaths you shine,
  And tune your soft melodious notes,
You seem a sister of the Nine,
  Or Phœbus' self in petticoats.

I fancy, when your song you sing,
  (Your song you sing with so much art)
Your pen was plucked from Cupid's wing;
  For, ah! it wounds me like his dart.

"Why," says I, "this is a little nosegay of conceits, a very lump of salt: every verse has something in it that piques; and then the *dart* in the last line is certainly as pretty a sting in the tail of an epigram, for so I think you critics call it, as ever entered into the thought of a poet."

"Dear Mr. Bickerstaff," says he, shaking me by the hand, "everybody knows you to be a judge of these things; and to tell you truly, I read over Roscommon's translation of 'Horace's Art of Poetry,' three several times, before I sat down to write the sonnet which I have shown you. But you shall hear it again, and pray

---

OF LITERARY INTEREST

The Tatler and The Spectator

One day in 1709, there appeared in the London coffee houses a single news sheet called *The Tatler*, which bore the motto "Whatever men do is the subject of this book." Its author was Richard Steele, who had decided to make the education of the newly arrived middle class his main life task. *The Tatler's* news items and essays were soon being read by practically everybody.

One issue found its way to Ireland, where Joseph Addison, a former schoolmate of Steele, was employed in government service. Addison thought he recognized *The Tatler's* anonymous author and sent him a contribution for its columns. This was the beginning of a famous literary partnership.

When *The Tatler* was discontinued in 1711 because of political difficulties, Addison and Steele founded a daily paper called *The Spectator*. Still writing anonymously, the authors offered their comments on manners, morals, and literature through the character of "the Spectator."

observe every line of it; for not one of them shall pass without your approbation.

> When dressed in laurel wreaths you shine.

"That is," says he, "when you have your garland on; when you are writing verses." To which I replied, "I know your meaning: a metaphor!" "The same," said he, and went on:

> "And tune your soft melodious notes.

"Pray observe the gliding of that verse; there is scarce a consonant in it: I took care to make it run upon liquids. Give me your opinion of it."

"Truly," said I, "I think it as good as the former."

"I am very glad to hear you say so," says he; "but mind the next:

> You seem a sister of the Nine.

"That is," says he, "you seem a sister of the Muses; for if you look into ancient authors, you will find it was their opinion that there were nine of them." "I remember it very well," said I; "but pray proceed."

> "Or Phœbus' self in petticoats.

"Phœbus," says he, "was the God of Poetry. These little instances, Mr. Bickerstaff, show a gentleman's reading. Then to take off from the air of learning, which Phœbus and the Muses have given to this first stanza, you may observe how it falls all of a sudden into the familiar, 'in petticoats!'

> Or Phœbus' self in petticoats."

"Let us now," says I, "enter upon the second stanza. I find the first line is still a continuation of the metaphor:

> I fancy, when your song you sing."

"It is very right," says he; "but pray observe the turn of words in those two lines. I was a whole hour in adjusting of them, and have still a doubt upon me, whether in the second line it should be 'Your song you sing'; or, 'You sing your songs.' You shall hear them both:

> I fancy when your song you sing
> (Your song you sing with so much art).

Or,

> I fancy, when your song you sing
> (You sing your song with so much art.)"

"Truly," said I, "the turn is so natural either way that you have made me almost giddy with it."

"Dear sir," said he, grasping me by the hand, "you have a great deal of patience; but pray what do you think of the next verse:

A COFFEE HOUSE. RADIO TIMES HULTON PICTURE LIBRARY.

> Your pen was plucked from Cupid's wing?"

"Think!" says I; "I think you have made Cupid look like a little goose."

"That was my meaning," says he; "I think the ridicule is well enough hit off. But we now come to the last, which sums up the whole matter:

> For, ah! it wounds me like his dart.

"Pray, how do you like that 'Ah!' Does it not make a pretty figure in that place? *Ah!*——it looks as if I felt the dart, and cried out as being pricked with it!

> For, ah! it wounds me like his dart.

"My friend Dick Easy," continued he, "assured me, he would rather have written that *Ah!* than to have been the author of the Æneid. He indeed objected, that I made Mira's pen like a quill in one of the lines, and like a dart in the other. But as to that——"

"Oh! as to that," says I, "it is but supposing Cupid to be like a porcupine, and his quills and darts will be the same thing."

He was going to embrace me for the hint; but half a dozen critics coming into the room, whose faces he did not like, he conveyed the sonnet into his pocket, and whispered me in the ear, "he would show it me again as soon as his man had written it over fair."

DISSECTION OF A BEAU'S HEAD

The Spectator, No. 275.   *January 15, 1712*

I was yesterday engaged in an assembly of virtu-osos,[1] where one of them produced many curious observations which he had lately made in the anat-omy of an human body. Another of the company communicated to us several wonderful discoveries, which he had also made on the same subject, by the help of very fine glasses. This gave birth to a great variety of uncommon remarks, and furnished dis-course for the remaining part of the day.

The different opinions which were started on this occasion presented to my imagination so many new ideas that, by mixing with those which were already there, they employed my fancy all the last night, and composed a very wild extravagant dream.

I was invited, methought, to the dissection of a beau's head, and of a coquette's heart, which were both of them laid on a table before us. An imaginary operator opened the first with a great deal of nicety, which, upon a cursory and superficial view, ap-peared like the head of another man; but, upon applying our glasses to it, we made a very odd dis-covery, namely, that what we looked upon as brains, were not such in reality, but an heap of strange materials wound up in that shape and texture, and packed together with wonderful art in the several cavities of the skull. For, as Homer tells us that the blood of the gods is not real blood, but only some-thing like it; so we found that the brain of a beau is not real brain, but only something like it.

The pineal gland, which many of our modern philosophers suppose to be the seat of the soul, smelt very strong of essence and orange-flower water, and was encompassed with a kind of horny substance, cut into a thousand little faces or mirrors, which were imperceptible to the naked eye; inso-much that the soul, if there had been any here, must have been always taken up in contemplating her own beauties.

We observed a large antrum or cavity in the sin-ciput, that was filled with ribbons, lace, and em-broidery, wrought together in a most curious piece of network, the parts of which were likewise impercep-tible to the naked eye. Another of these antrums or cavities was stuffed with invisible billet-doux,[2] love-letters, pricked dances,[3] and other trumpery of the same nature. In another we found a kind of powder, which set the whole company a sneezing, and by the scent discovered itself to be right Spanish.[4] The several other cells were stored with commodities of the same kind, of which it would be tedious to give the reader an exact inventory.

There was a large cavity on each side of the head, which I must not omit. That on the right side was filled with fictions, flatteries, and falsehoods, vows, promises, and protestations; that on the left with oaths and imprecations. There issued out a duct from each of these cells, which ran into the root of the tongue, where both joined together, and passed for-ward in one common duct to the tip of it. We dis-covered several little roads or canals running from the ear into the brain, and took particular care to trace them out through their several passages. One of them extended itself to a bundle of sonnets and little musical instruments. Others ended in several bladders which were filled either with wind or froth. But the large canal entered into a great cavity of the skull, from whence there went another canal into the tongue. This great cavity was filled with a kind of spongy substance, which the French anatomists call *galimatias,* and the English nonsense.

The skins of the forehead were extremely tough and thick, and, what very much surprised us, had not in them any single blood-vessel that we were able to discover, either with or without our glasses; from whence we concluded that the party when alive must have been entirely deprived of the faculty of blushing.

The *os cribriforme* was exceedingly stuffed, and in some places damaged with snuff. We could not but take notice in particular of that small muscle, which is not often discovered in dissections, and draws the nose upwards, when it expresses the contempt which the owner of it has, upon seeing anything he does not like, or hearing anything he does not under-stand. I need not tell my learned reader, this is that muscle which performs the motion so often men-

---

1. *virtuosos,* men interested in science.

2. *billet-doux* (bil′ ā dü′), love letters (French).
3. *pricked dances,* dance-cards or dance programs marked to in-dicate which dances are taken.
4. *right Spanish,* a type of snuff.

tioned by the Latin poets, when they talk of a man's cocking his nose, or playing the rhinoceros.

We did not find anything very remarkable in the eye, saving only that the *musculi amatorii,* or as we may translate it into English, the ogling muscles, were very much worn and decayed with use; whereas on the contrary, the elevator, or the muscle which turns the eye toward heaven, did not appear to have been used at all.

I have only mentioned in this dissection such new discoveries as we were able to make, and have not taken any notice of those parts which are to be met with in common heads. As for the skull, the face, and indeed the whole outward shape and figure of the head, we could not discover any difference from what we observe in the heads of other men. We were informed, that the person to whom this head belonged, had passed for a man above five and thirty years; during which time he ate and drank like other people, dressed well, talked loud, laughed frequently, and on particular occasions had acquitted himself tolerably at a ball or an assembly; to which

one of the company added, that a certain knot of ladies took him for a wit. He was cut off in the flower of his age by the blow of a paring-shovel, having been surprised by an eminent citizen, as he was tendering some civilities to his wife.

When we had thoroughly examined this head with all its apartments, and its several kinds of furniture, we put up the brain, such as it was, into its proper place, and laid it aside under a broad piece of scarlet cloth, in order to be prepared, and kept in a great repository of dissections; our operator telling us that the preparation would not be so difficult as that of another brain, for that he had observed several of the little pipes and tubes which ran through the brain were already filled with a kind of mercurial substance, which he looked upon to be true quicksilver.

He applied himself in the next place to the coquette's heart, which he likewise laid open with great dexterity. There occurred to us many particularities in this dissection; but, being unwilling to burden my reader's memory too much, I shall reserve this subject for the speculation of another day.   □

DISCUSSION

1. Both *The Tatler* and *The Spectator* aimed at correcting some of the follies of their age.

(a) What follies are treated in the selections included here?

(b) Which selection is more effective? Why?

(c) Which selection is most relevant to modern readers? Why?

2. To avoid boring their readers, the periodical essayists used a variety of literary forms, such as fables, allegories, visions, conversational anecdotes, tales, and letters from real or imaginary correspondents.

(a) Which of the forms can you identify in the selections included here?

(b) Would either of the selections be more effective in a different form? Explain.

3. How does the beau's head indicate his character and the life he lived?

4. (a) Based on Ned Softly's explication of his sonnet, what sort of English teacher would he make?

(b) What is your reaction to Bickerstaff's ironical comments?

(c) Is Softly aware of any of them? Explain.

WRITING

1. Try your hand at a periodical essay satirizing one of the follies of the modern world. The class may wish to collect and reproduce the best of these in a modern *Tatler* or *Spectator*.
2. Try a literary dissection of the head of a modern beau, or any other modern character type.
3. According to Addison and Steele, the objectives of their literary periodicals were "to enliven morality with wit, and to temper wit with morality." In a short paper, discuss how well the selections you have read carry out these objectives.

Alexander Pope 1688 / 1744

THE RAPE OF THE LOCK
An Heroi-Comical Poem

The Rape of the Lock was written to help end a quarrel between two families that resulted when a young lord cut off a lock of a young lady's hair. The poem follows the epic form, but it is a "mock epic," a kind of burlesque, treating trivial matters in ultraserious or elevated language and style. In traditional epics such as *Beowulf* or Homer's *Iliad* and *Odyssey* or Milton's *Paradise Lost*, impressive creatures of supernatural powers (gods, monsters, angels) enter into and affect the action. Pope introduced in their stead small creatures such as sylphs and gnomes. He explained: "The gnomes, or daemons of earth, delight in mischief; but the sylphs, whose habitation is in the air, are the best-conditioned creatures imaginable." In the poem the sylphs are assigned the task of defending the heroine, Belinda, and her precious locks of hair.

CANTO I

What dire offense from am'rous causes springs,
What mighty contests rise from trivial things,
I sing—This verse to Caryll,[1] Muse! is due;
This, ev'n Belinda may vouchsafe to view:
5 Slight is the subject, but not so the praise,
If she inspire, and he approve my lays.
    Say what strange motive, Goddess! could compel
A well-bred lord t' assault a gentle belle?
O say what stranger cause, yet unexplored,
10 Could make a gentle belle reject a lord?
In tasks so bold, can little men engage,
And in soft bosoms dwells such mighty rage?
    Sol through white curtains shot a tim'rous ray,
And oped those eyes that must eclipse the day;
15 Now lap dogs give themselves the rousing shake.
And sleepless lovers, just at twelve, awake:
Thrice rung the bell, the slipper knocked the ground,
And the pressed watch returned a silver sound.[2]
Belinda still her downy pillow pressed,
20 Her guardian Sylph prolonged the balmy rest.

'Twas he had summoned to her silent bed
The morning dream that hovered o'er her head.
A youth more glittering than a Birth-night beau,[3]
(That ev'n in slumber caused her cheek to glow)
25 Seemed to her ear his winning lips to lay,
And thus in whispers said, or seemed to say. . . .
(As Belinda dreams, her guardian sylph, Ariel, delivers a long speech explaining the life of the sylphs, and concludes with a grave warning.)
    "Of these am I, who thy protection claim,
A watchful sprite, and Ariel is my name.
Late, as I ranged the crystal wilds of air,
30 In the clear mirror of thy ruling star
I saw, alas! some dread event impend,
Ere to the main this morning sun descend,
But heav'n reveals not what, or how, or where:
Warned by the Sylph, oh pious maid, beware!
35 This to disclose is all thy guardian can:
Beware of all, but most beware of man!"
    He said; when Shock, who thought she slept too long,
Leaped up, and waked his mistress with his tongue.
'Twas then, Belinda, if report say true,
40 Thy eyes first opened on a billet-doux;
Wounds, charms, and ardors were no sooner read,
But all the vision vanished from thy head.
    And now, unveiled, the toilet[4] stands displayed,
Each silver vase in mystic order laid.
45 First, robed in white, the nymph intent adores,
With head uncovered, the cosmetic powers.
A heav'nly image in the glass appears,
To that she bends, to that her eye she rears;
Th' inferior priestess, at her altar's side,
50 Trembling, begins the sacred rites of pride.
Unnumbered treasures ope at once, and here
The various off'rings of the world appear;
From each she nicely culls with curious toil,
And decks the goddess with the glitt'ring spoil.
55 This casket India's glowing gems unlocks,
And all Arabia breathes from yonder box.
The tortoise here and elephant unite,
Transformed to combs, the speckled and the white.

---

1. *Caryll,* John Caryll, who suggested that Pope write the poem to heal the breach between the two families.
2. *pressed . . . sound,* a type of watch in which a pressure on the stem would cause the watch to strike the last hour again.

3. *Birth-night beau,* a gentleman dressed in fine clothes for the sovereign's birthday ball.
4. *toilet,* dressing table.

Here files of pins extend their shining rows,
60 Puffs, powders, patches, Bibles, billet-doux.
Now awful Beauty puts on all its arms;
The fair each moment rises in her charms,
Repairs her smiles, awakens ev'ry grace,
And calls forth all the wonders of her face;
65 Sees by degrees a purer blush arise,
And keener lightnings quicken in her eyes.
The busy Sylphs surround their darling care;
These set the head, and those divide the hair,
Some fold the sleeve, while others plait the gown;
70 And Betty's[5] praised for labors not her own.

CANTO II

(After her elaborate preparations at the dressing
table, Belinda sets out, "launched on the bosom of
the silver Thames," on her way to Hampton Court,
one of the royal palaces near London, and the center
of her delightful, sophisticated, and trivial social
life.)

This nymph, to the destruction of mankind,
Nourished two locks, which graceful hung behind
In equal curls, and well conspired to deck
With shining ringlets the smooth iv'ry neck.
75 Love in these labyrinths his slaves detains,
And mighty hearts are held in slender chains.
With hairy springes[6] we the birds betray,
Slight lines of hair surprise the finny prey,
Fair tresses man's imperial race ensnare,
80 And beauty draws us with a single hair.
Th' adventurous Baron the bright locks admired;
He saw, he wished, and to the prize aspired.
Resolved to win, he meditates the way,
By force to ravish, or by fraud betray;
85 For when success a lover's toils attends,
Few ask, if fraud or force attained his ends.
(The sylph Ariel, aware of the threat to Belinda,
summons his fellow sylphs and sends them to their
various stations about Belinda to guard her every
precious possession.)
"This day, black omens threat the brightest Fair
That e'er deserved a watchful spirit's care;
Some dire disaster, or by force, or slight;
90 But what, or where, the Fates have wrapped in night.
Whether the nymph shall break Diana's law,[7]

Or some frail china jar receive a flaw;
Or stain her honor, or her new brocade;
Forget her prayers, or miss a masquerade;
95 Or lose her heart, or necklace, at a ball;
Or whether Heav'n has doomed that Shock must fall.
Haste, then, ye spirits! to your charge repair:
The fluttering fan be Zephyretta's care;
The drops[8] to thee, Brillante, we consign;
100 And, Momentilla, let the watch be thine:
Do thou, Crispissa, tend her fav'rite lock;
Ariel himself shall be the guard of Shock.
"To fifty chosen Sylphs, of special note,
We trust th' important charge, the petticoat:
105 Oft have we known that sev'nfold fence to fail,
Though stiff with hoops, and armed with ribs of
        whale;
Form a strong line about the silver bound,
And guard the wide circumference around.
"Whatever spirit, careless of his charge,
110 His post neglects, or leaves the fair at large,
Shall feel sharp vengeance soon o'ertake his sins,
Be stopped in vials, or transfixed with pins;
Or plunged in lakes of bitter washes lie,
Or wedged whole ages in a bodkin's eye:
115 Gums and pomatums[9] shall his flight restrain,
While clogged he beats his silken wings in vain;
Or alum styptics[10] with contracting power
Shrink his thin essence like a rivelled flower:
Or, as Ixion[11] fixed, the wretch shall feel
120 The giddy motion of the whirling mill,
In fumes of burning chocolate shall glow,
And tremble at the sea that froths below!"
He spoke; the spirits from the sails descend;
Some, orb in orb, around the nymph extend,
125 Some thrid[12] the mazy ringlets of her hair,
Some hang upon the pendants of her ear;
With beating hearts the dire event they wait,
Anxious, and trembling for the birth of Fate.

CANTO III

Close by those meads, for ever crowned with flow'rs,
130 Where Thames with pride surveys his rising tow'rs,
There stands a structure of majestic frame,

---

5. Betty, Belinda's maid.
6. springes, nooses to catch birds.
7. Diana's law, chastity. Diana was the goddess of maidenhood.

8. drops, pendant earrings.
9. pomatums, perfumed ointments to keep the hair in place.
10. alum styptics, astringents.
11. Ixion, in Greek myth, fastened to an endlessly revolving wheel
in Hades as punishment for making love to Juno, queen of the gods.
12. thrid, thread; pass through.

Which from the neighb'ring Hampton takes its name.
Here Britain's statesmen oft the fall foredoom
Of foreign tyrants, and of nymphs at home;
135 Here thou, great Anna![13] whom three realms obey,
Dost sometimes counsel take—and sometimes tea.
　Hither the heroes and the nymphs resort,
To taste awhile the pleasures of a court;
In various talk th' instructive hours they passed,
140 Who gave the ball, or paid the visit last;
One speaks the glory of the British Queen,
And one describes a charming Indian screen;
A third interprets motions, looks, and eyes;
At ev'ry word a reputation dies.
145 Snuff, or the fan, supply each pause of chat,
With singing, laughing, ogling, and all that.
　Meanwhile, declining from the noon of day,
The sun obliquely shoots his burning ray;
The hungry judges soon the sentence sign,
150 And wretches hang that jurymen may dine; . . .
(Belinda joins the pleasure-seekers at Hampton
Court, and wins at a card game, ombre, over the
Baron who covets her locks. But as the game ends,

and they all partake of refreshments, the Baron
seizes his opportunity.)
　But when to mischief mortals bend their will,
How soon they find fit instruments of ill!
Just then, Clarissa drew with tempting grace
A two-edged weapon[14] from her shining case;
155 So ladies in romance assist their knight,
Present the spear, and arm him for the fight.
He takes the gift with rev'rence, and extends
The little engine on his fingers' ends;
This just behind Belinda's neck he spread,
160 As o'er the fragrant steams she bends her head:
Swift to the lock a thousand sprites repair,
A thousand wings, by turns, blow back the hair;
And thrice they twitched the diamond in her ear;
Thrice she looked back, and thrice the foe drew near.
165 Just in that instant, anxious Ariel sought
The close recesses of the virgin's thought;
As on the nosegay in her breast reclined,
He watched th' ideas rising in her mind,
Sudden he viewed, in spite of all her art,
170 An earthly lover lurking at her heart.

---

13. *Anna,* Queen Anne (1702–1714).

14. *two-edged weapon,* scissors.

OF LITERARY INTEREST

Satire

Satire is the literary art of making a subject ridiculous by arousing towards it feelings of contempt, amusement, and scorn. While humor has the evocation of amusement as its sole end, satire often employs the comic to the end of pointing up human faults and effecting some improvement in humanity or human institutions. The butt of satire may be an individual (as in Dryden's *MacFlecknoe,* a mock epic whose victim is playwright Thomas Shadwell), a type of person (Addison's "Dissection of a Beau's Head"), a particular social evil (as in Swift's *A Modest Proposal*), or even the entire race of mankind (Swift's *Gulliver's Travels).*

The most frequently used satirical techniques are *irony, sarcasm, burlesque,* and *parody. Irony* is a technique in which the attitudes stated differ from what is really meant. For example, words of praise can be used to imply blame. *A Modest Proposal* is one of the most effective and savage examples of sustained ironic tone in English literature.

Sarcasm is more caustic, crude, and heavy-handed than irony, of which it is a form. Sarcasm also tends to be more personally directed than irony.

Burlesque is an imitation of a person or subject which, by ridiculous exaggeration or distortion, aims to amuse. The quality which characterizes this technique is a discrepancy between the subject matter and the style in which it is treated. For example, a frivolous subject may be treated with mock dignity, or, conversely, a weighty subject might be handled in a trivial style. Mock epics, such as Pope's *The Rape of the Lock,* use the elaborate and elevated style of the epic to make a trivial subject laughable.

Parody differs from burlesque in that it derides not a person or subject, but a specific literary work or style, by imitating features and applying them to trivial or incongruous materials. The poem "Father William" in *Alice in Wonderland* (page 454) is a funny and successful parody of Southey's poem "The Old Man's Comforts."

Satire has existed at least since the classical literature of Greece and Rome. It achieved a golden age in eighteenth-century England, when poetry, drama, essays, and criticism all took on the satiric tone at the hands of such masters as Dryden, Pope, Addison, Steele, and Swift. Satire continues to be an important medium for social commentary in our time. A well-known modern example is George Orwell's *Animal Farm.* The English satiric spirit has also been maintained by such authors as G. B. Shaw, Evelyn Waugh, and Aldous Huxley and such magazines as *Punch;* in the United States, periodicals like *Mad* and *The National Lampoon* present social and political satire.

Amazed, confused, he found his pow'r expired,
Resigned to fate, and with a sigh retired.
   The peer now spreads the glittering forfex[15] wide,
T' inclose the lock; now joins it, to divide.
175 Ev'n then, before the fatal engine closed,
A wretched Sylph too fondly interposed;
Fate urged the shears, and cut the Sylph in twain
(But airy substance soon unites again).
The meeting points the sacred hair dissever
180 From the fair head, for ever, and for ever!
   Then flashed the living lightning from her eyes,
And screams of horror rend th' affrighted skies.
Not louder shrieks to pitying Heav'n are cast,
When husbands or when lap dogs breathe their last;
185 Or when rich China vessels fallen from high,
In glitt'ring dust and painted fragments lie!
   "Let wreaths of triumph now my temples twine,"
(The victor cried) "the glorious prize is mine!
While fish in streams, or birds delight in air,
190 Or in a coach and six the British fair,
As long as *Atalantis*[16] shall be read,
Or the small pillow grace a lady's bed,
While visits shall be paid on solemn days,
When numerous wax-lights in bright order blaze,
195 While nymphs take treats, or assignations give,
So long my honor, name, and praise shall live!

---

15. *forfex*, scissors.
16. *Atalantis*, a popular book of court scandal and gossip.

What time would spare, from steel receives its
   date,
And monuments, like men, submit to fate!
Steel could the labor of the gods destroy,
200 And strike to dust th' imperial tow'rs of Troy;
Steel could the works of mortal pride confound,
And hew triumphal arches to the ground.
What wonder then, fair nymph! thy hairs should feel
The conquering force of unresisted steel?"

CANTO IV

(Confusion and hysteria result from the Baron's dastardly deed of cutting off Belinda's lock of hair, and Belinda delivers to the Baron a speech of elevated indignation.)

205   "For ever curs'd be this detested day,
Which snatched my best, my fav'rite curl away!
Happy! ah ten times happy had I been,
If Hampton Court these eyes had never seen!
Yet am not I the first mistaken maid,
210 By love of courts to num'rous ills betrayed.
Oh had I rather unadmired remained
In some lone isle, or distant northern land;
Where the gilt chariot never marks the way,
Where none learn ombre, none e'er taste bohea!
215 There kept my charms concealed from mortal eye,
Like roses that in deserts bloom and die.

DANCING THE MINUET AT A FASHIONABLE BALL. RADIO TIMES HULTON PICTURE LIBRARY.

OF HUMAN INTEREST

What finally happened?

Pope's mock epic apparently succeeded in its purpose of healing the breach between the families involved. Only one of the minor characters depicted was offended; in fact, Arabella Fermor ("Belinda") was pleased with the attention given her. While it would have made the story complete if the real-life hero and heroine had married and lived happily ever after, this was not to be. The "Baron" (Lord Petre) married a younger and richer heiress, but died of smallpox within a year. Arabella married another gentleman and became the mother of six children.

What moved my mind with youthful lords to roam?
Oh had I stayed, and said my prayers at home!
'Twas this, the morning omens seemed to tell:
220 Thrice from my trembling hand the patchbox fell;
The tottering china shook without a wind,
Nay, Poll sat mute, and Shock was most unkind!
A Sylph too warned me of the threats of fate,
In mystic visions, now believed too late!
225 See the poor remnants of these slighted hairs!
My hands shall rend what ev'n thy rapine spares:
These, in two sable ringlets taught to break,
Once gave new beauties to the snowy neck.
The sister-lock now sits uncouth, alone,
230 And in its fellow's fate foresees its own;
Uncurled it hangs, the fatal shears demands;
And tempts, once more, thy sacrilegious hands.
Oh hadst thou, cruel! been content to seize
Hairs less in sight, or any hairs but these!"

CANTO V

(Such a treacherous deed as the rape of a lock of lady's hair inevitably results in an "epic" battle.)
235 "To arms, to arms!" the fierce virago cries,
And swift as lightning to the combat flies.
All side in parties, and begin th' attack;
Fans clap, silks rustle, and tough whalebones crack;
Heroes' and heroines' shouts confus'dly rise,
240 And bass, and treble voices strike the skies.
No common weapons in their hands are found,
Like gods they fight, nor dread a mortal wound.
(Belinda attacks the Baron, but to no avail. They are both deprived of the precious lock as it rises

into the skies immortalized and transfigured into a heavenly body.)
See fierce Belinda on the Baron flies,
With more than usual lightning in her eyes;
245 Nor feared the chief th' unequal fight to try,
Who sought no more than on his foe to die.
But this bold lord, with manly strength endued,
She with one finger and a thumb subdued:
Just where the breath of life his nostrils drew,
250 A charge of snuff the wily virgin threw;
The Gnomes direct, to every atom just,
The pungent grains of titillating dust.
Sudden, with starting tears each eye o'erflows,
And the high dome re-echoes to his nose.
255 "Now meet thy fate," incensed Belinda cried,
And drew a deadly bodkin[17] from her side.
(The same, his ancient personage to deck,
Her great-great-grandsire wore about his neck
In three seal rings; which after, melted down,
260 Formed a vast buckle for his widow's gown:
Her infant grandame's whistle next it grew,
The bells she jingled, and the whistle blew;
Then in a bodkin graced her mother's hairs,
Which long she wore, and now Belinda wears.)
265 "Boast not my fall" (he cried) "insulting foe!
Thou by some other shalt be laid as low.
Nor think, to die dejects my lofty mind;
All that I dread is leaving you behind!
Rather than so, ah let me still survive,
270 And burn in Cupid's flames—but burn alive."
"Restore the lock!" she cries; and all around
"Restore the lock!" the vaulted roofs rebound.
Not fierce Othello in so loud a strain
Roared for the handkerchief that caused his pain.[18]
275 But see how oft ambitious aims are crossed,
And chiefs contend till all the prize is lost!
The lock, obtained with guilt, and kept with pain,
In ev'ry place is sought, but sought in vain:
With such a prize no mortal must be blest,
280 So Heav'n decrees! with Heav'n who can contest?
Some thought it mounted to the lunar sphere,
Since all things lost on earth, are treasured there.
There heroes' wits are kept in pond'rous vases,
And beaux' in snuffboxes and tweezer-cases.
285 There broken vows, and deathbed alms are found,
And lovers' hearts with ends of riband bound;

---

17. *bodkin,* ornamental hairpin shaped like a stiletto.
18. *Othello . . . pain.* In Shakespeare's play, Othello becomes enraged when his wife Desdemona fails to produce a highly-prized handkerchief and is convinced she has given it to her supposed lover.

The courtier's promises and sick man's prayers,
The smiles of harlots, and the tears of heirs.
Cages for gnats, and chains to yoke a flea,
290 Dried butterflies, and tomes of casuistry.[19]
    But trust the Muse—she saw it upward rise,
Though marked by none but quick poetic eyes:
(So Rome's great founder to the heav'ns withdrew,
To Proculus alone confessed in view.)[20]
295 A sudden star, it shot through liquid air,
And drew behind a radiant trail of hair.
Not Berenice's lock[21] first rose so bright,
The heav'ns bespangling with disheveled light.
The Sylphs behold it kindling as it flies,
300 And pleased pursue its progress through the skies.
    This the beau monde shall from the Mall[22]
        survey,

And hail with music its propitious ray.
This, the blest lover shall for Venus take,
And send up vows from Rosamonda's lake.[23]
305 This Partridge soon shall view in cloudless skies,
When next he looks through Galileo's eyes;
And hence th' egregious wizard shall foredoom
The fate of Louis, and the fall of Rome.[24]
    Then cease, bright nymph! to mourn thy ravished
        hair
310 Which adds new glory to the shining sphere!
Not all the tresses that fair head can boast
Shall draw such envy as the lock you lost.
For, after all the murders of your eye,
When, after millions slain, your self shall die;
315 When those fair suns shall set, as set they must,
And all those tresses shall be laid in dust;
This lock, the Muse shall consecrate to fame,
And 'midst the stars inscribe Belinda's name.

---

19. *tomes of casuistry,* books of oversubtle reasoning about conscience and conduct.
20. *So Rome's . . . view.* Proculus, a Roman senator, saw Romulus, the founder of Rome, taken to heaven.
21. *Berenice's lock.* The Egyptian queen Berenice dedicated a lock of her beautiful hair to Venus for the safe return of her husband from war; the hair was turned into a comet. There is a constellation known as *Coma Berenicis,* Berenice's hair.
22. *Mall,* a promenade in St. James's Park in London.

---

23. *Rosamonda's lake,* in St. James's Park.
24. *Partridge . . . Rome.* John Partridge (1644–1715) was an astrologer and almanac-maker who annually predicted the downfall of the King of France and of the Pope.

DISCUSSION

1. (a) In *The Rape of the Lock,* what devices are used to make Belinda seem like a goddess? to seem like an Amazon or other female warrior?
(b) How does Pope make these appropriate to a *mock* epic?
2. The Baron's feelings about Belinda are clear. What are her feelings about him?
3. How important are the Sylphs to the plot of the poem? to the atmosphere? Explain.
4. In what respects has the war between the sexes remained unchanged from the time of *The Rape of the Lock* to the present day? In what respects has it changed?

5. Explain how *The Rape of the Lock* could be popular with the real-life principals involved, at the same time that it pointed out the ridiculousness of their quarrel.
6. Pope's mock epic depends for its effect on the juxtaposition of the serious and the trivial. Cite at least five instances.

WRITING

1. Prepare a newspaper story describing the loss of Belinda's lock.
2. Write a letter of apology from the Baron to Belinda, and her reply to it.
3. In a paper of about 500 words, discuss how Pope adapted some of the following devices of the epic for his mock epic: invocation to the muse; statement of theme; statement of the

epic question; elevated language; intervention of supernatural beings; a hero who seems "larger than life"; boastful speeches by great warriors; descriptions of armor; detailed history of heroes' weapons; great battles; personal combats.

READERS' THEATER

Join with other students in presenting a dramatic reading of this version of *The Rape of the Lock.* You will need the following parts: narrator, Ariel, Belinda, the Baron. You may wish to divide the narrator's lines. If the entire poem seems too ambitious a project, select portions of it.

QUOTABLE POPE

Next to Shakespeare, Pope is probably the most frequently quoted of English poets. The following remarks are from his *Essay on Criticism,* a long poem which expressed in polished heroic couplets (pairs of rhyming lines in iambic pentameter) the eighteenth century's basic rules for poetry.

1. 'Tis with our judgments as our watches; none
   Go just alike, yet each believes his own.

2. Let such teach others who themselves excel,
   And censure freely who have written well.

3. Music resembles poetry; in each
   Are nameless graces which no methods teach.

4. Those oft are stratagems which errors seem,
   Nor is it Homer nods, but we that dream.

5. Of all the causes which conspire to blind
   Man's erring judgment, and misguide the mind,
   What the weak head with strongest bias rules,
   Is pride, the never-failing vice of fools.

6. Trust not yourself: but your defects to know,
   Make use of every friend—and every foe.

7. A little learning is a dangerous thing;
   Drink deep, or taste not the Pierian spring.[1]
   There shallow draughts intoxicate the brain,
   And drinking largely sobers us again.

8. 'Tis not a lip, or eye, we beauty call,
   But the joint force and full result of all.

9. True wit is Nature to advantage dressed,
   What oft was thought, but ne'er so well expressed.

10. As shades more sweetly recommend the light,
    So modest plainness sets off sprightly wit.

11. Words are like leaves; and where they most abound,
    Much fruit of sense beneath is rarely found.

12. True ease in writing comes from art, not chance,
    As those move easiest who have learned to dance.

13. Those heads, as stomachs, are not sure the best
    Which nauseate all, and nothing can digest.

14. Be not the first by whom the new are tried,
    Nor yet the last to lay the old aside.

15. Where'er you find "the cooling western breeze,"
    In the next line, it "whispers through the trees";
    If crystal streams "with pleasing murmurs creep,"
    The reader's threatened (not in vain) with "sleep."

16. Some praise at morning what they blame at night,
    But always think the last opinion right.

17. We think our fathers fools, so wise we grow;
    Our wiser sons, no doubt, will think us so.

18. Envy will merit, as its shade, pursue.
    But like a shadow, proves the substance true.

19. Good nature and good sense must ever join;
    To err is human, to forgive divine.

KNOW THEN THYSELF
From AN ESSAY ON MAN

Know then thyself, presume not God to scan:
The proper study of mankind is man.
Placed on this isthmus of a middle state,
A being darkly wise, and rudely great:
5 With too much knowledge for the skeptic side,
With too much weakness for the Stoic's pride,
He hangs between: in doubt to act, or rest;
In doubt to deem himself a god, or beast;
In doubt his mind or body to prefer;
10 Born but to die, and reas'ning but to err;
Alike in ignorance, his reason such,
Whether he thinks too little, or too much:
Chaos of thought and passion, all confused;
Still by himself abused, or disabused;
15 Created half to rise, and half to fall;
Great lord of all things, yet a prey to all;
Sole judge of truth, in endless error hurled:
The glory, jest, and riddle of the world!

EPIGRAM

Engraved on the Collar of a Dog Which I Gave to His Royal Highness

I am his Highness' dog at Kew;
Pray tell me sir, whose dog are you?

---

1. *Pierian spring,* i.e. inspiration; from Pieria, where the Muses were born.

DISCUSSION

1. Many of the excerpts from *An Essay on Criticism* can be read in two senses: as advice to writers or critics, and as general maxims for living. Select three of them and explain their use in both senses.

2. Everyone agrees that Pope's "Epigram Engraved on the Collar of a Dog" is clever, but just where *does* its cleverness lie?

3. What is the tone of "Know Then Thyself"? Does the speaker think that man will ever be able to understand himself? Explain.

WRITING

1. Select any of the excerpts from *An Essay on Criticism* and use it as the basis for a composition in which you draw on your own experience to explain and illustrate its applicability.

2. Try your hand at writing some two-line epigrams. Current news events or public figures are good targets for this sort of writing.

Samuel Johnson   1709 / 1784

NATIONAL PORTRAIT GALLERY, LONDON

Johnson's reputation as a scholar and writer was established in 1755 with the publication of his *Dictionary*, which was as much a revelation of its author's personality as an attempt to stabilize the English language.

From
THE DICTIONARY

alliga'tor. The crocodile. This name is chiefly used for the crocodile of America, between which, and that of Africa, naturalists have laid down this difference, that one moves the upper, and the other the lower jaw; but this is now known to be chimerical, the lower jaw being equally moved by both.

bu'lly. (Skinner derives this word from *burly*, as a corruption in the pronunciation; which is very probably right; or from *bulky*, or *bull-eyed*; which are less probable. May it not come from *bull*, the pope's letter, implying the insolence of those who came invested with authority from the papal court?) A noisy, blustering, quarrelling fellow: it is generally taken for a man that has only the appearance of courage.

bu'tterfly. A beautiful insect, so named because it first appears at the beginning of the season for butter.

chi'cken. (3) A term for a young girl.

chiru'rgeon. One that cures ailments, not by internal medicines, but outward applications. It is now generally pronounced, and by many written, *surgeon*.

cough. A convulsion of the lungs, vellicated by some sharp serosity. It is pronounced *coff*.

cu'ckoo. (1) A bird which appears in the spring; and is said to suck the eggs of other birds, and lay her own to be hatched in their place; from which practice, it was usual to alarm a husband at the approach of an adulterer by calling *cuckoo*, which, by mistake, was in time applied to the husband. This bird is remarkable for the uniformity of his note, from which his name in most tongues seems to have been formed.

to cu'rtail. (*curto*, Latin. It was anciently written *curtal*, which perhaps is more proper; but dogs that had their tails cut, being called *curtal* dogs, the word was vulgarly conceived to mean originally *to cut the tail*, and was in time written according to that notion.) (1) To cut off; to cut short; to shorten.

dedica'tion. (2) A servile address to a patron.

den. (1) A cavern or hollow running horizontally, or with a small obliquity, under ground; distinct from a hole, which runs down perpendicularly.

dull. (8) Not exhilarating; not delightful; as, *to make dictionaries is dull work.*

e'ssay. (2) A loose sally of the mind; an irregular indigested piece; not a regular and orderly composition.

exci'se. A hateful tax levied upon commodities, and adjudged not by the common judges of property, but wretches hired by those to whom excise is paid.[1]

fa'vourite. (2) One chosen as a companion by his superiour; a mean wretch whose whole business is by any means to please.

fun. (A low cant word.) Sport; high merriment; frolicksome delight.

ga'mbler. (A cant word, I suppose, for *game*, or *gamester*.) A knave whose practice it is to invite the unwary to game and cheat them.

to gi'ggle. To laugh idly; to titter; to grin with merry levity. It is retained in Scotland.

goat. A ruminant animal that seems a middle species between deer and sheep.

gob. A small quantity. A low word.

gra'vy. The serous juice that runs from flesh not much dried by the fire.

gru'bstreet. Originally the name of a street in Moorfields in London, much inhabited by writers of small histories, dictionaries, and temporary poems; whence any mean production is called grubstreet.

to hiss. To utter a noise like that of a serpent and some other animals. It is remarkable, that this word cannot be pronounced without making the noise which it signifies.

itch. (1) A cutaneous disease extremely contagious, which overspreads the body with small pustules filled with a thin serum, and raised as microscopes have discovered by a small animal. It is cured by sulphur.

lexico'grapher. A writer of dictionaries; a harmless drudge, that busies himself in tracing the original, and detailing the signification of words.

lunch, lu'ncheon. As much food as one's hand can hold.

ne'twork. Any thing reticulated or decussated, at equal distances, with interstices between the intersections.

oats. A grain, which in England is generally given to horses, but in Scotland supports the people.

pa'rasite. One that frequents rich tables, and earns his welcome by flattery.

pa'stern. (1) The knee of an horse.[2]

pa'tron. (1) One who countenances, supports, or protects. Commonly a wretch who supports with insolence, and is paid with flattery.

pe'nsioner. (2) A slave of state hired by a stipend to obey his master.

sa'tire. A poem in which wickedness or folly is censured. Proper *satire* is distinguished, by the generality of the reflections, from a *lampoon* which is aimed against a particular person; but they are too frequently confounded.

shre'wmouse. A mouse of which the bite is generally supposed venomous, and to which vulgar tradition assigns such malignity, that she is said to lame the foot over which she runs. I am informed that all these reports are calumnious, and that her feet and teeth are equally harmless with those of any other little mouse. Our ancestors however looked on her with such terrour, that they are supposed to have given her name to a scolding woman, whom for her venom they call a *shrew*.

so'nnet. (1) A short poem consisting of fourteen lines, of which the rhymes are adjusted by a particular rule. It is not very suitable to the English language, and has not been used by any man of eminence since Milton.

to'ry. (A cant term, derived, I suppose, from an Irish word signifying a savage.) One who adheres to the ancient constitution of the state, and the apostolical hierarchy of the church of England, opposed to a whig.[3]

whig. (2) The name of a faction.

wi'tticism. A mean attempt at wit.

to worm. (2) To deprive a dog of something, nobody knows what, under his tongue, which is said to prevent him, nobody knows why, from running mad.

---

1. *excise.* Johnson's father had had trouble with the commissioners of excise, in the conduct of his business as a bookseller and maker of parchment.

2. *pastern.* (1) In fact, part of the foot of a horse. When a lady asked Johnson how he came to define the word in this way, he answered, "Ignorance, Madam, pure ignorance." But he didn't bother to correct his definition until eighteen years later.

3. Johnson himself was a Tory.

JOHNSON'S LETTER TO CHESTERFIELD

When Johnson, in 1746, first proposed the idea of compiling a dictionary, he discussed the project with Lord Chesterfield, one of the most cultivated noblemen of the age and a man with some scholarly knowledge of language and literature. Chesterfield expressed interest, and in accordance with the custom of literary patronage, gave Johnson a gift of £10. Johnson then addressed to him a detailed *Plan of a Dictionary*, in which Chesterfield is referred to as the patron of the project. Chesterfield read and approved the document before it was published, and apparently promised Johnson his continued assistance and financial support. This, however, never materialized. When the *Dictionary* finally appeared in 1755, Chesterfield expressed the desire to be regarded as its patron. This is the letter Johnson wrote him.

NATIONAL PORTRAIT GALLERY, LONDON

To the Right Honorable
the Earl of Chesterfield

February 7, 1755.

My Lord: I have lately been informed by the proprietor of *The World*,[1] that two papers, in which my *Dictionary* is recommended to the public, were written by your lordship. To be so distinguished is an honor which, being very little accustomed to favors from the great, I know not well how to receive, or in what terms to acknowledge.

When, upon some slight encouragement, I first visited your lordship, I was overpowered, like the rest of mankind, by the enchantment of your address; and I could not forbear to wish that I might boast myself *"Le vainqueur du vainqueur de la terre"*,[2] that I might obtain that regard for which I saw the world contending; but I found my attendance so little encouraged, that neither pride nor modesty would suffer me to continue it. When I had once addressed your lordship in public, I had exhausted all the art of pleasing which a retired and uncourtly scholar can possess. I had done all that I could; and no man is well pleased to have his all neglected, be it ever so little.

Seven years, my lord, have now passed, since I waited in your outward rooms, or was repulsed from your door; during which time I have been pushing on my work through difficulties, of which it is useless to complain, and have brought it at last to the verge of publication, without one act of assistance, one word of encouragement, or one smile of favor. Such treatment I did not expect, for I never had a patron before.

The shepherd in Vergil grew at last acquainted with Love, and found him a native of the rocks.[3]

Is not a patron, my lord, one who looks with unconcern on a man struggling for life in the water, and, when he has reached ground, encumbers him with help? The notice which you have been pleased to take of my labors, had it been early, had been kind; but it has been delayed till I am indifferent and cannot enjoy it; till I am solitary, and cannot impart it; till I am known, and do not want it. I hope it is no very cynical asperity not to confess obligations where no benefit has been received, or to be unwilling that the public should consider me as owing that to a patron, which Providence has enabled me to do for myself.

Having carried on my work thus far with so little obligation to any favorer of learning, I shall not be disappointed though I should conclude it, if less be possible, with less; for I have been long wakened from that dream of hope, in which I once boasted myself with so much exaltation,

> My Lord,
> Your Lordship's most humble,
> Most Obedient servant,
>
> SAM. JOHNSON

---

1. *The World*, a newspaper run by a friend of Johnson.
2. *Le vainqueur . . . de la terre.* The conqueror of the conqueror of the world (French).

3. *The shepherd . . . rocks.* Johnson is referring to a pastoral poem by Vergil which speaks of the cruelty and inhumanity of love.

VULTURES TALK ABOUT MEN

The Idler, No. 22—September 9, 1758

"The Idler" was a weekly essay which Johnson wrote for *The Universal Chronicle*, a weekly newspaper, from 1758–1760. The essays were twice collected and reprinted during Johnson's lifetime, but both editions omitted No. 22, possibly because of the unsavory picture it presents of mankind.

MANY naturalists are of opinion that the animals which we commonly consider as mute have the power of imparting their thoughts to one another. That they can express general sensations is very certain; every being that can utter sounds has a different voice for pleasure and for pain. The hound informs his fellows when he scents his game; the hen calls her chickens to their food by her cluck, and drives them from danger by her scream.

Birds have the greatest variety of notes; they have indeed a variety which seems almost sufficient to make a speech adequate to the purposes of a life which is regulated by instinct and can admit little change or improvement. To the cries of birds curiosity or superstition has been always attentive; many have studied the language of the feathered tribes, and some have boasted that they understood it.

The most skilful or most confident interpreters of the silvan dialogues have been commonly found among the philosophers of the East, in a country

---

OF HUMAN INTEREST

Johnson's pride

Lord Chesterfield maintained repeatedly that he had never knowingly refused to see Dr. Johnson. Some Johnson biographers believe that if Johnson had persisted, Chesterfield no doubt would have received him. But Johnson, once rebuffed, was too proud to continue efforts to see Chesterfield. Boswell, in his *Life of Johnson*, reports: "[Dr. Adams] insisted on Lord Chesterfield's general affability and easiness of access, especially to literary men. 'Sir, (said Johnson) that is not Lord Chesterfield; he is the proudest man this day existing.' 'No, (said Dr. Adams) there is one person, at least, as proud; I think, by your own account you are the prouder man of the two.' 'But mine (replied Johnson instantly) was *defensive* pride.'"

where the calmness of the air and the mildness of the seasons allow the student to pass a great part of the year in groves and bowers. But what may be done in one place by peculiar opportunities, may be performed in another by peculiar diligence. A shepherd of Bohemia has, by long abode in the forests, enabled himself to understand the voice of birds; at least he relates with great confidence a story of which the credibility may be considered by the learned.

"As I was sitting, (said he) within a hollow rock, and watching my sheep that fed in the valley, I heard two vultures interchangeably crying on the summit of the cliff. Both voices were earnest and deliberate. My curiosity prevailed over my care of the flock; I climbed slowly and silently from crag to crag, concealed among the shrubs, till I found a cavity where I might sit and listen without suffering or giving disturbance.

"I soon perceived that my labour would be well repaid; for an old vulture was sitting on a naked prominence, with her young about her, whom she was instructing in the arts of a vulture's life and preparing, by the last lecture, for their final dismission to the mountains and the skies.

"'My children,' said the old vulture, 'you will the less want my instructions because you have had my practice before your eyes; you have seen me snatch from the farm the household fowl, you have seen me seize the leveret in the bush, and the kid in the pasture; you know how to fix your talons, and how to balance your flight when you are laden with your prey. But you remember the taste of more delicious food; I have often regaled you with the flesh of man.'

"'Tell us,' said the young vultures, 'where man may be found, and how he may be known; his flesh is surely the natural food of a vulture. Why have you never brought a man in your talons to the nest?'

"'He is too bulky,' said the mother; 'when we find a man, we can only tear away his flesh and leave his bones upon the ground.'

"'Since man is so big,' said the young ones, 'how do you kill him? You are afraid of the wolf and of the bear; by what power are vultures superior to man, is man more defenseless than a sheep?'

"'We have not the strength of man,' returned the mother, 'and I am sometimes in doubt whether we have the subtilty; and the vultures would seldom feast upon his flesh, had not nature, that devoted him to our uses, infused into him a strange ferocity, which I have never observed in any other being that feeds upon the earth. Two herds of men will often meet and shake the earth with noise, and fill the air with fire. When you hear noise and see fire which flashes along the ground, hasten to the place with your swiftest wing, for men are surely destroying one another; you will then find the ground smoking with blood and covered with carcasses, of which many are dismembered and mangled for the convenience of the vulture.'

"'But when men have killed their prey,' said the pupil, 'why do they not eat it? When the wolf has killed a sheep he suffers not the vulture to touch it till he has satisfied himself. Is not man another kind of wolf?'

"'Man,' said the mother, 'is the only beast who kills that which he does not devour, and this quality makes him so much a benefactor to our species.'

"'If men kill our prey and lay it in our way,' said the young one, 'what need shall we have of labouring for ourselves?'

"'Because man will, sometimes,' replied the mother, 'remain for a long time quiet in his den. The old vultures will tell you when you are to watch his motions. When you see men in great numbers moving close together, like a flight of storks, you may conclude that they are hunting, and that you will soon revel in human blood.'

"'But still,' said the young one, 'I would gladly know the reason of this mutual slaughter. I could never kill what I could not eat.'

"'My child,' said the mother, 'this is a question which I cannot answer, tho' I am reckoned the most subtile bird of the mountain. When I was young I used frequently to visit the ayry of an old vulture who dwelt upon the Carpathian rocks; he had made many observations; he knew the places that afforded prey round his habitation, as far in every direction as the strongest wing can fly between the rising and setting of the summer sun; he had fed year after year on the entrails of men. His opinion was that men had only the appearance of animal life, being really vegetables with the power of motion; and that as the boughs of an oak are dashed together by the storm, that swine may fatten upon the falling acorns, so men are by some unaccountable power driven one against another, till they lose their motion, that vultures may be fed. Others think they have observed something of contrivance and policy among these mischievous beings, and those that hover more closely round them pretend that there is, in every herd, one that gives directions to the rest, and seems to be more eminently delighted with a wide carnage. What it is that entitles him to such preëminence we know not; he is seldom the biggest or the swiftest, but he shews by his eagerness and diligence that he is, more than any of the others, a friend to vultures.'"

□

DISCUSSION

1. The excerpts from the *Dictionary* provide a cross-section of Johnson's personality as well as his work. Find examples that:

(a) illustrate his whimsy.

(b) show his learning.

(c) display the beliefs of his age.

(d) have undergone great change in meaning or in acceptability since his day.

(e) indicate the timelessness of some colloquial or substandard words or expressions.

(f) demonstrate his thoroughness.

(g) reveal his prejudices.

(h) show his ability to enjoy a joke at his own expense.

2. (a) Which of the expressions in Johnson's letter to Chesterfield do you consider to be "masterful put-downs"?

(b) Compare the *Dictionary* definition of *patron* with that in the letter. Which do you prefer?

(c) How do you suppose Lord Chesterfield reacted to Johnson's letter? To see how successful a guesser you are, consult Boswell's *Life of Johnson* or an encyclopedia or literary history to find what Chesterfield's reaction was.

3. (a) In "Vultures Talk about Men," the Bohemian shepherd's account uses a device popular with all story-tellers: that of the naive narrator (in this case the old vulture) whose simplicity increases the impact of the moral of the story. Explain specifically how this device operates in "The Idler" No. 22.

(b) Reread Johnson's definition of *essay*. How well does it apply to "Vultures Talk about Men"?

WRITING

1. Take a dozen or so words of your own choice and prepare personalized definitions of them in the manner of Johnson's *Dictionary*.

2. Assume you are Lord Chesterfield and write an answer to Johnson's letter.

3. Compose a fable exposing some evil or folly of the modern world, in the manner of "The Idler" No. 22.

LLOYD'S COFFEE HOUSE, LLOYD'S, LONDON.

From LONDON

The year after he came to the city, Johnson published, anonymously, a long satirical poem which he labeled "A poem in imitation of the third satire of Juvenal." Juvenal was a Roman (A.D. 60?–130?) who wrote bitter denunciations of the society, culture, and politics of his day.

By numbers, here, from shame or censure free,[1]
All crimes are safe, but hated poverty.
This, only this, the rigid law pursues,
This, only this, provokes the snarling Muse;
5   The sober trader, at a tattered cloak,
Wakes from his dream and labors for a joke;
With brisker air the silken courtiers gaze,
And turn the varied taunt a thousand ways.
Of all the griefs that harass the distressed
10 Sure the most bitter is a scornful jest
Fate never wounds more deep the gen'rous heart
Than when a blockhead's insult points the dart. . . .

  Prepare for death, if here at night you roam,
And sign your will before you sup from home.
15 Some fiery fop, with new commission vain,
Who sleeps on brambles till he kills his man;[2]
Some frolic drunkard, reeling from a feast,
Provokes a broil and stabs you for a jest.
Yet ev'n these heroes, mischievously gay,
20 Lords of the street and terrors of the way,

Flushed as they are with folly, youth and wine,
Their prudent insults to the poor confine:
Afar they mark the flambeau's bright approach,
And shun the shining train and golden coach.
25   In vain, these dangers past, your doors you close,
And hope the balmy blessings of repose:
Cruel with guilt, and daring with despair,
The midnight murd'rer bursts the faithless bar,
Invades the sacred hour of silent rest,
30 And plants, unseen, a dagger in your breast.
   Scarce can our fields—such crowds at Tyburn[3] die—
With hemp the gallows and the fleet supply.
Propose your schemes, ye senatorian band,
Whose "Ways and Means"[4] support the sinking land,
35 Lest ropes be wanting, in the tempting Spring,
To rig another convoy for the King.

---

3. *Tyburn*, place where criminals were executed.
4. *Ways and Means*, term used in the House of Commons for methods of raising money.

---

1. *By numbers . . . free*, free from shame or censure because they (crimes) are so frequent.
2. *Who sleeps . . . man*, who cannot rest until he kills his man.

DISCUSSION

1. (a) Compare the evils described in "London" with those described by Swift in "A Modest Proposal."

(b) How does the modern age compare with the age described in "London"?

2. Keeping in mind the violence that Johnson describes, write either, in prose or in rhymed couplets a satire on the violence of our modern age (perhaps "Ten Suggestions for Staying Alive in America Today").

James Boswell 1740 / 1795

From
THE LIFE OF
SAMUEL JOHNSON, LL.D.

As I had the honor and happiness of enjoying Dr. Johnson's friendship for upwards of twenty years; as I had the scheme of writing his life constantly in view; as he was well apprised of this circumstance, and from time to time obligingly satisfied my inquiries by communicating to me the incidents of his early years; as I acquired a facility in recollecting, and was very assiduous in recording, his conversation, of which the extraordinary vigor and vivacity constituted one of the first features of his character; and as I have spared no pains in obtaining materials concerning him from every quarter where I could discover that they were to be found, and have been favored with the most liberal communications by his friends, I flatter myself that few biographers have entered upon such a work as this with more advantages; independent of literary abilities, in which I am not vain enough to compare myself with some great names who have gone before me in this kind of writing. . . .

Boswell's Introduction to Johnson (1763)

This is to me a memorable year, for in it I had the happiness to obtain the acquaintance of that extraordinary man whose memoirs I am now writing; an acquaintance which I shall ever esteem as one of the most fortunate circumstances in my life. . . .

Mr. Thomas Davies the actor, who then kept a bookseller's shop in Russel-street, Covent-garden, told me that Johnson was very much his friend, and came frequently to his house, where he more than once invited me to meet him; but by some unlucky accident or other he was prevented from coming to us.

At last, on Monday the 16th of May, when I was sitting in Mr. Davies's back-parlor, after having drunk tea with him and Mrs. Davies, Johnson unexpectedly came into the shop; and Mr. Davies having perceived him through the glass-door in the room in which we were sitting, advancing towards us—he announced his aweful approach to me, somewhat in the manner of an actor in the part of Horatio, when he addresses Hamlet on the appearance of his father's ghost, "Look, my Lord, it comes."

I found that I had a very perfect idea of Johnson's figure, from the portrait of him painted by Sir Joshua Reynolds soon after he had published his *Dictionary*, in the attitude of sitting in his easy chair in deep meditation, which was the first picture his friend did for him, which Sir Joshua kindly presented to me. Mr. Davies mentioned my name, and respectfully introduced me to him. I was much agitated, and recollecting his prejudice against the Scotch, of which I had heard much, I said to Davies, "Don't tell where I come from."

"From Scotland," cried Davies roguishly.

"Mr. Johnson, (said I) I do indeed come from Scotland, but I cannot help it." I am willing to flatter myself that I meant this as light pleasantry to soothe and conciliate him, and not as an humiliating abasement at the expense of my country. But however that might be, this speech was somewhat unlucky, for with that quickness of wit for which he was so remarkable, he seized the expression "come from Scotland" which I used in the sense of being of that country, and, as if I had said that I had come away from it, or left it, retorted, "That, Sir, I find, is what a very great many of your countrymen cannot help."

This stroke stunned me a good deal; and when we had sat down, I felt myself not a little embarrassed, and apprehensive of what might come next. He then addressed himself to Davies: "What do you think of Garrick?[1] He has refused me an order for the play

In these excerpts, punctuation and paragraphing have been slightly modernized.

1. *Garrick,* David Garrick, the most famous actor of his day, and a former pupil of Johnson's.

for Miss Williams,[2] because he knows the house will be full, and that an order would be worth three shillings."

Eager to take any opening to get into conversation with him, I ventured to say, "O, Sir, I cannot think Mr. Garrick would grudge such a trifle to you."

"Sir (said he, with a stern look), I have known David Garrick longer than you have done: and I know no right you have to talk to me on the subject."

Perhaps I deserved this check, for it was rather presumptuous in me, an entire stranger, to express any doubt of the justice of his animadversion upon his old acquaintance and pupil. I now felt myself much mortified, and began to think that the hope which I had long indulged of obtaining his acquaintance was blasted. And, in truth, had not my ardor been uncommonly strong, and my resolution uncommonly persevering, so rough a reception might have deterred me for ever from making any further attempts. Fortunately, however, I remained upon the field not wholly discomfited; and was soon rewarded by hearing some of his conversation, of which I preserved the following short minute, without marking the questions and observations by which it was produced.

"People (he remarked) may be taken in once, who imagine that an author is greater in private life than other men. Uncommon parts[3] require uncommon opportunities for their exertion."

"In barbarous society, superiority of parts is of real consequence. Great strength or great wisdom is of much value to an individual. But in more polished times there are people to do every thing for money; and then there are a number of other superiorities, such as those of birth and fortune, and rank, that dissipate men's attention, and leave no extraordinary share of respect for personal and intellectual superiority. This is wisely ordered by Providence, to preserve some equality among mankind.". . .

I was highly pleased with the extraordinary vigor of his conversation, and regretted that I was drawn away from it by an engagement at another place. I had, for a part of the evening, been left alone with him, and had ventured to make an observation now and then, which he received very civilly; so that I

---

2. *Miss Williams*, an indigent elderly lady who lived in Johnson's household and on his bounty.
3. *parts*, personal qualities; abilities or talents.

was satisfied that though there was a roughness in his manner, there was no ill-nature in his disposition. Davies followed me to the door, and when I complained to him a little of the hard blows which the great man had given me, he kindly took upon him to console me by saying, "Don't be uneasy. I can see he likes you very well."

A few days afterwards I called on Davies, and asked him if he thought I might take the liberty of waiting on Mr. Johnson at his Chambers in the Temple. He said I certainly might, and that Mr. Johnson would take it as a compliment. So upon Tuesday the 24th of May, I boldly repaired to Johnson. His Chambers were on the first floor of No. 1, Inner-Temple-lane, and I entered them with an impression given me by the Reverend Dr. Blair, of Edinburgh, who had been introduced to him not long before, and described his having "found the Giant in his den"; an expression which, when I came to be pretty well acquainted with Johnson, I repeated to him, and he was diverted by this picturesque account of himself.

He received me very courteously; but it must be confessed that his apartment, and furniture, and morning dress were sufficiently uncouth. His brown suit of clothes looked very rusty; he had on a little old shrivelled unpowdered wig, which was too small for his head; his shirt-neck and knees of his breeches were loose; his black worsted stockings ill drawn up; and he had a pair of unbuckled shoes by way of slippers. But all these slovenly peculiarities were forgotten the moment that he began to talk. Some gentlemen whom I do not recollect were sitting with him; and when they went away, I also rose; but he said to me, "Nay, don't go."

"Sir, (said I) I am afraid that I intrude upon you. It is benevolent to allow me to sit and hear you."

He seemed pleased with this compliment, which I sincerely paid him, and answered, "Sir, I am obliged to any man who visits me." I have preserved the following short minute of what passed this day:

"Madness frequently discovers itself merely by unnecessary deviation from the usual modes of the world. My poor friend Smart shewed the disturbance of his mind by falling upon his knees and saying his prayers in the street or in any other unusual place. Now although, rationally speaking, it is greater madness not to pray at all than to pray as Smart did, I am afraid there are so many who do not pray that their understanding is not called in question."

Concerning this unfortunate poet, Christopher Smart, who was confined in a mad-house, he had, at another time, the following conversation with Dr. Burney:

BURNEY. "How does poor Smart do, Sir; is he likely to recover?"

JOHNSON. "It seems as if his mind had ceased to struggle with the disease, for he grows fat upon it."

BURNEY. "Perhaps, Sir, that may be from want of exercise."

JOHNSON. "No, Sir; he has partly as much exercise as he used to have, for he digs in the garden. Indeed, before his confinement, he used for exercise to walk to the ale-house; but he was *carried* back again. I did not think he ought to be shut up. His infirmities were not noxious to society. He insisted on people praying with him; and I'd as lief pray with Kit Smart as any one else. Another charge was that he did not love clean linen; and I have no passion for it."

Johnson continued, "Mankind have a great aversion to intellectual labor; but even supposing knowledge to be easily attainable, more people would be content to be ignorant than would take even a little trouble to acquire it."

"The morality of an action depends on the motive from which we act. If I fling half a crown to a beggar with intention to break his head, and he picks it up and buys victuals with it, the physical effect is good; but, with respect to me, the action is very wrong."

Johnson on Fathers and Sons (July 1763)

Feeling myself now quite at ease as his companion, though I had all possible reverence for him, I expressed a regret that I could not be so easy with my father, though he was not much older than Johnson, and certainly however respectable had not more learning and greater abilities to depress me. I asked him the reason of this.

JOHNSON. "Why, Sir, I am a man of the world. I live in the world, and I take, in some degree, the color of the world as it moves along. Your father is a Judge in a remote part of the island, and all his notions are taken from the old world. Besides, Sir, there must always be a struggle between a father and son, while one aims at power and the other at independence."

I said I was afraid my father would force me to be a lawyer.

JOHNSON. "Sir, you need not be afraid of his forcing you to be a laborious practising lawyer; that is not in his power. For as the proverb says, 'One man may lead a horse to the water, but twenty cannot make him drink.' He may be displeased that you are not what he wishes you to be; but that displeasure will not go far. If he insists only on your having as much law as is necessary for a man of property, and then endeavors to get you into Parliament, he is quite right."

On Young People

At night Mr. Johnson and I supped in a private room at the Turk's Head coffee-house in the Strand. "I encourage this house (said he) for the mistress of it is a good civil woman, and has not much business."

"Sir, I love the acquaintance of young people; because, in the first place, I don't like to think myself growing old. In the next place, young acquaintances must last longest, if they do last; and then, Sir, young men have more virtue than old men; they have more generous sentiments in every respect. I love the young dogs of this age: they have more wit and humor and knowledge of life than we had; but then the dogs are not so good scholars. Sir, in my early years I read very hard. It is a sad reflection, but a true one, that I knew almost as much at eighteen as I do now. My judgment, to be sure, was not so good; but I had all the facts. I remember very well, when I was at Oxford, an old gentleman said to me, 'Young man, ply your book diligently now, and acquire a stock of knowledge; for when years come upon you, you will find that poring upon books will be but an irksome task.'"

On Eating (August 1763)

At supper this night he talked of good eating with uncommon satisfaction. "Some people (said he) have a foolish way of not minding, or pretending not to mind, what they eat. For my part, I mind my belly very studiously, and very carefully; for I look upon it that he who does not mind his belly will hardly mind anything else."

He now appeared to me *Jean Bull philosophe*,[4] and he was, for the moment, not only serious but

---

4. *Jean Bull philosophe*, John Bull the philosopher (French). John Bull is the personification of the English nation, the typical Englishman. Boswell probably means that Johnson was philosophizing in the English vein.

vehement. Yet I have heard him, upon other occasions, talk with great contempt of people who were anxious to gratify their palates; and the 206th number of his *Rambler* is a masterly essay against gulosity. His practice, indeed, I must acknowledge, may be considered as casting the balance of his different opinions upon this subject, for I never knew any man who relished good eating more than he did. When at table, he was totally absorbed in the business of the moment; his looks seemed rivetted to his plate; nor would he, unless when in very high company, say one word, or even pay the least attention to what was said by others, till he had satisfied his appetite, which was so fierce, and indulged with such intenseness, that while in the act of eating, the veins of his forehead swelled, and generally a strong perspiration was visible. To those whose sensations were delicate, this could not but be disgusting; and it was doubtless not very suitable to the character of a philosopher, who should be distinguished by self-command. But it must be owned that Johnson, though he could be rigidly *abstemious,* was not a *temperate* man either in eating or drinking. He could refrain, but he could not use moderately. He told me that he had fasted two days without inconvenience, and that he had never been hungry but once. They who beheld with wonder how much he eat upon all occasions when his dinner was to his taste could not easily conceive what he must have meant by hunger, and not only was he remarkable for the extraordinary quantity which he eat, but he was, or affected to be, a man of very nice discernment in the science of cookery. He used to descant critically on the dishes which had been at table where he had dined or supped, and to recollect minutely what he had liked.

When invited to dine, even with an intimate friend, he was not pleased if something better than a plain dinner was not prepared for him. I have heard him say on such an occasion, "This was a good dinner enough, to be sure; but it was not a dinner to *ask* a man to." On the other hand, he was wont to express, with great glee, his satisfaction when he had been entertained quite to his mind.

On Equality of the Sexes (April 1778)

Mrs. Knowles affected to complain that men had much more liberty allowed them than women.

JOHNSON. "Why, Madam, women have all the liberty they should wish to have. We have all the labor and the danger, and the women all the ad-

vantage. We go to sea, we build houses, we do everything, in short, to pay our court to the women.''

MRS. KNOWLES. ''The Doctor reasons very wittily, but not convincingly. Now, take the instance of building; the mason's wife, if she is ever seen in liquor, is ruined; the mason may get himself drunk as often as he pleases, with little loss of character; nay, may let his wife and children starve.''

JOHNSON. ''Madam, you must consider, if the mason does get himself drunk, and let his wife and children starve, the parish will oblige him to find security for their maintenance. We have different modes of restraining evil. Stocks for the men, a ducking-stool for women, and a pound for beasts. If we require more perfection from women than from ourselves, it is doing them honor. And women have not the same temptations that we have: they may always live in virtuous company; men must mix in the world indiscriminately. If a woman has no inclination to do what is wrong, being secured from it is no restraint to her. I am at liberty to walk into the Thames; but if I were to try it, my friends would restrain me in Bedlam, and I should be obliged to them.''

MRS. KNOWLES. ''Still, Doctor, I cannot help thinking it a hardship that more indulgence is allowed to men than to women. It gives a superiority to men, to which I do not see how they are entitled.''

JOHNSON. ''It is plain, Madam, one or other must have the superiority. As Shakespeare says, 'If two men ride on a horse, one must ride behind.'''

DILLY. ''I suppose, Sir, Mrs. Knowles would have them to ride in panniers, one on each side.''

JOHNSON. ''Then, Sir, the horse would throw them both.''

MRS. KNOWLES. ''Well, I hope that in another world the sexes will be equal.''

BOSWELL. ''That is being too ambitious, Madam. *We* might as well desire to be equal with the angels. We shall all, I hope, be happy in a future state, but we must not expect to be all happy in the same degree. It is enough if we be happy according to our several capacities. A worthy carman will get to heaven as well as Sir Isaac Newton. Yet, though equally good, they will not have the same degrees of happiness.''

JOHNSON. ''Probably not.''　□

SEE ALSO THE ARTICLE ''BOSWELL AS BIOGRAPHER'' BEGINNING ON PAGE 332.

BOSWELL AND JOHNSON AS TRAVEL WRITERS

In 1773, Johnson and Boswell made an extended journey from Edinburgh through the more remote parts of Scotland to the Hebrides, or Western Islands, a region then almost totally isolated from the rest of Europe. Both men wrote of their experiences. Johnson's account, *A Journey to the Western Islands of Scotland*, was published in 1775. In 1785, after Johnson's death, Boswell published a heavily edited version of the journal he had kept on the tour. The version used here, however, is from the recently recovered manuscript journal (see the article beginning on page 332), and presents, in Boswell's natural, private style, what he actually wrote in 1773.

Excerpts from the beginning of Boswell's journal are given here, and then parallel passages from Boswell's and Johnson's accounts of the same events.

From Boswell's
*Journal of a Tour to the Hebrides
with Samuel Johnson, LL.D.*

DR. Johnson had for many years given me hopes that we should go together and visit the Hebrides. Martin's Account of those islands had impressed us with a notion that we might there contemplate a system of life almost totally different from what we had been accustomed to see; and to find simplicity and wildness, and all the circumstances of remote time or place, so near to our native great island, was an object within the reach of reasonable curiosity. . . . We reckoned there would be some inconveniences and hardships, and perhaps a little danger; but these we were persuaded were magnified in the imagination of everybody. When I was at Ferney in 1764, I mentioned our design to Voltaire.[1] He looked at me as if I had talked of going to the North Pole, and said, "You do not insist on my accompanying you?" "No, sir." "Then I am very willing you

should go." I was not afraid that our curious expedition would be prevented by such apprehensions, but I doubted that it would not be possible to prevail on Dr. Johnson to relinquish for some time the felicity of a London life. . . .

He had disappointed my expectations so long that I began to despair; but in spring, 1773, he talked of coming to Scotland that year with so much firmness that I hoped he was at last in earnest. I knew that if he were once launched from the metropolis, he would go forward very well; and I got our common friends there to assist in setting him afloat. To Mrs. Thrale in particular, whose enchantment over him seldom failed, I was much obliged. . . .

Dr. Johnson's prejudice against Scotland was announced almost as soon as he began to appear in the world of letters. . . . The truth is, like the ancient Greeks and Romans, he allowed himself to look upon all nations but his own as barbarians. If he was particularly prejudiced against the Scots, it was because they were more in his way; because he thought their success in England rather exceeded the due proportion of their real merit. . . .

To Scotland, however, he ventured; and he returned from it in great good humor, with his prejudices much lessened, and with very grateful feelings of the hospitality with which he was treated, as is evident from that admirable work, his *Journey to the Western Islands of Scotland*. . . .

[*Boswell and Johnson arrived separately in Edinburgh, Johnson traveling there in post-chaises with a Mr. Scott of Oxford.*]

On Saturday the fourteenth of August, 1773, late in the evening, I received a note from him that he was arrived at Boyd's Inn, at the head of the Canongate. I went to him directly. He embraced me cordially, and I exulted in the thought that I now had him actually in Caledonia.[2] Mr. Scott's amiable manners and attachment to our Socrates at once united me to him. He told me that before I came in the Doctor had unluckily had a bad specimen of Scottish cleanliness. He then drank no fermented liquor. He asked to have his lemonade made sweeter, upon which the waiter with his greasy fingers lifted a lump of sugar and put it into it. The Doctor in indignation threw it out of the window. Scott said

---

From *Boswell's The Journal of a Tour to the Hebrides* edited by Frederick A. Pottle & Charles H. Bennett. Copyright © 1961 by Yale University. Used with permission of McGraw-Hill Book Company, Yale University and William Heinemann Limited.
1. *Voltaire,* (1694–1778), French satirist, philosopher, historian, dramatist, and poet, considered one of the most influential men in the history of thought and very famous in his own day.

2. *Caledonia,* Latin name for Scotland.

he was afraid he would have knocked the waiter down. Mr. Johnson told me that such another trick was played him at the house of a lady in Paris.

He was to do me the honour to lodge under my roof. I regretted sincerely that I had not also a room for Mr. Scott. Mr. Johnson and I walked arm-in-arm up the High Street to my house in James's Court; it was a dusky night; I could not prevent his being assailed by the evening effluvia of Edinburgh. I heard a late baronet of some distinction in the political world in the beginning of the present reign observe that "walking the streets of Edinburgh at night was pretty perilous and a good deal odoriferous." The peril is much abated by the care which the magistrates have taken to enforce the city laws against throwing foul water from the windows; but, from the structure of the houses in the old town, which consist of many storeys in each of which a different family lives, and there being no covered sewers, the odor still continues. . . .

ANOCH—TUESDAY 31 AUGUST, 1773

Between twelve and one we set out and travelled eleven wild miles till we came to a house in Glenmoriston kept by one Macqueen. Our landlord was a sensible fellow. He had learnt his grammar,[3] and Dr. Johnson justly observed that a man is the better for that as long as he lives. There were some books here: a treatise against drunkenness, translated from the French, a volume of the *Spectator*, a volume of Prideaux' *Connexion, Cyrus's Travels*. Macqueen said he had more volumes, and his pride seemed to be piqued that we were surprised at his having books.

Near to this, we had passed a party of soldiers under a sergeant at work upon the road. We gave them two shillings to drink. They came to this house and made merry in the barn. We went out, Mr. Johnson saying, "Come, let's go and give 'em another shilling apiece." We did so, and he was saluted "My Lord" by all of 'em. He is really generous, loves influence, and has the way of gaining it. He said he was quite feudal. Here I agree with him. I said I regretted I was not head of a clan. I would make my tenants follow me. I could not be a *patriarchal* chief. But I'd be a *feudal* chief.

The poor soldiers got too much liquor. Some of

DR. JOHNSON IN HIS TRAVELLING DRESS. FROM A CONTEMPORARY ENGRAVING.

'em fought and left blood upon the spot, and cursed whisky next morning. The house here was built of thick turfs and thatched with thinner turfs and heath. It had three rooms in length, and a little room projected. Where we sat, the side-walls were *wainscotted*, as Mr. Johnson said, with wands very well plaited. Our landlord had made all with his own hand. We had a broiled chicken, mutton collops or chops, mutton sausage, and eggs, of which Mr. Johnson eat five and nothing else. I eat four, some chicken and some sausage, and drank some rum and water and sugar. Joseph had lemons for Mr. Johnson, so he had lemonade. Mr. Johnson said he was a fine fellow: a civil man and a wise man.

Macqueen, our landlord, sat by us awhile and talked with us. He said all Glenmoriston's people would bleed for him if they were well used. But

---

3. *learnt his grammar*, i.e., he had studied Latin.

that seventy men had gone out of the Glen to America. That he himself intended to go next year, for that his farm, which twenty-five years ago was only £5 a year, was now raised to £20. That he could pay £10 and live, but no more. Mr. Johnson said he wished Macqueen Laird of Glenmoriston, and Glenmoriston to go to America. Macqueen very generously said he should be sorry for it, for Glenmoriston could not shift for himself in America as he could do.

I talked of the officers whom we had left today: how much service they had seen and how little they got for it, even of fame. Mr. Johnson said, "Sir, a soldier gets as little as any man can get." I observed that Goldsmith had more fame than all the officers last war who were not generals. JOHNSON. "Why, sir, you will get ten thousand to do what they did before you get one who does what Goldsmith has done. You must consider a thing is valued according to its rarity. A pebble that paves the street is in itself more useful than the diamond upon a lady's finger." I wish Goldie had heard this.

He said yesterday when I wondered how John Hay, one of our guides, who had been pressed aboard a man-of-war, did not choose to continue longer than nine months, after which time he got off: "Why, sir, no man will be a sailor who has contrivance to get himself into a jail, for being in a ship is being in a jail with the chance of being drowned."

We had tea in the afternoon, and our landlord's daughter, a modest civil girl very neatly dressed, made it to us. She told us she had been a year at Inverness and learnt reading and writing, sewing, knotting, working lace, and pastry. Mr. Johnson made her a present of a book of arithmetic which he had bought at Inverness.

The room had some deals laid as a kind of ceiling.

There were two beds in the room. A woman's gown was hung on a rope to make a curtain of separation between them. Joseph had the sheets which we brought with us laid on them. We had much hesitation whether to undress or lie down with our clothes on. I said at last, "I'll plunge in! I shall have less room for vermin to settle about me when I strip!" Mr. Johnson said he was like one hesitating whether to go into the cold bath. At last he resolved too. I observed he might serve a campaign. Said he, "I could do all that can be done by patience. Whether I should have strength enough, I know not." He was in excellent humor. To see the Rambler as I saw him tonight was really a curiosity. . . .

Tonight each offered up his private devotions. After we had chatted a little from our beds, Dr. Johnson said, "God bless us both for Jesus Christ's sake. Good night." I pronounced "Amen." Mr. Johnson fell asleep immediately. I could not have that good fortune for a long time. I fancied myself bit by innumerable vermin under the clothes, and that a spider was travelling from the *wainscot* towards my mouth. At last I fell into insensibility.

WEDNESDAY 1 SEPTEMBER. I awaked very early. I began to imagine that the landlord, being about to emigrate, might murder us to get our money and lay it upon the soldiers in the barn. Such groundless fears will arise in the mind before it has resumed its vigour after sleep! Mr. Johnson had had the same kind of ideas; for he told me afterwards that he considered so many soldiers, having seen us, would be witnesses should any harm be done; and the thought of that, I suppose, he considered would make us secure. When I got up, I found him sound asleep in his miserable sty, I may say, with a coloured handkerchief tied round his head. With difficulty could I get him up. . . .

From Johnson's JOURNEY TO THE WESTERN ISLANDS OF SCOTLAND

EARLY in the afternoon we came to Anoch, a village in *Glenmollison* of three huts, one of which is distinguished by a chimney. Here we were to dine and lodge, and were conducted through the first room, that had the chimney, into another lighted by a small glass window. The landlord attended us with great civility, and told us what he could give us to eat and drink. I found some books on a shelf, among which were a volume or more of Prideaux's Connection.[1]

This I mentioned as something unexpected, and perceived that I did not please him. I praised the propriety of his language, and was answered that I need not wonder, for he had learned it by grammar.

By subsequent opportunities of observation, I found that my host's diction had nothing peculiar. Those Highlanders that can speak English, commonly speak it well, with few of the words and little of the tone by which a Scotchman is distinguished. Their language seems to have been learned in the army or the navy, or by some communication with those who could give them good examples of accent and pronunciation. By their Lowland neighbours they would not willingly be taught; for they have long considered them as a mean and degenerate race. These prejudices are wearing fast away; but so much of them still remains, that when I asked a very learned minister in the islands which they considered as their most savage clans: "*Those,* said he, *that live next the lowlands.*"

As we came hither early in the day, we had time sufficient to survey the place. The house was built like other huts of loose stones, but the part in which we dined and slept was lined with turf and wattled with twigs, which kept the earth from falling. Near it was a garden of turnips and a field of potatoes. It stands in a glen, or valley, pleasantly watered by a winding river. But this country, however it may delight the gazer or amuse the naturalist, is of no great advantage to its owners. Our landlord told us of a gentleman who possesses lands eighteen Scotch miles in length and three in breadth, a space con-

taining at least a hundred square English miles. He has raised his rents, to the danger of depopulating his farms, and he fells his timber, and by exerting every art of augmentation, has obtained an yearly revenue of four hundred pounds, which for a hundred square miles is three halfpence an acre.

Some time after dinner we were surprised by the entrance of a young woman, not inelegant either in mien or dress, who asked us whether we would have tea. We found that she was the daughter of our host, and desired her to make it. Her conversation, like her appearance, was gentle and pleasing. We knew that the girls of the Highlands are all gentlewomen, and treated her with great respect, which she received as customary and due, and was neither elated by it, nor confused, but repaid my civilities without embarrassment, and told me how much I honoured her country by coming to survey it.

She had been at *Inverness* to gain the common female qualifications, and had, like her father, the English pronunciation. I presented her with a book, which I happened to have about me, and should not be pleased to think that she forgets me.

In the evening the soldiers whom we had passed on the road came to spend at our inn the little money that we had given them. They had the true military impatience of coin in their pockets, and had marched at least six miles to find the first place where liquor could be bought. Having never been before in a place so wild and unfrequented, I was glad of their arrival, because I knew that we had made them friends, and to gain still more of their good will, we went to them, where they were carousing in the barn, and added something to our former gift. All that we gave was not much, but it detained them in the barn, either merry or quarrelling, the whole night, and in the morning they went back to their work, with great indignation at the bad qualities of whisky.

We had gained so much the favour of our host that, when we left his house in the morning, he walked by us a great way, and entertained us with conversation both on his own condition, and that of the country. His life seemed to be merely pastoral, except that he differed from some of the ancient Nomades in having a settled dwelling. His wealth consists of one hundred sheep, as many goats,

---

1. *Prideaux's Connection.* Humphrey Prideaux (1648–1728) was a cleric and oriental scholar whose *Connection* was a scholarly work on the interval between the Old and New Testaments.

twelve milk-cows, and twenty-eight beeves ready for the drover.

From him we first heard of the general dissatisfaction which is now driving the Highlanders into the other hemisphere; and when I asked him whether they would stay at home if they were well treated, he answered with indignation that no man willingly left his native country. Of the farm which he himself occupied, the rent had, in twenty-five years, been advanced from five to twenty pounds, which he found himself so little able to pay that he would be glad to try his fortune in some other place. Yet he owned the reasonableness of raising the Highland rents in a certain degree, and declared himself willing to pay ten pounds for the ground which he had formerly had for five.

Our host having amused us for a time, resigned us to our guides. . . . □

DISCUSSION

1. In *The Life of Samuel Johnson*, Boswell's professed objective is to write Johnson's biography so that "he will be seen as he really was," to "delineate him without reserve."

(a) To what extent did he carry out this intent?

(b) What are some of the unpleasant aspects of the picture of Johnson that Boswell presents? What is your reaction to these aspects of Johnson?

(c) What seems to be Boswell's attitude toward Johnson?

(d) Does Boswell succeed in making Johnson come alive for you? Explain.

2. Reread for comparison the parallel passages on Anoch from Johnson's and Boswell's journals.

(a) In what respects are they similar? In what ways are they different?

(b) What differences in the characters of the two narrators emerge from these accounts?

(c) Which account do you prefer? Why?

WRITING

1. Some of the ideas Johnson expounded to Boswell are still being talked about today. Select one or two of these and write a brief essay in which you discuss the extent to which our ideas are similar to or different from those of Johnson's day. Possibilities: the generation gap as discussed in the "On Fathers and Sons" section of the *Life*; "Women's Lib" as presented by Mrs. Knowles, and the validity of Johnson's reactions.

2. Assume you are a modern Boswell and write a description of an imaginary meeting between yourself and some modern figure you admire.

3. The American critic J. Donald Adams has commented on Johnson's *Dictionary*: "Steeped in prejudice and tinged with mulishness as some of the definitions were, they are at least always the product of a sharp and honest mind. It is one of Johnson's great—and one of his most engaging—qualities, that he never indulged in double talk, that he never soft-soaped anyone. . . . Behind this book there is a man." In a brief essay, discuss the applicability of this statement, not only to the *Dictionary*, but to the picture of Johnson that emerges from all the writings by or about him in this section.

READERS' THEATER

1. Prepare and present a dramatized version of Boswell's first meeting with Johnson.

2. Prepare and present an original conversation between Johnson and Boswell dealing with some topic of current interest.

Thomas Gray
1716 / 1771

ELEGY WRITTEN IN A COUNTRY CHURCHYARD

The curfew tolls the knell of parting day,
  The lowing herd wind slowly o'er the lea,
The plowman homeward plods his weary way,
  And leaves the world to darkness and to me.

5 Now fades the glimmering landscape on the sight,
  And all the air a solemn stillness holds,
Save where the beetle wheels his droning flight,
  And drowsy tinklings lull the distant folds;

Save that from yonder ivy-mantled tower
10 The moping owl does to the moon complain
Of such as, wandering near her secret bower,
  Molest her ancient solitary reign.

Beneath those rugged elms, that yew-tree's shade,
  Where heaves the turf in many a moldering heap,
15 Each in his narrow cell forever laid,
  The rude forefathers of the hamlet sleep.

The breezy call of incense-breathing Morn,
  The swallow twittering from the strawbuilt shed,
The cock's shrill clarion, or the echoing horn,[1]
20 No more shall rouse them from their lowly bed.

For them no more the blazing hearth shall burn,
  Or busy housewife ply her evening care;
No children run to lisp their sire's return,
  Or climb his knees the envied kiss to share.

25 Oft did the harvest to their sickle yield,
  Their furrow oft the stubborn glebe has broke;
How jocund did they drive their team afield!
  How bowed the woods beneath their sturdy
    stroke!

Let not Ambition mock their useful toil,
30 Their homely joys, and destiny obscure;
Nor Grandeur hear, with a disdainful smile,
  The short and simple annals of the poor.

The boast of heraldry, the pomp of power,
  And all that beauty, all that wealth e'er gave,
35 Awaits alike the inevitable hour:
  The paths of glory lead but to the grave.

Nor you, ye proud, impute to these the fault,
  If Memory o'er their tomb no trophies raise,
Where through the long-drawn aisle and fretted vault
40 The pealing anthem swells the note of praise.

Can storied urn[2] or animated[3] bust
  Back to its mansion call the fleeting breath?
Can Honor's voice provoke the silent dust,
  Or Flattery soothe the dull cold ear of Death?

45 Perhaps in this neglected spot is laid
  Some heart once pregnant with celestial fire;
Hands that the rod of empire might have swayed,
  Or waked to ecstasy the living lyre.

But Knowledge to their eyes her ample page
50 Rich with the spoils of time did ne'er unroll;
Chill Penury repressed their noble rage,
  And froze the genial current of the soul.

Full many a gem of purest ray serene
  The dark unfathomed caves of ocean bear;
55 Full many a flower is born to blush unseen,
  And waste its sweetness on the desert air.

---

1. *horn,* the huntsman's horn.

2. *storied urn,* an urn decorated with pictures that tell a story.
3. *animated,* lifelike.

Some village Hampden[4] that with dauntless breast
   The little tyrant of his fields withstood;
Some mute inglorious Milton here may rest,
60   Some Cromwell guiltless of his country's blood.

The applause of listening senates to command,
   The threats of pain and ruin to despise,
To scatter plenty o'er a smiling land,
   And read their history in a nation's eyes,

65 Their lot forbade; nor circumscribed alone
   Their growing virtues, but their crimes confined;
Forbade to wade through slaughter to a throne,
   And shut the gates of mercy on mankind,

The struggling pangs of conscious truth to hide,
70   To quench the blushes of ingenuous shame,
Or heap the shrine of Luxury and Pride
   With incense kindled at the Muse's flame.

Far from the madding crowd's ignoble strife,
   Their sober wishes never learned to stray;
75 Along the cool sequestered vale of life
   They kept the noiseless tenor of their way.

Yet ev'n these bones from insult to protect
   Some frail memorial still erected nigh,
With uncouth[5] rimes and shapeless sculpture
    decked,
80   Implores the passing tribute of a sigh.

Their name, their years, spelt by the unlettered
    Muse,
   The place of fame and elegy supply;
And many a holy text around she strews,
   That teach the rustic moralist to die.

85 For who, to dumb Forgetfulness a prey,
   This pleasing anxious being e'er resigned,
Left the warm precincts of the cheerful day,
   Nor cast one longing, lingering look behind?

On some fond breast the parting soul relies,
90   Some pious drops the closing eye requires;
Ev'n from the tomb the voice of Nature cries,
   Ev'n in our ashes live their wonted fires.

For thee,[6] who mindful of the unhonored dead
   Dost in these lines their artless tale relate;
95 If chance, by lonely Contemplation led,
   Some kindred spirit shall inquire thy fate,

Haply some hoary-headed swain may say,
   "Oft have we seen him at the peep of dawn
Brushing with hasty steps the dews away
100   To meet the sun upon the upland lawn,

"There at the foot of yonder nodding beech,
   That wreathes its old fantastic roots so high,
His listless length at noontide would he stretch,
   And pore upon the brook that babbles by.

105 "Hard by yon wood, now smiling as in scorn,
   Muttering his wayward fancies he would rove,
Now drooping, woeful wan, like one forlorn,
   Or crazed with care, or crossed in hopeless love.

"One morn I missed him on the customed hill,
110   Along the heath, and near his favorite tree;
Another came; nor yet beside the rill,
   Nor up the lawn, nor at the wood was he;

"The next with dirges due in sad array
   Slow through the church-way path we saw him
    borne.
115 Approach and read (for thou canst read) the lay,
   Graved on the stone beneath yon aged thorn."

THE EPITAPH

Here rests his head upon the lap of Earth
   A youth to Fortune and to Fame unknown.
Fair Science frowned not on his humble birth,
120   *And Melancholy marked him for her own.*

Large was his bounty, and his soul sincere,
   Heaven did a recompense as largely send;
He gave to Misery all he had, a tear,
   He gained from Heaven ('twas all he wished) a
    friend.

125 *No farther seek his merits to disclose,*
   Or draw his frailties from their dread abode.
(There they alike in trembling hope repose),
   The bosom of his Father and his God.

4. *Hampden*, John Hampden (1594–1643), member of the Puritan
or Roundhead party who spoke out against royal taxes.
5. *uncouth*, strange, odd.

6. *thee*, Gray himself.

ODE ON THE DEATH OF A FAVOURITE CAT, DROWNED IN A TUB OF GOLD FISHES

'Twas on a lofty vase's side,
Where China's gayest art had dyed
   The azure flowers, that blow;
Demurest of the tabby kind,
5 The pensive Selima reclined,
   Gazed on the lake below.

Her conscious tail her joy declared;
The fair round face, the snowy beard,
   The velvet of her paws,
10 Her coat, that with the tortoise vies,
Her ears of jet, and emerald eyes,
   She saw; and purred applause.

Still had she gazed; but 'midst the tide
Two angel forms were seen to glide,
15   The Genii of the stream:
Their scaly armour's Tyrian hue
Thro' richest purple to the view
   Betrayed a golden gleam.

The hapless Nymph with wonder saw:
20 A whisker first and then a claw,
   With many an ardent wish,

She stretched in vain to reach the prize.
What female heart can gold despise?
   What Cat's averse to fish?

25 Presumptuous Maid! with looks intent
Again she stretched, again she bent,
   Nor knew the gulf between.
(Malignant Fate sat by, and smiled)
The slipp'ry verge her feet beguiled,
30   She tumbled headlong in.

Eight times emerging from the flood
She mewed to ev'ry wat'ry God,
   Some speedy aid to send.
No Dolphin came, no Nereid stirred:
35 Nor cruel *Tom*, nor *Susan* heard.
   A Fav'rite has no friend!

From hence, ye Beauties, undeceived,
Know, one false step is ne'er retrieved,
   And be with caution bold.
40 Not all that tempts your wand'ring eyes
And heedless hearts, is lawful prize;
   Nor all, that glisters, gold.

DISCUSSION

1. (a) What words in the first stanza of the Elegy contribute to the air of melancholy that pervades the poem?

(b) How do the second and third stanzas add to this melancholy?

2. The fourth stanza introduces the subject of the poem, the "rude forefathers of the hamlet."

(a) What is the speaker's attitude toward them as contrasted with his attitude toward the great of the world?

(b) To what extent were the rude forefathers' poverty and lack of education a handicap?

(c) To what extent were they a blessing?

3. One critical opinion holds that Gray's poem is "an elegy for Man, or at least for all 'average' and obscure men." Comment on this opinion.

4. If the "rude forefathers of the hamlet" may be said to be the protagonists of the poem, who or what are the antagonists?

5. Reread the poem and list lines and phrases that strike you as most quotable. To what do you attribute this preponderance of quotable material?

6. According to the epitaph which ends the poem, how satisfactory a life did the speaker live?

7. (a) At what points in "Ode on the Death of a Favorite Cat" does Gray turn aside from the cat to point a moral for his female readers?

(b) Comment on the appropriateness of the form and tone to the subject matter of the "Ode."

(c) Compare and contrast Gray's adaptation of a traditional ode with Pope's adaptation of a traditional epic in "The Rape of the Lock."

WRITING

1. Write a free verse poem or prose composition in which you celebrate the virtues of some humble moderns who, like Gray's villagers, would otherwise be overlooked and forgotten.

2. Write a short paper in which you discuss Gray's careful selection of words for their sounds and connotations so that they contribute actively to the theme and mood of his Elegy.

3. Write a brief parody of Gray's Elegy. Suggestions: "The hall-bell clangs the end of history . . ." or "The alarm shrieks the start of blue Monday. . . ." You can probably think of better subjects.

Robert Burns   1759 / 1796

A RED, RED ROSE

O my luve is like a red, red rose
    That's newly sprung in June.
O my luve is like the melodie
    That's sweetly played in tune.

5 As fair art thou, my bonie lass,
    So deep in luve am I,
And I will luve thee still, my dear,
    Till a' the seas gang dry.

Till a' the seas gang dry, my dear,
10   And the rocks melt wi' the sun!
And I will luve thee still, my dear,
    While the sands o' life shall run.

And fare thee weel, my only luve,
    And fare thee weel a while!
15 And I will come again, my luve,
    Tho' it were ten thousand mile!

TO A MOUSE

on turning her up in her nest
with the plow, November, 1785

WEE, sleekit,° cow'rin', tim'rous beastie,   sleek
O what a panic's in thy breastie!
Thou need na start awa sae hasty,
        Wi' bickering brattle!°   short race
5 I wad be laith to rin an' chase thee
        Wi' murd'ring pattle!°   plow-spade

I'm truly sorry man's dominion
Has broken Nature's social union,
An' justifies that ill opinion
10   Which makes thee startle
At me, thy poor earth-born companion,
        An' fellow-mortal!

I doubt na, whiles,° but thou may thieve;   sometimes
What then? poor beastie, thou maun live!
15 A daimen-icker in a thrave[1]
        'S a sma' request:
I'll get a blessin' wi' the lave,°   the rest
        And never miss 't!

Thy wee bit housie, too, in ruin!
20 Its silly wa's° the win's are strewin'!   simple walls
An' naething, now, to big° a new ane,   build
        O' foggage° green!   coarse grass
An' bleak December's win's ensuin',
        Baith snell° an' keen!   biting

25 Thou saw the fields laid bare and waste.
An' weary winter comin' fast,
An' cozie here, beneath the blast,
        Thou thought to dwell,
Till crash! the cruel coulter° past   plowshare
30   Out-thro' thy cell.

That wee bit heap o' leaves an' stibble
Has cost thee mony a weary nibble!
Now thou's turn'd out, for a' thy trouble,
        But house or hald,°   abode
35 To thole the winter's sleety dribble,
        An' cranreuch° cauld!   hoarfrost

But, Mousie, thou art no thy lane,°   alone
In proving foresight may be vain:
The best laid schemes o' mice an' men
40   Gang aft a-gley,°   go awry
An' lea'e us nought but grief an' pain
        For promis'd joy.

Still thou art blest compar'd wi' me!
The present only toucheth thee:
45 But oh! I backward cast my e'e
        On prospects drear!
An' forward tho' I canna see,
        I guess an' fear!

---

1. *A daimen-icker in a thrave*, an occasional ear or head of grain
in a shock.

TO A LOUSE

on seeing one on a lady's bonnet at church

1

HA! wh'are ye gaun, ye crowlin' ferlie!°   *crawling wonder*
Your impudence protects you sairly;°   *greatly*
I canna say but ye strunt° rarely,   *strut*
     Owre gauze and lace;
5 Tho' faith! I fear ye dine but sparely
     On sic a place.

2

Ye ugly, creepin', blastit wonner,
Detested, shunned by saunt an' sinner!
How dare ye set your fit° upon her,   *foot*
10   Sae fine a lady?
Gae somewhere else, and seek your dinner
     On some poor body.

3

Swith! in some beggar's haffet squattle;[1]
There ye may creep, and sprawl, and sprattle°   *struggle*
15 Wi' ither kindred jumping cattle,
     In shoals and nations;
Where horn nor bane° ne'er dare unsettle   *comb nor poison*
     Your thick plantations.

4

Now haud° ye there, ye're out o' sight,   *hold*
20 Below the fatt'rels,° snug an' tight;   *ribbon-ends*
Na, faith ye yet! ye'll no be right
     Till ye've got on it,
The very tapmost tow'ring height
     O' Miss's bonnet.

5

25 My sooth! right bauld ye set your nose out,
As plump and gray as onie grozet;°   *gooseberry*
O for some rank mercurial rozet,°   *rosin*
     Or fell red smeddum!°   *dust*
I'd gie you sic a hearty doze o't,
30   Wad dress your droddum![2]

6

I wad na been surprised to spy
You on an auld wife's flannen toy;°   *flannel cap*
Or aiblins° some bit duddie° boy,   *perhaps / ragged*
     On 's wyliecoat;°   *undervest*
35 But Miss's fine Lunardi![3] fie,
     How daur ye do't?

7

O Jenny, dinna toss your head,
An' set your beauties a' abroad!
Ye little ken what cursèd speed
40   The blastie's makin'!
Thae winks and finger-ends, I dread,
     Are notice takin'!

8

O wad some Power the giftie gie us
To see oursels as others see us!
45 It wad frae mony a blunder free us,
     And foolish notion:
What airs in dress an' gait wad lea'e us,
     And ev'n devotion!

---

1. *Swith! . . squattle.* Quick! on some beggar's temple sprawl.
2. *Wad dress your droddum,* would fix you proper.
3. *Lunardi,* balloon bonnet, named after a famous balloonist.

EPITAPHS AND EPIGRAMS

EPITAPH ON A SCHOOLMASTER

HERE lie Willie Michie's banes;
  O Satan, when ye tak him,
Gie him the schoolin' of your weans,°   children
  For clever deils° he'll mak them!   devils

ON THE DEATH OF A LAP-DOG *named Echo*

In wood and wild, ye warbling throng,
  Your heavy loss deplore;
Now half-extinct your powers of song,
  Sweet Echo is no more.

5 Ye jarring, screeching things around,
  Scream your discordant joys;
Now half your din of tuneless sound
  With Echo silent lies.

POVERTY

IN politics if thou wouldst mix,
  And mean thy fortunes be;
Bear this in mind,—be deaf and blind,
  Let great folks hear and see.

THE BOOK-WORMS

THROUGH and through the inspired leaves,
  Ye maggots, make your windings;
But, oh! respect his lordship's taste,
  And spare his golden bindings.

IMPROMPTU

How daur ye ca' me howlet-face,°   owl-face
  Ye ugly, glowering spectre?
My face was but the keekin' glass,°   mirror
  An' there ye saw your picture.

TO AN ARTIST

DEAR —, I'll gie ye some advice
  You'll tak it no uncivil:
You shouldna paint at angels mair,
  But try and paint the devil.
5 To paint an angel's kittle° wark,   ticklish
  Wi' auld Nick there's less danger;
You'll easy draw a weel-kent° face,   well-known
  But no sae weel a stranger.

THE SELKIRK GRACE

SOME hae meat, and canna eat,
  And some was eat that want it,
But we hae meat and we can eat,
  And sae the Lord be thankit.

ON HEARING THAT THERE WAS FALSEHOOD IN THE REV. DR. BABINGTON'S VERY LOOKS

THAT there is falsehood in his looks
  I must and will deny;
They say their master is a knave—
  And sure they do not lie.

EXTEMPORE *on passing a lady's carriage*

IF you rattle along like your mistress's tongue,
  Your speed will out-rival the dart:
But, a fly for your load, you'll break down on the
    road,
  If your stuff be as rotten's her heart.

EPITAPH ON A HENPECKED COUNTRY SQUIRE

As father Adam first was fooled
  (A case that's still too common),
Here lies a man a woman ruled,
  —The Devil ruled the woman.

ON SCARING SOME WATER FOWL

in Loch-Turit, a wild scene
among the hills of Ochtertyre

WHY, ye tenants of the lake,
For me your wat'ry haunt forsake?
Tell me, fellow-creatures, why
At my presence thus you fly?
5 Why disturb your social joys,
Parent, filial, kindred ties?—
Common friend to you and me,
Nature's gifts to all are free:
Peaceful keep your dimpling wave,
10 Busy feed, or wanton lave;
Or, beneath the sheltering rock,
Bide the surging billow's shock.
    Conscious, blushing for our race,
Soon, too soon, your fears I trace.
15 Man, your proud, usurping foe,
Would be lord of all below;
Plumes himself in Freedom's pride,
Tyrant stern to all beside.
    The eagle, from the cliffy brow,
20 Marking you his prey below,

In his breast no pity dwells,
Strong necessity compels.
But man, to whom alone is giv'n
A ray direct from pitying Heav'n,
25 Glories in his heart humane—
And creatures for his pleasure slain.
    In these savage, liquid plains,
Only known to wand'ring swains,
Where the mossy riv'let strays,
30 Far from human haunts and ways;
All on Nature you depend,
And life's poor season peaceful spend.
    Or, if man's superior might
Dare invade your native right,
35 On the lofty ether borne,
Man with all his pow'rs you scorn;
Swiftly seek, on clanging wings,
Other lakes and other springs;
And the foe you cannot brave,
40 Scorn at least to be his slave.

DISCUSSION

1. (a) What has occasioned the writing of "A Red, Red Rose"?

(b) How old do the lovers appear to be?

(c) How serious is the speaker? Explain.

2. (a) What bit of philosophy is contained in the second stanza of "To a Mouse"? in the seventh? in the eighth?

(b) What is gained by having such philosophical thoughts initiated by the plight of the mouse?

3. (a) Contrast "To a Louse" with "To a Mouse" with regard to situation, tone of speaker, and mood of poem.

(b) Which of the two poems comes across to you more strongly? Why?

4. About whom is "To a Louse" really written—the louse? Jenny? the speaker? all of these? something more than all of these?

5. (a) In what respects is "On Scaring Some Water Fowl" as topical today as it was when Burns wrote it?

(b) With what other Burns poem you have read may it best be compared?

6. (a) Which of the "Epigrams and Epitaphs" are *not* satirical in intent?

(b) Which are most satirical? Explain.

(c) Which are most humorous?

(d) Are you conscious of any difference between those written in Scots dialect and those written in English? Explain.

WRITING

1. Recast the ideas conveyed in one (or more) of Burns' poems in prose form. For instance, "To a Mouse" might be retold as a fable, "To a Louse" as a gossip item for a local newspaper, "A Red, Red Rose" as a short love story.

2. Develop a brief essay in which you discuss the ways in which Burns' life as a poor farmer enriched his poetry.

3. Although Burns is the most famous of the Scots poets, he is by no means the only one. Investigate and write a report on some other Scots poets, ancient or modern.

4. Discuss the ways in which Burns' songs and poems continue the tradition of the medieval lyric and ballad.

William Blake 1757 / 1827

From SONGS OF INNOCENCE

INTRODUCTION

Piping down the valleys wild,
Piping songs of pleasant glee
On a cloud I saw a child,
And he laughing said to me:

5 Pipe a song about a Lamb!
So I piped with merry cheer.
Piper pipe that song again—
So I piped, he wept to hear.

Drop thy pipe thy happy pipe
10 Sing thy songs of happy cheer.
So I sung the same again
While he wept with joy to hear.

Piper sit thee down and write
In a book that all may read—
15 So he vanished from my sight,
And I plucked a hollow reed,

And I made a rural pen,
And I stained the water clear,
And I wrote my happy songs,
20 Every child may joy to hear.

THE LAMB

Little Lamb, who made thee?
  Dost thou know who made thee?
Gave thee life, & bid thee feed
By the stream & o'er the mead;
5 Gave thee clothing of delight,
Softest clothing, wooly, bright;
Gave thee such a tender voice,
Making all the vales rejoice?
  Little Lamb, who made thee?
10   Dost thou know who made thee?

  Little Lamb, I'll tell thee,
  Little Lamb, I'll tell thee:
He is callèd by thy name,
For he calls himself a Lamb.
15 He is meek, & he is mild;
He became a little child.
I a child, & thou a lamb,
We are callèd by his name.
  Little Lamb, God bless thee!
20   Little Lamb, God bless thee!

**OF LITERARY
INTEREST**

Blake—the first multimedia artist?

Songs of Innocence first appeared in 1789. Blake completed Songs of Experience five years later, and combined the two sets of poems into a single volume which he called *Songs of Innocence and Experience: Shewing the Two Contrary States of the Human Soul.* Although not all the Songs of Innocence have counterparts in Songs of Experience, Blake obviously intended that many of the poems be matched.

Not only did Blake compose the poems, but he prepared his own illustrative engravings by a process he himself developed, inscribed the poems in his own handwriting instead of resorting to movable type, reproduced each engraved page by hand, and either himself tinted, or had his wife tint, each illustration. The result was something comparable to the illuminated manuscripts of medieval times.

THE CHIMNEY SWEEPER

When my mother died I was very young,
And my father sold me while yet my tongue
Could scarcely cry "'weep! 'weep! 'weep! 'weep!"
So your chimneys I sweep, & in soot I sleep.

5 There's little Tom Dacre, who cried when his head,
That curled like a lamb's back, was shav'd: so I said
"Hush, Tom! never mind it, for when your head's bare
You know that the soot cannot spoil your white hair."

And so he was quiet, & that very night,
10 As Tom was a-sleeping, he had such a sight!
That thousands of sweepers, Dick, Joe, Ned, & Jack,
Were all of them locked up in coffins of black.

And by came an Angel who had a bright key,
And he opened the coffins & set them all free;
15 Then down a green plain leaping, laughing, they run,
And wash in a river, and shine in the Sun.

Then naked & white, all their bags left behind,
They rise upon clouds and sport in the wind;
And the Angel told Tom, if he'd be a good boy,
20 He'd have God for his father, & never want joy.

And so Tom awoke; and we rose in the dark,
And got with our bags & our brushes to work.
Tho' the morning was cold, Tom was happy & warm;
So if all do their duty they need not fear harm.

THE LITTLE BOY LOST

"Father! father! where are you going?
O do not walk so fast.
Speak, father, speak to your little boy,
Or else I shall be lost."

5 The night was dark, no father was there;
The child was wet with dew;
The mire was deep, & the child did weep,
And away the vapour flew.

THE LITTLE BOY FOUND

The little boy lost in the lonely fen,
Led by the wand'ring light,
Began to cry; but God, ever nigh,
Appeared like his father in white.

5 He kissed the child & by the hand led
And to his mother brought,
Who in sorrow pale, thro' the lonely dale,
Her little boy weeping sought.

THE DIVINE IMAGE

To Mercy, Pity, Peace, and Love
All pray in their distress;
And to these virtues of delight
Return their thankfulness.

5 For Mercy, Pity, Peace, and Love
Is God, our father dear,
And Mercy, Pity, Peace, and Love
Is Man, his child and care.

For Mercy has a human heart,
10 Pity a human face,
And Love, the human form divine,
And Peace, the human dress.

Then every man, of every clime,
That prays in his distress,
15 Prays to the human form divine,
Love, Mercy, Pity, Peace.

And all must love the human form,
In heathen, turk, or jew;
Where Mercy, Love, & Pity dwell
20 There God is dwelling too.

HOLY THURSDAY

'Twas on a Holy Thursday,[1] their innocent faces clean,
The children walking two & two, in red & blue &
    green,
Grey-headed beadles walked before, with wands as
    white as snow,
Till into the high dome of Paul's they like Thames'
    waters flow.

5 O what a multitude they seemed, these flowers of
    London town!
Seated in companies they sit with radiance all their
    own.
The hum of multitudes was there, but multitudes of
    lambs,
Thousands of little boys & girls raising their innocent
    hands.

Now like a mighty wind they raise to heaven the
    voice of song,
10 Or like harmonious thunderings the seats of Heaven
    among.
Beneath them sit the agèd men, wise guardians of
    the poor;
Then cherish pity, lest you drive an angel from your
    door.

---

1. *Holy Thursday,* Ascension Day, the 40th day after Easter, when
children in orphanages were brought to St. Paul's Cathedral to give
thanks for the charity of God, of which human charity is supposedly
a reflection.

INFANT JOY

I have no name
I am but two days old.—
What shall I call thee?
I happy am
5 Joy is my name,—
Sweet joy befall thee!

Pretty joy!
Sweet joy but two days old.
Sweet joy I call thee:
10 Thou dost smile.
I sing the while
Sweet joy befall thee.

NURSE'S SONG

When the voices of children are heard on the green
And laughing is heard on the hill,
My heart is at rest within my breast
    And everything else is still.

5 "Then come home, my children, the sun is gone
    down
And the dews of night arise;
Come, come, leave off play, and let us away
Till the morning appears in the skies."

"No, no, let us play, for it is yet day
10 And we cannot go to sleep;
Besides, in the sky the little birds fly
And the hills are all covered with sheep."

"Well, well, go & play till the light fades away
And then go home to bed."
15 The little ones leaped & shouted & laughed
    And all the hills ecchoed.

OF HUMAN
INTEREST

Blake's obscurities

Few people of his own day understood or appreciated
Blake's writings or his drawings. In a letter to a Dr. Trusler
whose writings he was asked to illustrate and who objected
to the obscurity of his designs, he wrote: "You say that I
want somebody to Elucidate my Ideas. What is Grand is
necessarily obscure to Weak men. That which can be made
Explicit to the Idiot is not worthy my care. The wisest of
the Ancients considered what is not too Explicit as the
fittest for Instruction, because it rouzes the faculties to act.
I name Moses, Solomon, Esop, Homer, Plato."

But in the same letter he also says: "But I am happy to
find a Great Majority of Fellow Mortals who can Elucidate
My Visions, & Particularly they have been elucidated by
Children, who have taken a greater delight in contemplat-
ing my Pictures than I even hoped. Neither Youth nor
Childhood is Folly or Incapacity."

From SONGS OF EXPERIENCE

INTRODUCTION

Hear the voice of the Bard!
Who Present, Past, and Future sees
Whose ears have heard
The Holy Word,
5   That walk'd among the ancient trees.

Calling the lapsed Soul[1]
And weeping in the evening dew:
That might controll
The starry pole:
10   And fallen fallen light renew!

O Earth O Earth return!
Arise from out the dewy grass:
Night is worn,
And the morn
15   Rises from the slumberous mass.

Turn away no more:
Why wilt thou turn away
The starry floor
The wat'ry shore
20   Is giv'n thee till the break of day.

---

1.   *lapsed Soul,* soul fallen from grace after
the fall of Adam and Eve.

NURSE'S SONG

When the voices of children are heard on the green
And whisp'rings are in the dale,
The days of my youth rise fresh in my mind,
My face turns green and pale.

5   Then come home, my children, the sun is gone down,
And the dews of night arise;
Your spring & your day are wasted in play,
And your winter and night in disguise.

THE TYGER

Tyger! Tyger! burning bright
In the forests of the night,
What immortal hand or eye
Could frame thy fearful symmetry?

5   In what distant deeps or skies
Burnt the fire of thine eyes?
On what wings dare he aspire?
What the hand dare sieze the fire?

And what shoulder, & what art,
10   Could twist the sinews of thy heart?
And when thy heart began to beat,
What dread hand? & what dread feet?

What the hammer? what the chain?
In what furnace was thy brain?
15   What the anvil? what dread grasp
Dare its deadly terrors clasp?

When the stars threw down their spears,
And watered heaven with their tears,
Did he smile his work to see?
20   Did he who made the Lamb make thee?

Tyger! Tyger! burning bright
In the forests of the night,
What immortal hand or eye
Dare frame thy fearful symmetry?

FROM BLAKE'S ORIGINAL ENGRAVING

THE CHIMNEY SWEEPER

A little black thing among the snow,
Crying "'weep! 'weep!" in notes of woe!
"Where are thy father & mother? say?"
"They are both gone up to the church to pray.

5 "Because I was happy upon the heath,
And smiled among the winter's snow,
They clothed me in the clothes of death,
And taught me to sing the notes of woe.

"And because I am happy & dance & sing,
10 They think they have done me no injury,
And are gone to praise God & his Priest & King,
Who make up a heaven of our misery."

20 They stripped him to his little shirt,
And bound him in an iron chain;

And burned him in a holy place,
Where many had been burned before:
The weeping parents wept in vain.
Are such things done on Albion's shore?

A LITTLE BOY LOST

"Nought loves another as itself,
Nor venerates another so,
Nor is it possible to Thought
A greater than itself to know:

5 "And Father, how can I love you
Or any of my brothers more?
I love you like the little bird
That picks up crumbs around the door."

The Priest sat by and heard the child,
.10 In trembling zeal he siezed his hair:
He led him by his little coat,
And all admired the Priestly care.

And standing on the altar high,
"Lo! what a fiend is here!" said he,
15 "One who sets reason up for judge
Of our most holy Mystery."

The weeping child could not be heard,
The weeping parents wept in vain;

THE HUMAN ABSTRACT

Pity would be no more
If we did not make somebody Poor;
And Mercy no more could be
If all were as happy as we.

5 And mutual fear brings peace,
Till the selfish loves increase:
Then Cruelty knits a snare,
And spreads his baits with care.

He sits down with holy fears,
10 And waters the ground with tears;
Then Humility takes its root
Underneath his foot.

Soon spreads the dismal shade
Of Mystery over his head;
15 And the Catterpiller and Fly
Feed on the Mystery.

And it bears the fruit of Deceit,
Ruddy and sweet to eat;
And the Raven his nest has made
20 In its thickest shade.

The Gods of the earth and sea
Sought thro' Nature to find this Tree;
But their search was all in vain:
There grows one in the Human Brain.

HOLY THURSDAY

Is this a holy thing to see
In a rich and fruitful land,
Babes reduced to misery,
Fed with cold and usurous hand?

5 Is that trembling cry a song?
Can it be a song of joy?
And so many children poor?
It is a land of poverty!

And their sun does never shine,
10 And their fields are bleak & bare,
And their ways are filled with thorns:
It is eternal winter there.

For where-e'er the sun does shine,
And where-e'er the rain does fall,
15 Babe can never hunger there,
Nor poverty the mind appall.

LONDON

I wander thro' each chartered street,
Near where the chartered Thames does flow,
And mark in every face I meet
Marks of weakness, marks of woe.

5 In every cry of every Man,
In every Infant's cry of fear,
In every voice, in every ban,
The mind-forged manacles I hear.

How the Chimney-sweeper's cry
10 Every black'ning Church appalls;
And the hapless Soldier's sigh
Runs in blood down Palace walls.

But most thro' midnight streets I hear
How the youthful Harlot's curse
15 Blasts the new born Infant's tear,
And blights with plagues the Marriage hearse.

THE FLY

Little Fly,
Thy summer's play
My thoughtless hand
Has brushed away.

5 Am not I
A fly like thee?
Or art not thou
A man like me?

For I dance,
10 And drink, & sing,
Till some blind hand
Shall brush my wing.

If thought is life
And strength & breath,
15 And the want
Of thought is death;

Then am I
A happy fly,
If I live
20 Or if I die.

THE CLOD AND THE PEBBLE

"Love seeketh not Itself to please,
Nor for itself hath any care,
But for another gives its ease,
And builds a Heaven in Hell's despair."

5 So sung a little Clod of Clay
Trodden with the cattle's feet,
But a Pebble of the brook
Warbled out these metres meet:

"Love seeketh only Self to please,
10 To bind another to Its delight,
Joys in another's loss of ease,
And builds a Hell in Heaven's despite."

INFANT SORROW

My mother groaned! my father wept,
Into the dangerous world I leapt:
Helpless, naked, piping loud:
Like a fiend hid in a cloud.

5 Struggling in my father's hands:
Striving against my swaddling bands:
Bound and weary I thought best
To sulk upon my mother's breast.

THE SICK ROSE

O rose, thou art sick!
The invisible worm
That flies in the night,
In the howling storm,

5 Has found out thy bed
Of crimson joy,
And his dark secret love
Does thy life destroy.

A DIVINE IMAGE

Cruelty has a Human Heart,
And Jealousy a Human Face;
Terror the Human Form Divine,
And Secrecy the Human Dress.

5 The Human Dress is forged Iron,
The Human Form a fiery Forge,
The Human Face a Furnace sealed,
The Human Heart its hungry Gorge.

A POISON TREE

I was angry with my friend:
I told my wrath, my wrath did end.
I was angry with my foe:
I told it not, my wrath did grow.

5 And I watered it in fears,
Night & morning with my tears;
And I sunned it with smiles,
And with soft deceitful wiles.

And it grew both day and night,
10 Till it bore an apple bright;
And my foe beheld it shine,
And he knew that it was mine,

And into my garden stole
When the night had veiled the pole:
15 In the morning glad I see
My foe outstretched beneath the tree.

FROM BLAKE'S ORIGINAL ENGRAVING

PROVERBS OF HELL

From The Marriage of Heaven and Hell

In seed time learn, in harvest teach, in winter
    enjoy.

Drive your cart and your plow over the bones of
    the dead.

The road of excess leads to the palace of wisdom.

Prudence is a rich, ugly old maid courted by
    Incapacity.

5 The cut worm forgives the plow.

A fool sees not the same tree that a wise man sees.

He whose face gives no light, shall never become a
    star.

Eternity is in love with the productions of time.

All wholesome food is caught without a net or a
    trap.

10 No bird soars too high, if he soars with his own
    wings.

If the fool would persist in his folly he would
    become wise.

Shame is pride's cloak.

Excess of sorrow laughs. Excess of joy weeps.

The roaring of lions, the howling of wolves, the
    raging of the stormy sea, and the destructive
    sword, are portions of eternity, too great
    for the eye of man.

15 Let man wear the fell of the lion, woman the fleece
    of the sheep.

The bird a nest, the spider a web, man friendship.

What is now proved was once only imagined.

Every thing possible to be believed is an image of
    truth.

The fox provides for himself, but God provides for
    the lion.

20 Think in the morning. Act in the noon. Eat in the
    evening. Sleep in the night.

The tygers of wrath are wiser than the horses of
    instruction.

Expect poison from the standing water.

You never know what is enough unless you
    know what is more than enough.

The weak in courage is strong in cunning.

25 Damn braces. Bless relaxes.

The crow wished every thing was black, the owl
    that every thing was white.

Improvement makes strait roads; but the crooked
    roads without improvement are roads of
    Genius.

Truth can never be told so as to be understood, and
    not be believed.

OF LITERARY INTEREST

Blake's ideas

There is no use denying the difficulties of Blake's poetry—though they should no longer keep anyone from discovering its exuberant beauty. All the tangled ramifications of Blake's thought spring from a single idea . . . that man, born free, is everywhere in chains. But this is only one aspect of Blake's multidimensioned view of human experience—of mankind once whole and happy, now fallen into discord and tyranny, from which it must be rescued by some revolutionary or apocalyptic upheaval. In theological terms, this is the familiar story of man's fall from Eden into a world of sin—which Blake, a dissenting Protestant, saw also in ecclesiastical terms, as the negation of Christ's

From "The Framing of His Fearful Symmetry" by Aileen Ward as taken from *Book Week* (January 23, 1966). Used by permission of the *Chicago Tribune*.

"Everlasting Gospel" by the dogmas of the church. In intellectual terms, it is the decline from the wisdom of the ancients to the dead logic of Locke, the dead science of Newton; in artistic terms, from the sublime example of the Bible to the "stolen and perverted" tradition of the classics. In society, it is the change from universal brotherhood to the inequalities of monarchy; in economics, from the primitive state in which every man was an "earth-owner" to the present divisions of rich and poor; in technology, from the craftsmanship of the guild system to the factory methods of capitalism. Fundamentally, it is an inner or psychological fall, from the unself-conscious integrity of "Infant Joy" with its innocent sensuality to the self-tormenting self-divisions of adulthood and the battle of the sexes.

Blake's insight into the evils of his time was extraordinary in its scope; his dedication to the struggle against them was heroic. But as with all prophets, the times seemed to belie his vision, and he remained without honor in his country for many years after his death.

DISCUSSION

1. (a) In the Introduction to *Songs of Innocence*, the speaker is both piper and poet. In the Introduction to *Songs of Experience*, there is no identifiable speaker, but the reader is instructed to listen to the voice of the bard, who is also a prophet. How is each an appropriate figure for the group of poems he introduces?

(b) In the Introduction to *Innocence*, the child directs the poet; in the Introduction to *Experience*, the Holy Word calls the lapsed soul. How is each an appropriate figure for his subject matter?

(c) The setting of the Introduction to *Innocence* is daytime; that in the Introduction to *Experience* ranges from evening to daybreak. What do these settings connote?

(d) The Introduction to *Experience* contains indications, other than the setting, that the lapsed soul is not entirely lost, that the situation may be reversed. What are some of these indications?

2. "The Lamb" and "The Tyger" are also matched poems.

(a) How is each connected with the Introduction to its category?

(b) How are these two matched poems related to each other by content?

(c) Many theories have been advanced as to what the lamb and the tyger symbolize. What do they mean to you?

3. The matched "Chimney Sweeper" poems differ vastly in tone.

(a) How do their last stanzas contrast?

(b) Which is the more powerful poem? Why?

4. (a) Which of the two *Experience* poems, "A Divine Image" or "The Human Abstract," is a better contrast to "The Divine Image" in *Innocence*? Explain.

(b) "A Divine Image" is the last poem in *Experience*. Do you agree with its placement there? Explain.

5. (a) What effect does Blake gain through the contrasting views of the children in the matched "Holy Thursday" poems?

(b) When these poems are considered in conjunction with the matched "Chimney Sweeper" poems and "London" (*Experience*), what do they reveal about London in Blake's day?

6. Consider the matched "Nurse's Song" poems. Do both have the same speaker, or are two different speakers involved? Explain.

7. (a) What differences are there between the state of the infant in stanzas 1 and 2 of "Infant Sorrow"?

(b) Are there any such differences in "Infant Joy"?

(c) Do these matched poems represent the joyful and sorrowful infant, or the infancy of joy and sorrow? Explain.

8. "Little Boy Lost" and "Little Boy Found" (*Innocence*) may be read at several different levels. Give at least two plausible interpretations of them.

9. (a) Account for the placement of the following poems under *Experience:* "The Sick Rose," "The Fly," "The Clod and the Pebble," "A Poison Tree."

(b) Which poem do you find most impressive? Why?

10. If, as Blake claims, the "Proverbs of Hell" do "show the nature of Infernal wisdom," what *is* the nature of that wisdom?

WRITING

1. Write an overall comparison of *Songs of Innocence* and *Songs of Experience*, focusing on any one of the following: tone, major symbols, or verse forms and rhythm—or another area of focus approved by your teacher.

2. Select any of the "Proverbs of Hell" and write a composition illustrating it. If you wish, your composition may take the form of a fable or illustrative anecdote.

3. Write a paper discussing William Blake as a social critic, or as a humanitarian.

READERS' THEATER

1. Prepare the matched poems in *Songs of Innocence and of Experience* for dramatic reading in class. Be careful to select voices appropriate to each poem.

2. For a more ambitious undertaking, present a "Blake Poetry Festival," in which one student serves as Blake, introducing other students who read selected poems, perhaps with a musical background. Conclude the program with renditions of "Memo" and "Lullaby for William Blake" on the following page.

SEE ALSO THE ARTICLE "WHAT DID BLAKE MEAN BY INNOCENCE AND EXPERIENCE?" BEGINNING ON PAGE 335.

Many modern poets have paid tribute to William Blake. Here are two examples.

MEMO

by Michael Horovitz

(from Wm Blake
to sundry   psychedelinquent   whizz kids
assuming   his name   in vain):

Stop bleating
5 about the bush
little lambs

Get wean'd
Or get   stufft

(in some body
10 else's   pram—

LULLABY FOR WILLIAM BLAKE

by Adrian Mitchell

Blakehead, babyhead,
Your head is full of light.
You sucked the sun like a gobstopper.
Blakehead, babyhead,
5 High as a satellite on sunflower seeds,
First man-powered man to fly the Atlantic,
Inventor of the poem which kills itself,
The poem which gives birth to itself,
The human form, jazz, Jerusalem
10 And other luminous, luminous galaxies.
You out-spat your enemies.
You irradiated your friends.
Always naked, you shaven, shaking tyger-lamb,
Moon-man, moon-clown, moon-singer, moon-
      drinker,
15 You never killed anyone.
Blakehead, babyhead,
Accept this mug of crude red wine—
I love you.

From *Children of Albion*, published by Penguin Books Ltd. Reprinted by permission of the author.

From *Out Loud*, published by Cape Goliard, distributed in America by Grossman Publishers, Inc. Reprinted by permission of Jonathan Cape Ltd.

"THE RANELAGH ROTUNDA" BY ANTONIO CANALE (CANALETTO). THE ROTUNDA WAS BUILT FOR CONCERTS AND FESTIVITIES BY THE EARL OF RANELAGH.
ITS OPULENCE FITTED THE LIFE-STYLE OF AN EIGHTEENTH-CENTURY LORD. REPRODUCED BY COURTESY OF THE TRUSTEES, THE NATIONAL GALLERY, LONDON.

BACKGROUND

The Eighteenth Century

WHILE it was partly a reaction against the social and political chaos of the preceding century, the passion for order that characterized the first half of the eighteenth century was mainly the outgrowth of a new enlightenment in science (Newton) and in philosophy (Locke) which revived the old belief that the natural laws of the universe were discoverable and could be used by men for the better understanding and regulation of their lives. On the whole, the Augustan Age gives the impression of assured elegance and refinement, decorous social behavior, and propriety, grace, and a certain rigidity in the arts. But beneath the puffery of wigs and beribboned silks, beneath the restrained and witty conversation there remained a very human zest for living—at times even a touch of boorishness. There was also a pronounced uneasiness about the supposedly settled state of things.

This subsurface instability is evident in the contrasts of the age. While the beaux and belles were carried in their coaches or brocaded sedan chairs for an evening's entertainment, the poor lived with filth and stench and wondered what they would eat next day. The contrasts extended to the lofty figures of the age as well. The portrait of Dr. Johnson which comes to us, both through his own writings and the reports of Boswell and others, indicates that this great man of letters who had such a sure touch and such apparently set opinions was actually tortured by deep personal struggles. The satire of Dean Swift betrays distrust in reason, human nature, and social progress. Even the lighter satire of Pope and Addison hints at some misgivings about the settled nature of things and the ideals of reasonable human behavior.

There was an energetic restlessness in the age which pushed at established limits. The frontiers of the British empire were extended deeper into America, Africa, and Asia. London was growing into an ever greater urban center of trade, its creative and commercial life focusing on the smoky din of its coffee houses where merchants, lawyers, writers, brokers, and men of affairs, as well as the "pretty fellows" of fashion, gathered to bargain, argue, swear (with restraint, of course), laugh, gossip, and read the latest poem, pamphlet, or journal.

The eighteenth century was also a time of earnest party politics and shifting centers of political power. During the early years of the century the middle class, which had already begun to merge with the landed gentry through intermarriage and common concerns for wealth and property, moved into a position of political dominance. Representative of this enlarged and newly powerful group was the Whig party which gained great power in Parliament. When Queen Anne, the last of the Stuart monarchs, died without an heir in 1714, the Whigs threw the Tory or conservative party out of office and granted the royal succession to Anne's cousins from the small German kingdom of Hanover.

The first kings of the House of Hanover—George I (1714–1727) and George II (1727–1760)—were, contrary to common belief, competent if limited rulers, but their power rested to a large extent in the hands of their cabinet ministers, Townshend, Walpole, and the two Pitts, who were masterful wielders of political influence and effective in keeping Parliament in line. When George III came to the throne in 1760 he tried unsuccessfully to reëstablish the Tory party and to loosen Parliamentary curbs on monarchial power. His obstinacy in asserting himself over Parliament and in insisting on Parliament's power over the American colonies caused a long period of political instability in England and a prolonged war in America. By 1788 George III had already begun to show signs of progressive blindness and madness, and for the last two decades of his reign his life was enshrouded in the darkness of insanity.

By the end of the eighteenth century England had already suffered the first major loss to her colonial empire; war with America had drawn her into war with France; the industrial revolution which was to blacken Britain's skies had already begun; and the truths which had seemed so self-evident at the beginning of the century were being questioned by those with a new vision of man's role in the world.

□

BOSWELL AS BIOGRAPHER
by James L. Clifford

BOSWELL'S *Life of Johnson* has been universally acknowledged as one of the great books of the Western world. Yet only in the last half century have we had any clear idea of the nature of Boswell's achievement, or of the way in which he worked. Generally accepted for most of the nineteenth century was Macaulay's theory that the *Life* was an accidental masterpiece, produced by a fool who happened to have a perfect subject. No one ever thought of him as a major creative artist.

Abridged from James L. Clifford, Ed., *Twentieth Century Interpretations of Boswell's Life of Johnson*, © 1970. Reprinted by permission of Prentice-Hall, Inc., Englewood Cliffs, N.J.

In the 1920's, following the fantastic discovery of a portion of Boswell's archives at Malahide Castle outside Dublin, and the subsequent further discoveries there and in Scotland, the emphasis gradually began to change. For one thing, Boswell's reputation as a revealing diarist steadily mounted. His London journal, discovered at Fettercairn House in Scotland in 1930, but not published until twenty years later, became a best seller and was widely hailed as one of the most fascinating autobiographical documents in all literature.

In addition to changing Boswell's reputation as a

creative writer, the new discoveries provide extensive evidence concerning Boswell's method of recording conversations, the question of basic accuracy, and his particular technique in combining all his diverse material into a readable biography.

Boswell and Johnson

When Boswell met Samuel Johnson in May 1763, the pensioned lexicographer and essayist was thirty years his senior. Inevitably the relationship was that of a youthful admirer to an eccentric middle-aged celebrity. But it soon became more than that, for the youthful Scot, for all his levity and rakish propensities, had a serious side. This Johnson soon found out, as he grew to respect the keen intelligence behind Boswell's gay exterior. Through Boswell's revealing accounts it is fascinating to watch the development of their close friendship.

It is not certain when Boswell first considered writing the life of Johnson. The earliest indication comes in an entry in his journal for October 12, 1780. But it was not until after Johnson's death in December 1784 that Boswell began seriously to consider the actual writing of the biography. Even then he was slow in starting. Despite the solicitation of his publisher, who was eager to have him provide at once a rival volume to the numerous journalistic lives which were beginning to appear, he refused to be hurried. Nevertheless, he was eager to give the public a taste of what was coming. The obvious answer was to bring out a version of the journal he had kept during the tour to the Hebrides in 1773, the longest single period during which he had been in close contact with Johnson. The volume appeared in the early fall of 1785. It was an immediate sensation, stirring up intense controversy, largely on ethical grounds concerned with his revelations of Johnson's casual conversations.

Happily, the attacks did not turn Boswell from his main purpose, though they may have induced him to be a little more careful when including material about persons who were extremely sensitive to publicity. But he was now certain of just what he wanted to do, and in a leisurely fashion he set about his task.

Boswell interviewed many of Johnson's old friends; he sent a special questionnaire to Edmund Hector, Johnson's old schoolmate, with blanks left for the answers. He gathered all the letters of Johnson he could find. He got what he could from Frank Barber, Johnson's servant, and most of the Club members, as well as many others, cooperated with Boswell's efforts. Thus he gradually assembled a huge mass of material.

When a first version was finally prepared, it was then rigorously revised, further corrections being made in proof. At last *The Life of Samuel Johnson, LL.D.* was published on May 16, 1791, exactly twenty-eight years after the first meeting in 1763. It was widely read, and was a definite financial success.

Boswell's Method of Keeping a Journal

When Boswell came to London in 1762, the last thing before he went to bed or the first thing in the morning, he was accustomed to write out short memoranda to himself outlining what he intended to do during the day. Every so often he would arrange to stay home and write up his full journal, and no doubt these little memoranda helped to remind him of what had happened. Yet there were obvious discrepancies. For example, on May 16, 1763, the surviving memorandum contains various items about sending out his breeches to be mended, about what to eat for breakfast, about getting money and seeing people, and even what frame of mind to be in, but there is no mention whatsoever of what has been called "the most important single event in Boswell's life"—his meeting with Samuel Johnson.

Once Boswell recognized that these notes were not of much use in writing up his journal, he changed his practice. Normally he waited until the end of the day, and then summed up briefly what had actually occurred. These notes were vital to him when he came to write a full account in his journal.

In the later 1770's what survives is often a sequence of very brief notations, some of the most cryptic kind, along with others (the majority) fairly long and quite intelligible. When Boswell fell behind, instead of going back and trying to catch up, he would write a long entry for the day before, or for a few days before, and then cover up the gap with rough notes. There are long periods when there are only intermittent entries. Thus sometimes we have fully written journals, sometimes only the condensed, suggestive notes or half-expanded versions, and sometimes nothing at all.

The Question of Accuracy of Reporting

So long as the old theory was accepted—that Boswell was little more than an energetic reporter—the matter of the verbal accuracy of his versions did not stir up much controversy. Other evidence which was available seemed to confirm his reports, and that was that. But now, with the general agreement on Boswell's remarkable creative gifts, there are some questions which need to be discussed. Exactly how did Boswell's memory work? What part of the dramatic scenes in the *Life* represents Boswell's imaginative coloring, and how much is purely factual?

Frederick A. Pottle, who knows more about Boswell than anyone today, believes that Boswell had a very special kind of mind. Once it was given a jog —by a note or in some other way—the whole of an earlier event came back to him in great detail. Given the proper reminder, Boswell was just as capable of bringing back little details after ten years as after two weeks. Pottle cites various evidence to support his position, including the findings of modern psychologists who have studied people with similar memories.

Some readers may wonder if there are any dependable ways of checking Boswell's reporting of Johnson's conversation. The answer is that there are. Occasionally other people were present who also had the itch to write down what was said by the Doctor, and some of these other reports catch the same "Johnsonian aether." In general when two accounts are compared, there is surprising agreement as to the main ideas expressed, although inevitably there are variations in wording.

Gathering Material for the Life

That Boswell had a keen interest in securing accurate facts has never been doubted. As he bragged in the "Advertizement" to the first edition of the *Life*, he was quite ready to "run half over London" to verify a date. And it is now evident that he used admirable skepticism in regard to casual anecdotes which he secured from others.

The wealth of evidence now available makes clear that Boswell did not use all the material he collected, even when it was relevant. Thus he omitted an amusing story told him by Hector of a night in Birmingham when Johnson as a young man may have been drunk. Other small details which Boswell felt were either irrelevant or not characteristic of the great moralist he was describing were silently omitted.

This does not mean that Boswell was consciously distorting character or falsifying evidence. Like all great biographers, he was presenting the essential truth as he saw it.

Contemporary Reception

Because the *Tour to the Hebrides* and the *Life of Johnson* have for so long been recognized as masterpieces, we sometimes forget that when they first appeared they were subjected to the same kind of abuse that is leveled against some candid biographers today. The *Tour* when it appeared in 1785 was constantly under attack in the newspapers.

In fashionable and conservative circles what shocked many readers was Boswell's willingness to report exactly what people said in private conversation. This attitude was summed up by one letter-writer: "Johnson's faults were balanced by many and great virtues; and when that is the case, the virtues only should be remembered, and the faults entirely forgotten." Biography according to this position should embalm, not re-create.

On the appearance of the *Life,* almost six years later, there was the same kind of shock over the frankness of the personal revelations it contained. We now know that Boswell tried hard not to hurt the feelings of Johnson's close friends, and had been willing to do some significant censoring, but none of this was apparent to the general reader. On the surface it appeared that he was indiscreetly telling everything. And many thought that such lack of taste not only hurt others, but was injurious to the reputation of Johnson himself. There is even some indication that in later years Boswell himself was not graciously received in certain circles, for fear that he would write down what was said and perhaps publish it.

At the same time, many general readers were quite ready to accept the new approach with enthusiasm. A writer in the *Monthly Review* replied to objectors as follows:

. . . where the biographer has for his subject the life and sentiments of so eminent an instructor of mankind as Samuel Johnson, and so immense a store-house of mental treasure to open and disclose . . . there can be no just exception taken against the number and variety of the objects exhibited. . . . To the reporter, would he not say "Give us *all;* suppress nothing; lest, in rejecting that which, in your estimation, may seem to be of inferior value, you unwarily throw away gold with the dross."

Before the late eighteenth century, there was little significant criticism concerning the art and ethical principles of biography. Life-writing had simply not been accepted as a major literary genre. It was not until the extended arguments stirred up by Boswell's thorough and revealing coverage of Johnson's private life that biography gradually took its place as one of the important kinds of writing worthy of searching critical examination.

With the argument over Boswell's *Life of Johnson* the whole issue as to how much a biographer should tell was finally brought into the open. Even though the next century kept insisting on reticence and good taste, the possibilities of three-dimensional re-creation of character, both psychological and factual, were now apparent. ☐

WHAT DID BLAKE MEAN
BY INNOCENCE AND EXPERIENCE?
by Morton D. Paley

WHAT are the two Contrary States and what is the relationship between them? *Innocence* and *Experience* are not, first of all, a direct record of Blake's spiritual autobiography. Anyone who thinks the *Songs of Innocence* reflect Blake's own world view at the time of composition should carefully read the prose satire *An Island in the Moon,* which Blake wrote in 1784 and in which versions of three *Songs of Innocence* first appear. In this anything-but-innocent narrative, the simplicity of "Holy Thursday," "Nurse's Song," and "Little Boy Lost" contrast sharply with the egotism and pretentiousness of the characters. Of course we cannot know whether Blake had the *Songs of Experience* in mind when he wrote the *Songs of Innocence,* but we do know that four of the earlier group seemed to him sufficiently poems of Experience to be shifted to the latter group in 1794: "The School Boy," "The Little Girl Lost," "The Little Girl Found," and "The Voice of the An-

cient Bard." These poems had already burst the bounds of the state of Innocence, all of them presenting themes more appropriate to the Contrary State—institutional restraint, the prophetic function of the poet, the growth of self-awareness. Innocence *demands* Experience: both are phases in the spiritual development of man and, at the same time, perennial ways of looking at the world.

The state of Innocence is compounded of the pagan Age of Gold and the Judeo-Christian Eden. Externally and generically, it applies to the condition of man before the Fall; internally and psychologically to the child who has not yet experienced the inner divisions of human life. Its literary forebears are the worlds of the pastoral and the Psalms. Blake's Innocence also has a special relationship to the thought of the Swedish visionary Emanuel Swedenborg, whose works Blake annotated with great interest in the 1780's and who conceived of Innocence in terms peculiarly appropriate to Blake's: as an inner state, taking images such as the child and the lamb as correspondences.

Experience, too, is an inner state externalized in a

Abridged from the Introduction by Morton D. Paley, Ed., *Twentieth Century Interpretations of Songs of Innocence and of Experience:* A Collection of Critical Essays, © 1969. By permission of Prentice-Hall, Inc., Englewood Cliffs, New Jersey.

world of images—chains, thorns, spears, graves, briars, blood, and roots, to name a few—all of which correspond to felt qualities in life. In Experience, which is the world of normal adult life, people try to analyze and codify their feelings, and as a result they become incapable of spontaneity. The traditional hierarchy of society, seen as benevolent in *Innocence,* is now regarded as a vast exploitative deceit. With all this suffering, however, Experience also brings a bitter wisdom. Experience, then, is not wholly negative. The harmony of Innocence has been lost, but insight comes in its place. In the wisdom of Experience, as embodied in the voice of the prophetic Bard of the second group of Songs, lies the possibility of reorganizing man's divided self and, if not of regaining the lost world of Innocence, then of forging a new unity. "Man is so created," Swedenborg wrote, "as to be during his childhood in external innocence, and when he becomes old in internal innocence, to the end that he may come by means of the former into the latter, and from the latter into the former." "Unorganized Innocence," according to Blake, is "an Impossibility. Innocence dwells with Wisdom, but never with Ignorance."

The transition from Innocence to Experience may be seen as a version of what medieval theologians call The Fortunate Fall—the idea that the fall of Adam and Eve was in a paradoxical sense a "happy sin," in that otherwise Christ would not have been born to save mankind. For Blake, the fall into Experience was if not happy at least necessary.

As Blake tells us in *The Marriage of Heaven and Hell,* "without Contraries is no progression." In this case, progression is toward a condition of being in which the harmony lost in the fall from Innocence is regained. The agent of regeneration is Energy. In the fallen world of Experience, this Energy is present as the wrath of the Tyger.

The Victorians at times mistook Blake's simplicity for naivete and were, accordingly, disposed toward an overly literal view of the poems. We, by contrast, may be tempted to find complexities that are not there, to over-read, to discover myths hidden in the shrubbery as if the poem were an ingenious puzzle.

□

The Changing English Language

IN KEEPING with the spirit of the Age of Reason, the movement in language in the eighteenth century was toward greater regulation of expression and greater precision in word usage and pronunciation. By the beginning of the century there had already grown up among those in fashionable society a disdain for the extravagant flourishes and conceits of seventeenth-century speech; emphasis came to be placed on refined, polite discourse based on "common sense." Those caught in the surge toward refinement—among them Swift, Steele, Addison, Johnson, and Lord Chesterfield—tended to disparage what they called "cant" or "low speech" with an assurance in the rightness of their judgments which today strikes us as immodest. However, these arbiters of language realized, as did many of their time, that the English language was in a muddle that the disputes over grammar of the previous centuries had failed to solve: words still had widely variant meanings, spellings, and pronunciations, and the general instability of the language was a barrier to clear communication. In the mishandling of the language the educated and well-to-do seem to have been as guilty as any. Defoe complained in one of his works that "gentlemen of fortunes and families . . . can hardly write their own names" and when they can write they "can't spell their mother tongue." A favorite point made by satirists of the day was that the one member of a great household most likely to read and write the King's English was either the butler or the serving woman.

The urge to bring the language more into accord with Natural Law is evident in hundreds of projects undertaken during the course of the century and typified by this statement of Lord Chesterfield's published in *The World* in 1754, a year before the appearance of Johnson's *Dictionary:*

It must be owned that our language is, at present, in a state of anarchy, and hitherto, perhaps, it may not have been the worse for it. During our free and open trade, many words and expressions have been imported, adopted, and naturalized from other languages, which have greatly enriched our own. . . . The time for discrimination seems to be now come. Toleration, adoption, and naturalization, have run their lengths. Good order and authority are now necessary. But where shall we find them, and at the same time, the obedience due to them? We must have recourse to the old Roman expedient in times of confusion, and choose a dictator. Upon this principle, I give my vote for Mr. Johnson to fill that great and arduous post. . . .

Johnson's ponderous two-volume *Dictionary*, great achievement though it was, offered only a partial solution to the problems of normalizing the language, and before the century ended there were many other attempts. The efforts at standardization spilled over into literary texts. One mid-eighteenth-century editor announced that Shakespeare's works were an "unweeded Garden grown to Seed," and confidently set about the cultivation and pruning he thought necessary. Another overearnest reformer named Bentley tackled Milton's poetry, and got for his pains Pope's ridicule for being a scribbler "whose unwearied pains / Made Horace dull, and humbled Milton's strains." If there was widespread agreement that the English language needed polishing, there was little agreement about how it should be done, and the controversy continued throughout the century.

One characteristic of the many arguments for purification of English was a sort of intellectual elitism that rejected the living language of the mob (the word *mob* is itself an eighteenth-century coinage used by those who wished to emphasize their social exclusivity). The more common words of Anglo-Saxon derivation were frowned upon as low, slangy, or imprecise, and in their place many Latinisms were substituted (see Johnson's definition of *network* on page 299), largely because words derived from Latin were supported by the "authority" of classical writers, and also because they were suited for expressing the abstractions that dominated eighteenth-century thinking.

While neoclassicism did much to tone down the bizarre and freakish aspects of seventeenth-century speech, it did not, in spite of its insistence on rules and rigidity, stamp out the rich variety which makes English a vital instrument of communication. Although both Johnson and Swift objected to the use of such words as *humbug, prig, doodle, bamboozle, fib, bully, fop, banter, stingy, fun, prude*, they continued in use then as they do today, evidence of the fact that people, not grammar books or dictionaries, make and perpetuate language.   □

BIOGRAPHIES

Joseph Addison   1672 / 1719

An Oxford graduate and classical scholar of some note, Addison was also a Member of Parliament from 1708 until his death, and briefly held the office of Secretary of State in the last years of his life. He varied his political activity with literary endeavors, contributing periodical essays to Richard Steele's *Tatler*, and later joining with Steele to produce the *Spectator* (1711–1712). Addison's life was the epitome of Neoclassical virtues: he sought in his writings to reform the manners and tastes of his time, he was politically active, and he was a model of reasonableness and rationality. His periodical essays are polished, gently humorous, and unobtrusively moral in tone.

William Blake   1757 / 1827

William Blake was not only a poet, but a painter, an engraver, and a spiritual visionary. He claimed to have seen the prophet Ezekiel in a tree when only a child, and believed that much of his later poetry was dictated to him by a spiritual amanuensis. He lived all but three years of his life in London, where he earned a moderate—sometimes barely sufficient—income as an engraver. Between 1783 and 1793 he wrote, illustrated, and printed his most famous lyrics, *Songs of Innocence and Experience*, and also one major prose work, *The Marriage of Heaven and Hell*.

From 1800 to 1803 he lived at Flepham on the Sussex coast, under the patronage of a wealthy amateur artist,

William Hayley, who tried to convert him into a more conventional craftsman. Blake, always temperamental about his personal freedom, soon quarreled with Hayley and returned to London, but not before an event occurred which left a permanent mark on his life. He was charged with sedition by a soldier who had a personal grudge against him. Though he was acquitted after a harrowing trial and escaped hanging, he lived for the rest of his life under the conviction that dark and uncontrollable powers were at work in the world, a view that affected his later prophetic poems, *Milton* (1804) and *Jerusalem* (1820).

Blake's later years were largely happy and peaceful; after the age of sixty he gave up poetry in favor of painting, illustrating the poetry of Dante and Chaucer and the Book of Job. During his lifetime, Blake's visual productions were almost unknown to the public, and his poetry was entirely ignored. The recent increase in his popularity can probably be attributed to recognition of his humanitarian (even revolutionary) beliefs, and interest in his mysticism.

James Boswell   1740 / 1795

The discovery and recent publication of Boswell's personal journals have done much to correct the caricature of Boswell, pencil in hand and ear cocked, dancing attendance on the great Samuel Johnson and his circle. It is now clear that there was mutual respect and affection between the two, in spite of Boswell's sometimes absurd antics which drew harsh words from Johnson.

The son of a judge with the honorary title Lord Auchinleck, Boswell studied law at the University of Edinburgh, traveled widely on the continent, where he met and captivated Rousseau and Voltaire, and was technically a member of the gentry who could meet Johnson's circle on equal footing. He was also a man of genius with a remarkable memory and an instinct for unsparing portrayal of himself and others. His *Life of Johnson* (1791) and *Journal of a Tour to the Hebrides* (1785) reveal Johnson the whole man, not only the public figure in its most favorable aspects.

Robert Burns   1759 / 1796

When Burns' first volume of poetry appeared in 1786, he was immediately hailed as a "plowman poet," a rude untutored singer of Scottish native song. The realities of his early life in Ayrshire, Scotland, were harsh enough: in his early teens he was called upon to do a man's work as a farmer to help support his six younger brothers and sisters, his mother, and his ailing father. But Burns was no uneducated country bumpkin. He had received the foundations of an education and had read widely on his own, even teaching himself French. When the popularity of his first poetry thrust him into public light, he became known in

Edinburgh social circles as a charming and brilliant conversationalist. However, his liberal views and irreverent attitude toward the stern Scottish Presbyterian morality of the times (he had several illegitimate children) so outraged the good citizens of Edinburgh that his social success was brief. In 1788 he secured a government post and settled down with Jean Armour as a married man. He tried his hand at farming to supplement his government salary, failed, and died in his mid thirties, his constitution weakened by the rigors of his early life.

Burns wrote or rewrote over 200 songs in Scots dialect, as well as some in English. His longer poems reveal a versatile lyrical talent, a sharp and sometimes merciless sense of humor, and deep sensitivity to the natural world.

Daniel Defoe   1659 / 1731

The son of a butcher named Foe, Daniel Defoe was a man who seized, without undue scruples, whatever opportunities presented themselves. A Presbyterian, he was hampered his whole life long by his dissenting views. As a young man he set up business as a merchant but soon found himself bankrupt. He then turned to writing political verses and pamphlets, and was pilloried, fined, and jailed for a stinging satire on the Church of England's methods of treating nonconformists like himself. In his middle years he was a political adventurer, a spy and informer, serving one Robert Harley with his journalistic talents. A Whig by conviction, Defoe had few misgivings about switching parties when Harley became head of the Tory ministry in 1710. When the Tories fell from power in 1714, Defoe switched back to the Whig side with equal ease.

From a total of more than 250 works, Defoe is best known for those he wrote in later life, among them *Robinson Crusoe* (1719), *Moll Flanders* (1722), and *A Journal of the Plague Year* (1722). Purporting to be not fiction but true accounts, they have a realistic bite that makes them read like fact.

Thomas Gray   1716 / 1771

Gray is known today primarily for his "Elegy Written in a Country Churchyard" which, when it was published in 1750, immediately established his reputation. Its supposed setting, the churchyard of Stoke Poges, a village in Buckinghamshire, became Gray's own final resting place.

Gray studied at Cambridge, left without a degree to travel abroad, and then returned to the university where he completed his studies and lived for the rest of his life. In his later years he was appointed Professor of Modern History, but he never felt called upon to give a lecture in that subject, devoting himself instead to a life of quiet retirement and various scholarly pursuits. His poetic output was relatively small. His shy, affectionate nature and gentle humor are preserved in his letters, now considered among the best from an age in which letter writing was an art.

Samuel Johnson   1709 / 1784

Boswell's *Life* presents a picture of Johnson that is at least life-size—and Johnson was a huge man. Perhaps part of his future was shaped by his being the son of a Lichfield bookseller; perhaps still more, by his contracting scrofula, probably from his nurse, when he was barely out of infancy. The disease impaired his eyesight and left his face horribly marred. He attended Oxford but did not take a degree because family financial crises recalled him to Lichfield. When he was 26 he married a widow considerably older than himself, to whom he remained devoted for years after her death in 1752. For a while he operated a private school, but when that failed he went to London with one of his pupils, David Garrick, who was destined to become the greatest actor of his day. After doing some periodical writing, and publishing several works independently, among them *London* (1738), he issued the plan for his great *Dictionary*, a work which he finally finished in 1755. While working on the *Dictionary* he continued to write, and in 1750 started the *Rambler*, which ran for two years. Publication of the *Dictionary* won him a leading place among English men of letters. From 1758 to 1760 he wrote the "Idler" essays for the *Universal Chronicle*. In 1765 he completed his second extended project, the editing of Shakespeare's works. In 1763 he met Boswell, and in 1764 founded the Literary Club, which numbered among its members Goldsmith, Garrick, and Boswell. Johnson's trip to the Hebrides with Boswell in 1773 resulted in the publication of his *Journey to the Western Islands of Scotland* (1775). From 1777 to 1781 he was engaged in his third and last extended project: writing *The Lives of the English Poets*.

Alexander Pope   1688 / 1744

Despite personal handicaps that would have caused a man of less determination to give up, Pope rose to be the leading literary figure of his day. He was a Roman Catholic in an age when adherence to the "Old Faith" prevented him from receiving a university education, voting, or holding public office, and when the tax burden on Roman Catholics was sufficiently high to drive many once well-to-do families

into bankruptcy. In addition, at the age of 12 Pope was stricken with a disease that left him dwarfed, crippled, and in almost constant pain. By sheer power of will, he managed to educate himself and to become admired as a poet and feared as a satirist. Pope earned a large income through his poetry, editorial work, and translations of the *Iliad* and the *Odyssey*. He was instrumental in forming the Scriblerus Club, a group of writers (including Swift) who met on occasion to satirize the pretensions of learned men. In an age of satire Pope was often subjected to vituperous literary attacks, but he always gave at least as good as he got, cutting down his enemies with sharply honed heroic couplets. Among his best-known works are *Essay on Criticism* (1711), published when he was only 23; *The Rape of the Lock* (1714); *Essay on Man* (1733–34); and *Moral Essays* (1731–35), all written in heroic couplets.

Jonathan Swift   1667 / 1745

Born in Dublin of English parents, Swift was educated in Ireland, receiving his degree from Trinity College, Dublin, "by special grace" after he had been censured for offenses against college discipline. He fled with many of his fellow Anglo-Irish when James II invaded Ireland, and took refuge in England in the household of a kinsman, Sir William Temple. There he remained, with only a few visits to Ireland, from 1689 to 1699, reading widely and writing his first powerful satires. At some point during his stay with Temple he decided, with some reluctance, to make the Church his career, and so was ordained an Anglican minister in 1694.

Swift soon became a convinced churchman and upheld in spirited pamphlets and conversation the causes of both the Anglican Church and the Crown against all dissenters. In 1710 he became a Tory, and in 1713 was appointed Dean of St. Patrick's Cathedral in Dublin. There he established himself as an able administrator, though he disliked living in Ireland, largely because he had formed friendships with many prominent men in England and found his Irish friends less polished.

In his later years, Swift was afflicted with a rare disease which caused dizziness, deafness, and nausea. Nevertheless he continued to write prolifically, and kept his wit and his extraordinarily keen eye for human foibles and social corruption until the last few years of his life, when disease and old age closed in. *Gulliver's Travels* (1726), the only work for which he ever received payment, and *A Modest Proposal* (1729) were written at the height of his mature years.

(OVERLEAF) DETAIL FROM "IN A SHOREHAM GARDEN," BY SAMUEL PALMER. BY COURTESY OF THE VICTORIA AND ALBERT MUSEUM, LONDON, CROWN COPYRIGHT.

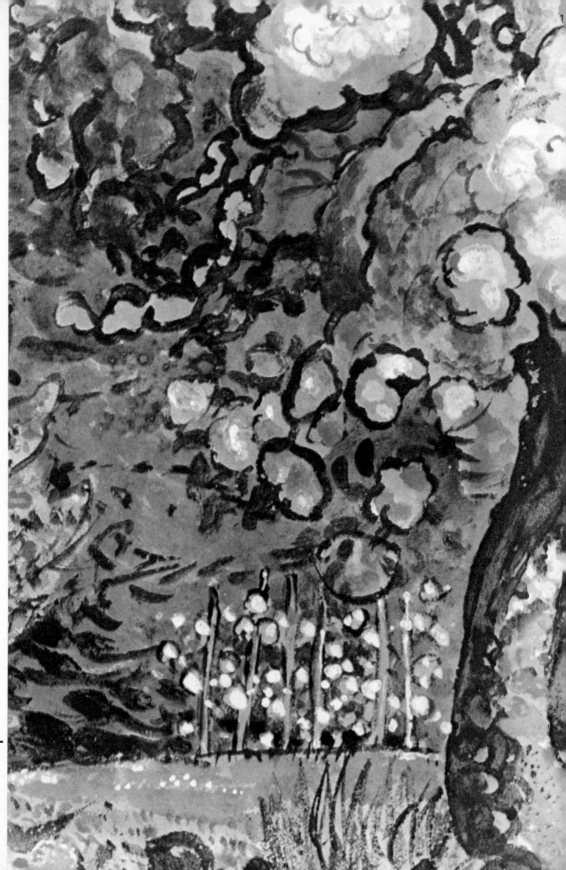

THE ROMANTICS 1798–1837

chapter six

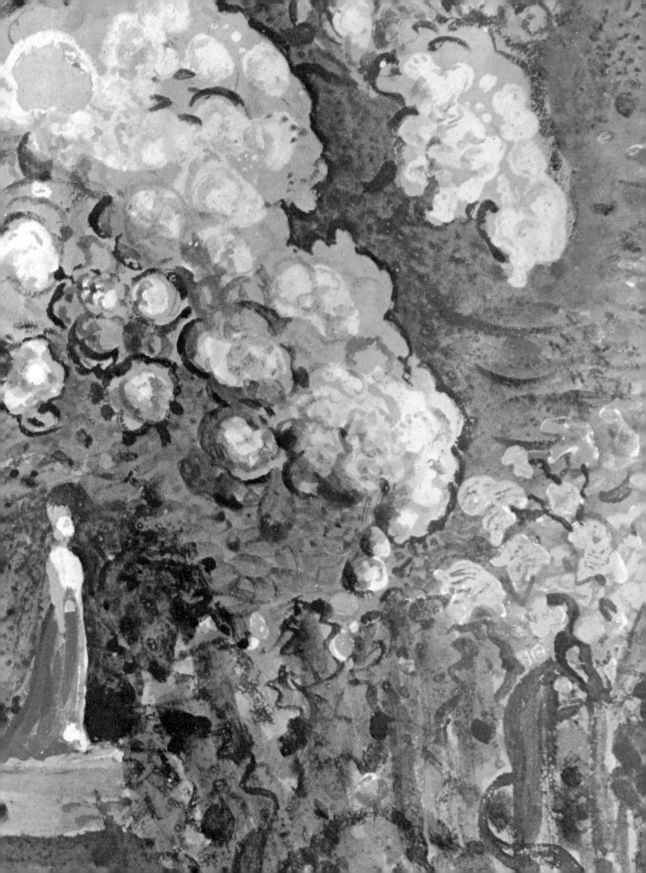

William Wordsworth
1770 / 1850

COMPOSED UPON WESTMINSTER BRIDGE, SEPTEMBER 3, 1802

[handwritten: the city is beautiful. Even it can be quiet when it is quiet and the nature there]

[handwritten scansion marks over first line]

Earth has not anything to show more fair: *[handwritten: and the nature there]*
Dull would he be of soul who could pass by *[handwritten: common people]*
A sight so touching in its majesty:
This City now doth, like a garment, wear
5 The beauty of the morning; silent, bare,
Ships, towers, domes, theaters, and temples lie
Open unto the fields, and to the sky;
All bright and glittering in the smokeless air.
Never did sun more beautifully steep
10 In his first splendor, valley, rock, or hill;
Ne'er saw I, never felt, a calm so deep!
The river glideth at his own sweet will:
Dear God! the very houses seem asleep;
And all that mighty heart is lying still!

LONDON, 1802

[handwritten: An ode to Milton] *[handwritten: ruling class]*

Milton! thou shouldst be living at this hour.
England hath need of thee; she is a fen
Of stagnant waters: altar, sword, and pen,
Fireside, the heroic wealth of hall and bower,
5 Have forfeited their ancient English dower
Of inward happiness. We are selfish men;
Oh! raise us up, return to us again,
And give us manners, virtue, freedom, power.
Thy soul was like a star, and dwelt apart:
10 Thou hadst a voice whose sound was like the sea;
Pure as the naked heavens, majestic, free,
So didst thou travel on life's common way,
In cheerful godliness; and yet thy heart
The lowliest duties on herself did lay.

THE WORLD IS TOO MUCH WITH US

[handwritten: getting into spending depletes ability to appreciate nature]

The world is too much with us; late and soon, A
Getting and spending, we lay waste our powers: B
Little we see in Nature that is ours; B
We have given our hearts away, a sordid boon! A
5 The sea that bares her bosom to the moon, A *[handwritten: moonlight on sea]*
The winds that will be howling at all hours, B
And are up-gathered now like sleeping flowers; B
For this, for everything, we are out of tune; A
It moves us not.—Great God! I'd rather be C
10 A Pagan suckled in a creed outworn; B
So might I, standing on this pleasant lea, C
Have glimpses that would make me less forlorn; D
Have sight of Proteus rising from the sea; C
Or hear old Triton[1] blow his wreathèd horn. D

IT IS A BEAUTEOUS EVENING

[handwritten: children are closer to God because they are not corrupt by society.]

It is a beauteous evening, calm and free, A
The holy time is quiet as a Nun B
Breathless with adoration; the broad sun B
Is sinking down in its tranquillity; A
5 The gentleness of heaven broods o'er the Sea: A
Listen! the mighty Being is awake, C
And doth with his eternal motion make C
A sound like thunder—everlastingly. A
Dear Child![1] dear Girl; that walkest with me here, D
10 If thou appear untouched by solemn thought, E
Thy nature is not therefore less divine: F
Thou liest in Abraham's bosom[2] all the year; D
And worshipp'st at the temple's inner shrine, F
God being with thee when we know it not. E

---

1. *Proteus . . . Triton*, sea gods in Greek mythology.

1. *Dear Child*, Wordsworth's French daughter, Caroline.
2. *in Abraham's bosom*, in the presence or favor of God. See Luke 16:22.

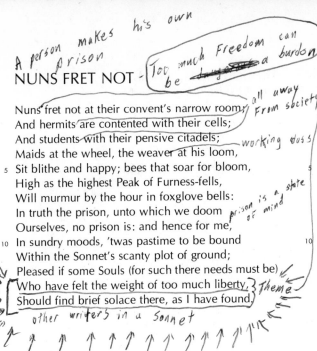

NUNS FRET NOT — PERSUASION

(handwritten annotations:)
A person makes his own prison
Too much Freedom can be a burden

Nuns fret not at their convent's narrow room, *(all away from society)*	"Man's life is like a Sparrow, mighty King! *(About soul)*
And hermits are contented with their cells;	That—while at banquet with your Chiefs you sit
And students with their pensive citadels; *(working class)*	Housed near a blazing fire—is seen to flit
Maids at the wheel, the weaver at his loom,	Safe from the wintry tempest. Fluttering,
5 Sit blithe and happy; bees that soar for bloom,	5 Here did it enter; there, on hasty wing,
High as the highest Peak of Furness-fells,	Flies out, and passes on from cold to cold;
Will murmur by the hour in foxglove bells:	But whence it came we know not, nor behold *(we don't no where it came From)*
In truth the prison, unto which we doom *(prison is a state of mind)*	Whither it goes. Even such, that transient Thing, *(or where it's going)*
Ourselves, no prison is: and hence for me,	The human Soul; not utterly unknown
10 In sundry moods, 'twas pastime to be bound	10 While in the Body lodged, her warm abode;
Within the Sonnet's scanty plot of ground;	But from what world She came, what woe or weal *(sparrow and soul)*
Pleased if some Souls (for such there needs must be)	On her departure waits, no tongue hath shown; *(heaven or hell)*
Who have felt the weight of too much liberty, *(Theme)*	This mystery if the Stranger[1] can reveal,
Should find brief solace there, as I have found.	His be a welcome cordially bestowed!"

(handwritten: other writers in a Sonnet)

---

1. *Stranger*, Paulinus, who converted King Edwin. See Bede's account on page 51.

DISCUSSION

Composed upon Westminster Bridge
1. What qualities in the sleeping city would you describe as natural rather than artificial? How is Wordsworth's view of the sleeping city related to his view of nature?
2. Compare this sonnet with William Blake's "London" (page 326). What similar features of the city do both poems note? What differences in tone are there between the two poems?

The World Is Too Much with Us
1. What aspects of the world does Wordsworth view as positive, and what as negative? With what aspects are we "out of tune"? What aspects are "too much with us"? Do you feel that Wordsworth's theme has as much validity today?
2. Where in the sonnet does the most dramatic break occur? How would you read the sonnet aloud to give this break maximum effect?
3. What personifications does Wordsworth use to present various aspects

of nature? Does his use of personification make the natural world seem more intimate, or more distant?

London, 1802
1. What qualities does Wordsworth ascribe to Milton? What qualities of life in 1802 does he mention as contrast?

It Is a Beauteous Evening
1. List the words in the sonnet which most directly convey its mood and discuss the sonnet in terms of them.
2. How does the mood of this sonnet compare with "Composed upon Westminster Bridge"?
3. What effect does Wordsworth create through the evening-nun simile?
4. How are the last six lines connected with the preceding eight? What "solemn thoughts" make Wordsworth turn to address his daughter?

Nuns Fret Not
1. What paradox is Wordsworth working out in this sonnet? How is it

related to the constraints of the sonnet form?
2. Wordsworth notes that there must be some who have felt the "weight of too much liberty." What does he mean here? Is there such a thing as "too much liberty"?
3. Discuss the implications of the statement "In truth the prison, unto which we doom / Ourselves, no prison is."

Persuasion
Compare this sonnet with the words of "another of the king's chief men" as reported by Bede on page 53. Which presentation do you prefer? Why? Does Wordsworth's use of the sonnet form improve the original?

WRITING

Write your own version of "The World Is Too Much with Us" (in free verse), commenting on aspects of the modern world with which you feel we are "out of tune."

LUCY POEMS

Love poem to Lucy: if he lost her...

STRANGE FITS OF PASSION
HAVE I KNOWN

strong emotional feelings

Strange fits of passion have I known:
And I will dare to tell,
But in the Lover's ear alone, *he only tells his lover*
What once to me befell.

5 When she I loved looked every day *love*
Fresh as a rose in June, *passionate love*
I to her cottage bent my way,
Beneath an evening-moon. *night time*

Upon the moon I fixed my eye,
10 All over the wide lea;
With quickening pace my horse drew nigh
Those paths so dear to me.

And now we reached the orchard-plot;
And, as we climbed the hill,
15 The sinking moon to Lucy's cot *bed*
Came near, and nearer still.

In one of those sweet dreams I slept,
Kind Nature's gentlest boon!
And all the while my eyes I kept
20 On the descending moon.

My horse moved on; hoof after hoof
He raised, and never stopped:
When down behind the cottage roof,
At once, the bright moon dropped.

25 What fond and wayward thoughts will slide
Into a Lover's head!
"O mercy!" to myself I cried,
"If Lucy should be dead!"

his love for Lucy and her death

SHE DWELT AMONG
THE UNTRODDEN WAYS

She dwelt among the untrodden ways A
    Beside the springs of Dove, B
A Maid whom there were none to praise A
    And very few to love: B

---

2 metaphors Lucy — violet and a star

5 A violet by a mossy stone A
    Half hidden from the eye! B
—Fair as a star, when only one A
    Is shining in the sky. B

She lived unknown, and few could know A
10   When Lucy ceased to be; B
But she is in her grave, and, oh, A
    The difference to me! B

She's dead and he is changed

I TRAVELLED AMONG
UNKNOWN MEN

his love for Lucy

I travelled among unknown men,
    In lands beyond the sea;
Nor, England! did I know till then
    What love I bore to thee.

5 'Tis past, that melancholy dream!
    Nor will I quit thy shore
A second time; for still I seem
    To love thee more and more.

Among thy mountains did I feel
10   The joy of my desire;
And she I cherished turned her wheel
    Beside an English fire.

Thy mornings showed, thy nights concealed,
    The bowers where Lucy played;
15 And thine too is the last green field
    That Lucy's eyes surveyed.

A SLUMBER DID MY SPIRIT SEAL

Lucy's death

A slumber did my spirit seal;
    I had no human fears:
She seemed a thing that could not feel
    The touch of earthly years.

5 No motion has she now, no force;
    She neither hears nor sees;
Rolled round in earth's diurnal course,
    With rocks, and stones, and trees.

OF CRITICAL INTEREST

"She dwelt among the untrodden ways"

Samuel Butler, nineteenth-century author and critic, wrote the following speculations on the meaning of Wordsworth's poem. Is he serious or spoofing?

"Anyone imbued with the spirit of modern science will read Wordsworth's poem with different eyes from those of a mere literary critic. He will note that Wordsworth is most careful not to explain the nature of the difference which the death of Lucy will occasion to him. He tells us that there will be a difference; but there the matter ends. The superficial reader takes it that he was very sorry she was dead; it is, of course, possible that he may have actually been so, but he has not said this. On the contrary, he has hinted plainly that she was ugly, and generally disliked; she was only like a violet when she was half-hidden from the view, and only fair as a star when there were so few stars out that it was practically impossible to make an invidious comparison. If there were as many as even two stars the likeness was felt to be at an end. If Wordsworth had imprudently promised to marry this young person during a time when he had been unusually long in keeping to good resolutions, and had afterwards seen someone whom he liked better, then Lucy's death would undoubtedly have made a considerable difference to him, and this is all that he has ever said that it would do. What right have we to put glosses upon the masterly reticence of a poet, and credit him with feelings

From "Quis Desiderio . . . ?" by Samuel Butler. First published in the *Universal Review*, July 1888.

possibly the very reverse of those he actually entertained?

"Sometimes, indeed, I have been inclined to think that a mystery is being hinted at more dark than any critic has suspected. I do not happen to possess a copy of the poem, but the writer, if I am not mistaken, says that 'few could know when Lucy ceased to be.' 'Ceased to be' is a suspiciously euphemistic expression, and the words 'few could know' are not applicable to the ordinary peaceful death of a domestic servant such as Lucy appears to have been. No matter how obscure the deceased, any number of people commonly can know the day and hour of his or her demise, whereas in this case we are expressly told it would be impossible for them to do so. Wordsworth was nothing if not accurate, and would not have said that few could know, but that few actually did know, unless he was aware of circumstances that precluded all but those implicated in the crime of her death from knowing the precise moment of its occurrence. If Lucy was the kind of person not obscurely portrayed in the poem; if Wordsworth had murdered her, either by cutting her throat or smothering her, in concert, perhaps, with his friends Southey and Coleridge; and if he had thus found himself released from an engagement which had become irksome to him, or possibly from the threat of an action for breach of promise, then there is not a syllable in the poem with which he crowns his crime that is not alive with meaning. On any other supposition to the general reader it is unintelligible. . . ."

DISCUSSION

1. Discuss how the Lucy poems differ from each other, taking into account the mood (how do the natural objects mentioned fit the mood of each poem?) and the emotional tone (what kinds of feelings—determination, grief, consolation, fear, foreboding, etc.—does each poem deal with?).
2. The first poem ("Strange Fits of Passion") has been called "hallucinatory." What kind of hallucination takes place? How is it induced? What is the suggestion behind the line "At once, the bright moon dropped"?

WRITING

1. Can you detect any progression in action and time—a plot—implied in the Lucy poems presented here? Construct a hypothetical story around them. What is your reaction to Samuel Butler's hypothesis in the Extension?
2. The Lucy poems have been parodied many times. Choose one poem and write a parody of it.

EXPOSTULATION AND REPLY

[handwritten: present views and ideas]

"Why, William, on that old grey stone,
Thus for the length of half a day,
Why, William, sit you thus alone,
And dream your time away?

5 "Where are your books?—that light bequeathed
To Beings else forlorn and blind!
Up! up! and drink the spirit breathed
From dead men to their kind.

"You look round on your Mother Earth,
10 As if she for no purpose bore you;
As if you were her first-born birth,
And none had lived before you!"

One morning thus, by Esthwaite lake,
When life was sweet, I knew not why,
15 To me my good friend Matthew spake,
And thus I made reply:

"The eye—it cannot choose but see;
We cannot bid the ear be still;
Our bodies feel, where'er they be,
20 Against or with our will.

"Nor less I deem that there are Powers
Which of themselves our minds impress;
That we can feed this mind of ours
In a wise passiveness.

[handwritten: you can learn by just watching and listening.]

25 "Think you, 'mid all this mighty sum
Of things for ever speaking,
That nothing of itself will come,
But we must still be seeking?

"—Then ask not wherefore, here, alone,
30 Conversing as I may,
I sit upon this old grey stone,
And dream my time away."

THE SOLITARY REAPER

[handwritten: alone / harvester]

Behold her, single in the field,
Yon solitary Highland lass!
Reaping and singing by herself;
Stop here, or gently pass!
5 Alone she cuts and binds the grain,
And sings a melancholy strain;
O listen! for the vale profound
Is overflowing with the sound.

No nightingale did ever chaunt
10 More welcome notes to weary bands
Of travelers in some shady haunt,
Among Arabian sands:
A voice so thrilling ne'er was heard
In springtime from the cuckoo-bird,
15 Breaking the silence of the seas
Among the farthest Hebrides.

Will no one tell me what she sings?—
Perhaps the plaintive numbers flow
For old, unhappy, far-off things,
20 And battles long ago;
Or is it some more humble lay,
Familiar matter of today?
Some natural sorrow, loss, or pain,
That has been, and may be again?

25 Whate'er the theme, the maiden sang
As if her song could have no ending;
I saw her singing at her work,
And o'er the sickle bending;—
I listened, motionless and still;
30 And, as I mounted up the hill,
The music in my heart I bore,
Long after it was heard no more.

From

PREFACE TO LYRICAL BALLADS - *intellectual*

Summary of romaticisim

Partly to answer the criticisms which met the first edition of *Lyrical Ballads* (see the biography of Wordsworth on page 385), and partly to explain his own theories of poetry, Wordsworth wrote a Preface to the second (1800) edition. Here are two passages from this Preface.

THE principal object . . . proposed in these Poems was to choose incidents and situations from common life, and to relate or describe them throughout, as far as was possible, in a selection of language really used by men, and, at the same time, to throw over them a certain colouring of imagination, whereby ordinary things should be presented to the mind in an unusual aspect; and further, and above all, to make these incidents and situations interesting by tracing in them, truly though not ostentatiously, the primary laws of our nature: chiefly, as far as regards the manner in which we associate ideas in a state of excitement. [Humble and rustic life was generally chosen, because in that condition the essential passions of the heart find a better soil in which they can attain their maturity, are less under restraint, and speak a plainer and more emphatic language; because in that condition of life our elementary feelings coexist in a state of greater simplicity] and, consequently, may be more accurately contemplated, and more forcibly communicated; because the manners of rural life germinate from those elementary feelings, and, from the necessary character of rural occupations, are more easily comprehended, and are more durable; and, lastly, because in that condition the passions of men are incorporated with the beautiful and permanent forms of nature. The language, too, of these men has been adopted (purified indeed from what appear to be its real defects, from all lasting and rational causes of dislike or disgust) because such men hourly communicate with the best objects from which the best part of language is originally derived; and because, from their rank in society and the sameness and narrow circle of their intercourse, being less under the influence of social vanity, they convey their feelings and notions in simple and unelaborated expressions. Accordingly, such a language, arising out of repeated experience and regular feelings, is a more permanent, and a far more philosophical language, than that which is frequently substituted for it by Poets, who think that they are conferring honour upon themselves and their art, in proportion as they separate themselves from the sympathies of men, and indulge in arbitrary and capricious habits of expression, in order to furnish food for fickle tastes and fickle appetites of their own creation.

. . . .

Poetry is the spontaneous overflow of powerful feelings: it takes its origin from emotion recollected in tranquillity: the emotion is contemplated till, by a species of reaction, the tranquillity gradually disappears, and an emotion, kindred to that which was before the subject of contemplation, is gradually produced, and does itself actually exist in the mind.

DISCUSSION

Expostulation and Reply
What "Powers" or "things forever speaking" do you think Wordsworth had in mind when he wrote this poem? What are these "Powers" contrasted with?

The Solitary Reaper
1. Describe in as much detail as you can *imagine* (you won't find much explicit detail in the poem) the setting in which the lone woman reaps the grain. What overtones of mood does Wordsworth give the scene?
2. Read the excerpt from Wordsworth's "Preface to Lyrical Ballads" on this page. To what extent, in this poem, has he used the "language really used by men" or a situation taken from "humble and rustic" life?

LINES COMPOSED A FEW MILES
ABOVE TINTERN ABBEY

FIVE years have past; five summers,
    with the length
Of five long winters! and again I hear
These waters, rolling from their mountain springs
With a soft inland murmur. Once again
5 Do I behold these steep and lofty cliffs
That on a wild secluded scene impress
Thoughts of more deep seclusion and connect
The landscape with the quiet of the sky.
The day is come when I again repose
10 Here, under this dark sycamore, and view
These plots of cottage ground, these orchard tufts,
Which at this season, with their unripe fruits,
Are clad in one green hue, and lose themselves
Mid groves and copses. Once again I see
15 These hedgerows, hardly hedgerows, little lines
Of sportive wood run wild; these pastoral farms,
Green to the very door; and wreaths of smoke
Sent up, in silence, from among the trees,
With some uncertain notice, as might seem
20 Of vagrant dwellers in the houseless woods,
Or of some hermit's cave, where by his fire
The hermit sits alone.
                    These beauteous forms,
Through a long absence, have not been to me
As is a landscape to a blind man's eye;
25 But oft, in lonely rooms, and 'mid the din
Of towns and cities, I have owed to them,
In hours of weariness, sensations sweet,
Felt in the blood, and felt along the heart;
And passing even into my purer mind,
30 With tranquil restoration—feelings too
Of unremembered pleasure, such, perhaps,
As have no slight or trivial influence
On that best portion of a good man's life,
His little, nameless, unremembered acts
35 Of kindness and of love. Nor less, I trust,
To them I may have owed another gift,
Of aspect more sublime; that blessèd mood,
In which the burthen of the mystery,
In which the heavy and the weary weight
40 Of all this unintelligible world,
Is lightened—that serene and blessèd mood,
In which the affections gently lead us on—
Until, the breath of this corporeal frame
And even the motion of our human blood

45 Almost suspended, we are laid asleep
In body, and become a living soul;
While with an eye made quiet by the power
Of harmony, and the deep power of joy,
We see into the life of things.
                                If this
50 Be but a vain belief, yet, oh! how oft—
In darkness and amid the many shapes
Of joyless daylight; when the fretful stir
Unprofitable, and the fever of the world,
Have hung upon the beatings of my heart—
55 How oft, in spirit, have I turned to thee,
O sylvan Wye! thou wanderer through the woods,
How often has my spirit turned to thee!
And now, with gleams of half-extinguished thought,
With many recognitions dim and faint,
60 And somewhat of a sad perplexity,
The picture of the mind revives again;
While here I stand, not only with the sense
Of present pleasure, but with pleasing thoughts
That in this moment there is life and food
65 For future years. And so I dare to hope,
Though changed, no doubt, from what I was when
            first
I came among these hills, when like a roe
I bounded o'er the mountains, by the sides
Of the deep rivers, and the lonely streams,
70 Wherever nature led—more like a man
Flying from something that he dreads than one
Who sought the thing he loved. For nature then
(The coarser pleasures of my boyish days,
And their glad animal movements all gone by)
75 To me was all in all. —I cannot paint
What then I was. The sounding cataract
Haunted me like a passion; the tall rock,
The mountain, and the deep and gloomy wood,
Their colors and their forms, were then to me
80 An appetite, a feeling and a love,
That had no need of a remoter charm,
By thought supplied, nor any interest
Unborrowed from the eye. —That time is past,
And all its aching joys are now no more,
85 And all its dizzy raptures. Not for this
Faint I, nor mourn nor murmur; other gifts
Have followed; for such loss, I would believe,
Abundant recompense. For I have learned
To look on nature, not as in the hour
90 Of thoughtless youth, but hearing often times
The still, sad music of humanity,
Nor harsh nor grating, though of ample power

To chasten and subdue. And I have felt
A presence that disturbs me with the joy
95 Of elevated thoughts; a sense sublime
Of something far more deeply interfused,
Whose dwelling is the light of setting suns,
And the round ocean and the living air,
And the blue sky, and in the mind of man;
100 A motion and a spirit, that impels
All thinking things, all objects of all thought,
And rolls through all things. Therefore am I still
A lover of the meadows and the woods,
And mountains; and of all that we behold
105 From this green earth; of all the mighty world
Of eye, and ear—both what they half create,
And what perceive; well pleased to recognize
In nature and the language of the sense
The anchor of my purest thoughts, the nurse,
110 The guide, the guardian of my heart, and soul
Of all my moral being.
                              Nor perchance,
If I were not thus taught, should I the more
Suffer my genial spirits to decay;
For thou art with me here upon the banks
115 Of this fair river; thou my dearest friend,[1]
My dear, dear friend; and in thy voice I catch
The language of my former heart, and read
My former pleasures in the shooting lights
Of thy wild eyes. Oh! yet a little while
120 May I behold in thee what I was once,
My dear, dear sister! and this prayer I make,
Knowing that nature never did betray
The heart that loved her; 'tis her privilege,
Through all the years of this our life, to lead

---

1. *my dearest friend,* Wordsworth's sister, Dorothy.

125 From joy to joy; for she can so inform
The mind that is within us, so impress
With quietness and beauty, and so feed
With lofty thoughts, that neither evil tongues,
Rash judgments, nor the sneers of selfish men,
130 Nor greetings where no kindness is, nor all
The dreary intercourse of daily life,
Shall e'er prevail against us, or disturb
Our cheerful faith, that all which we behold
Is full of blessings. Therefore let the moon
135 Shine on thee in thy solitary walk;
And let the misty mountain winds be free
To blow against thee; and, in after years,
When these wild ecstasies shall be matured
Into a sober pleasure, when thy mind
140 Shall be a mansion for all lovely forms,
Thy memory be as a dwelling place
For all sweet sounds and harmonies; oh! then,
If solitude, or fear, or pain, or grief,
Should be thy portion, with what healing thoughts
145 Of tender joy wilt thou remember me,
And these my exhortations! Nor, perchance—
If I should be where I no more can hear
Thy voice, nor catch from thy wild eyes these gleams
Of past existence—wilt thou then forget
150 That on the banks of this delightful stream
We stood together; and that I, so long
A worshiper of nature, hither came
Unwearied in that service—rather say
With warmer love—oh! with far deeper zeal
155 Of holier love. Nor wilt thou then forget
That after many wanderings, many years
Of absence, these steep woods and lofty cliffs,
And this green pastoral landscape, were to me
More dear, both for themselves and for thy sake! □

DISCUSSION

1. How is nature presented in the first twenty-two lines of the poem? Are there any signs of human habitation? How are these presented?

2. Read the sonnet "The World Is Too Much with Us" against lines 23–65. What similarities of theme can you detect? What "gifts" or sustenance does Wordsworth find in nature? How does he view city life?

3. How is Wordsworth's affection for his sister connected with the themes of the poem?

4. Do you think we can in any way view nature today as Wordsworth does in this poem? What, if anything, has changed in the natural world and our view of it?

WRITING

1. In a sense this poem is about the passage of time and the changes in attitude toward nature that Wordsworth experienced between boyhood and manhood. In lines 65–111, trace the stages of his development. What did nature mean to him as a boy? as a grown man? (In your essay, you might use the contrast between "powerful feelings" and "tranquility" which Wordsworth brings up in his definition of poetry in the "Preface to Lyrical Ballads.")

2. In prose or poetry, write a description of your feelings on returning, after an absence of months or years, to some place you have felt close to.

From THE PRELUDE, Book 1

— 3 experiences from his childhood (handwritten annotation)

Wordsworth referred to *The Prelude*, on which he worked
for almost fifty years, as "a history of the author's mind."
This excerpt describes boyhood adventures which made
a profound impression on him.

To support (handwritten annotation, left margin)

F AIR seed-time had my soul, and I grew up
Fostered alike by beauty and by fear:
Much favoured in my birth-place, and no less   *long* (annotation)
In that belovèd Vale[1] to which erelong *— before* (annotation)
5   We were transplanted;—there were we let loose
For sports of wider range. Ere I had told
Ten birth-days, when among the mountain slopes
Frost, and the breath of frosty wind, had snapped
The last autumnal crocus, 't was my joy
10 With store of springes[2] o'er my shoulder hung
To range the open heights where woodcocks run
Along the smooth green turf. Through half the night,
Scudding away from snare to snare, I plied
That anxious visitation;—moon and stars
15 Were shining o'er my head. I was alone,
And seemed to be a trouble to the peace
That dwelt among them. Sometimes it befell
In these night wanderings, that a strong desire
O'erpowered my better reason, and the bird
20 Which was the captive of another's toil
Became my prey; and when the deed was done
I heard among the solitary hills
Low breathings coming after me, and sounds
Of undistinguishable motion, steps
25 Almost as silent as the turf they trod.

     Nor less, when spring had warmed the cultured
          Vale,
Moved we as plunderers where the mother-bird
Had in high places built her lodge; though mean
Our object and inglorious, yet the end
30 Was not ignoble. Oh! when I have hung
Above the raven's nest, by knots of grass
And half-inch fissures in the slippery rock
But ill sustained, and almost (so it seemed)
Suspended by the blast that blew amain,
35 Shouldering the naked crag, oh, at that time
While on the perilous ridge I hung alone,
With what strange utterance did the loud dry wind
Blow through my ear! the sky seemed not a sky

---

1. *Vale*, Esthwaite Vale in Lancashire, near Wordsworth's boyhood home.
2. *springes*, snares for catching birds.

Of earth—and with what motion moved the clouds!
40 Dust as we are, the immortal spirit grows
Like harmony in music; there is a dark
Inscrutable workmanship that reconciles
Discordant elements, makes them cling together
In one society. How strange, that all
The terrors, pains, and early miseries   *(annotation)*
Regrets, vexations, lassitudes interfused
Within my mind, should e'er have borne a part,
And that a needful part, in making up
The calm existence that is mine when I
50 Am worthy of myself! Praise to the end!
Thanks to the means which Nature deigned to
          employ;
Whether her fearless visitings, or those
That came with soft alarm, like hurtless light
Opening the peaceful clouds; or she would use
55 Severer interventions, ministry
More palpable, as best might suit her aim.
    obvious (annotation)

     One summer evening (led by her) I found
A little boat tied to a willow tree
Within a rocky cove, its usual home.
60 Straight I unloosed her chain, and stepping in   *secrecy* (annotation)
Pushed from the shore. It was an act of stealth
And troubled pleasure, nor without the voice
Of mountain-echoes did my boat move on;
Leaving behind her still, on either side,
65 Small circles glittering idly in the moon,
Until they melted all into one track
Of sparkling light. But now, like one who rows,
Proud of his skill, to reach a chosen point
With an unswerving line, I fixed my view
70 Upon the summit of a craggy ridge,
The horizon's utmost boundary; far above
Was nothing but the stars and the grey sky.
She was an elfin pinnace; lustily   *small boat* (annotation)
I dipped my oars into the silent lake,
75 And, as I rose upon the stroke, my boat
Went heaving through the water like a swan;
When, from behind that craggy steep till then
The horizon's bound, a huge peak, black and huge,
As if with voluntary power instinct,
80 Upreared its head. I struck and struck again,   *size* (annotation)
And growing still in stature the grim shape
Towered up between me and the stars, and still,
For so it seemed, with purpose of its own
And measured motion like a living thing,
85 Strode after me. With trembling oars I turned,

[right margin handwritten annotations: "we all came from nothing", "growing", "am not move"]

And through the silent water stole my way
Back to the covert of the willow tree;   *boat*
There in her mooring-place I left my bark,—
And through the meadows homeward went, in grave
90 And serious mood; but after I had seen
That spectacle, for many days, my brain
Worked with a dim and undetermined sense
Of unknown modes of being; o'er my thoughts
There hung a darkness, call it solitude
95 Or blank desertion. No familiar shapes
Remained, no pleasant images of trees,
Of sea or sky, no colours of green fields;
But huge and mighty forms, that do not live
Like living men, moved slowly through the mind
100 By day, and were a trouble to my dreams.   □

DISCUSSION

1. What guises does nature take as the "teacher" of young Wordsworth? Is nature presented as pleasant and harmless, or as a threatening force? What imagery in the passage supports your view?
2. What feelings of guilt are evident in this passage? How and where are they presented?

Samuel Taylor Coleridge   *—stoner weirdo*

1772 / 1834

NATIONAL PORTRAIT GALLERY, LONDON

THE EXCHANGE

We pledged our hearts, my love and I,—
    I in my arms the maiden clasping;
I could not guess the reason why,
    But, oh! I trembled like an aspen.

5 Her father's love she bade me gain;
    I went, but shook like any reed!
I strove to act the man—in vain!
    We had exchanged our hearts indeed.

COLOGNE

In Köhln,[1] a town of monks and bones,*a*
And pavements fanged with murderous stones*a*
And rags, and hags, and hideous wenches;*b*
I counted two and seventy stenches,*b*
5 All well defined, and several stinks!*c*
Ye Nymphs that reign o'er sewers and sinks,*c*
The river Rhine, it is well known, *d*
Doth wash your city of Cologne;*d*
But tell me, Nymphs, what power divine *e*
10 Shall henceforth wash the river Rhine? *e*

---

1.   *Köhln*, the German name for Cologne.

SONG   *♪ love is a sword*

Though veiled in spires of myrtle-wreath,
Love is a sword which cuts its sheath,
And through the clefts itself has made,
We spy the flashes of the blade!

5 But through the clefts itself has made
We likewise see Love's flashing blade,
By rust consumed, or snapt in twain;
And only hilt and stump remain.

KUBLA KHAN *opium Trip*

In Xanadu did Kubla Khan
A stately pleasure dome decree:
Where Alph, the sacred river, ran
Through caverns measureless to man
5   Down to a sunless sea.
So twice five miles of fertile ground
With walls and towers were girdled round:
And there were gardens bright with sinuous rills,
Where blossomed many an incense-bearing tree;
10 And here were forests ancient as the hills,
Enfolding sunny spots of greenery.

But oh! that deep romantic chasm which slanted
Down the green hill athwart a cedarn cover!
A savage place! as holy and enchanted
15 As e'er beneath a waning moon was haunted
By woman wailing for her demon lover!
And from this chasm, with ceaseless turmoil seething,
As if this earth in fast thick pants were breathing,
A mighty fountain momently was forced:
20 Amid whose swift half-intermitted burst
Huge fragments vaulted like rebounding hail,
Or chaffy grain beneath the thresher's flail:
And 'mid these dancing rocks at once and ever
It flung up momently the sacred river.
25 Five miles meandering with a mazy motion
Through wood and dale the sacred river ran,
Then reached the caverns measureless to man,

And sank in tumult to a lifeless ocean:
And 'mid this tumult Kubla heard from far
30 Ancestral voices prophesying war!
    The shadow of the dome of pleasure
    Floated midway on the waves;
    Where was heard the mingled measure
    From the fountain and the caves.
35 It was a miracle of rare device,
A sunny pleasure dome with caves of ice!

    A damsel with a dulcimer
    In a vision once I saw:
    It was an Abyssinian maid,
40   And on her dulcimer she played,
    Singing of Mount Abora.
Could I revive within me
Her symphony and song,
To such a deep delight 'twould win me,
45 That with music loud and long,
I would build that dome in air,
That sunny dome! those caves of ice!
And all who heard should see them there,
And all should cry, Beware! Beware!
50 His flashing eyes, his floating hair!
Weave a circle round him thrice,
And close your eyes with holy dread,
For he on honeydew hath fed,
And drunk the milk of Paradise.

OF LITERARY INTEREST

Coleridge's remarks about "Kubla Khan"

The following fragment is here published at the request of a poet of great and deserved celebrity,[1] and, as far as the author's own opinions are concerned, rather as a psychological curiosity, than on the ground of any supposed *poetic* merits.

In the summer of the year 1797, the author, then in ill health, had retired to a lonely farmhouse between Porlock and Linton, on the Exmoor confines of Somerset and Devonshire. In consequence of a slight indisposition, an anodyne had been prescribed, from the effects of which he fell asleep in his chair at the moment that he was reading the following sentence, or words of the same substance, in *Purchas's*

1. *poet . . . celebrity*, Byron.

Pilgrimage: "Here the Khan Kubla commanded a palace to be built, and a stately garden thereunto. And thus ten miles of fertile ground were inclosed with a wall."[2] The author continued for about three hours in a profound sleep, at least of the external senses, during which time he has the most vivid confidence that he could not have composed less than from two to three hundred lines; if that

2. *"Here the Khan . . . with a wall."* The actual sentence in *Purchas his Pilgrimage* (1613) reads "In Xamdu did Cublai Can build a stately Palace, encompassing sixteene miles of plaine ground with a wall, wherein are fertile Meddowes, pleasant springs, delightfull Streames, and all sorts of beasts of chase and game, and in the middest thereof a sumptuous house of pleasure, which may be removed from place to place." The historical Kubla Khan founded the Mongol dynasty in China in the thirteenth century.

FROST AT MIDNIGHT

[handwritten: - a promise to his son. he wants his son to grow in nature]

The Frost performs its secret ministry,
Unhelped by any wind. The owlet's cry
Came loud—and hark, again! loud as before.
The inmates of my cottage, all at rest,
5 Have left me to that solitude, which suits *[handwritten: meditating]*
Abstruser musings: save that at my side
My cradled infant[1] slumbers peacefully.
'Tis calm indeed! so calm, that it disturbs
And vexes meditation with its strange
10 And extreme silentness. Sea, hill, and wood,
This populous village! Sea, and hill, and wood,
With all the numberless goings-on of life,
Inaudible as dreams! the thin blue flame
Lies on my low-burnt fire, and quivers not;
15 Only that film,[2] which fluttered on the grate,
Still flutters there, the sole unquiet thing.
Methinks its motion in this hush of nature
Gives it dim sympathies with me who live,
Making it a companionable form,

20 Whose puny flaps and freaks the idling Spirit
By its own moods interprets, everywhere
Echo or mirror seeking of itself,
And makes a toy of Thought.

                But O! how oft,
How oft, at school, with most believing mind,
25 Presageful, have I gazed upon the bars,
To watch that fluttering *stranger!* and as oft
With unclosed lids, already had I dreamt
Of my sweet birthplace, and the old church tower,
Whose bells, the poor man's only music, rang
30 From morn to evening, all the hot fair-day,
So sweetly, that they stirred and haunted me
With a wild pleasure, falling on mine ear
Most like articulate sounds of things to come!
So gazed I, till the soothing things, I dreamt,
35 Lulled me to sleep, and sleep prolonged my dreams!
And so I brooded all the following morn, *[handwritten: teacher]*
Awed by the stern preceptor's face, mine eye
Fixed with mock study on my swimming book:
Save if the door half opened, and I snatched
40 A hasty glance, and still my heart leaped up,
For still I hoped to see the *stranger's* face,
Townsman, or aunt, or sister more beloved,
My playmate when we both were clothed alike![3]

    Dear Babe, that sleepest cradled by my side,
45 Whose gentle breathings, heard in this deep calm,
Fill up the interspersèd vacancies
And momentary pauses of the thought!
My babe so beautiful! it thrills my heart
With tender gladness, thus to look at thee,
50 And think that thou shalt learn far other lore,
And in far other scenes! For I was reared
In the great city, pent 'mid cloisters dim,
And saw nought lovely but the sky and stars.
But *thou*, my babe! shalt wander like a breeze
55 By lakes and sandy shores, beneath the crags
Of ancient mountain, and beneath the clouds,

---

1. *My cradled infant*, Coleridge's son, Hartley.
2. *film*, a film of soot. Coleridge's note on this reads: "In all parts of the kingdom these films are called *strangers* and are supposed to portend the arrival of some absent friend."

/

indeed can be called composition in which all the images rose up before him as *things*, with a parallel production of the correspondent expressions, without any sensation or consciousness of effort. On awaking he appeared to himself to have a distinct recollection of the whole, and taking his pen, ink, and paper, instantly and eagerly wrote down the lines that are here preserved. At this moment he was unfortunately called out by a person on business from Porlock, and detained by him above an hour, and on his return to his room, found, to his no small surprise and mortification, that though he still retained some vague and dim recollection of the general purport of the vision, yet, with the exception of some eight or ten scattered lines and images, all the rest had passed away like the images on the surface of a stream into which a stone has been cast. . . .

---

3. *when we both were clothed alike*, i.e., when both Coleridge and his sister Ann wore infant clothes.

Which image in their bulk both lakes and shores
And mountain crags: so shalt thou see and hear
The lovely shapes and sounds intelligible
60 Of that eternal language, which thy God
Utters, who from eternity doth teach
Himself in all, and all things in himself.
Great universal Teacher! he shall mold
Thy spirit, and by giving make it ask.

65   Therefore all seasons shall be sweet to thee,
Whether the summer clothe the general earth
With greenness, or the redbreast sit and sing
Betwixt the tufts of snow on the bare branch
Of mossy apple tree, while the nigh thatch
70 Smokes in the sun-thaw; whether the eave-drops fall
Heard only in the trances of the blast,
Or if the secret ministry of frost
Shall hang them up in silent icicles,
Quietly shining to the quiet Moon.   □

OF HUMAN INTEREST

A son's reply

In this sonnet, Coleridge's son Hartley alludes to "Frost at Midnight."

Dedicatory Sonnet To S. T. Coleridge

Father, and Bard revered! to whom I owe,
Whate'er it be, my little art of numbers,
Thou, in thy night-watch o'er my cradled slumbers,
Didst meditate the verse that lives to show,
5 (And long shall live, when we alike are low)
Thy prayer how ardent, and thy hope how strong,
That I should learn of Nature's self the song,
The lore which none but Nature's pupils know.

    The prayer was heard I "wandered like a breeze,"
10 By mountain brooks and solitary meres,[1]
And gathered there the shapes and phantasies
Which, mixed with passions of my sadder years,
Compose this book. If good therein there be,
That good, my sire, I dedicate to thee.

---
1. *meres,* lakes.

DISCUSSION

Kubla Khan

1. What instances of exotic imagery do you find in this poem? Can you factually describe or explain them—for example, can you describe what a "pleasure dome" is? Or do you *feel* the meaning, rather than "see" it in detail? What qualities of language add to your impression?

2. Readers of "Kubla Khan" have often commented that in spite of the luxuriance of the scenes described, the poem has foreboding or sinister undertones. Do you find any? What lines or phrases suggest them to you?

3. What does Coleridge suggest, in the last thirteen lines of the poem, as possible effects of reviving or completing his dream vision?

Frost at Midnight

1. What is the pervasive mood of this poem? What types of imagery help convey this mood?
2. What role does the "stranger" play? What memories does it recall?
3. What do Coleridge's memories suggest about his boyhood? In what ways are they related to (or contrasted with) his wishes for his infant son?

4. In the first and last lines of the poem, Coleridge refers to the "secret ministry of frost." What are the implications of this phrase? What particular overtones do you find in the word "ministry"? What does the phrase suggest about Coleridge's attitude toward nature?

WRITING

Read Hartley Coleridge's "Dedicatory Sonnet" and the words addressed to him in "Frost at Midnight." What do the two poems together suggest regarding the relationship between father and son?

George Gordon, Lord Byron —the crippled lover

1788 / 1824

WHEN WE TWO PARTED

An affair that went bad

When we two parted 4
   In silence and tears, 8
Half broken-hearted 4
   To sever for years 8
5 Pale grew thy cheek and cold, C
   Colder thy kiss; D
Truly that hour foretold C
   Sorrow to this. D

The dew of the morning
10   Sunk chill on my brow—
It felt like the warning
   Of what I feel now.
Thy vows are all broken,
   And light is thy fame;
15 I hear thy name spoken,
   And share in its shame.

They name thee before me,
   A knell to mine ear;
A shudder comes o'er me—
20   Why wert thou so dear?
They know not I knew thee,
   Who knew thee too well:—
Long, long shall I rue thee,
   Too deeply to tell. *regret*

25 In secret we met—
   In silence I grieve
That thy heart could forget,
   Thy spirit deceive.
If I should meet thee
30   After long years,
How should I greet thee?—
   With silence and tears.

SO WE'LL GO NO MORE A-ROVING

He's not going to go out anymore

So we'll go no more a-roving
   So late into the night,
Though the heart be still as loving,
   And the moon be still as bright.

5 For the sword outwears its sheath,
   And the soul wears out the breast,
And the heart must pause to breathe,
   And Love itself have rest.

Though the night was made for loving,
10   And the day returns too soon,
Yet we'll go no more a-roving
   By the light of the moon.

SHE WALKS IN BEAUTY

She walks in beauty, like the night,
   Of cloudless climes and starry skies;
And all that's best of dark and bright
   Meet in her aspect and her eyes:
5 Thus mellowed to that tender light
   Which heaven to gaudy day denies.

One shade the more, one ray the less,
   Had half impaired the nameless grace
Which waves in every raven tress,— *hair*
10   Or softly lightens o'er her face;
Where thoughts serenely sweet express
   How pure, how dear their dwelling place.

And on that cheek, and o'er that brow,
   So soft, so calm, yet eloquent,—
15 The smiles that win, the tints that glow,
   But tell of days in goodness spent,
A mind at peace with all below,
   A heart whose love is innocent!

DARKNESS — *The end of the world*

I HAD a dream, which was not all a dream.
The bright sun was extinguished, and the stars
Did wander darkling in the eternal space,
Rayless, and pathless, and the icy earth
5 Swung blind and blackening in the moonless air;
Morn came and went—and came, and brought no day,
And men forgot their passions in the dread
Of this their desolation; and all hearts
Were chilled into a selfish prayer for light:
10 And they did live by watchfires—and the thrones,
The palaces of crownèd kings—the huts,
The habitations of all things which dwell,
Were burnt for beacons; cities were consumed,
And men were gathered round their blazing homes
15 To look once more into each other's face;
Happy were those who dwelt within the eye
Of the volcanoes, and their mountain torch:
A fearful hope was all the world contained;
Forests were set on fire—but hour by hour
20 They fell and faded—and the crackling trunks
Extinguished with a crash—and all was black.
The brows of men by the despairing light
Wore an unearthly aspect, as by fits
The flashes fell upon them; some lay down
25 And hid their eyes and wept; and some did rest
Their chins upon their clenchèd hands, and smiled;
And others hurried to and fro, and fed
Their funeral piles with fuel, and looked up
With mad disquietude on the dull sky,
30 The pall of a past world; and then again
With curses cast them down upon the dust,
And gnashed their teeth and howled: the wild birds shrieked
And, terrified, did flutter on the ground,
And flap their useless wings; the wildest brutes
35 Came tame and tremulous; and vipers crawled
And twined themselves among the multitude,
Hissing, but stingless—they were slain for food;
And War, which for a moment was no more,
Did glut himself again—a meal was bought
40 With blood, and each sate sullenly apart
Gorging himself in gloom: no love was left;
All earth was but one thought—and that was death
Immediate and inglorious; and the pang
Of famine fed upon all entrails—men

45 Died, and their bones were tombless as their flesh;
The meager by the meager were devoured,
Even dogs assailed their masters, all save one,
And he was faithful to a corse, and kept
The birds and beasts and famished men at bay,
50 Till hunger clung them, or the dropping dead
Lured their lank jaws; himself sought out no food,
But with a piteous and perpetual moan,
And a quick desolate cry, licking the hand
Which answered not with a caress—he died.
55 The crowd was famished by degrees; but two
Of an enormous city did survive,
And they were enemies: they met beside
The dying embers of an altar place.
Where had been heaped a mass of holy things
60 For an unholy usage; they raked up,
And shivering scraped with their cold skeleton hands
The feeble ashes, and their feeble breath
Blew for a little life, and made a flame
Which was a mockery; then they lifted up
65 Their eyes as it grew lighter, and beheld
Each other's aspects—saw, and shrieked, and died—
Even of their mutual hideousness they died,
Unknowing who he was upon whose brow
Famine had written Fiend. The world was void,
70 The populous and the powerful was a lump
Seasonless, herbless, treeless, manless, lifeless—
A lump of death—a chaos of hard clay.
The rivers, lakes, and ocean all stood still,
And nothing stirred within their silent depths;
75 Ships sailorless lay rotting on the sea,
And their masts fell down piecemeal: as they dropped
They slept on the abyss without a surge—
The waves were dead; the tides were in their grave,
The Moon, their mistress, had expired before;
80 The winds were withered in the stagnant air,
And the clouds perished; Darkness had no need
Of aid from them—She was the Universe. ☐

DISCUSSION

She Walks in Beauty

What quality of beauty does Byron emphasize in this portrait? Is it physical or spiritual beauty?

When We Two Parted

What words or phrases most vividly convey the feelings experienced by the speaker? What specifically is that feeling—has the speaker completely rejected the person addressed in the poem?

Darkness

1. Do you find anything in this poem which relieves its pessimism? What?
2. What sound effects make this poem so powerful in expression? Select six lines and examine them closely in terms of word choice, assonance, and alliteration.

WRITING

Darkness

Write a paragraph or two on the overtones of meaning you find in the first line. What aspects of possible reality are there in this poem for modern readers?

a sattire (teaches you something) is always long

From DON JUAN, CANTO 1 *Epic*

Sattire of Epic

1

I WANT a hero: an uncommon want,
  When every year and month sends forth a new one,
Till, after cloying the gazettes with cant,
  The age discovers he is not the true one;
5 Of such as these I should not care to vaunt,
  I'll therefore take our ancient friend Don Juan—
We all have seen him, in the pantomime,
Sent to the devil somewhat ere his time.

6

middle of things

Most epic poets plunge "in medias res"
10 (Horace makes this the heroic turnpike road),
And then your hero tells, whene'er you please,
  What went before—by way of episode,
While seated after dinner at his ease,
  Beside his mistress in some soft abode,
15 Palace, or garden, paradise, or cavern,
Which serves the happy couple for a tavern.

7

That is the usual method, but not mine—
  My way is to begin with the beginning;
The regularity of my design
20 Forbids all wandering as the worst of sinning,
And therefore I shall open with a line
  (Although it cost me half an hour in spinning)
Narrating somewhat of Don Juan's father,
And also of his mother, if you'd rather.

8

25 In Seville was he born, a pleasant city,
  Famous for oranges and women—he
Who has not seen it will be much to pity,
  So says the proverb—and I quite agree;
Of all the Spanish towns is none more pretty,
30 Cadiz, perhaps—but that you soon may see:—
Don Juan's parents lived beside the river,
A noble stream, and called the Guadalquivir.

9

His father's name was Jóse—*Don*, of course,
  A true Hidalgo,[1] free from every stain
35 Of Moor or Hebrew blood, he traced his source
  Through the most Gothic gentlemen of Spain;
A better cavalier ne'er mounted horse,
  Or, being mounted, e'er got down again,
Than Jóse, who begot our hero, who
40 Begot—but that's to come—Well, to renew:

10

His mother was a learned lady, famed
  For every branch of every science known—
In every Christian language ever named,
  With virtues equalled by her wit alone:
45 She made the cleverest people quite ashamed,
  And even the good with inward envy groan,
Finding themselves so very much exceeded
In their own way by all the things that she did.

1. *Hidalgo,* a member of the lower Spanish nobility.

13

She knew the Latin—that is, "the Lord's prayer,"
50   And Greek—the alphabet—I'm nearly sure;
She read some French romances here and there,
     Although her mode of speaking was not pure;
For native Spanish she had no great care,
     At least her conversation was obscure;
55 Her thoughts were theorems, her words a problem,
As if she deemed that mystery would ennoble 'em.

15

Some women use their tongues—she *looked* a lecture,
     Each eye a sermon, and her brow a homily,
An all-in-all sufficient self-director,
60   Like the lamented late Sir Samuel Romilly,[2]
The Law's expounder, and the State's corrector,
     Whose suicide was almost an anomaly—
One sad example more, that "All is vanity,"—
(The jury brought their verdict in "Insanity.")

17

65 Oh! she was perfect past all parallel—
     Of any modern female saint's comparison;
So far above the cunning powers of hell,
     Her guardian angel had given up his garrison;
Even her minutest motions went as well
70   As those of the best time-piece made by Harrison:[3]
In virtues nothing earthly could surpass her,
Save thine "incomparable oil," Macassar![4]

18

Perfect she was, but as perfection is
     Insipid in this naughty world of ours,
75 Where our first parents never learned to kiss
     Till they were exiled from their earlier bowers,
Where all was peace, and innocence, and bliss
     (I wonder how they got through the twelve hours),
Don Jóse, like a lineal son of Eve,
80 Went plucking various fruit without her leave.

19

He was a mortal of the careless kind,
     With no great love for learning, or the learned,
Who chose to go where'er he had a mind,
     And never dreamed his lady was concerned;

85 The world, as usual, wickedly inclined
     To see a kingdom or a house o'erturned,
Whispered he had a mistress, some said *two,*
But for domestic quarrels *one* will do.

20

Now Donna Inez had, with all her merit,
90   A great opinion of her own good qualities;
Neglect, indeed, requires a saint to bear it,
     And such, indeed, she was in her moralities;
But then she had a devil of a spirit,
     And sometimes mixed up fancies with realities,
95 And let few opportunities escape
Of getting her liege lord into a scrape.

23

Don Jóse and his lady quarrelled—*why,*
     Not any of the many could divine,
Though several thousand people chose to try,
100   'Twas surely no concern of theirs nor mine;
I loathe that low vice—curiosity;
     But if there's anything in which I shine,
'Tis in arranging all my friends' affairs,
Not having, of my own, domestic cares.

24

105 And so I interfered, and with the best
     Intentions, but their treatment was not kind;
I think the foolish people were possessed,
     For neither of them could I ever find,
Although their porter afterwards confessed—
110   But that's no matter, and the worst's behind,
For little Juan o'er me threw, down stairs,
A pail of housemaid's water unawares.

25

A little curly-headed, good-for-nothing,
     And mischief-making monkey from his birth;
115 His parents ne'er agreed except in doting
     Upon the most unquiet imp on earth;
Instead of quarrelling, had they been but both in
     Their senses, they'd have sent young master forth
To school, or had him soundly whipped at home,
120 To teach him manners for the time to come.

26

Don Jóse and the Donna Inez led
     For some time an unhappy sort of life,
Wishing each other, not divorced, but dead;
     They lived respectably as man and wife,

---

2. *Sir Samuel Romilly*, an English lawyer who represented Byron's
wife in her suit for divorce; he committed suicide in 1818.
3. *Harrison*, John Harrison (1693–1776), watchmaker and scientific inventor.
4. *Macassar*, a fragrant oil used as hair dressing.

Their conduct was exceedingly well-bred,
    And gave no outward signs of inward strife,
Until at length the smothered fire broke out,
And put the business past all kind of doubt.

27

For Inez called some druggists and physicians,
    And tried to prove her loving lord was *mad,*
But as he had some lucid intermissions,
    She next decided he was only *bad;*
Yet when they asked her for her depositions,
    No sort of explanation could be had,
Save that her duty both to man and God
Required this conduct—which seemed very odd.

32

Their friends had tried at reconciliation,
    Then their relations, who made matters worse,
('Twere hard to tell upon a like occasion
    To whom it may be best to have recourse—
I can't say much for friend or yet relation):
    The lawyers did their utmost for divorce,
But scarce a fee was paid on either side
Before, unluckily, Don Jóse died.

33

He died: and most unluckily, because,
    According to all hints I could collect
From counsel learned in those kinds of laws
    (Although their talk's obscure and circumspect),
His death contrived to spoil a charming cause;
    A thousand pities also with respect
To public feeling, which on this occasion
Was manifested in a great sensation.

37

Dying intestate, Juan was sole heir
    To a chancery suit, and messuages,[5] and lands,
Which, with a long minority and care,
    Promised to turn out well in proper hands:
Inez became sole guardian, which was fair,
    And answered but to nature's just demands;
An only son left with an only mother
Is brought up much more wisely than another.

38

Sagest of women, even of widows, she
    Resolved that Juan should be quite a paragon,

---

5. *messuages,* houses together with adjacent buildings.

And worthy of the noblest pedigree:
    (His sire was of Castile, his dam from Aragon).
Then for accomplishments of chivalry,
    In case our lord the king should go to war again,
He learned the arts of riding, fencing, gunnery,
    And how to scale a fortress—or a nunnery.

39

But that which Donna Inez most desired,
    And saw into herself each day before all
The learned tutors whom for him she hired,
    Was, that his breeding should be strictly moral:
Much into all his studies she inquired,
    And so they were submitted first to her, all,
Arts, sciences, no branch was made a mystery
To Juan's eyes, excepting natural history.

40

The languages, especially the dead,
    The sciences, and most of all the abstruse,
The arts, at least all such as could be said
    To be the most remote from common use,
In all these he was much and deeply read;
    But not a page of anything that's loose,
Or hints continuation of the species,
Was ever suffered, lest he should grow vicious.

41

His classic studies made a little puzzle,
    Because of filthy loves of gods and goddesses,
Who in the earlier ages raised a bustle,
    But never put on pantaloons or bodices;
His reverend tutors had at times a tussle,
    And for their Æneids, Iliads, and Odysseys,
Were forced to make an odd sort of apology,
For Donna Inez dreaded the Mythology.

44

Juan was taught from out the best edition,
    Expurgated by learned men, who place,
Judiciously, from out the schoolboy's vision,
    The grosser parts; but, fearful to deface
Too much their modest bard by this omission,
    And pitying sore this mutilated case,
They only add them all in an appendix,
Which saves, in fact, the trouble of an index;

45

For there we have them all "at one fell swoop,"
    Instead of being scattered through the pages;

They stand forth marshalled in a handsome troop,
    To meet the ingenuous youth of future ages,
205 Till some less rigid editor shall stoop
    To call them back into their separate cages,
    Instead of standing staring all together,
    Like garden gods—and not so decent either.

47

Sermons he read, and lectures he endured,
210   And homilies, and lives of all the saints;
    To Jerome and to Chrysostom inured,
        He did not take such studies for restraints;
    But how faith is acquired, and then ensured,
        So well not one of the aforesaid paints
215 As Saint Augustine in his fine Confessions,[6]
    Which make the reader envy his transgressions.

48

This, too, was a sealed book to little Juan—
    I can't but say that his mamma was right,
If such an education was the true one.
220   She scarcely trusted him from out her sight;
    Her maids were old, and if she took a new one,
        You might be sure she was a perfect fright;
    She did this during even her husband's life—
    I recommend as much to every wife.

49

225 Young Juan waxed in godliness and grace;
        At six a charming child, and at eleven
    With all the promise of as fine a face
        As e'er to man's maturer growth was given:
    He studied steadily and grew apace,
230   And seemed, at least, in the right road to heaven,
    For half his days were passed at church, the other
    Between his tutors, confessor, and mother.

50

At six, I said, he was a charming child,
        At twelve he was a fine, but quiet boy;
235 Although in infancy a little wild,
        They tamed him down amongst them: to destroy
    His natural spirit not in vain they toiled.
        At least it seemed so; and his mother's joy
    Was to declare how sage, and still, and steady,
240 Her young philosopher was grown already.

54

Young Juan now was sixteen years of age,
    Tall, handsome, slender, but well knit: he seemed
Active, though not so sprightly, as a page;
    And everybody but his mother deemed
245 Him almost man; but she flew in a rage
    And bit her lips (for else she might have screamed)
If any said so, for to be precocious
Was in her eyes a thing the most atrocious.

55

Amongst her numerous acquaintance, all
250   Selected for discretion and devotion,
There was the Donna Julia, whom to call
    Pretty were but to give a feeble notion
Of many charms in her as natural
    As sweetness to the flower, or salt to ocean,
255 Her zone to Venus, or his bow to Cupid,
(But this last simile is trite and stupid).

60

Her eye (I'm very fond of handsome eyes)
    Was large and dark, suppressing half its fire
Until she spoke, then through its soft disguise
260   Flashed an expression more of pride than ire,
    And love than either; and there would arise
    A something in them which was not desire,
But would have been, perhaps, but for the soul
Which struggled through and chastened down the
    whole.

61

265 Her glossy hair was clustered o'er a brow
    Bright with intelligence, and fair, and smooth;
Her eyebrow's shape was like the aërial bow,
    Her cheek all purple with the beam of youth,
Mounting, at times, to a transparent glow,
270   As if her veins ran lightning; she, in sooth,
    Possessed an air and grace by no means common:
Her stature tall—I hate a dumpy woman.

62

Wedded she was some years, and to a man
    Of fifty, and such husbands are in plenty;
275 And yet, I think, instead of such a ONE
    'Twere better to have TWO of five-and-twenty,
    Especially in countries near the sun:
        And now I think on't, "mi vien in mente,"[7]

---

6. *Saint Augustine . . . Confessions.* In his *Confessions* Saint
Augustine describes a variety of his youthful sins.

7. *mi vien in mente,* it comes to mind (Italian).

Ladies even of the most uneasy virtue
280 Prefer a spouse whose age is short of thirty.

69

Juan she saw, and, as a pretty child,
  Caressed him often—such a thing might be
Quite innocently done, and harmless styled,
  When she had twenty years, and thirteen he;
285 But I am not so sure I should have smiled
  When he was sixteen, Julia twenty-three;
These few short years make wondrous alterations,
Particularly amongst sun-burnt nations.

70

Whate'er the cause might be, they had become
290   Changed; for the dame grew distant, the youth shy,
Their looks cast down, their greetings almost dumb,
  And much embarrassment in either eye;
There surely will be little doubt with some
  That Donna Julia knew the reason why,
295 But as for Juan, he had no more notion
Than he who never saw the sea of ocean.

71

Yet Julia's very coldness still was kind,
  And tremulously gentle her small hand
Withdrew itself from his, but left behind
300   A little pressure, thrilling, and so bland
And slight, so very slight, that to the mind
  'Twas but a doubt; but ne'er magician's wand
Wrought change with all Armida's[8] fairy art
  Like what this light touch left on Juan's heart.

72

305 And if she met him, though she smiled no more,
  She looked a sadness sweeter than her smile,
As if her heart had deeper thoughts in store
  She must not own, but cherished more the while
For that compression in its burning core;
310   Even innocence itself has many a wile,
And will not dare to trust itself with truth,
And love is taught hypocrisy from youth.

75

Poor Julia's heart was in an awkward state;
  She felt it going, and resolved to make
315 The noblest efforts for herself and mate,

For honour's, pride's, religion's, virtue's sake.
Her resolutions were most truly great,
  And almost might have made a Tarquin[9] quake:
She prayed the Virgin Mary for her grace,
320 As being the best judge of a lady's case.

76

She vowed she never would see Juan more,
  And next day paid a visit to his mother,
And looked extremely at the opening door,
  Which, by the Virgin's grace, let in another;
325 Grateful she was, and yet a little sore—
  Again it opens, it can be no other,
'Tis surely Juan now—No! I'm afraid
That night the Virgin was no further prayed.

77

She now determined that a virtuous woman
330   Should rather face an overcome temptation,
That flight was base and dastardly, and no man
  Should ever give her heart the least sensation;
That is to say, a thought beyond the common
  Preference, that we must feel upon occasion,
335 For people who are pleasanter than others,
But then they only seem so many brothers.

78

And even if by chance—and who can tell?
  The devil's so very sly—she should discover
That all within was not so very well,
340   And, if still free, that such or such a lover
Might please perhaps, a virtuous wife can quell
  Such thoughts, and be the better when they're
    over;
And if the man should ask, 'tis but denial:
I recommend young ladies to make trial.

79

345 And then there are such things as love divine,
  Bright and immaculate, unmixed and pure,
Such as the angles think so very fine,
  And matrons, who would be no less secure,
Platonic, perfect, "just such love as mine":
350   Thus Julia said—and thought so, to be sure;
And so I'd have her think, were I the man
On whom her reveries celestial ran.

---

8. *Armida*, a sorceress mentioned in the work of Torquato Tasso, Italian Renaissance poet (1544–1595).

9. *a Tarquin*, one of the legendary kings of ancient Rome noted for their lustiness.

86

So much for Julia. Now we'll turn to Juan.
    Poor little fellow! he had no idea
355 Of his own case, and never hit the true one;
    In feelings quick as Ovid's Miss Medea,[10]
He puzzled over what he found a new one,
    But not as yet imagined it could be a
Thing quite in course, and not at all alarming,
360 Which, with a little patience, might grow charming.

87

Silent and pensive, idle, restless, slow,
    His home deserted for the lonely wood,
Tormented with a wound he could not know,
    His, like all deep grief, plunged in solitude:
365 I'm fond myself of solitude or so,
    But then, I beg it may be understood,
By solitude I mean a Sultan's, not
A hermit's, with a haram for a grot.

90

Young Juan wandered by the glassy brooks,
370 Thinking unutterable things; he threw
Himself at length within the leafy nooks
    Where the wild branch of the cork forest grew;

---

10. *Ovid's Miss Medea.* In the *Metamorphoses*, Ovid presents Medea as a quick-tempered woman who took dreadful revenge on Jason for deserting her.

There poets find materials for their books,
    And every now and then we read them through,
375 So that their plan and prosody are eligible,
    Unless, like Wordsworth, they prove unintelligible.

91

He, Juan (and not Wordsworth), so pursued
    His self-communion with his own high soul,
Until his mighty heart, in its great mood,
380   Had mitigated part, though not the whole
Of its disease; he did the best he could
    With things not very subject to control,
And turned, without perceiving his condition,
Like Coleridge, into a metaphysician.

92

385 He thought about himself, and the whole earth,
    Of man the wonderful, and of the stars,
And how the deuce they ever could have birth;
    And then he thought of earthquakes, and of wars,
How many miles the moon might have in girth,
390   Of air-balloons, and of the many bars
To perfect knowledge of the boundless skies;—
And then he thought of Donna Julia's eyes.

There are 132 more stanzas in the remainder of Canto I of Don Juan. *Between 1819 and 1823 Byron added fifteen more cantos to the poem.*

DISCUSSION

1. In stanza 7 Byron states that the regularity of his plans for his epic poem "Forbids all wandering as the worst of sinning." Is his poem that formal? Does he digress? Does he make "asides" or off-the-cuff remarks? How is the formality or informality of the poem reflected in his "poetic" diction?

2. Reread the portrait of Donna Inez (Don Juan's mother) in stanzas 10 – 18. Byron says "Oh! she was perfect past all parallel." Was she?

3. What plans does Donna Inez have for her son? What is Byron's attitude toward these plans? Is there any suggestion that Don Juan might become the kind of "paragon" his mother has in mind? that he might become another type of "paragon"?

4. Which do you feel is the most sympathetic portrait Byron paints in these stanzas from *Don Juan*? On what do you base your opinion?

5. Most of Byron's stanzas contain some sort of "punch line." Locate a few examples. What is their effect? Describe the effect in terms of any of the following words: mild, sharp, stinging, savage, childish, merely clever, showy, profound.

WRITING

1. In Canto IV of *Don Juan*, Byron writes "if I laugh at any mortal thing / 'Tis that I may not weep." Write a short essay classifying the selection in this book from *Don Juan*: is it merely designed for amusement, or is it an earnest criticism of human weaknesses, or is it something in between?

2. "Beneath each quick and glittering wit lies a vast, dark chasm of despair." Explore the meaning of this statement in reference to Byron and also in reference to your personal observations of everyday wit and humor.

3. Byron said that poetry is "the lava of the imagination whose eruption prevents an earthquake." Write a short paper in which you discuss the poems in this volume that he may have written for emotional release.

4. *Don Juan* is a mock epic (note its beginning: "I want a hero"). Compare and contrast it with *The Rape of the Lock*, another mock epic.

Percy Bysshe Shelley — *The radical* 1792 / 1822

ENGLAND IN 1819 *injustices of society*
Sonnet

seen An old, mad, blind, despised, and dying king[1]—
Princes, the dregs of their dull race, who flow
Through public scorn—mud from a muddy spring;
Rulers who neither see, nor feel, nor know,
5 But leechlike to their fainting country cling,
Till they drop, blind in blood, without a blow;
A people starved and stabbed in the untilled field—
An army, which liberticide and prey
Makes as a two-edged sword to all who wield;
10 Golden and sanguine laws which tempt and slay;
Religion Christless, Godless—a book sealed;
A Senate—Time's worst statute[2] unrepealed—
Are graves, from which a glorious Phantom[3] may
Burst, to illumine our tempestuous day.

---

1. *An old . . . king,* George III, who died in 1820, blind and insane.
2. *Time's worst statute,* the law restricting the civil liberties of Roman Catholics, which was not repealed until 1829.
3. *Phantom,* revolution.

OZYMANDIAS — *Nothing human lasts forever*

I met a traveller from an antique land
Who said: Two vast and trunkless legs of stone
Stand in the desert . . . Near them, on the sand,
Half sunk, a shattered visage lies, whose frown,
5 And wrinkled lip, and sneer of cold command,
Tell that its sculptor well those passions read
Which yet survive, stamped on these lifeless things,
The hand that mocked them, and the heart that fed:
And on the pedestal these words appear:
10 "My name is Ozymandias, king of kings:
Look on my works, ye Mighty, and despair!"
Nothing beside remains. Round the decay
Of that colossal wreck, boundless and bare
The lone and level sands stretch far away.

SONG TO THE MEN OF ENGLAND
Challenge to working men of England to unite

1
Men of England, wherefore plow
For the lords who lay ye low?
Wherefore weave with toil and care
The rich robes your tyrants wear?

2
5 Wherefore feed, and clothe, and save,
From the cradle to the grave,
Those ungrateful drones who would
Drain your sweat—nay, drink your blood?

3
Wherefore, Bees of England, forge
10 Many a weapon, chain, and scourge,
That these stingless drones may spoil
The forced produce of your toil?

4
Have ye leisure, comfort, calm,
Shelter, food, love's gentle balm?
15 Or what is it ye buy so dear
With your pain and with your fear?

rhetorical question (answer is in the question)

5
The seed ye sow, another reaps;
The wealth ye find, another keeps;
The robes ye weave, another wears;
20 The arms ye forge, another bears.

6
Sow seed—but let no tyrant reap;
Find wealth—let no impostor heap;
Weave robes—let not the idle wear;
Forge arms—in your defense to bear.

7
25 Shrink to your cellars, holes, and cells;
In halls ye deck another dwells.
Why shake the chains ye wrought? Ye see
The steel ye tempered glance on ye.

8
With plow and spade, and hoe and loom,
30 Trace your grave, and build your tomb,
And weave your winding-sheet, till fair
England be your sepulcher.

MUTABILITY — *something that changes*

We are as clouds that veil the midnight moon;
How restlessly they speed, and gleam, and quiver,
Streaking the darkness radiantly!—yet soon
Night closes round, and they are lost for ever:

5 Or like forgotten lyres, whose dissonant strings
Give various response to each varying blast,
To whose frail frame no second motion brings
One mood or modulation like the last.

We rest.—A dream has power to poison sleep;
10 We rise.—One wandering thought pollutes the day;
We feel, conceive or reason, laugh or weep;
Embrace fond woe, or cast our cares away:

It is the same!—For, be it joy or sorrow,
The path of its departure still is free:
15 Man's yesterday may ne'er be like his morrow;
Nought may endure but Mutability.

MUSIC, WHEN SOFT VOICES DIE

Just because something dies, there is still a memory of it

Music, when soft voices die,
Vibrates in the memory—
Odours, when sweet violets sicken,
Live within the sense they quicken.

5 Rose leaves, when the rose is dead,
Are heaped for the belovèd's bed;
And so thy thoughts, when thou art gone,
Love itself shall slumber on.

A DIRGE — *a funeral song*

death fall

Rough wind, that moanest loud
Grief too sad for song;
Wild wind, when sullen cloud
Knells all the night long;
5 Sad storm, whose tears are vain,
Bare woods, whose branches strain,
Deep caves and dreary main—
Wail, for the world's wrong!

DETAIL FROM "CALAIS PIER, WITH FRENCH POISSARDS PREPARING FOR SEA: AN ENGLISH PACKET ARRIV[ING]" BY JOSEPH M. W. TURNER (EXHIBITED IN 1803). REPRODUCED BY COURTESY OF THE TRUSTEES, THE NATIONAL GALLERY, LONDON.

ODE TO THE WEST WIND

-The wind's effect on nature, him, ~~and~~ the power of the wind

1

O WILD West Wind, thou breath of Autumn's
    being,
Thou, from whose unseen presence the leaves dead
Are driven, like ghosts from an enchanter fleeing,

Yellow, and black, and pale, and hectic red,
5 Pestilence-stricken multitudes: O thou,
Who chariotest to their dark wintry bed

The wingèd seeds, where they lie cold and low,
Each like a corpse within its grave, until
Thine azure sister of the Spring shall blow
    'Blue
10 Her clarion o'er the dreaming earth, and fill
(Driving sweet buds like flocks to feed in air)
With living hues and odors plain and hill:

Wild Spirit, which art moving everywhere;
Destroyer and preserver; hear, oh, hear!

2

15 Thou on whose stream, mid the steep sky's
    commotion,
Loose clouds like earth's decaying leaves are shed,
Shook from the tangled boughs of Heaven and
    Ocean,

Angels of rain and lightning: there are spread
On the blue surface of thine aëry surge,
20 Like the bright hair uplifted from the head

Of some fierce Maenad,[1] even from the dim verge
Of the horizon to the zenith's height,
The locks of the approaching storm. Thou dirge *-funereal song*

Of the dying year, to which this closing night
25 Will be the dome of a vast sepulcher, *-tomb*
Vaulted with all thy congregated might

Of vapors, from whose solid atmosphere
Black rain, and fire, and hail will burst: oh hear!

3

Thou who didst waken from his summer dreams
30 The blue Mediterranean, where he lay,
Lulled by the coil of his crystalline streams,

Beside a pumice isle in Baiae's bay,[2]
And saw in sleep old palaces and towers
Quivering within the wave's intenser day,

35 All overgrown with azure moss and flowers
So sweet, the sense faints picturing them! Thou
For whose path the Atlantic's level powers

Cleave themselves into chasms, while far below
The sea-blooms and the oozy woods which wear
40 The sapless foliage of the ocean, know

Thy voice, and suddenly grow gray with fear,
And tremble and despoil themselves: oh, hear!

4

If I were a dead leaf thou mightest bear,
If I were a swift cloud to fly with thee;
45 A wave to pant beneath thy power, and share

The impulse of thy strength, only less free
Than thou, O uncontrollable! If even
I were as in my boyhood, and could be

The comrade of thy wanderings over Heaven,
50 As then, when to outstrip thy skyey speed
Scarce seemed a vision; I would ne'er have striven

As thus with thee in prayer in my sore need.
Oh, lift me as a wave, a leaf, a cloud!
I fall upon the thorns of life! I bleed!

                       (more)

---

1. *Maenad* (mē′nad), a priestess of Bacchus, god of wine.

2. *Baiae's* (bä′yäz) *bay*. The village of Baia is a seaport about ten miles from Naples in Italy.

55 A heavy weight of hours has chained and bowed
One too like thee: tameless, and swift, and proud.

5

Make me thy lyre, even as the forest is:
What if my leaves are falling like its own!
The tumult of thy mighty harmonies

60 Will take from both a deep, autumnal tone,
Sweet though in sadness. Be thou, Spirit fierce,
My spirit! Be thou me, impetuous one!

Drive my dead thoughts over the universe
Like withered leaves to quicken a new birth!
65 And, by the incantation of this verse,

Scatter, as from an unextinguished hearth
Ashes and sparks, my words among mankind!
Be through my lips to unawakened earth

The trumpet of a prophecy! O Wind,
70 If Winter comes, can Spring be far behind?

DISCUSSION

England in 1819

1. What is the literal "argument" of this sonnet?
2. What imagery in the sonnet gives the argument its strongest impact, in your opinion?

Ozymandias

1. What is the irony of the inscription on the pedestal?
2. How does the imagery of the poem reinforce the double meaning of the word "despair"?

Song to the Men of England

1. What in your opinion is Shelley's general attitude toward the men of England? Is he sympathetic, or contemptuous?
2. Compare this song with the sonnet "England in 1819." Is there any similarity of tone or theme between the two? Which uses the stronger imagery?

Mutability

Which of the following statements do you think best embodies the theme of "Mutability"? (a) Tomorrow and tomorrow and tomorrow creeps in its petty pace from day to day. (b) The only certainty is change. (c) Sad today, glad tomorrow. Support your choice by referring to the poem.

A Dirge

Reread "Westron Wind" on page 105 and compare it with this lyric. What differences do you find? Which poem do you prefer? Why?

Ode to the West Wind

1. What two contradictory forces does the West Wind represent? What echoes of this paradox do you find throughout the poem? In what sense is the West Wind a spirit "moving everywhere"?
2. Choose from the poem what you consider the two or three most dramatic images of the West Wind's intensity. What qualities of language or physical description convey the idea or feeling of force?

John Keats *sad life: died of T.B.* 1795 / 1821

NATIONAL PORTRAIT GALLERY, LONDON

WHEN I HAVE FEARS
Sonnet — *Afraid of dying before he has a chance to do what he wants*

When I have fears that I may cease to be
Before my pen has gleaned my teeming brain,
Before high-pilèd books, in charact'ry,
Hold like rich garners the full-ripened grain;
5 When I behold, upon the night's starred face,
Huge cloudy symbols of a high romance,
And think that I may never live to trace
Their shadows, with the magic hand of chance;
And when I feel, fair creature of an hour,
10 That I shall never look upon thee more,
Never have relish in the faery power
Of unreflecting love!—then on the shore
Of the wide world I stand alone, and think
Till Love and Fame to nothingness do sink.

BRIGHT STAR, WOULD I WERE STEDFAST
— Be permanent not temporary and die

Bright star, would I were stedfast as thou art—
Not in lone splendour hung aloft the night
And watching, with eternal lids apart,
Like nature's patient, sleepless Eremite,[1]
5 The moving waters at their priestlike task
Of pure ablution round earth's human shores,
Or gazing on the new soft-fallen mask
Of snow upon the mountains and the moors—
No—yet still stedfast, still unchangeable,
10 Pillowed upon my fair love's ripening breast,
To feel for ever its soft fall and swell,
Awake for ever in a sweet unrest,
Still, still to hear her tender-taken breath,
And so live ever—or else swoon to death.

---

1. *Eremite,* hermit; guardian.

THIS LIVING HAND[1]
— She shouldn't worry about his death

This living hand, now warm and capable
Of earnest grasping, would, if it were cold
And in the icy silence of the tomb,
So haunt thy days and chill thy dreaming nights
5 That thou would[st] wish thine own heart dry of
    blood
So in my veins red life might stream again,
And thou be conscience-calm'd—see here it is—
I hold it towards you.

---

1. This poem was supposedly written for Fanny Brawne, with whom Keats was in love.

ON FIRST LOOKING INTO CHAPMAN'S HOMER
Sonnet

Much have I travelled in the realms of gold,
And many goodly states and kingdoms seen;
Round many western islands have I been
Which bards in fealty to Apollo hold.
5 Oft of one wide expanse had I been told
That deep-brow'd Homer ruled as his demesne;[1]
Yet did I never breathe its pure serene
Till I heard Chapman speak out loud and bold:
Then felt I like some watcher of the skies
10 When a new planet swims into his ken;
Or like stout Cortez when with eagle eyes
He stared at the Pacific—and all his men
Looked at each other with a wild surmise—
Silent, upon a peak in Darien.

---

1. *demesne*, domain.

OF CRITICAL INTEREST

Did Keats make an ignorant blunder?

The fact that Balboa, not Cortez, first discovered the Pacific has disturbed commentators on Keats's sonnet "On First Looking into Chapman's Homer" for many years. Why does Keats, who was a voracious reader from boyhood and acquainted with most of the available literature on historic voyages, use Cortez as his symbol of discovery? Perhaps he deliberately chose Cortez to imply that one need not be "the first" to make a discovery for that discovery to have profound personal significance. After all, Keats was not the first to read Chapman's famous translation of Homer (which had been in print for two centuries), nor was his discovery of Chapman's version his first contact with Homer (he had read Pope's translation). Yet the force of his discovery was such that it left him overwhelmed by a kind of personal illumination grasped for the first time.

The story is that Keats stayed up the whole night reading the translation with his friend and former teacher, Charles Cowden Clarke. Keats walked home at dawn, and Clarke received the sonnet in the mail later the same morning.

We who live in a competitive age of rapidly proliferating "firsts"—first man on the moon, first heart transplant—may think it strange of Keats to mention Cortez, who was second. But Keats was not talking about outward accomplishments; he was talking about the satisfactions of an inner voyage, where "first" no longer counts.

TO AUTUMN — *about autumn (dying)*

1

Season of mists and mellow fruitfulness,
Close bosom-friend of the maturing sun;
Conspiring with him how to load and bless
With fruit the vines that round the thatch-eaves run;
5 To bend with apples the mossed cottage-trees,
And fill all fruit with ripeness to the core;
To swell the gourd, and plump the hazel shells
With a sweet kernel; to set budding more,
And still more, later flowers for the bees,
10 Until they think warm days will never cease,
For Summer has o'er-brimmed their clammy cells.

2

Who hath not seen thee oft amid thy store?
Sometimes whoever seeks abroad may find
Thee sitting careless on a granary floor,
15 Thy hair soft-lifted by the winnowing wind;
Or on a half-reaped furrow sound asleep,
Drowsed with the fume of poppies, while thy hook
Spares the next swath and all its twinèd flowers:
And sometimes like a gleaner thou dost keep
20 Steady thy laden head across a brook;
Or by a cider-press, with patient look,
Thou watchest the last oozings hours by hours.

3

Where are the songs of Spring? Aye, where are they?
Think not of them, thou hast thy music too—
25 While barred clouds bloom the soft-dying day,
And touch the stubble-plains with rosy hue;
Then in a wailful choir the small gnats mourn
Among the river sallows,[1] borne aloft
Or sinking as the light wind lives or dies;
30 And full-grown lambs loud bleat from hilly bourn;
Hedge crickets sing; and now with treble soft
The redbreast whistles from a garden croft;
And gathering swallows twitter in the skies.

———————
1. *sallows,* willows.

DISCUSSION

This Living Hand
Compare these lines with the sonnet "When I Have Fears." Which is the more direct statement of "unreflecting love"? Which is more convincing?

Bright Star. . . .
What is the one word in this sonnet which emphasizes its theme? State that theme in one or two sentences.

On First Looking into Chapman's Homer
What does the last line—"Silent, upon a peak in Darien"—suggest about the feelings Keats experienced when he first read the book?

To Autumn
1. Shortly after this poem was composed on September 19, 1819, Keats wrote to a friend: "I never liked stubble fields so much as now—Aye, better than the chilly green of the spring. Somehow a stubble field looks warm. . . ." What in the poem would explain Keats's preference?
2. Compare Keats's attitude toward autumn with Shelley's in "Ode to the West Wind." What differences do you find?
3. Discuss "To Autumn" in the context of Keats's life and in terms of this opinion: "Keats's Ode overflows with all the sensations of those warm and drowsy days just before the onslaught of winter, when the world and one's relation to it seem a promise totally fulfilled. During that short season one lives every day as if it were an unexpected reprieve, knowing full well what it will be like after the first killing frost."

WRITING

The poet symbolizes Autumn as a mythic person; yet describes the signs of Fall in very real terms. How would you describe or personify this season? Write a brief essay or poem, using an image that seems to you to best portray Autumn. Let your imagination run free.

Praise of a Vase (old greek vase, used for cremated ashes, water, oil, wine)

ODE ON A GRECIAN URN

represents eternal life

THOU still unravished *(raped)* bride of quietness,
  Thou foster child of Silence and slow Time,
Sylvan historian, who canst thus express
A flowery tale more sweetly than our rime—
5 What leaf-fringed legend haunts about thy shape
  Of deities or mortals, or of both,
    In Tempe[1] or the dales of Arcady?[2]
    What men or gods are these? What maidens loath?
What mad pursuit? What struggle to escape?
10   What pipes and timbrels? What wild ecstasy?

Heard melodies are sweet, but those unheard
  Are sweeter; therefore, ye soft pipes, play on;
Not to the sensual ear, but, more endeared,
  Pipe to the spirit ditties of no tone.
15 Fair youth, beneath the trees, thou canst not leave
  Thy song, nor ever can those trees be bare;
    Bold lover, never, never canst thou kiss,
    Though winning near the goal—yet, do not grieve;
She cannot fade, though thou hast not thy bliss,
20   Forever wilt thou love, and she be fair!

Ah, happy, happy boughs! that cannot shed
  Your leaves, nor ever bid the spring adieu;
And, happy melodist, unwearièd,
  Forever piping songs forever new.
25 More happy love! more happy, happy love!

Forever warm and still to be enjoyed,
  Forever panting, and forever young;
All breathing human passion far above,
That leaves a heart high-sorrowful and cloyed,
30   A burning forehead, and a parching tongue.

Who are these coming to the sacrifice?
  To what green altar, O mysterious priest,
Lead'st thou that heifer lowing at the skies,
  And all her silken flanks with garlands dressed?
35 What little town by river or seashore,
  Or mountain-built with peaceful citadel,
    Is emptied of this folk, this pious morn?
    And, little town, thy streets forevermore
Will silent be; and not a soul to tell
40   Why thou art desolate, can e'er return.

O Attic shape![3] Fair attitude! with brede[4]
  Of marble men and maidens overwrought,
With forest branches and the trodden weed;
  Thou, silent form! dost tease us out of thought
45 As doth eternity: Cold pastoral!
  When old age shall this generation waste,
  Thou shalt remain, in midst of other woe
Than ours, a friend to man, to whom thou say'st,
"Beauty is truth, truth beauty—that is all
50   Ye know on earth, and all ye need to know."

---

1. *Tempe*, a beautiful valley in Thessaly in Greece.
2. *Arcady*, Arcadia, a part of ancient Greece, celebrated in pastoral poetry as the home of an ideal shepherd life.

3. *Attic shape*, a shape representing the simple, elegant taste of Athens.
4. *brede*, embroidery.

DISCUSSION

1. What specifically is the source of the "happiness" that Keats sees in the scene depicted on the urn? How is such "happiness" related to the statement: "Heard melodies are sweet, but those unheard / Are sweeter"? Why might Keats's final judgment of the urn be: "*Cold* pastoral"?

2. Describe the scenes depicted on the urn in as much detail as the poem allows. Do you get a clear picture, or an indistinct one?
3. What truths do you think the urn conveys about the human condition? What might Keats mean by "beauty"?

Pretty lady that doesn't have any pity

LA BELLE DAME SANS MERCI[1]

1
O what can ail thee, Knight at arms,
   Alone and palely loitering?
The sedge has withered from the Lake
   And no birds sing!

2
5 O what can ail thee, Knight at arms,
   So haggard, and so woebegone?
The squirrel's granary is full
   And the harvest's done.

3
I see a lily on thy brow
10 With anguish moist and fever dew,
And on thy cheeks a fading rose
   Fast withereth too.

4
I met a Lady in the Meads,
   Full beautiful, a faery's child,
15 Her hair was long, her foot was light
   And her eyes were wild.

5
I made a Garland for her head,
  · And bracelets too, and fragrant Zone;[2]
She looked at me as she did love
20 And made sweet moan.

6
I set her on my pacing steed
   And nothing else saw all day long,
For sidelong would she bend and sing
   A faery's song.

7
25 She found me roots of relish sweet,
   And honey wild, and manna dew,
And sure in language strange she said
   "I love thee true."

8
She took me to her elfin grot
30 And there she wept and sighed full sore,
And there I shut her wild wild eyes
   With kisses four.

9
And there she lullèd me asleep,
   And there I dreamed, Ah Woe betide!
35 The latest dream I ever dreamt
   On the cold hill side.

10
I saw pale Kings, and Princes too,
   Pale warriors, death-pale were they all;
They cried, "La belle dame sans merci
40 Thee hath in thrall!"

11
I saw their starved lips in the gloam
   With horrid warning gapèd wide,
And I awoke, and found me here
   On the cold hill's side.

12
45 And this is why I sojourn here,
   Alone and palely loitering;
Though the sedge is withered from the Lake
   And no birds sing.

1. The title means "The Lovely Lady Without Pity."
2. *Zone*, girdle.

DISCUSSION

1. What kind of "enthrallment" does the lady impose? Is it the imprisonment of physical love, or the confinements of a world of misleading fancy? Might it be the confines of a temporal world where youth and youthful love grow into withered old age? Other theories?

2. What effects has this "enthrallment" had on the knight? What are the overtones of the last two lines of the poem in respect to his condition?

Keats comes very close to death

ODE TO A NIGHTINGALE

Summer

My heart aches, and a drowsy numbness pains
    My sense, as though of hemlock[1] I had drunk,
Or emptied some dull opiate to the drains
    One minute past, and Lethe-wards[2] had sunk.
5 'Tis not through envy of thy happy lot,
    But being too happy in thine happiness—
        That thou, light-wingèd Dryad[3] of the trees,
            In some melodious plot
Of beechen green, and shadows numberless,
10   Singest of summer in full-throated ease.

Turn to drinking

O for a draft of vintage! that hath been
    Cooled a long age in the deep-delvèd earth,
Tasting of Flora[4] and the country green,
    Dance, and Provencal song,[5] and sunburnt mirth!
15 O for a beaker full of the warm South,
    Full of the true, the blushful Hippocrene,[6]
        With beaded bubbles winking at the brim,
            And purple-stainèd mouth;
That I might drink, and leave the world unseen,
20   And with thee fade away into the forest dim—

nightingale

Fade far away/dissolve, and quite forget
    What thou among the leaves hast never known,
The weariness, the fever, and the fret
    Here, where men sit and hear each other groan;
25 Where palsy shakes a few, sad, last gray hairs,
    Where youth grows pale, and specter-thin, and
        dies;
    Where but to think is to be full of sorrow
        And leaden-eyed despairs,
Where Beauty cannot keep her lustrous eyes,
30   Or new love pine at them beyond tomorrow.

Away! away! for I will fly to thee,
    Not charioted by Bacchus[7] and his pards,
But on the viewless[8] wings of poesy, *poetry*

Though the dull brain perplexes and retards.
35 Already with thee! tender is the night,
    And haply the Queen-Moon is on her throne,
        Clustered around by all her starry fays;
            But here there is no light,
Save what from heaven is with the breezes blown
40   Through verdurous glooms and winding mossy
            ways.

branches

I cannot see what flowers are at my feet,
    Nor what soft incense hangs upon the boughs,
But, in embalmèd darkness, guess each sweet
    Wherewith the seasonable month endows
45 The grass, the thicket, and the fruit tree wild;
    White hawthorn, and the pastoral eglantine;
        Fast fading violets covered up in leaves;
            And mid-May's eldest child,
The coming muskrose, full of dewy wine,
50   The murmurous haunt of flies on summer eves.

Death

Darkling I listen; and, for many a time,
    I have been half in love with easeful Death,
Called him soft names in many a musèd rime,
    To take into the air my quiet breath;
55 Now more than ever seems it rich to die,
    To cease upon the midnight with no pain,
        While thou art pouring forth thy soul abroad
            In such an ecstasy!
Still wouldst thou sing, and I have ears in vain—
60   To thy high requiem become a sod.

Thou wast not born for death, immortal Bird!
    No hungry generations tread thee down;
The voice I hear this passing night was heard
    In ancient days by emperor and clown;[9]
65 Perhaps the selfsame song that found a path
    Through the sad heart of Ruth, when sick for home,
        She stood in tears amid the alien corn;[10]
            The same that ofttimes hath
Charmed magic casements, opening on the foam
70   Of perilous seas, in faery lands forlorn.

---

1. *hemlock*, a poison.
2. *Lethe-wards*, towards Lethe, the river of forgetfulness in Hades.
3. *Dryad*, a tree nymph.
4. *Flora*, goddess of the flowers and the spring.
5. *Provençal song*. Provence in southern France was famous in the Middle Ages for the songs of its troubadours.
6. *Hippocrene*, a fountain on Mt. Helicon in Greece, sacred to the Muses.
7. *Bacchus*, god of wine, who was often represented as riding in a carriage drawn by leopards (pards).
8. *viewless*, invisible.

9. *clown*, peasant.
10. *Ruth . . . corn*. According to the Bible story, Ruth left her homeland to go with Naomi, her mother-in-law, to Judah, a foreign country to her, where she worked in the corn (wheat) fields (Ruth 2:1–23).

Forlorn! the very word is like a bell
    To toll me back from thee to my sole self.
Adieu! the fancy cannot cheat so well
    As she is famed to do, deceiving elf.
75 Adieu! adieu! thy plaintive anthem fades

Past the near meadows, over the still stream,
    Up the hillside; and now 'tis buried deep
        In the next valley glades.
    Was it a vision, or a waking dream?
80   Fled is that music.—Do I wake or sleep?   □

DISCUSSION

1. What are the probable causes of Keats's sense of "heartache" and "drowsy numbness" as given in the poem?
2. In what sense can this poem be called a reverie about "escaping" from the world? What possible means of escape are suggested? Why does Keats finally reject them all?
3. What role do the poet, the nightingale, and Ruth play?
4. What does Keats mean by lines 73–74: "the fancy cannot cheat so well / As she is famed to do"? How is this related to his "forlorn" state?

THE EVE OF ST. AGNES

St. Agnes, who was martyred in Rome around A.D. 300 at the age of thirteen, was the patron saint of virgins. In the Middle Ages there developed the legend on which this poem is based—that by following a certain ritual on St. Agnes' Eve (January 20), a virtuous maiden might see her future husband in a dream.

1
St. AGNES' Eve—Ah, bitter chill it was!
The owl, for all his feathers, was a-cold;
The hare limped trembling through the frozen grass,
And silent was the flock in woolly fold:
5 Numb were the Beadsman's[1] fingers while he told
His rosary, and while his frosted breath,
Like pious incense from a censer old,
Seemed taking flight for heaven, without a death,
Past the sweet Virgin's picture, while his prayer he
        saith.

2
10 His prayer he saith, this patient, holy man;
Then takes his lamp, and riseth from his knees,
And back returneth, meager, barefoot, wan,
Along the chapel aisle by slow degrees:
The sculptured dead, on each side, seem to freeze,
15 Imprisoned in black, purgatorial rails:

---

1. *Beadsman*, a dependent whose whole duty was to pray for his benefactor.

Knights, ladies, praying in dumb orat'ries,
He passeth by, and his weak spirit fails
To think how they may ache in icy hoods and mails.

3
Northward he turneth through a little door,
20 And scarce three steps, ere Music's golden tongue
Flattered to tears this aged man and poor;
But no—already had his death-bell rung:
The joys of all his life were said and sung:
His was harsh penance on St. Agnes' Eve:
25 Another way he went, and soon among
Rough ashes sat he for his soul's reprieve,
And all night kept awake, for sinners' sake to grieve.

4
That ancient Beadsman heard the prelude soft;
And so it chanced, for many a door was wide,
30 From hurry to and fro. Soon, up aloft,
The silver, snarling trumpets 'gan to chide:
The level chambers, ready with their pride,
Were glowing to receive a thousand guests.

The carved angels, ever eager-eyed,
35 Stared, where upon their heads the cornice rests,
With hair blown back, and wings put crosswise on
        their breasts.

5

At length burst in the argent revelry,
With plume, tiara, and all rich array,
Numerous as shadows haunting faerily
40 The brain new-stuffed, in youth, with triumphs gay
Of old romance. These let us wish away,
And turn, sole-thoughted, to one Lady there,
Whose heart had brooded, all that wintry day,
On love, and winged St. Agnes' saintly care,
45 As she had heard old dames full many times declare.

6

They told her how, upon St. Agnes' Eve,
Young virgins might have visions of delight,
And soft adorings from their loves receive
Upon the honeyed middle of the night,
50 If ceremonies due they did aright;
As, supperless to bed they must retire,
And couch supine their beauties, lily white;
Nor look behind, nor sideways, but require
Of Heaven with upward eyes for all that they desire.

7

55 Full of this whim was thoughtful Madeline:
The music, yearning like a God in pain,
She scarcely heard: her maiden eyes divine,
Fixed on the floor, saw many a sweeping train
Pass by—she heeded not at all: in vain
60 Came many a tiptoe, amorous cavalier,
And back retired; not cooled by high disdain,
But she saw not: her heart was otherwhere;
She sighed for Agnes' dreams, the sweetest of the
        year.

8

She danced along with vague, regardless eyes,
65 Anxious her lips, her breathing quick and short:
The hallowed hour was near at hand: she sighs
Amid the timbrels, and the thronged resort
Of whisperers in anger or in sport;
'Mid looks of love, defiance, hate, and scorn,
70 Hoodwinked with faery fancy; all amort,[2]
Save to St. Agnes and her lambs unshorn,[3]
And all the bliss to be before tomorrow morn.

---

2. *amort*, deadened.
3. *St. Agnes and her lambs unshorn.* St. Agnes' day was originally
celebrated by the sacrifice of two lambs, their wool to be woven
later by chosen nuns.

9

So, purposing each moment to retire,
She lingered still. Meantime, across the moors,
75 Had come young Porphyro, with heart on fire
For Madeline. Beside the portal doors,
Buttressed from moonlight, stands he, and implores
All saints to give him sight of Madeline,
But for one moment in the tedious hours,
80 That he might gaze and worship all unseen;
Perchance speak, kneel, touch, kiss—in sooth such
        things have been.

10

He ventures in: let no buzzed whisper tell,
All eyes be muffled, or a hundred swords
Will storm his heart, Love's feverous citadel:
85 For him, those chambers held barbarian hordes,
Hyena foemen, and hot-blooded lords,
Whose very dogs would execrations howl
Against his lineage; not one breast affords
Him any mercy in that mansion foul,
90 Save one old beldame, weak in body and in soul.

11

Ah, happy chance! the aged creature came,
Shuffling along with ivory-headed wand,
To where he stood, hid from the torch's flame,
Behind a broad hall pillar, far beyond
95 The sound of merriment and chorus bland.
He startled her: but soon she knew his face,
And grasped his fingers in her palsied hand,
Saying, "Mercy, Porphyro! hie thee from this place;
They are all here tonight, the whole blood-thirsty
        race!

12

100 "Get hence! get hence! there's dwarfish Hildebrand:
He had a fever late, and in the fit
He cursed thee and thine, both house and land:
Then there's that old Lord Maurice, not a whit
More tame for his gray hairs—Alas me! flit!
105 Flit like a ghost away."—"Ah, Gossip[4] dear,
We're safe enough; here in this arm-chair sit,
And tell me how—" "Good saints! not here, not here!
Follow me, child, or else these stones will be
        thy bier."

13

He followed through a lowly archèd way,
110 Brushing the cobwebs with his lofty plume;

---

4. *Gossip*, friend.

And as she muttered "Well-a—well-a-day!"
He found him in a little moonlight room,
Pale, latticed, chill, and silent as a tomb.
"Now tell me where is Madeline," said he,
115 "O tell me, Angela, by the holy loom
Which none but secret sisterhood may see,
When they St. Agnes' wool are weaving piously."

14

"St. Agnes! Ah! it is St. Agnes' Eve—
Yet men will murder upon holy days.
120 Thou must hold water in a witch's sieve,[5]
And be liege-lord of all the Elves and Fays
To venture so: it fills me with amaze
To see thee, Porphyro!—St. Agnes' Eve!
God's help! my lady fair the conjurer plays
125 This very night: good angels her deceive!
But let me laugh awhile,—I've mickle time to grieve."

15

Feebly she laugheth in the languid moon,
While Porphyro upon her face doth look,
Like puzzled urchin on an aged crone
130 Who keepeth closed a wondrous riddlebook,
As spectacled she sits in chimney nook.
But soon his eyes grew brilliant, when she told
His lady's purpose; and he scarce could brook
Tears, at the thought of those enchantments cold,
135 And Madeline asleep in lap of legends old.

16

Sudden a thought came like a full-blown rose,
Flushing his brow, and in his pained heart
Made purple riot: then doth he propose
A stratagem, that makes the beldame start:
140 "A cruel man and impious thou art!
Sweet lady, let her pray, and sleep and dream
Alone with her good angels, far apart
From wicked men like thee. Go, go! I deem
Thou canst not surely be the same that thou didst
    seem."

17

145 "I will not harm her, by all saints I swear!"
Quoth Porphyro: "O may I ne'er find grace
When my weak voice shall whisper its last prayer,
If one of her soft ringlets I displace,
Or look with ruffian passion in her face.

150 Good Angela, believe me, by these tears;
Or I will, even in moment's space,
Awake, with horrid shout, my foemen's ears,
And beard them, though they be more fanged than
    wolves and bears."

18

"Ah! why wilt thou affright a feeble soul?
155 A poor, weak, palsy-stricken, churchyard thing,
Whose passing-bell may ere the midnight toll;
Whose prayers for thee, each morn and evening,
Were never missed." Thus plaining, doth she bring
A gentler speech from burning Porphyro;
160 So woeful, and of such deep sorrowing,
That Angela gives promise she will do
Whatever he shall wish, betide her weal or woe.

19

Which was, to lead him, in close secrecy,
Even to Madeline's chamber, and there hide
165 Him in a closet, of such privacy
That he might see her beauty unespied,
And win perhaps that night a peerless bride,
While legioned fairies paced the coverlet,
And pale enchantment held her sleepy-eyed.
170 Never on such a night have lovers met,
Since Merlin paid his Demon all the monstrous debt.[6]

20

"It shall be as thou wishest," said the Dame:
"All cates and dainties shall be stored there
Quickly on this feast-night: by the tambour frame
175 Her own lute thou wilt see: no time to spare,
For I am slow and feeble, and scarce dare
On such a catering trust my dizzy head.
Wait here, my child, with patience: kneel in prayer
The while. Ah! thou must needs the lady wed,
180 Or may I never leave my grave among the dead."

21

So saying she hobbled off with busy fear.
The lover's endless minutes slowly passed;
The dame returned, and whispered in his ear
To follow her; with aged eyes aghast
185 From fright of dim espial. Safe at last
Through many a dusky gallery, they gain
The maiden's chamber, silken, hushed and chaste;

5. *hold water . . . sieve,* a sign of supernatural power.

6. *Since Merlin . . . debt.* Merlin, the famous wizard of King Arthur's court, was the son of a demon. He was killed by the sorceress Vivien who used a spell he himself had taught her.

Where Porphyro took covert, pleased amain.
His poor guide hurried back with agues in her brain.

22

190 Her faltering hand upon the balustrade,
Old Angela was feeling for the stair,
When Madeline, St. Agnes' charmed maid,
Rose, like a missioned spirit, unaware:
With silver taper's light, and pious care,
195 She turned and down the aged gossip led
To a safe level matting. Now prepare,
Young Porphyro, for gazing on that bed;
She comes, she comes again, like ring-dove frayed[7] and fled.

23

Out went the taper as she hurried in;
200 Its little smoke, in pallid moonshine, died:
She closed the door, she panted, all akin
To spirits of the air, and visions wide:
No uttered syllable, or, woe betide!
But to her heart, her heart was voluble,
205 Paining with eloquence her balmy side;
As though a tongueless nightingale should swell
Her throat in vain, and die, heart-stifled, in her dell.

24

A casement high and triple-arched there was,
All garlanded with carven imageries,
210 Of fruits, and flowers, and bunches of knotgrass,
And diamonded with panes of quaint device,
Innumerable of stains and splendid dyes,
As are the tiger-moth's deep-damasked wings,
And in the midst, 'mong thousand heraldries,
215 And twilight saints, and dim emblazonings,
A shielded scutcheon blushed with blood of queens and kings.

25

Full on this casement shone the wintry moon,
And threw warm gules[8] on Madeline's fair breast,
As down she knelt for Heaven's grace and boon;
220 Rose-bloom fell on her hands, together prest,
And on her silver cross soft amethyst,
And on her hair a glory, like a saint:
She seemed a splendid angel, newly drest,
Save wings, for heaven:—Porphyro grew faint:
225 She knelt, so pure a thing, so free from mortal taint.

26

Anon his heart revives: her vespers done,
Of all its wreathed pearls her hair she frees;
Unclasps her warmed jewels one by one;
Loosens her fragrant bodice; by degrees
230 Her rich attire creeps rustling to her knees:
Half-hidden, like a mermaid in sea-weed,
Pensive awhile she dreams awake, and sees,
In fancy, fair St. Agnes in her bed,
But dares not look behind, or all the charm is fled.

27

235 Soon, trembling in her soft and chilly nest,
In sort of wakeful swoon, perplexed she lay,
Until the poppied warmth of sleep oppressed
Her soothed limbs, and soul fatigued away;
Flown, like a thought, until the morrow-day;
240 Blissfully havened both from joy and pain;
Clasped like a missal where swart Paynims pray;[9]
Blinded alike from sunshine and from rain,
As though a rose should shut, and be a bud again.

28

Stolen to this paradise, and so entranced,
245 Porphyro gazed upon her empty dress,
And listened to her breathing, if it chanced
To wake into a slumberous tenderness;
Which when he heard, that minute did he bless,
And breathed himself: then from the closet crept,
250 Noiseless as fear in a wide wilderness,
And over the hushed carpet, silent, stept,
And 'tween the curtains peeped, where, lo!—how fast she slept.

29

Then by the bed-side, where the faded moon
Made a dim, silver twilight, soft he set
255 A table, and, half anguished, threw thereon
A cloth of woven crimson, gold and jet:—
O for some drowsy Morphean amulet![10]
The boisterous, midnight, festive clarion,
The kettle-drum, and far-heard clarinet,
260 Affray his ears, though but in dying tone:—
The hall-door shuts again, and all the noise is gone.

---

7. *frayed,* frightened.
8. *gules,* red colors from the stained glass.

9. *Clasped . . . pray,* shut like a prayer book which pagans would have no occasion to open.
10. *Morphean amulet,* a sleep-producing charm. Morpheus was the god of sleep.

30

And still she slept an azure-lidded sleep,
In blanched linen, smooth, and lavendered,
While he from forth the closet brought a heap
265 Of candied apple, quince, and plum, and gourd;
With jellies soother than the creamy curd,
And lucent syrops, tinct with cinnamon;
Manna and dates, in argosy transferred
From Fez; and spiced dainties, every one,
270 From silken Samarcand to cedared Lebanon.

31

These delicates he heaped with glowing hand
On golden dishes and in baskets bright
Of wreathed silver: sumptuous they stand
In the retired quiet of the night,
275 Filling the chilly room with perfume light.—
"And now, my love, my seraph fair, awake!
Thou art my heaven, and I thine eremite:[11]
Open thine eyes, for meek St. Agnes' sake,
Or I shall drowse beside thee, so my soul doth ache."

32

280 Thus whispering, his warm, unnerved arm
Sank in her pillow. Shaded was her dream
By the dusk curtains:—'twas a midnight charm
Impossible to melt as iced stream:
The lustrous salvers in the moonlight gleam;
285 Broad golden fringe upon the carpet lies:
It seemed he never, never could redeem
From such a stedfast spell his lady's eyes;
So mused awhile, entoiled in woofed phantasies.

33

Awakening up, he took her hollow lute,—
290 Tumultuous,—and, in chords that tenderest be,
He played an ancient ditty, long since mute,
In Provence called, "La belle dame sans mercy":
Close to her ear touching the melody;—
Wherewith disturbed, she uttered a soft moan;
295 He ceased—she panted quick—and suddenly
Her blue affrayed eyes wide open shone:
Upon his knees he sank, pale as smooth-sculptured
    stone.

34

Her eyes were open, but she still beheld,
Now wide awake, the vision of her sleep:

---

11. *eremite*, devoted follower.

300 There was a painful change, that nigh expelled
The blisses of her dream so pure and deep
At which fair Madeline began to weep,
And moan forth witless words with many a sigh,
While still her gaze on Porphyro would keep:
305 Who knelt, with joined hands and piteous eye,
Fearing to move or speak, she looked so dreamingly.

35

"Ah, Porphyro!" said she, "but even now
Thy voice was at sweet tremble in mine ear,
Made tuneable with every sweetest vow;
310 And those sad eyes were spiritual and clear:
How changed thou art! how pallid, chill, and drear!
Give me that voice again, my Porphyro,
Those looks immortal, those complainings dear!
Oh, leave me not in this eternal woe,
315 For if thou diest, my Love, I know not where to go."

36

Beyond a mortal man impassioned far
At these voluptuous accents, he arose,
Ethereal, flushed, and like a throbbing star
Seen 'mid the sapphire heaven's deep repose;
320 Into her dream he melted, as the rose
Blendeth its odor with the violet,—
Solution sweet: meantime the frost-wind blows
Like Love's alarum, pattering the sharp sleet
Against the window-panes; St. Agnes' moon hath set.

37

325 'Tis dark: quick pattereth the flaw-blown sleet.
"This is no dream, my bride, my Madeline!"
'Tis dark: the iced gusts still rave and beat:
"No dream, alas! alas! and woe is mine!
Porphyro will leave me here to fade and pine.
330 Cruel! what traitor could thee hither bring?
I curse not, for my heart is lost in thine,
Though thou forsakest a deceived thing;—
A dove forlorn and lost with sick unpruned wing."

38

"My Madeline! sweet dreamer! lovely bride!
335 Say, may I be for aye thy vassal blest?
Thy beauty's shield, heart-shaped and vermeil-dyed?
Ah, silver shrine, here will I take my rest
After so many hours of toil and quest,
A famished pilgrim,—saved by miracle.
340 Though I have found, I will not rob thy nest,
Saving of thy sweet self; if thou think'st well
To trust, fair Madeline, to no rude infidel.

39

"Hark! 'tis an elfin-storm from faery land,
Of haggard seeming, but a boon indeed:
345 Arise—arise! the morning is at hand;—
The bloated wassailers will never heed;—
Let us away, my love, with happy speed;
There are no ears to hear, or eyes to see,—
Drowned all in Rhenish and the sleepy mead:
350 Awake! arise! my love, and fearless be,
For o'er the southern moors I have a home for thee."

40

She hurried at his words, beset with fears,
For there were sleeping dragons all around,
At glaring watch, perhaps, with ready spears—
355 Down the wide stairs a darkling way they found;
In all the house was heard no human sound.
A chain-drooped lamp was flickering by each door;
The arras, rich with horseman, hawk, and hound,
Fluttered in the besieging wind's uproar;
360 And the long carpets rose along the gusty floor.

41

They glide, like phantoms, into the wide hall;
Like phantoms, to the iron porch they glide,
Where lay the Porter, in uneasy sprawl,
With a huge empty flagon by his side:
365 The wakeful bloodhound rose, and shook his hide,
But his sagacious eye an inmate owns:
By one, and one the bolts full easy slide:—
The chains lie silent on the footworn stones;
The key turns, and the door upon its hinges groans.

42

370 And they are gone: aye, ages long ago
These lovers fled away into the storm.
That night the Baron dreamt of many a woe,
And all his warrior-guests with shade and form
Of witch, and demon, and large coffin-worm,
375 Were long be-nightmared. Angela the old
Died palsy-twitched, with meager face deform;
The Beadsman, after thousand aves told,
For aye unsought-for slept among his ashes cold. □

DISCUSSION

1. What kinds of images appear most frequently in the first three stanzas? What general effect do these stanzas have on you?
2. What might the Beadsman represent? What one other character in the poem is most closely associated with him? In what ways? With whom are these two most strongly contrasted?
3. Choose the one passage which you think most effectively brings out the rich texture and coloring of the medieval scene, and show how imagery and language are used to create these effects.

4. If you had to interpret this poem as either "dream" or "reality," which would you choose? What elements contribute to the poem's dreamlike quality? to its realistic qualities?
5. How do you interpret the ending? Are the two lovers stepping out into a future that is to be lived "happily ever after" or are they headed for a different fate? What in the poem supports your view?
6. The theme of "La Belle Dame Sans Merci" is raised at one point in this poem. Is Madeline in any way comparable to the fair lady without pity in Keats's other poem? Are there any similarities between the poems as a whole?

7. There are hints of cruelty in the poem. Where do you find them? Would you characterize Porphyro as cruel in any way?

WRITING

The Eve of St. Agnes touches on themes that run through much English and continental literature, from folk tales like "Sleeping Beauty" to high tragedy like Shakespeare's Romeo and Juliet. Discuss the similarities of these and other works you can think of to The Eve of St. Agnes. How are they parallel, how different?

Charles Lamb   1775 / 1834

Although the romantic spirit found its most striking expression in lyric poetry, prose was also affected by the new influence. An essayist like Charles Lamb, for example, no longer felt he had to write in the scholarly style of the classicists. His writing became personal, whimsical, full of figure and fancy. His subjects bore no resemblance to those of eighteenth-century essays—they became only launching pads for the expression of personality. This new approach to prose writing is known as the _familiar essay_. Lamb was a master of this new art.

DREAM CHILDREN

CHILDREN love to listen to stories about their elders, when _they_ were children; to stretch their imagination to the conception of a traditionary great-uncle, or grandame, whom they never saw. It was in this spirit that my little ones crept about me the other evening to hear about their great-grandmother Field, who lived in a great house in Norfolk (a hundred times bigger than that in which they and papa lived) which had been the scene—so at least it was generally believed in that part of the country—of the tragic incidents which they had lately become familiar with from the ballad of "The Children in the Wood." Certain it is that the whole story of the children and their cruel uncle was to be seen fairly carved out in wood upon the chimney piece of the great hall, the whole story down to the Robin Redbreasts,[1] till a foolish rich person pulled it down to set up a marble one of modern invention in its stead, with no story upon it. Here Alice put out one of her dear mother's looks, too tender to be called upbraiding.

Then I went on to say how religious and how good their great-grandmother Field was, how beloved and respected by everybody, though she was not indeed the mistress of this great house, but had only the charge of it (and yet in some respects she might be said to be mistress of it too) committed to her by the owner, who preferred living in a newer and more fashionable mansion which he had purchased somewhere in the adjoining county; but still she lived in it in a manner as if it had been her own and kept up the dignity of the great house in a sort while she lived, which afterward came to decay and was nearly pulled down, and all its old ornaments were stripped and carried away to the owner's other house, where they were set up and looked as awkward as if someone were to carry away the old tombs they had seen lately at the Abbey[2] and stick them up in Lady C.'s tawdry gilt drawing room. Here John smiled, as much as to say, "That would be foolish, indeed."

And then I told how, when she came to die, her funeral was attended by a concourse of all the poor, and some of the gentry too, of the neighborhood for many miles round, to show their respect for her memory, because she had been such a good and religious woman—so good indeed, that she knew all the Psaltery[3] by heart, aye, and a great part of the Testament besides. Here little Alice spread her hands.

Then I told what a tall, upright, graceful person their great-grandmother Field once was, and how in her youth she was esteemed the best dancer—here Alice's little right foot played an involuntary move-

---

1. _Robin Redbreasts_. At the end of the ballad the robins cover the bodies of the murdered children with leaves.

2. _Abbey_, Westminster Abbey in London, where many famous Englishmen are buried.
3. _Psaltery_, the version of the Psalms in the _Book of Common Prayer_.

ment, till upon my looking grave, it desisted—the best dancer, I was saying, in the county, till a cruel disease, called a cancer, came and bowed her down with pain; but it could never bend her good spirits, or make them stoop, because she was so good and religious.

Then I told how she was used to sleep by herself in a lone chamber of the great lone house, and how she believed that an apparition of two infants was to be seen at midnight gliding up and down the great staircase near where she slept, but she said "those innocents would do her no harm"; and how frightened I used to be, because I was never half so good or religious as she—and yet I never saw the infants. Here John tried to look courageous.

Then I told how good she was to all her grandchildren, having us to the great house in the holidays, where I in particular used to spend many hours by myself in gazing upon the old busts of the twelve Caesars that had been emperors of Rome, till the old marble heads would seem to live again or I to be turned into marble with them; how I never could be tired with roaming about that huge mansion with its vast, empty rooms, with their worn-out hangings, fluttering tapestry, and carved oaken panels, with the gliding almost rubbed out—sometimes in the spacious old-fashioned gardens, which I had almost to myself, unless when now and then a solitary gardening man would cross me—and how the nectarines and peaches hung upon the walls without my ever offering to pluck them, because they were forbidden fruits, unless now and then—and because I had more pleasure in strolling about among the old melancholy-looking yew trees, or the firs, and picking up the red berries and the fir apples,[4] which were good for nothing but to look at—or in lying about upon the fresh grass, with all the fine garden smells around me—or basking in the orangery, till I could almost fancy myself ripening too along with the oranges and the limes in that grateful warmth—or in watching the dace that darted to and fro in the fishpond, at the bottom of the garden, with here and there a great sulky pike hanging midway down the water in silent state, as if it mocked at their impertinent friskings—I had more pleasure in these busy-idle diversions than in all the sweet flavors of peaches, nectarines, oranges, and suchlike common baits of children. Here John slyly deposited back

---

4. *fir apples,* pine cones.

upon the plate a bunch of grapes which, not unobserved by Alice, he had meditated dividing with her, and both seemed willing to relinquish them for the present as irrelevant.

Then in somewhat a more heightened tone, I told how, though their great-grandmother Field loved all her grandchildren, yet in an especial manner she might be said to love their uncle, John L_____,[5] because he was so handsome and spirited a youth,

---

5. *John L* _____, Lamb's brother John.

OF HUMAN INTEREST

Lamb's family tragedy

On September 27, 1796, Charles Lamb wrote this disconnected letter with its strange postscript to his friend Samuel Coleridge:

My dearest friend—White or some of my friends or the public papers by this time may have informed you of the terrible calamities that have fallen on our family. I will only give you the outlines. My poor dear dearest sister in a fit of insanity has been the death of her own mother. I was at hand only time enough to snatch the knife out of her grasp. She is at present in a mad house, from whence I fear she must be moved to an hospital. God has preserved to me my senses,—I eat and drink and sleep, and have my judgment I believe very sound.

My poor father was slightly wounded, and I am left to take care of him and my aunt. Mr. Norris of the Bluecoat school has been very kind to us, and we have no other friend, but thank God I am very calm and composed and able to do the best that remains to do. Write,—as religious a letter as possible—but no mention of what is gone and done with—with me the former things are passed away, and I have something more to do that [than] to feel——

God almighty

have us all in
his keeping.——

C. LAMB.

mention nothing of poetry. I have destroyed every vestige of past vanities of that kind. Do as you please, but if you publish, publish mine (I give free leave) without name or initial, and never send me a book, I charge you, you [your] own judgment will convince you not to take any notice of this yet to your dear wife.—You look after your family,— I have my reason and strength left to take care of mine. I charge you don't think of coming to see me. Write. I will not see you if you come. God almighty love you and all of us——

and a king to the rest of us; and, instead of moping about in solitary corners, like some of us, he would mount the most mettlesome horse he could get, when but an imp no bigger than themselves, and make it carry him half over the county in a morning, and join the hunters when there were any out—and yet he loved the old great house and gardens too, but had too much spirit to be always pent up within their boundaries—and how their uncle grew up to man's estate as brave as he was handsome, to the admiration of everybody, but of their great-grandmother Field most especially; and how he used to carry me upon his back when I was a lame-footed boy—for he was a good bit older than me—many a mile when I could not walk for pain; and how in afterlife he became lame-footed too, and I did not always (I fear) make allowance enough for him when he was impatient, and in pain, nor remember sufficiently how considerate he had been to me when I was lame-footed; and how when he died, though he had not been dead an hour, it seemed as if he had died a great while ago, such a distance there is betwixt life and death; and how I bore his death as I thought pretty well at first, but afterward it haunted and haunted me; and though I did not cry or take it to heart as some do, and as I think he would have done if I had died, yet I missed him all day long, and knew not till then how much I had loved him. I missed his kindness, and I missed his crossness, and wished him to be alive again, to be quarreling with him (for we quarreled sometimes), rather than not have him again, and was as uneasy without him as he, their poor uncle, must have been when the doctor took off his limb. Here the children fell a-crying and asked if their little mourning, which they had on, was not for Uncle John; and they looked up and prayed me not to go on about their uncle, but to tell them some stories about their pretty dead mother.

Then I told how for seven long years, in hope sometimes, sometimes in despair, yet persisting ever, I courted the fair Alice W_____n; and, as much as children could understand, I explained to them what coyness and denial meant in maidens—when suddenly, turning to Alice, the soul of the first Alice looked out at her eyes with such a reality of representment, that I became in doubt which of them stood there before me, or whose that bright hair was; and while I stood gazing, both the children gradually grew fainter to my view, receding, and still receding, till nothing at last but two mournful features were seen in the uttermost distance, which, without speech, strangely impressed upon me the effects of speech: "We are not of Alice, nor of thee, nor are we children at all. We are nothing; less than nothing, and dreams. We are only what might have been, and must wait upon the tedious shores of Lethe millions of ages before we have existence and a name"—and immediately awaking, I found myself quietly seated in my bachelor armchair, where I had fallen asleep, with the faithful Bridget unchanged by my side—but John L. (or James Elia)[6] was gone forever.

---

6. *Bridget . . . James Elia,* names given by Lamb to his sister Mary and his brother John.

DISCUSSION

1. Explain the title of this essay.
2. "Lamb's reverie is not much more than the sentimental musings of a pathetic and aging bachelor." Agree or disagree with this opinion, supporting your argument with details from the essay.
3. What qualities of spirit do Grandmother Field and Uncle John represent? What similarities are there between the two portraits?

WRITING

"Every man is beset, his whole life long, with the difficulty of accepting what has been and what is and reconciling these realities with what might have been." Discuss Lamb's essay in terms of this statement and the biographical sketch of his life on pages 384–385.

BACKGROUND

JOSEPH M. W. TURNER, "PEACE: BURIAL AT SEA" EXHIBITED 1842. THE TATE GALLERY, LONDO

The Romantic Age

TOWARD the end of the eighteenth century the certainties and rigidities of the Augustan Age began to crumble under the influence of revolutionary and humanitarian ideals which swept across America, Europe, and England. The serene and symmetrical neoclassical facade had already toppled by the time Frenchmen stormed the Bastille in 1789. By the last decades of the century the Romantic literary movement in England was well under way; it had been foreshadowed by the nature poets Goldsmith, Gray, and Burns, and been given its first intense thrust by

the visionary William Blake. By 1815, when Napoleon was finally defeated at the Battle of Waterloo, the revolutionary fervor which inspired English Romanticism had already begun to cool.

The Romantic period was thus one of very short duration. The bulk of its great poetry was written between 1795 and 1830. Each of the major figures in it knew, or knew of, the others. Wordsworth and Coleridge collaborated on a volume of poetry; Shelley and Byron spent time together on the continent; and the cross-fertilization of minds in conversation, letters, reviews, and criticism that took place during these short decades was to change, as no previous period had, the shape and nature of literature. As a revolutionary period it had its eccentrics, some of whom displayed outright disregard for social convention, others who were quiet renegades. It was, in short, an age of individualists who seem to have taken their cue from the French Romantic philosopher Rousseau who said, "I may not be better than other people, but at least I'm different."

An even more prominent trait was the high seriousness and vigorous humanitarianism of the period. By the end of the eighteenth century the abuses of the Industrial Revolution and the need for social reform had become clear. Although legislative reforms were slow in coming—most were established in the late nineteenth century—the reforming spirit is evident in most Romantic writing, in its concern for the humble lives of the poor and its outright rejection of materialism and rationalism. It became clear to the Romantic that all was not right with the world, as the eighteenth-century rationalist had professed, and for merely logical reasoning he substituted personal "feeling" and conviction. The chief characteristic of the period was thus a tremendous increase in awareness (what the Romantics called "sensibility") not only of the sublime power and beauty of nature unsullied by man's hand, but also of man's intimate connection with the natural world, and of the social ills that result when that world is corrupted or man's "first-born affinities" with it are severed.

The literature of this brief period is richer and more powerful in the statement of these basic themes than any which preceded or followed it. It has about it a deep personal earnestness, a sensuous delight in the most common and natural (and most overlooked) things of this world, a blend of intensely lived joy and dejection, a yearning for ideal states of being and a probing interest in mysterious and mystical experience. If the Romantic vision of the world was occasionally tinged with bitterness or outrage, it was because the Romantic confronted the implications of a mechanical and materialistic society which threatened to extinguish man's awareness of his vital relationship with his fellow men and with the rhythms of nature that mold his life. Romantic protests, in fact, remain as persuasive today as they did a century and a half ago, and the challenges and questions implied in Romantic literature remain still valid, and still unanswered. □

BIOGRAPHIES

George Noel Gordon, Lord Byron   1788 / 1824

Lord Byron was born lame, a fate to which he was never able to reconcile himself. Born only remotely to nobility, he inherited his title at age 11 on the death of a great-uncle. When he entered Cambridge at 17, he was well-read in Latin and Greek, excelled in swimming and boxing, and had already fallen in love twice. After graduation he traveled throughout Europe and Asia Minor. Returning to London when he was 23, he published the first two cantos of *Childe Harold,* made a brilliant speech in the House of Lords defending workers who had wrecked machinery that threatened their jobs, and became famous overnight.

He relished his role as the favorite of London society. After several love affairs, he married the nobly born, very proper Annabella Milbanke, but at the end of the first year of marriage Annabella took their newborn daughter and returned to her parents. Byron was outraged. Londoners, appalled at Byron's egotistical conduct, ostracized him. Bitter about the hypocricies of society, he left England in 1816, never to return.

Byron wandered about the continent, doing precisely as he pleased, hobnobbing with prominent people, befriending Shelley, and carrying on intrigues with ladies, one of whom, Claire Claremont, bore him a daughter. He finished *Childe Harold*, began his masterpiece, *Don Juan*, and wrote many shorter poems. His verses sold well, but while his fortunes prospered, his health, always poor, began to fail.

A foe of despotism anywhere, Byron in 1823 joined the Greek war for independence from the Turks, devoting much time and money to the effort. But before he could see battle, he caught fever and died in camp at Missolonghi, embittered and old at 36.

To his contemporaries Byron was more a colorful and scandalous personality than a poet. His poetry reflects the paradoxes of his life. He was a fiery rebel and a conventional aristocrat, an idealist and a cynic, a cad to his countrymen and a hero to the Greeks. His power as a poet is due to his sharp eye for human foibles and hypocrisy; his satire was the best produced in England since Pope's.

Samuel Taylor Coleridge   1772 / 1834

The youngest of twelve children, Coleridge was an imaginative and precocious child. Although his family was poor, he was sent to Cambridge, where he read everything he thought worth while and fascinated the students with eloquent monologues, full of mysticism and radical politics. ("Charles, did you ever hear me preach?" he once asked his friend Lamb. "I never heard you do anything else," Lamb replied.) However, he found university life boring, ran up debts, and recklessly left school in his second year to join His Majesty's Fifteenth Light Dragoons under the name of Silas Tomkyn Comberbacke. The harsh discipline of military life was too much for him; fortunately his brothers and friends rescued him, paid his debts, and had him reinstated in college. But he was not to remain at the university.

In June 1794, Coleridge met Robert Southey, a young poet who had become inspired by the French Revolution. The two made elaborate plans to migrate to America and found a colony based on brotherly love, simple living, and high thinking. But they never reached America. Southey settled in Lisbon; Coleridge, newly married to Sara Fricker and practically destitute, wandered about the English countryside. He started a magazine and wrote a play. The magazine failed within two months; the play was not published.

In 1797 he met Wordsworth; stimulated by his encouragement and their shared plans for *Lyrical Ballads*, he produced in one year almost all his greatest poetry, including "The Rime of the Ancient Mariner," "Christabel," and "Kubla Khan." At about this time he began taking opium, first for relief from the excruciating pains of neuralgia and other ailments, then compulsively to allay the frustrations of a marriage gone sour (he fell in love with Sara Hutchinson, sister of Wordsworth's wife) and recurrent feelings of personal inadequacy. By the age of 30 he was no longer capable of sustained creative effort; at 35 he separated from his wife. The remainder of his life was an agonizing struggle against the addictive grip of opium. Nevertheless, in his later years he managed to produce significant works of literary criticism and philosophy and established a reputation as a brilliant lecturer and conversationalist.

John Keats   1795 / 1821

John Keats was born in London, the oldest son of a cockney stable keeper. His father was killed in a riding accident when the boy was 9; six years later his mother died of tuberculosis. That same year he was taken out of school and apprenticed to a physician. Although he spent some time in London hospitals and qualified to practice as an apothecary, he finally abandoned medicine for literature.

With support from such people as Wordsworth and Lamb, the 21-year-old Keats began his literary career in earnest, full of the exuberance of youth. Suddenly came disappointment and tragedy: one brother left for America, the other died of tuberculosis. The publication of *Endymion*, his first sustained poetic effort, was met with vicious and unwarranted criticism. His cockney heritage and medical training were ridiculed. Bad publicity kept his poetry from selling and Keats was soon destitute; in 1818 his suspicion that he had tuberculosis was confirmed. Ill, depressed, Keats fell in love with Fanny Brawne, but knowing he could never marry, and under orders from his physician to give up all work, he left England for the warmer climate of Italy in a last desperate attempt to regain his health. There he died in 1821. He was buried in the Protestant Cemetery in Rome under the epitaph he himself had composed: "Here lies one whose name was writ in water."

Unlike Wordsworth and Shelley, Keats was not caught up in the zeal for reform that accompanied the French Revolution. Throughout his short creative life he was chary of poetry "that has designs upon us." Instead of using poetry to state ideas, he struggled for an intuitive vision of truth in poetic beauty. Hence the lushness of the imagery in his best poetry, its sustained melodious flow. In the course of his short life, Keats learned to use language with a range and felicity equalled only by the greatest poets.

Charles Lamb   1775 / 1834

Born in a medieval quarter of old London, Lamb drew as much inspiration from the city as Wordsworth found in the countryside. London was the center of his world; there he lived, worked, and died. He was miserable only when well-meaning friends took him for visits to the country. An easy-going, light-hearted man, his personal life was marred by frustration. Because of a stammer, he was unable to take an examination at his preparatory school to qualify for a university. Lack of education forced him to take a job as a low-salaried clerk for The East India Company, where he worked until 1825. His sister Mary had several attacks of madness, during one of which she killed their mother. Rather than confine her to a miserable life in a sanitarium, Lamb abandoned hope of marriage and devoted the rest of his life to her care and comfort.

Lamb did not really begin to find himself as a writer until he reached middle age. His first book of familiar essays, entitled *Essays of Elia*, was published when he was 48. The book's humor, whimsy, and faint overtones of sadness made Lamb immediately popular with nineteenth-century readers. It is from this first volume that "Dream Children" comes.

Percy Bysshe Shelley   1792 / 1822

Percy Shelley was the black sheep of a conventional, wealthy family; he stepped lightly over religious, political, social, and moral boundaries, seemingly unaware of their existence. He was a brilliant student, but resentful of all authority, and did not hesitate to express nonconformist views while at Eton, a fashionable boys' school, where he was at odds with everyone. He fared no better at Oxford, where he published a pamphlet entitled "The Necessity of Atheism," for which he was expelled.

By the time he was 21 he was married (to Harriet West-brooke) and a father, and had already published his first important poem, *Queen Mab*, a diatribe against orthodox religion and morality. After several years he began to find his marriage dull, and eloped with Mary Godwin, daughter of the radical William Godwin, whose revolutionary zeal Shelley shared. In 1816 Harriet committed suicide, and shortly thereafter Shelley married Mary (who had already borne two of his children), but he never fully recovered from the scorn the English public heaped upon him for his actions. In 1818 he and Mary left for Italy. In 1822 he was drowned while sailing in a small boat off the Italian coast. His body was discovered some ten days later and was cremated on the beach. As the funeral pyre burned low, Mary, according to some accounts, snatched her husband's heart from the ashes. The heart is buried in the Protestant Cemetery in Rome under the inscription "Cor Cordium!" (Heart of Hearts!).

Shelley wrote most of his greatest poetry in the four years he spent in Italy. Throughout his lifetime he was filled with schemes for reforming the world, and he remained a firm believer in the purity of his intentions and the soundness of his views. However, his greatness lies not so much in the themes of reform and revolution that run through much of his poetry as in his powerful imagination and his over-brimming lyric power.

William Wordsworth   1770 / 1850

As a restless young man Wordsworth became caught up in the radical causes of the French Revolution; as an old man, established as poet laureate of England, he became an ultraconservative whose rigid opinions many found unattractive.

Wordsworth's life was not untroubled. His mother died when he was 7, his father when he was 13. Yet his boyhood days were free, perhaps the happiest of his life. He attended the village school at Hawkshead and ranged through the countryside during vacations. He read widely on his own; his sensibilities became sharpened, his sympathies enlarged, his intimate knowledge of natural things strengthened. At Cambridge he found the classical curriculum a bore, and graduated in 1791 without distinction and with no particular plans.

During a European walking tour in the summer of 1790 his sympathies for the French Revolution had been aroused. After graduation he set out again for France, where he met and fell in love with Annette Vallon, who bore him a daughter, Caroline. In 1792, he was unexpectedly summoned to England, and when war broke out between France and England it was impossible for him to return to France. He did not see Annette or Caroline again until 1802, when he made arrangements for Caroline's financial support. Then he married Mary Hutchinson, a friend since boyhood days.

From 1797 to 1807, a period considered his most productive, Wordsworth worked closely with Coleridge, a relationship quickened by Wordsworth's sister Dorothy. *Lyrical Ballads*, published anonymously in 1798, contained poems by both men, according to the following scheme: Wordsworth was to "give the charm of novelty to subjects of everyday life"; Coleridge was to let his imagination roam over more unusual and supernatural subject matter. Though the book included such poems as Coleridge's "Rime of the Ancient Mariner" and Wordsworth's "Tintern Abbey" (now considered among the finest in the English language), it was at first contemptuously received by critics. In 1800 an expanded edition was published with a preface written by Wordsworth to explain his theories of poetry.

By 1810 Wordsworth's extraordinary powers of awareness had begun to fade. He became estranged from Coleridge for several years; his revolutionary fervor dulled; and he never again achieved the intensity of his earlier work. Yet when he died at the age of 80 he had not lost his fierce dedication to his role as poet and visionary which gives his best lines their unequaled power.

THE VICTORIANS
1837–1901

chapter seven

"AN ENGLISH AUTUMN AFTERNOON" BY FORD MADOX BROWN. BY PERMISSION OF THE BIRMINGHAM MUSEUM AND ART GALLERY.

I. EARLY VICTORIAN POETS

Alfred, Lord Tennyson
"Who am I?"
"What can I believe in?"

1809 / 1892

ULYSSES · old age · how ulysses deals with it.

I T LITTLE profits that an idle king,
By this still hearth, among these barren crags,
Matched with an aged wife, I mete and dole
Unequal laws unto a savage race,
5 That hoard, and sleep, and feed, and know not me.
I cannot rest from travel; I will drink
Life to the lees. All times I have enjoyed
Greatly, have suffered greatly, both with those
That loved me, and alone; on shore, and when
10 Through scudding drifts the rainy Hyades[1]
Vexed the dim sea. I am become a name;
For always roaming with a hungry heart
Much have I seen and known—cities of men
And manners, climates, councils, governments,
15 Myself not least, but honored of them all—
And drunk delight of battle with my peers,
Far on the ringing plains of windy Troy.
I am part of all that I have met;
Yet all experience is an arch wherethrough
20 Gleams that untraveled world whose margin fades
Forever and forever when I move.
How dull it is to pause, to make an end,
To rust unburnished, not to shine in use!
As though to breathe were life! Life piled on life
25 Were all too little, and of one to me
Little remains; but every hour is saved
From that eternal silence, something more,
A bringer of new things; and vile it were
For some three suns to store and hoard myself,
30 And this gray spirit yearning in desire
To follow knowledge like a sinking star,
Beyond the utmost bound of human thought.
   This is my son, mine own Telemachus,

To whom I leave the scepter and the isle—
35 Well-loved of me, discerning to fulfill
This labor, by slow prudence to make mild
A rugged people, and through soft degrees
Subdue them to the useful and the good.
Most blameless is he, centered in the sphere
40 Of common duties, decent not to fail
In offices of tenderness, and pay
Meet adoration to my household gods,
When I am gone. He works his work, I mine.
   There lies the port; the vessel puffs her sail;
45 There gloom the dark, broad seas. My mariners,
Souls that have toiled, and wrought, and thought
      with me—
That ever with a frolic welcome took
The thunder and the sunshine, and opposed
Free hearts, free foreheads—you and I are old;
50 Old age hath yet his honor and his toil.
Death closes all; but something ere the end,
Some work of noble note, may yet be done,
Not unbecoming men that strove with gods.
The lights begin to twinkle from the rocks;
55 The long day wanes; the slow moon climbs; the
      deep
Moans round with many voices. Come, my friends.
'Tis not too late to seek a newer world.
Push off, and sitting well in order smite
The sounding furrows; for my purpose holds
60 To sail beyond the sunset, and the baths
Of all the western stars, until I die.
It may be that the gulfs will wash us down;
It may be we shall touch the Happy Isles,[2]
And see the great Achilles, whom we knew.
65 Though much is taken, much abides; and though
We are not now that strength which in old days
Moved earth and heaven, that which we are, we
      are—
One equal temper of heroic hearts,
Made weak by time and fate, but strong in will
70 To strive, to seek, to find, and not to yield.

---

1. *rainy Hyades* (hī′ ə dēz), a group of seven stars once associated with the rainy season.

2. *Happy Isles,* the mythical Islands of the Blessed where the souls of the good were supposed to dwell after death.

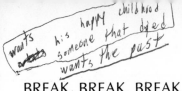

wants his happy childhood
wants ~~who~~ someone that died
wants the past

BREAK, BREAK, BREAK

Break, break, break,
  On thy cold gray stones, O Sea!
And I would that my tongue could utter
  The thoughts that arise in me.

5 O well for the fisherman's boy,
  That he shouts with his sister at play!
O well for the sailor lad,
  That he sings in his boat on the bay!

And the stately ships go on
10   To their haven under the hill;
But O for the touch of a vanished hand,
  And the sound of a voice that is still!

Break, break, break,
  At the foot of thy crags, O Sea!
15 But the tender grace of a day that is dead
  Will never come back to me.

when he dies he doesn't want
anyone to be sad.
He wants to see God

CROSSING THE BAR

Sunset and evening star,
  And one clear call for me!
And may there be no moaning of the bar,[1]
  When I put out to sea,

5 But such a tide as moving seems asleep,
  Too full for sound and foam,
When that which drew from out the boundless deep
  Turns again home.

Twilight and evening bell,
10   And after that the dark!
And may there be no sadness of farewell,
  When I embark;

For though from out our bourn of time and place
  The flood may bear me far,
15 I hope to see my Pilot face to face
  When I have crossed the bar.

---

1. *no moaning of the bar.* A sandbar sometimes obstructs the passage of a ship from the harbor into open water. An old superstition held that, whenever a death occurred, the outgoing tide moaned as it rolled over the bar.

in memory of...

From IN MEMORIAM

7 He misses his Friend

Dark house, by which once more I stand
  Here in the long unlovely street,
  Doors, where my heart was used to beat
So quickly, waiting for a hand,

5 A hand that can be clasped no more—
  Behold me, for I cannot sleep,
  And like a guilty thing I creep
At earliest morning to the door.

He is not here; but far away
10   The noise of life begins again,
  And ghastly thro' the drizzling rain
On the bald street breaks the blank day.

alliteration

34 - why do people live if they are going to die

My own dim life should teach me this,
  That life shall live for evermore,
15   Else earth is darkness at the core,
And dust and ashes all that is;

This round of green, this orb of flame,
  Fantastic beauty; such as lurks
  In some wild poet, when he works
20 Without a conscience or an aim.

What then were God to such as I?
  'T were hardly worth my while to choose
  Of things all mortal, or to use
A little patience ere I die;

25 'T were best at once to sink to peace,
  Like birds the charming serpent draws,
  To drop head-foremost in the jaws
Of vacant darkness and to cease.

96 doubt vs. faith

You say, but with no touch of scorn,
30   Sweet-hearted, you, whose light blue eyes
  Are tender over drowning flies,
You tell me, doubt is Devil-born.

I know not: one indeed I knew
  In many a subtle question versed,
35   Who touched a jarring lyre at first,
But ever strove to make it true;

Perplext in faith, but pure in deeds,
   At last he beat his music out.
   There lives more faith in honest doubt,
40 Believe me, than in half the creeds.

He fought his doubts and gathered strength,
   He would not make his judgment blind,
   He faced the spectres of the mind
   And laid them; thus he came at length

45 To find a stronger faith his own,
   And Power was with him in the night,
   Which makes the darkness and the light,
   And dwells not in the light alone,

But in the darkness and the cloud,
50   As over Sinai's peaks of old,
   While Israel made their gods of gold,
   Altho' the trumpet blew so loud.

THE DAWN

"You are but children"
—EGYPTIAN PRIEST TO SOLON

         Red of the Dawn!
Screams of a babe in the red-hot palms of a Moloch[1] of Tyre,
   Man with his brotherless dinner on man in the tropical wood,
   Priests in the name of the Lord passing souls through fire to the fire,
5 Head-hunters and boats of Dahomey[2] that float upon human blood.

         Red of the Dawn!
Godless fury of peoples, and Christless frolic of kings,
   And the bolt of war dashing down upon cities and blazing farms,
   For Babylon was a child newborn, and Rome was a babe in arms,
10 And London and Paris and all the rest are as yet but in leading strings.

         Dawn not Day,
While scandal is mouthing a bloodless name at *her* cannibal feast,
   And rake-ruined bodies and souls go down in a common wreck,
   And the Press of a thousand cities is prized for it smells of the beast,
15 Or easily violates virgin Truth for a coin or a check.

         Dawn not Day!
Is it Shame, so few should have climbed from the dens in the level below,
   Men, with a heart and a soul, no slaves of a four-footed will?
   But if twenty million of summers are stored in the sunlight still,
20 We are far from the noon of man, there is time for the race to grow.

         Red of the Dawn!
Is it turning a fainter red? So be it, but when shall we lay
   The Ghost of the Brute that is walking and haunting us yet, and be free?
   In a hundred, a thousand winters? Ah, what will *our* children be?
25 The men of a hundred thousand, a million summers away?

1. *Moloch*, a god to whom children were sacrificed.
2. *Dahomey*, a West African country in which human sacrifice still existed in the 19th century.

From GUINEVERE — story of Lancelot

In his *Idylls of the King*, Alfred, Lord Tennyson rewrote some of Malory's Arthurian tales in nineteenth-century Victorian verse infused with Victorian sensibility. His treatment of the love story of Lancelot and Guinevere, less robust and more delicate than that of Malory, places emphasis on Guinevere's ultimate retreat to a nunnery. In the passage quoted here, Tennyson opens with the scheming Modred [Mordred], eager to discredit Sir Lancelot and improve his own chances of succeeding his natural father as king, spying on Guinevere in hopes of catching her with her lover. The incidents that follow are essentially the same as those related in the Malory passage on pages 112–117. But note how Tennyson has shifted the emphasis.

For thus it chanced one morn when all the court,
Green-suited, but with plumes that mock'd the may,
Had been—their wont—a-maying and return'd,
That Modred still in green, all ear and eye,
25 Climb'd to the high top of the garden-wall
To spy some secret scandal if he might,
And saw the Queen who sat betwixt her best
Enid and lissome Vivien, of her court
The wiliest and the worst; and more than this
30 He saw not, for Sir Lancelot passing by
Spied where he couch'd, and as the gardener's hand
Picks from the colewort a green caterpillar,
So from the high wall and the flowering grove
Of grasses Lancelot pluck'd him by the heel,
35 And cast him as a worm upon the way;
But when he knew the prince tho' marr'd with dust,
He, reverencing king's blood in a bad man,
Made such excuses as he might, and these
Full knightly without scorn: for in those days
40 No knight of Arthur's noblest dealt in scorn;
But, if a man were halt, or hunch'd, in him
By those whom God had made full-limb'd and tall,
Scorn was allow'd as part of his defect,
And he was answer'd softly by the King
45 And all his Table. So Sir Lancelot holp
To raise the prince, who rising twice or thrice
Full sharply smote his knees, and smiled, and went:
But, ever after, the small violence done
Rankled in him and ruffled all his heart,
50 As the sharp wind that ruffles all day long
A little bitter pool about a stone
On the bare coast.

But when Sir Lancelot told

This matter to the Queen, at first she laugh'd
Lightly, to think of Modred's dusty fall,
55 Then shudder'd, as the village wife who cries,
"I shudder, some one steps across my grave";
Then laugh'd again, but faintlier, for indeed
She half-foresaw that he, the subtle beast,
Would track her guilt until he found, and hers
60 Would be for evermore a name of scorn.
Henceforward rarely could she front in hall,
Or elsewhere, Modred's narrow foxy face,
Heart-hiding smile, and gray persistent eye.
Henceforward too, the Powers that tend the soul,
65 To help it from the death that cannot die,
And save it even in extremes, began
To vex and plague her. Many a time for hours,
Beside the placid breathings of the King,
In the dead night, grim faces came and went
70 Before her, or a vague spiritual fear—
Like to some doubtful noise of creaking doors,
Heard by the watcher in a haunted house,
That keeps the rust of murder on the walls—
Held her awake: or if she slept she dream'd
75 An awful dream; for then she seem'd to stand
On some vast plain before a setting sun,
And from the sun there swiftly made at her
A ghastly something, and its shadow flew
Before it till it touch'd her, and she turn'd—
80 When lo! her own, that broadening from her feet,
And blackening, swallow'd all the land, and in it
Far cities burnt, and with a cry she woke.
And all this trouble did not pass but grew,
Till even the clear face of the guileless King,
85 And trustful courtesies of household life,
Became her bane; and at last she said,
"O Lancelot, get thee hence to thine own land,
For if thou tarry we shall meet again,
And if we meet again some evil chance
90 Will make the smouldering scandal break and blaze
Before the people and our lord the King."
And Lancelot ever promised, but remain'd,
And still they met and met. Again she said,
"O Lancelot, if thou love me get thee hence."
95 And then they were agreed upon a night—
When the good King should not be there—to meet
And part for ever. Vivien, lurking, heard.
She told Sir Modred. Passion-pale they met
And greeted. Hands in hands, and eye to eye,
100 Low on the border of her couch they sat
Stammering and staring. It was their last hour,
A madness of farewells. And Modred brought

His creatures to the basement of the tower
For testimony; and crying with full voice,
105 "Traitor, come out, ye are trapt at last," aroused
Lancelot, who rushing outward lionlike
Leapt on him, and hurl'd him headlong, and he fell
Stunn'd, and his creatures took and bare him off,
And all was still. Then she, "The end is come,
110 And I am shamed for ever"; and he said:
"Mine be the shame; mine was the sin: but rise,
And fly to my strong castle over-seas:
There will I hide thee till my life shall end,
There hold thee with my life against the world."
115 She answer'd: "Lancelot, wilt thou hold me so?
Nay, friend, for we have taken our farewells.
Would God that thou couldst hide me from myself!
Mine is the shame, for I was wife, and thou
Unwedded; yet rise now, and let us fly,
120 For I will draw me into sanctuary,
And bide my doom." So Lancelot got her horse,
Set her thereon, and mounted on his own,
And then they rode to the divided way,
There kiss'd, and parted weeping: for he past,

125 Love-loyal to the least wish of the Queen,
Back to his land; but she to Almesbury
Fled all night long by glimmering waste and weald,
And heard the spirits of the waste and weald
Moan as she fled, or thought she heard them moan:
130 And in herself she moan'd, "Too late, too late!"
Till in the cold wind that foreruns the morn,
A blot in heaven, the raven, flying high,
Croak'd, and she thought, "He spies a field of death;
For now the heathen of the Northern Sea,
135 Lured by the crimes and frailties of the court,
Begin to slay the folk and spoil the land."

And when she came to Almesbury she spake
There to the nuns, and said, "Mine enemies
Pursue me, but, O peaceful Sisterhood,
140 Receive and yield me sanctuary, nor ask
Her name to whom ye yield it till her time
To tell you"; and her beauty, grace, and power
Wrought as a charm upon them, and they spared
To ask it. . . .

□

DISCUSSION

1. (a) What emotional experience has the speaker of "Break, Break, Break" undergone, and how has it affected him?

(b) Which words in the poem intensify the effect of that experience?

(c) Evaluate the appropriateness of the poem's setting as a background for the speaker's emotion.

2. (a) What details in "Crossing the Bar" evoke a mood of peacefulness?

(b) What is the speaker's attitude toward death?

(c) How does this feeling contrast with that of "Break, Break, Break"? In which of the two poems do you think the emotion is more sincere?

3. (a) In "Guinevere," by what details is Modred made to appear repulsive?

(b) In general, how does Tennyson's account differ from that of Malory in "Slander and Strife" (page 114)?

4. (a) In "The Dawn," what is the Red of the Dawn? What is the Ghost of the Brute (line 23)?

(b) What does the speaker think of the past? the present?

(c) What is his unspoken hope for the future?

(d) How does this poem show the effect of the scientific thought of the Victorian Age?

(e) What appeal is the speaker making?

5. (a) In "Ulysses," how does Ulysses feel about his quiet life as ruler of Ithaca?

(b) What in his past might have made him feel that way?

(c) Do you agree with his philosophy of life? Explain.

(d) The last line of "Ulysses" has always been thought to be powerful. Analyze the ways in which the line achieves its effect, and show how this line has been prepared for by the rest of the poem.

6. Tennyson himself said that "In Memoriam" began with a funeral and ended with a wedding. This memorial to his friend Arthur Henry Hallam consists of 131 short poems written over a period of many years. The three included here (Nos. 7, "Dark House," 34, "My Own Dim Life," and 96, "You Say") come from the beginning, middle, and end of the series. Explain how they show the successive stages in the poet's first grief and slow recovery.

Robert Browning
1812 / 1889

PORPHYRIA'S LOVER

The rain set early in tonight,
    The sullen wind was soon awake,
It tore the elm-tops down for spite,
    And did its worst to vex the lake:
5   I listened with heart fit to break.
When glided in Porphyria; straight
    She shut the cold out and the storm,
And kneeled and made the cheerless grate
    Blaze up, and all the cottage warm;
10   Which done, she rose, and from her form
Withdrew the dripping cloak and shawl,
    And laid her soiled gloves by, untied
Her hat and let the damp hair fall,
    And, last, she sat down by my side
15   And called me. When no voice replied,
She put my arm about her waist,
    And made her smooth white shoulder bare,
And all her yellow hair displaced,
    And, stooping, made my cheek lie there,
20   And spread, o'er all, her yellow hair,
Murmuring how she loved me—she
    Too weak, for all her heart's endeavor,
To set its struggling passion free
    From pride, and vainer ties dissever,
25   And give herself to me forever.
But passion sometimes would prevail,
    Nor could tonight's gay feast restrain
A sudden thought of one so pale
    For love of her, and all in vain:
30   So, she was come through wind and rain.
Be sure I looked up at her eyes
    Happy and proud; at last I knew
Porphyria worshiped me: surprise
    Made my heart swell, and still it grew
35   While I debated what to do.
That moment she was mine, mine, fair,
    Perfectly pure and good: I found
A thing to do, and all her hair
    In one long yellow string I wound
40   Three times her little throat around,

And strangled her. No pain felt she;
    I am quite sure she felt no pain.
As a shut bud that holds a bee,
    I warily oped her lids: again
45   Laughed the blue eyes without a stain.
And I untightened next the tress
    About her neck; her cheek once more
Blushed bright beneath my burning kiss:
    I propped her head up as before,
50   Only, this time my shoulder bore
Her head, which droops upon it still:
    The smiling rosy little head,
So glad it has its utmost will,
    That all it scorned at once is fled,
55   And I, its love, am gained instead!
Porphyria's love: she guessed not how
    Her darling one wish would be heard.
And thus we sit together now,
    And all night long we have not stirred,
60   And yet God has not said a word!

MEMORABILIA

Ah, did you once see Shelley plain,
    And did he stop and speak to you
And did you speak to him again?
    How strange it seems and new!

5 But you were living before that,
    And also you are living after;
And the memory I started at—
    My starting moves your laughter.

I crossed a moor, with a name of its own
10   And a certain use in the world no doubt,
Yet a hand's-breadth of it shines alone
    'Mid the blank miles round about:

For there I picked up on the heather
    And there I put inside my breast
15 A moulted feather, an eagle-feather!
    Well, I forget the rest.

MY LAST DUCHESS

The time is the 16th century, the scene the city of Ferrara in northern Italy. The speaker is the Duke of Ferrara.

THAT'S my last duchess painted on the wall,
Looking as if she were alive. I call
That piece a wonder, now: Frà Pandolf's hands
Worked busily a day, and there she stands.
5 Will 't please you sit and look at her? I said
"Frà Pandolf" by design, for never read
Strangers like you that pictured countenance,
The depth and passion of its earnest glance,
But to myself they turned (since none puts by
10 The curtain I have drawn for you, but I)
And seemed as they would ask me, if they durst,
How such a glance came there; so, not the first
Are you to turn and ask thus. Sir, 'twas not
Her husband's presence only, called that spot
15 Of joy into the Duchess' cheek: perhaps
Frà Pandolf chanced to say "Her mantle laps
Over my lady's wrist too much," or "Paint
Must never hope to reproduce the faint
Half-flush that dies along her throat": such stuff
20 Was courtesy, she thought, and cause enough
For calling up that spot of joy. She had
A heart—how shall I say?—too soon made glad,
Too easily impressed; she liked whate'er
She looked on, and her looks went everywhere.
25 Sir, 'twas all one! My favor at her breast,
The dropping of the daylight in the West,
The bough of cherries some officious fool
Broke in the orchard for her, the white mule
She rode with round the terrace—all and each
30 Would draw from her alike the approving speech,
Or blush, at least. She thanked men—good! but thanked
Somehow—I know not how—as if she ranked
My gift of a nine-hundred-years-old name
With anybody's gift. Who'd stoop to blame
35 This sort of trifling? Even had you skill
In speech—which I have not—to make your will
Quite clear to such an one, and say, "Just this
Or that in you disgusts me; here you miss,
Or there exceed the mark"—and if she let
40 Herself be lessoned so, nor plainly set
Her wits to yours, forsooth, and made excuse—
E'en then would be some stooping; and I choose
Never to stoop. Oh sir, she smiled, no doubt,
Whene'er I passed her; but who passed without
45 Much the same smile? This grew; I gave commands;
Then all smiles stopped together. There she stands
As if alive. Will 't please you rise? We'll meet
The company below, then. I repeat,
The Count your master's known munificence
50 Is ample warrant that no just pretense
Of mine for dowry will be disallowed;
Though his fair daughter's self, as I avowed
At starting, is my object. Nay, we'll go
Together down, sir. Notice Neptune, though,
55 Taming a sea-horse, thought a rarity,
Which Claus of Innsbruck cast in bronze for me!

SUMMUM BONUM[1]

All the breath and bloom of the year in the bag of one bee;
    All the wonder and wealth of the mine in the heart of one gem;
In the core of one pearl all the shade and the shine of the sea:
    Breath and bloom, shade and shine—wonder, wealth, and—how far above them—
5   Truth, that's brighter than gem,
        Trust, that's purer than pearl—
Brightest truth, purest trust in the universe—all were for me
        In the kiss of one girl. — the best thing in the world

---

1. *Summum Bonum,* the highest good (Latin).

PROSPICE[1]

[handwritten annotations: "wants to get to / through death to / be with Eliz." and "Death—wants to / Fight death"]

Fear death?—to feel the fog in my throat,
  The mist in my face,
When the snows begin, and the blasts denote
  I am nearing the place,
5 The power of the night, the press of the storm,
  The post of the foe;
Where he stands, the Arch Fear in a visible form;
  Yet the strong man must go:
For the journey is done and the summit attained,
10   And the barriers fall,
Though a battle's to fight ere the guerdon be gained,
  The reward of it all.
I was ever a fighter, so—one fight more,
  The best and the last!

15 I would hate that Death bandaged my eyes, and
    forbore,
  And bade me creep past.
No! let me taste the whole of it, fare like my peers,
  The heroes of old,
Bear the brunt, in a minute pay glad life's arrears
20   Of pain, darkness and cold.
For sudden the worst turns the best to the brave.
  The black minute's at end,
And the elements' rage, the fiend voices that rave,
  Shall dwindle, shall blend,
25 Shall change, shall become first a peace out of
    pain.
Then a light, then thy breast,
O thou soul of my soul! I shall clasp thee again,
  And with God be the rest![2]

---

1. *Prospice* (pros′ pi chē), look forward (Latin).

2. *Then a light . . . be the rest.* These last three lines refer to Mrs. Browning, who had died shortly before the poem was written.

DISCUSSION

1. (a) Reread lines 1–15 of "Porphyria's Lover." What do Porphyria's actions indicate about her feelings for the speaker?

(b) What do lines 26–30 add to the portrait of Porphyria?

(c) What, then, prompts the speaker to strangle her?

(d) What is the meaning of the last line of the poem?

(e) What does the dramatic monologue reveal about Porphyria's lover?

2. (a) In "My Last Duchess," the only person we hear speak is the Duke, yet we come to dislike him. What devices has Browning used to cause the Duke inadvertently to reveal his evil nature?

(b) What is the situation in the poem —who is speaking to whom, what have they been discussing, where are they?

(c) Why has Browning selected this particular moment to present the Duke speaking?

(d) How much meaning may be read into the words in the opening lines that are here italicized: "That's *my last duchess* painted on the wall/ Looking *as if she were alive*"?

(e) Why does Browning include the remark about "Neptune. . . / Taming a sea horse" at the end of the poem?

3. (a) Compare the attitude toward death expressed in "Prospice" with that in Tennyson's "Crossing the Bar" and with John Donne's in "Death, be not proud." Which poem do you prefer? Why?

(b) To what extent is "Prospice" a love poem? What difference would there be if it ended with line 25?

(c) To what does Browning compare death in lines 1–12?

(d) Explain the meaning of *Arch Fear* (line 7), *journey* (line 9), and *guerdon* (line 11).

(e) The poem opens with a question, "Fear death?" which is not finally answered until line 17. Show how the poem is structured by this device of question and answer.

4. (a) In "Memorabilia," what is the speaker's attitude toward Shelley?

(b) Is the man to whom he is speaking successful in destroying his hero-worship? Explain.

(c) How do the last two stanzas of the poem illuminate the first two?

5. (a) One reader has dismissed "Summum Bonum" as "a bit of verbal fluff"; another has claimed it was "motivated by honest passion." With which reader do you agree, and why?

(b) Browning uses "the bag of one bee" to symbolize all the delights of fragrance and color that summer brings. Why is this an apt choice to symbolize all of summer? Explain the other natural symbols the poet uses. What relationship does he develop between the natural symbols in lines 1–4 and the rest of the poem?

(c) Why might Browning have used one word order in lines 1 and 2 and then reversed it in line 3?

WRITING

What report do you think the Count's emissary will bring back with him about the Duke in "My Last Duchess?" Write his report.

Matthew Arnold
1822 / 1888

[handwritten: something seperates he and Marguerite]

TO MARGUERITE

[handwritten: people are islands]

Yes! in the sea of life enisled,
With echoing straits between us thrown,
Dotting the shoreless watery wild,
We mortal millions live *alone*.
5 The islands feel the enclasping flow,
And then their endless bounds they know.

But when the moon their hollows lights,
And they are swept by balms of spring,
And in their glens, on starry nights,
10 The nightingales divinely sing;
And lovely notes, from shore to shore,
Across the sounds and channels pour—

Oh! then a longing like despair
Is to their farthest caverns sent;
15 For surely once, they feel, we were
Parts of a single continent!
Now round us spreads the watery plain—
Oh, might our marges meet again!

Who ordered, that their longing's fire
20 Should be, as soon as kindled, cooled?
Who renders vain their deep desire?—
A god, a god their severance ruled!
And bade betwixt their shores to be
The unplumbed, salt, estranging sea.

THE LAST WORD

Creep into thy narrow bed,
Creep, and let no more be said!
Vain thy onset! all stands fast.
Thou thyself must break at last.

5 Let the long contention cease!
Geese are swans, and swans are geese.
Let them have it how they will!
Thou art tired; best be still.

They out-talked thee, hissed thee, tore thee?
10 Better men fared thus before thee;
Fired their ringing shot and passed,
Hotly charged—and sank at last.

Charge once more, then, and be dumb!
Let the victors, when they come,
15 When the forts of folly fall,
Find thy body by the wall.

WEST LONDON *[handwritten: rich should give to the poor]*

Crouched on the pavement, close by Belgrave
    Square,
A tramp I saw, ill, moody, and tongue-tied.
A babe was in her arms, and at her side
A girl; their clothes were rags, their feet were bare.
Some labouring men, whose work lay somewhere
    there,
Passed opposite; she touched her girl, who hied
Across, and begged, and came back satisfied.
The rich she had let pass with frozen stare.
Thought I: "Above her state this spirit towers;
She will not ask of aliens, but of friends,
Of sharers in a common human fate.
She turns from that cold succour, which attends
The unknown little from the unknowing great,
And points us to a better time than ours."

DOVER BEACH

[handwritten: Be true to the one you love]

The sea is calm tonight,
The tide is full, the moon lies fair
Upon the straits; on the French coast the light
Gleams and is gone; the cliffs of England stand,
5 Glimmering and vast, out in the tranquil bay.
Come to the window, sweet is the night air!

Only, from the long line of spray
Where the sea meets the moon-blanched land,
Listen! you hear the grating roar
10 Of pebbles which the waves draw back, and fling,
At their return, up the high strand,
Begin, and cease, and then again begin,
With tremulous cadence slow, and bring
The eternal note of sadness in.

15 Sophocles[1] long ago
Heard it on the Aegean, and it brought
Into his mind the turbid ebb and flow
Of human misery; we
Find also in the sound a thought,
20 Hearing it by this distant northern sea.

The Sea of Faith
Was once, too, at the full, and round earth's shore
Lay like the folds of a bright girdle furled.
But now I only hear
25 Its melancholy, long, withdrawing roar,
Retreating, to the breath
Of the night wind, down the vast edges drear
And naked shingles[2] of the world.

Ah, love, let us be true
30 To one another! for the world, which seems
To lie before us like a land of dreams,
So various, so beautiful, so new,
Hath really neither joy, nor love, nor light,
Nor certitude, nor peace, nor help for pain;
35 And we are here as on a darkling plain
Swept with confused alarms of struggle and flight,
Where ignorant armies clash by night.

---

1. *Sophocles*, Greek dramatist (495–406 B.C.).
2. *shingles*, beaches.

SELF-DEPENDENCE

1

Weary of myself, and sick of asking
What I am, and what I ought to be,
At this vessel's prow I stand, which bears me
Forwards, forwards o'er the starlit sea.

2

5 And a look of passionate desire
O'er the sea and to the stars I send:
"Ye who from my childhood up have calmed me,
Calm me, ah, compose me to the end!

3

"Ah, once more," I cried, "ye stars, ye waters,
10 On my heart your mighty charm renew;
Still, still let me, as I gaze upon you,
Feel my soul becoming vast like you!"

4

From the intense, clear, star-sown vault of heaven,
Over the lit sea's unquiet way,
15 In the rustling night-air came the answer:
"Wouldst thou *be* as these are? *Live* as they.

5

"Unaffrighted by the silence round them,
Undistracted by the sights they see,
These demand not that the things without them
20 Yield them love, amusement, sympathy.

6

"And with joy the stars perform their shining,
And the sea its long moon-silvered roll;
For self-poised they live, nor pine with noting
All the fever of some differing soul.

7

25 "Bounded by themselves, and unregardful
In what state God's other works may be,
In their own tasks all their powers pouring,
These attain the mighty life you see."

8

O air-born voice! long since, severely clear,
30 A cry like thine in mine own heart I hear:
"Resolve to be thyself; and know that he
Who finds himself loses his misery!"

[handwritten: The way to be happy is to be yourself]

DISCUSSION

1. (a) According to the speaker in "To Marguerite," how do humans resemble islands?

(b) Does he feel these "islands" will ever be joined one to another?

(c) Compare his sentiments with those expressed by John Donne in "Meditation 17" (page 241).

2. Suppose that "The Last Word" is a soliloquy—that the speaker and "thou" are the same person. How would you interpret it?

3. In an Italian sonnet the first eight lines pose the proposition or problem, and the last six lines resolve it. Discuss how "West London" either follows or fails to follow this pattern.

4. (a) "Dover Beach" opens with a peaceful description; then the word *Only* (line 7) introduces a complete change in mood. What is that change?

(b) Trace further changes in mood which occur in the last two stanzas.

(c) What personal solution is suggested in the last stanza? Will the speaker find it satisfactory?

(d) "Dover Beach" is sometimes called "the first modern poem." Account for this comment.

(e) Is this predominantly a love poem, a philosophic poem, a meditative poem, or a combination? Explain.

5. (a) In "Self-Dependence" there are a number of speeches. Who is speaking in each case?

(b) Explore the meaning of the last two lines in stanza 6: "For self-poised they live, nor pine with noting / All the fever of some differing soul." Begin by defining the precise reference for "they." Relate these lines to the title and conclusion of the poem.

II. OTHER VICTORIAN POETS

From ~~love poems to her husband~~

SONNETS FROM THE PORTUGUESE
by Elizabeth Barrett Browning

22

WHEN our two souls stand up erect and strong,
Face to face, silent, drawing nigh and nigher,
Until the lengthening wings break into fire
At either curvèd point—what bitter wrong
5 Can the earth do to us, that we should not long
Be here contented? Think. In mounting higher,
The angels would press on us and aspire
To drop some golden orb of perfect song
Into our deep, dear silence. Let us stay
10 Rather on earth, Beloved—where the unfit
Contrarious moods of men recoil away
And isolate pure spirits, and permit
A place to stand and love in for a day,
With darkness and the death-hour rounding it.

28

My letters! all dead paper, mute and white!
And yet they seem alive and quivering
Against my tremulous hands which loose the string
And let them drop down on my knee to-night.
5 This said—he wished to have me in his sight
Once, as a friend: this fixed a day in spring
To come and touch my hand . . . a simple thing,
Yet I wept for it!—this, . . . the paper's light . . .
Said, *Dear I love thee*; and I sank and quailed
10 As if God's future thundered on my past.
This said, *I am thine*—and so its ink has paled
With lying at my heart that beat too fast.
And this . . . O Love, thy words have ill availed
If, what this said, I dared repeat at last!

43

How do I love thee? Let me count the ways.
I love thee to the depth and breadth and height
My soul can reach, when feeling out of sight
For the ends of Being and ideal Grace.
5 I love thee to the level of everyday's
Most quiet need, by sun and candlelight.
I love thee freely, as men strive for Right;
I love thee purely, as they turn from Praise.
I love thee with the passion put to use
10 In my old griefs, and with my childhood's faith,
I love thee with a love I seemed to lose
With my lost saints—I love thee with the breadth,
Smiles, tears, of all my life!—and, if God choose,
I shall but love thee better after death.

she'll love him after death

FALL, LEAVES, FALL

by Emily Brontë *she likes winter*

no quotes

Fall, leaves, fall; die, flowers, away;
Lengthen night and shorten day; *winter*
Every leaf speaks bliss to me
Fluttering from the autumn tree.
5 I shall smile when wreaths of snow
Blossom where the rose should grow;
I shall sing when night's decay
Ushers in a drearier day.

THE LATEST DECALOGUE

by Arthur Hugh Clough

Thou shalt have one God only; who
Would be at the expense of two?
No graven images may be
Worshipped, except the currency:
5 Swear not at all; for, for thy curse
Thine enemy is none the worse:
At church on Sunday to attend
Will serve to keep the world thy friend:
Honour thy parents; that is, all
10 From whom advancement may befall;
Thou shalt not kill; but need'st not strive
Officiously to keep alive:
Do not adultery commit;
Advantage rarely comes of it:
15 Thou shalt not steal; an empty feat,
When it's so lucrative to cheat:
Bear not false witness; let the lie
Have time on its own wings to fly:
Thou shalt not covet, but tradition
20 Approves all forms of competition.

THE FIRST DAY

wishes she could remember the First time she met this person.

by Christina Rossetti

I wish I could remember that first day,
First hour, first moment of your meeting me,
If bright or dim the season, it might be
Summer or Winter for aught I can say;
5 So unrecorded did it slip away,
So blind was I to see and to foresee,
So dull to mark the budding of my tree
That would not blossom yet for many a May.
If only I could recollect it, such
10 A day of days! I let it come and go
As traceless as a thaw of bygone snow;
It seemed to mean so little, meant so much;
If only now I could recall that touch,
First touch of hand in hand—Did one but know!

UP-HILL

Will there be room in heaven

by Christina Rossetti

Does the road wind up-hill all the way?
    Yes, to the very end.
Will the day's journey take the whole long day?
    From morn to night, my friend.

5 But is there for the night a resting-place?
    A roof for when the slow dark hours begin.
May not the darkness hide it from my face?
    You cannot miss that inn.

Shall I meet other wayfarers at night?
10   Those who have gone before.
Then must I knock, or call when just in sight?
    They will not keep you standing at that door.

Shall I find comfort, travel-sore and weak?
    Of labor you shall find the sum.
15 Will there be beds for me and all who seek?
    Yea, beds for all who come.

THE GARDEN OF PROSERPINE[1]

by Algernon Charles Swinburne

Here, where the world is quiet;
  Here, where all trouble seems
Dead winds' and spent waves' riot
  In doubtful dreams of dreams;
5 I watch the green field growing
  For reaping folk and sowing,
  For harvest-time and mowing,
    A sleepy world of streams.

I am tired of tears and laughter,
10   And men that laugh and weep;
Of what may come hereafter
  For men that sow to reap:
I am weary of days and hours,
  Blown buds of barren flowers,
15 Desires and dreams and powers
    And everything but sleep.

Here life has death for neighbor,
  And far from eye or ear
Wan waves and wet winds labor,
20   Weak ships and spirits steer;
They drive adrift, and whither
They wot not who make thither;
But no such winds blow hither,
    And no such things grow here.

25 No growth of moor or coppice,
   No heather-flower or vine,
But bloomless buds of poppies,
   Green grapes of Proserpine,
Pale beds of blowing rushes
30 Where no leaf blooms or blushes
Save this whereout she crushes
    For dead men deadly wine.

Pale, without name or number,
  In fruitless fields of corn,
35 They bow themselves and slumber
    All night till light is born;

And like a soul belated,
  In hell and heaven unmated,
  By cloud and mist abated
40   Comes out of darkness morn.

Though one were strong as seven,
   He too with death shall dwell,
Nor wake with wings in heaven,
  Nor weep for pains in hell;
45 Though one were fair as roses,
  His beauty clouds and closes;
And well though love reposes,
    In the end it is not well.

Pale, beyond porch and portal,
50   Crowned with calm leaves, she stands
Who gathers all things mortal
   With cold immortal hands;
Her languid lips are sweeter
Than love's who fears to greet her
55 To men that mix and meet her
    From many times and lands.

She waits for each and other,
   She waits for all men born;
Forgets the earth her mother,
60   The life of fruits and corn;
And spring and seed and swallow
Take wing for her and follow
Where summer song rings hollow
    And flowers are put to scorn.

65 There go the loves that wither,
   The old loves with wearier wings;
And all dead years draw thither,
   And all disastrous things;
Dead dreams of days forsaken,
70 Blind buds that snows have shaken,
Wild leaves that winds have taken,
    Red strays of ruined springs.

We are not sure of sorrow,
  And joy was never sure;
75 Today will die tomorrow;
   Time stoops to no man's lure,
And love, grown faint and fretful,
With lips but half regretful
Sighs, and with eyes forgetful
80   Weeps that no love endures.

---

1. *Proserpine* (pros′ ər pīn), in Roman mythology, the daughter of Zeus and the earth goddess Demeter, who was abducted by the god of the underworld and ruled with him there. Her Greek name is Persephone.

From too much love of living,
   From hope and fear set free,
We thank with brief thanksgiving
   Whatever gods may be
85 That no life lives for ever;
   That dead men rise up never;
   That even the weariest river
     Winds somewhere safe to sea.

   Then star nor sun shall waken,
90   Nor any change of light;
Nor sound of waters shaken,
   Nor any sound or sight;
Nor wintry leaves nor vernal,
Nor days nor things diurnal;
95 Only the sleep eternal
   In an eternal night.   ☐

SYMPHONY IN YELLOW
by Oscar Wilde

[handwritten: poem about yellow things]

An omnibus across the bridge
   Crawls like a yellow butterfly,
   And, here and there, a passer-by
Shows like a little restless midge.

5 Big barges full of yellow hay
   Are moved against the shadowy wharf,
   And, like a yellow silken scarf,
The thick fog hangs along the quay.

   The yellow leaves begin to fade
10   And flutter from the Temple elms,
   And at my feet the pale green Thames
Lies like a rod of rippled jade.

REQUIEM
by Robert Louis Stevenson

[handwritten: what he wants, written on his grave stone]

Under the wide and starry sky,
Dig the grave and let me lie.
Glad did I live and gladly die.
And I laid me down with a will.

This be the verse you grave for me:
Here he lies where he longed to be;—
Home is the sailor, home from the sea,
And the hunter home from the hill.

DISCUSSION

Elizabeth Barrett Browning
1. (a) In Sonnet 22, which facets of earthly love does the speaker praise most?
(b) Why doesn't she wish this love to mount any higher?
2. Describe in your own words the progress of the romance in Sonnet 28, "My letters all dead paper. . . ."
3. (a) Can you "count the ways" in which the speaker loves the person to whom Sonnet 43 is addressed? Is there any order or arrangement to the "ways"?
(b) What are "my lost saints" in line 12?

Emily Brontë
1. How does "Fall, Leaves" epitomize the feeling of pessimism that

is characteristic of much Victorian literature?

Arthur Hugh Clough
1. Explore the source of the irony that permeates this modern "adaptation" of the Ten Commandments.

Christina Rossetti
1. "The First Day" is quite specific in its utterances. On a deeper, generalized level, what is it referring to?
2. "Uphill" progresses in a series of questions and answers.
(a) Who might be asking the questions?
(b) Who is answering them?
(c) What does the poem mean?

Algernon Charles Swinburne
1. (a) In "The Garden of Proserpine," what comparison is made between life on earth and life in the underworld?
(b) Is this poem an expression of the universal death-wish, the desire for total oblivion?

Oscar Wilde
1. (a) In "Symphony in Yellow," what similes are used, and with what effect? What is the effect of the change in color in the last two lines?
(b) Compare the mood of this poem with that of Keats's "To Autumn."

Robert Louis Stevenson
1. "Requiem" is a poem about the speaker's death, yet it does not seem gloomy. Why?

From THE RUBÁIYÁT OF OMAR KHAYYÁM

by Edward Fitzgerald

"The Rubáiyát" is a translation of a work by the Persian
poet and mathematician Omar Khayyám, who died around
the year 1123. The original contained more than 400
quatrains, of which Fitzgerald translated 101. Experts
agree that the translation is faithful to the original in spirit
and idea, but very different in formal effect.

1

WAKE! For the Sun, who scattered into flight
The Stars before him from the Field of Night
   Drives Night along with them from Heav'n and
     strikes
The Sultàn's Turret with a Shaft of Light.

2

Come, fill the Cup, and in the fire of Spring
Your Winter garment of Repentance fling;
   The Bird of Time has but a little way
   To flutter—and the Bird is on the Wing.

3

A Book of Verses underneath the Bough,
10 A Jug of Wine, a Loaf of Bread—and Thou
   Beside me singing in the Wilderness—
Oh, Wilderness were Paradise enow!

4

Some for the Glories of This World, and some
Sigh for the Prophet's[1] Paradise to come;
15   Ah, take the Cash, and let the Credit go,
Nor heed the rumble of a distant Drum!

5

Look to the blowing[2] Rose about us—"Lo,
Laughing," she says, "into the world I blow,
   At once the silken tassel of my Purse
20 Tear, and its Treasure on the Garden throw."

6

And those who husbanded the Golden Grain,
And those who flung it to the winds like Rain,
   Alike to no such aureate Earth are turned

As, buried once, Men want dug up again.

7

25 Think, in this battered Caravanserai[3]
Whose Portals are alternate Night and Day,
   How Sultan after Sultàn with his Pomp
Abode his destined Hour, and went his way.

8

I sometimes think that never blows so red
30 The Rose as where some buried Caesar bled;
   That every Hyacinth[4] the Garden wears
Dropped in her Lap from some once lovely Head.

9

And this reviving Herb whose tender Green
Fledges the River-Lip on which we lean—
35   Ah, lean upon it lightly! for who knows
From what once lovely Lip it springs unseen!

10

Ah, make the most of what we yet may spend,
Before we too into the Dust descend;
   Dust into Dust, and under Dust, to lie,
40 Sans[5] Wine, sans Song, sans Singer, and—sans End!

11

Why, all the Saints and Sages who discussed
Of the Two Worlds so wisely—they are thrust
   Like foolish Prophets forth; their Words to Scorn
Are scattered, and their Mouths are stopped with
     Dust.

---

3. *Caravanserai*, an inn in the Orient where caravans put up for
the night.
4. *Hyacinth*, the flower named after Hyacinthus, a youth killed
by the god Apollo, and from whose blood the flower sprang.
5. *Sans*, without (French).

---

1. *Prophet's*, Mohammed's.
2. *blowing*, blossoming.

12

45 Myself when young did eagerly frequent
 Doctor and Saint, and heard great argument
  About it and about; but evermore
 Came out by the same door where in I went.

13

With them the seed of Wisdom did I sow,
50 And with mine own hand wrought to make it
   grow;
  And this was all the Harvest that I reaped—
 "I came like Water, and like Wind I go."

14

I sent my Soul through the Invisible,
Some letter of that Afterlife to spell;
55   And by and by my Soul returned to me,
 And answered, "I Myself am Heav'n and Hell"—

15

Heav'n but the Vision of fulfilled Desire,
And Hell the Shadow from a Soul on fire
  Cast on the Darkness into which Ourselves,
60 So late emerged from, shall so soon expire.

16

We are no other than a moving row
Of Magic Shadow-shapes that come and go
  Round with the Sun-illumined Lantern held
 In Midnight by the Master of the Show;

17

65 But helpless Pieces of the Game He plays
 Upon this Checkerboard of Nights and Days;
  Hither and thither moves, and checks, and slays,
 And one by one back in the Closet lays.

18

The Moving Finger writes, and, having writ,
70 Moves on; nor all your Piety nor Wit
  Shall lure it back to cancel half a line,
 Nor all your Tears wash out a Word of it.

19

Oh, Thou, who Man of Baser Earth didst make,
And ev'n with Paradise devise the Snake,
75   For all the Sin wherewith the Face of Man
 Is blackened—Man's forgiveness give—and take!

20

Yet, Ah, that Spring should vanish with the Rose!
That Youth's sweet-scented manuscript should close!
  The Nightingale that in the branches sang,
80 Ah whence, and whither flown again, who knows!

21

Would but some wingèd Angel ere too late
Arrest the yet unfolded Roll of Fate,
  And make the stern Recorder otherwise
Enregister, or quite obliterate!

22

85 Ah, Love! could you and I with Him conspire
To grasp this sorry Scheme of Things entire,
  Would not we shatter it to bits—and then
Remold it nearer to the Heart's Desire!

DISCUSSION

1. Discuss the symbolism of the imagery in stanza 3—the book of verses, the bough, the jug of wine, and "thou."

2. Relate "Ozymandias" (page 363) to some of the stanzas in this poem (especially stanza 7).

3. Discuss the meaning of line 48. Explain the aptness of the figure of the door.

4. Discuss the appropriateness and value of the metaphors of the "Magic Shadow-shapes" in line 62 and the "Moving Finger" in line 69.

III. LATE VICTORIAN POETS

Thomas Hardy
1840 / 1928

why am I here? who am I? [handwritten]

NATURE'S QUESTIONING

perfect victorian poem [handwritten]

When I look forth at dawning, pool,
    Field, flock, and lonely tree,
    All seem to gaze at me
Like chastened children sitting silent in a school;

5   Their faces dulled, constrained, and worn,
    As though the master's ways
    Through the long teaching days
Had cowed them till their early zest was overborne.

    Upon them stirs in lippings mere
10   (As if once clear in call,
    But now scarce breathed at all)—
"We wonder, ever wonder, why we find us here!

    "Has some Vast Imbecility,
    Mighty to build and blend,
15   But impotent to tend,
Framed us in jest, and left us now to hazardry?

    "Or come we of an Automaton
    Unconscious of our pains? . . .
    Or are we live remains
20 Of Godhead dying downwards, brain and eye now
    gone?

    "Or is it that some high Plan betides,
    As yet not understood,
    Of Evil stormed by Good,
We the Forlorn Hope over which Achievement
    strides?"

25   Thus things around. No answerer I. . .
    Meanwhile the winds, and rains,
    And Earth's old glooms and pains
Are still the same, and Life and Death are neigh-
    bours nigh.

HAP

If but some vengeful god would call to me
From up the sky, and laugh: "Thou suffering thing,
Know that thy sorrow is my ecstasy,
That thy love's loss is my hate's profiting!"

5 Then would I bear it, clench myself, and die,
Steeled by the sense of ire unmerited;
Half-eased in that a Powerfuller than I
Had willed and meted me the tears I shed.

But not so. How arrives it joy lies slain,
10 And why unblooms the best hope ever sown?
—Crass Casualty obstructs the sun and rain,
And dicing Time for gladness casts a moan. . .
These purblind Doomsters had as readily strown
Blisses about my pilgrimage as pain.

You live on in memory [handwritten]

HIS IMMORTALITY

    I saw a dead man's finer part
Shining with each faithful heart
Of those bereft. Then said I: "This must be
    His immortality."

5   I looked there as the seasons wore,
And still his soul continuously bore
A life in theirs. But less its shine excelled
    Than when I first beheld.

    His fellow-yearsmen passed, and then
10 In later hearts I looked for him again;
And found him—shrunk, alas! into a thin
    And spectral mannikin.

    Lastly I ask—now old and chill—
If aught of him remain unperished still;
15 And find, in me alone, a feeble spark,
    Dying amid the dark.

"Nature's Questioning," "Hap," and "His Immortality" from *Collected Poems* by Thomas Hardy. Reprinted with permission of The Macmillan Company; Macmillan London & Basingstoke; The Macmillan Company of Canada Limited, and the Trustees of the Hardy Estate. Copyright 1925 by The Macmillan Company.

When you die, life goes on and you are forgotten

"AH, ARE YOU DIGGING ON MY GRAVE?"

"Ah, are you digging on my grave
    My loved one?—planting rue?"
—"No: yesterday he went to wed
One of the brightest wealth has bred.
5 'It cannot hurt her now,' he said,
    'That I should not be true.'"

"Then who is digging on my grave?
    My nearest dearest kin?"
—"Ah, no: they sit and think, 'What use!
10 What good will planting flowers produce?
No tendance of her mound can loose
    Her spirit from Death's gin.'"

"But some one digs upon my grave?
    My enemy?—prodding sly?"
15 —"Nay: when she heard you had passed the Gate
That shuts on all flesh soon or late,
She thought you no more worth her hate,
    And cares not where you lie."

"Then, who is digging on my grave?
20   Say—since I have not guessed!"
—"O it is I, my mistress dear,
Your little dog, who still lives near,
And much I hope my movements here
    Have not disturbed your rest?"

25 "Ah, yes! *You* dig upon my grave . . .
    Why flashed it not on me
That one true heart was left behind!
What feeling do we ever find
To equal among human kind
30   A dog's fidelity!"

"Mistress, I dug upon your grave
    To bury a bone, in case
I should be hungry near this spot
When passing on my daily trot.
35 I am sorry, but I quite forgot
    It was your resting-place."

"Ah, Are You Digging on My Grave," "The Darkling Thrush," and
"Epitaph on a Pessimist" from *Collected Poems* by Thomas Hardy.
Reprinted with permission of The Macmillan Company; Macmillan
London & Basingstoke; The Macmillan Company of Canada Limited,
and the Trustees of the Hardy Estate. Copyright 1925 by The Mac-
millan Company.

THE DARKLING THRUSH

I leant upon a coppice gate
    When Frost was spectre-gray,
And Winter's dregs made desolate
    The weakening eye of day.
5 The tangled bine-stems scored the sky
    Like strings of broken lyres,
And all mankind that haunted nigh
    Had sought their household fires.

The land's sharp features seemed to be
10   The Century's corpse outleant;
His crypt the cloudy canopy,
    The wind his death-lament.
The ancient pulse of germ and birth
    Was shrunken hard and dry,
15 And every spirit upon earth
    Seemed fervourless as I.

At once a voice arose among
    The bleak twigs overhead
In a full-hearted evensong
20   Of joy illimited;
An aged thrush, frail, gaunt and small,
    In blast-beruffled plume,
Had chosen thus to fling his soul
    Upon the growing gloom.

25 So little cause for carolings
    Of such ecstatic sound
Was written on terrestrial things
    Afar or nigh around,
That I could think there trembled through
30   His happy good-night air
Some blessed Hope, whereof he knew
    And I was unaware.

He wishes his Father

EPITAPH ON A PESSIMIST

didn't know women so he wouldn't be born

I'm Smith of Stoke, aged sixty-odd,
    I've lived without a dame
From youth-time on; and would to God
    My dad had done the same.

                        From the French.

AT CASTLE BOTEREL

As I drive to the junction of lane and highway,
  And the drizzle bedrenches the waggonette,
I look behind at the fading byway,
  And see on its slope, now glistening wet,
5   Distinctly yet

Myself and a girlish form benighted
  In dry March weather. We climb the road
Beside a chaise. We had just alighted
  To ease the sturdy pony's load
10   When he sighed and slowed.

What we did as we climbed, and what we talked of
  Matters not much, nor to what it led—
Something that life will not be balked of
  Without rude reason till hope is dead,
15   And feeling fled.

It filled but a minute. But was there ever
  A time of such quality, since or before,
In that hill's story? To one mind never,
  Though it has been climbed, foot-swift, foot-sore,
20   By thousands more.

Primaeval rocks form the road's steep border,
  And much have they faced there, first and last,
Of the transitory in Earth's long order;
  But what they record in colour and cast
25   Is—that we two passed.

And to me, though Time's unflinching rigour,
  In mindless rote, has ruled from sight
The substance now, one phantom figure
  Remains on the slope, as when that night
30   Saw us alight.

I look and see it there, shrinking, shrinking,
  I look back at it amid the rain
For the very last time; for my sand is sinking,
  And I shall traverse old love's domain
35   Never again.

From *Collected Poems* by Thomas Hardy. Reprinted with permission of The Macmillan Company; Macmillan London & Basingstoke; The Macmillan Company of Canada Limited, and the Trustees of the Hardy Estate. Copyright 1925 by The Macmillan Company.

DISCUSSION

1. (a) What indications are there in the first three stanzas of "Nature's Questioning" that the world is old? How does the last stanza support this?

(b) The speaker mentions four aspects of the questions he imagines as being posed by the natural world: that it was created by "some Vast Imbecility," "an Automaton," "God-head dying downwards," or "some high Plan." Explain each of these aspects.

(c) How does the speaker view life?

2. (a) What does the speaker in "Hap" find even worse than the hatred of some vengeful god? Do you agree with him?

(b) Look up the meaning of the title in a dictionary and explain how it applies to the poem.

3. (a) In "Ah, Are You Digging on My Grave," has anyone—lover, family, enemy, or dog—really betrayed the buried girl, or are all behaving true to life's plans for them?

(b) This poem piles irony upon irony. Which do you think is the greatest irony?

(c) What does Hardy gain by keeping the tone of this poem so objective?

4. Comment on the character of Smith of Stoke in "Epitaph on a Pessimist." Limit yourself to 48 words—twice the number in the poem.

5. (a) In "The Darkling Thrush," contrast the speaker's mood with that of the thrush.

(b) Does the thrush affect the speaker's mood to any extent?

(c) Comment on the use of the word *darkling* in the title.

(d) What words and phrases suggest death?

6. How does the theme of "His Immortality" compare with the theme of immortality as treated by conventional sonneteers?

7. (a) In "At Castle Boterel," the speaker is revisiting a scene he knew years before. What happened on that earlier occasion?

(b) Was it something passing, or something relatively permanent? Explain.

(c) What is the point of bringing in the "Primaeval rocks" and the reference to "Time's unflinching rigour"?

(d) What is the theme of the poem?

Gerard Manley Hopkins 1844 / 1889

PIED BEAUTY [*Dappled things are great* — handwritten]

Glory be to God for dappled things—
  For skies of couple-color as a brinded cow;
    For rose-moles all in stipple upon trout that
      swim;
Fresh-firecoal chestnut-falls;[1] finches' wings;
5 Landscape plotted and pieced[2]—fold, fallow, and
      plow;
  And all trades, their gear and tackle and trim.

All things counter,[3] original, spare, strange;
  Whatever is fickle, freckled (who knows how?)
    With swift, slow; sweet, sour; adazzle, dim;
10 He fathers-forth whose beauty is past change:
      Praise him.

---

1. *chestnut-falls,* chestnuts newly stripped of their husks.
2. *plotted and pieced,* divided into fields.
3. *counter,* contrary to what is expected.

GOD'S GRANDEUR

The world is charged with the grandeur of God.
  It will flame out, like shining from shook foil;
  It gathers to a greatness, like the ooze of oil
Crushed.[1] Why do men then now not reck his rod?
5 Generations have trod, have trod, have trod;
  And all is seared with trade; bleared, smeared
      with toil;
  And wears man's smudge and shares man's smell:
      the soil
Is bare now, nor can foot feel, being shod.

And for[2] all this, nature is never spent;
10 There lives the dearest freshness deep down things;
  And though the last lights off the black West went
    Oh, morning, at the brown brink eastward, springs—
Because the Holy Ghost over the bent
    World broods with warm breast and with ah!
      bright wings.

---

1. *ooze . . . /Crushed,* oil from crushed olives.
2. *for,* despite.

SPRING AND FALL [*youth* — handwritten]

to a young child

Márgarét, are you gríeving
Over Goldengrove unleaving?
Leáves, líke the things of man, you
With your fresh thoughts care for, can you?
5 Áh! ás the heart grows older
It will come to such sights colder
By and by, nor spare a sigh
Though worlds of wanwood leafmeal lie;
And yet you wíll weep and know why.
10 Now no matter, child, the name:
Sórrow's spríngs áre the same.
Nor mouth had, no nor mind, expressed
What heart heard of, ghost guessed:
It ís the blight man was born for, [*man was borne* — handwritten]
15 It is Margaret you mourn for. [*For regreting loosing their childhood* — handwritten]

THOU ART INDEED JUST, LORD

Thou art indeed just, Lord, if I contend
With thee; but, sir, so what I plead is just.
Why do sinners' ways prosper? and why must
Disappointment all I endeavour end?
5 Wert thou my enemy, O thou my friend,
How wouldst thou worse, I wonder, than thou dost
Defeat, thwart me? Oh, the sots and thralls of lust
Do in spare hours more thrive than I that spend,
Sir, life upon thy cause. See, banks and brakes
10 Now, leavèd how thick! lacèd they are again
With fretty chervil, look, and fresh wind shakes
Them; birds build—but not I build; no, but strain,
Time's eunuch, and not breed one work that wakes.
Mine, O thou lord of life, send my roots rain.

"Pied Beauty," "God's Grandeur," "Spring and Fall," and "Thou Art Indeed Just, Lord" from *Poems of Gerard Manley Hopkins*, 4th Edition. Edited by W. H. Gardner and N. H. Mackenzie, 1967, published by Oxford University Press by arrangement with The Society of Jesus. Reprinted by permission.

THE WINDHOVER[1]

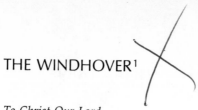

To Christ Our Lord

I caught this morning morning's minion, king-
    dom of daylight's dauphin, dapple-dawn-drawn Falcon, in his riding
    Of the rolling level underneath him steady air, and striding
High there, how he rung upon the rein of a wimpling wing
5 In his ecstasy! then off, off forth on swing,
    As a skate's heel sweeps smooth on a bow-bend—the hurl and gliding
    Rebuffed the big wind. My heart in hiding
Stirred for a bird—the achieve of, the mastery of the thing!

Brute beauty and valor and act, oh, air, pride, plume, here
10   Buckle! AND the fire that breaks from thee then, a billion
Times told lovelier, more dangerous, O my chevalier!
    No wonder of it: shéer plód makes plow down sillion
Shine, and blue-bleak embers, ah, my dear,
    Fall, gall themselves, and gash gold-vermilion.

From *Poems of Gerard Manley Hopkins*, 4th Edition. Edited by W. H. Gardner and N. H. Mackenzie, 1967, published by Oxford University Press by arrangement with The Society of Jesus. Reprinted by permission.
1. *Windhover*, a kestrel or sparrow-hawk.

DISCUSSION

1. (a) In "Pied Beauty," what specific aspects of nature are being praised?

(b) What physical characteristics do they have in common that causes Hopkins to praise them?

(c) What is the deeper reason for his praise?

2. (a) What is the complaint raised in the first eight lines of "God's Grandeur"?

(b) What is Hopkins' point in using words and images drawn from modern technology?

(c) How do the concluding six lines contrast with the first eight?

(d) Is the end result pessimistic or optimistic? Explain.

3. (a) According to "Spring and Fall," what is "the blight man was born for"?

(b) Explain how the poet uses the child's sorrow at seeing the falling autumn leaves to point out a universal truth.

(c) The words "Sorrow's springs" (line 11) have a dual function, based on two different meanings of the word *spring*. Explain this dual function.

(d) Discuss Hopkins' use of assonance (matching of vowel sounds), alliteration, and coined words such as *wanwood* (suggestive of *wan* and *wormwood*) and *leafmeal* (suggestive of *leaf* and *piecemeal*).

(e) What similarities can you find between "Spring and Fall" and Anglo-Saxon poetry?

4. (a) How does "The Windhover" try to capture the soaring, wheeling flight of the bird?

(b) Explain the subtitle, "To Christ our Lord."

(c) One reader has remarked that Hopkins' poems are like birdsong or the music of woodwinds—an ecstatic, trilling sigh, shaped and tempered by occasional plosive consonant sounds (d, g, k, t, p, b). Do you agree?

5. (a) What are the speaker's major complaints in "Thou Art Indeed Just"?

(b) How are these complaints similar to those expressed by Hardy in "Hap"?

(c) How are they different from Hardy's?

A. E. Housman
1859 / 1936

LOVELIEST OF TREES *not enough time in life to appreciate nature* (handwritten)

Loveliest of trees, the cherry now
Is hung with bloom along the bough,
And stands about the woodland ride,
Wearing white for Eastertide.

5 Now, of my threescore years and ten, *70 years* (handwritten)
Twenty will not come again,
And take from seventy springs a score,
It only leaves me fifty more.

And since to look at things in bloom
10 Fifty springs are little room,
About the woodlands I will go
To see the cherry hung with snow.

WHEN I WAS ONE-AND-TWENTY
It is more painful to give your heart away than your money (handwritten)

When I was one-and-twenty
 I heard a wise man say,
"Give crowns and pounds and guineas
 But not your heart away;
5 Give pearls away and rubies
 But keep your fancy free."
But I was one-and-twenty,
 No use to talk to me.

When I was one-and-twenty
10 I heard him say again,
"The heart out of the bosom
 Was never given in vain;
'Tis paid with sighs a plenty
 And sold for endless rue."
15 And I am two-and-twenty,
 And oh, 'tis true, 'tis true.

It is better to die before your Fame does (handwritten)

TO AN ATHLETE DYING YOUNG

The time you won your town the race
We chaired you through the market place;
Man and boy stood cheering by,
And home we brought you shoulder-high.

5 Today, the road all runners come,
Shoulder-high we bring you home,
And set you at your threshold down,
Townsman of a stiller town.

Smart lad, to slip betimes away
10 From fields where glory does not stay,
And early though the laurel grows
It withers quicker than the rose.

Eyes the shady night has shut
Cannot see the record cut,
15 And silence sounds no worse than cheers
After earth has stopped the ears.

Now you will not swell the rout
Of lads that wore their honors out, *Sadest thing that can happen to an athlete* (handwritten)
Runners whom renown outran
20 And the name died before the man.

So set, before its echoes fade,
The fleet foot on the sill of shade,
And hold to the low lintel up
The still-defended challenge cup.

25 And round that early-laureled head
Will flock to gaze the strengthless dead,
And find unwithered on its curls
The garland briefer than a girl's.

"Loveliest of Trees," "When I Was One-and-Twenty," and "To an Athlete Dying Young" from "A Shropshire Lad"—Authorised Edition—from *The Collected Poems of A. E. Housman*. Copyright 1939, 1940 © 1959 by Holt, Rinehart and Winston, Inc. Copyright © 1967, 1968 by Robert E. Symons. Reprinted by permission of Holt, Rinehart and Winston, Inc., and The Society of Authors as the literary representative of the Estate of A. E. Housman, and Jonathan Cape Ltd., publishers.

TERENCE, THIS IS STUPID STUFF

"Terence,[1] this is stupid stuff:
You eat your victuals fast enough;
There can't be much amiss, 'tis clear,
To see the rate you drink your beer.
5   But ho, good Lord, the verse you make,
It gives a chap the belly-ache.
The cow, the old cow, she is dead;
It sleeps well, the horned head:
We poor lads, 'tis our turn now
10 To hear such tunes as killed the cow.[2]
Pretty friendship 'tis to rhyme
Your friends to death before their time
Moping melancholy mad:
Come, pipe a tune to dance to, lad."

15   Why, if 'tis dancing you would be,
There's brisker pipes than poetry.
Say, for what were hop-yards meant,
Or why was Burton built on Trent?[3]
Oh many a peer of England brews
20 Livelier liquor than the Muse,
And malt does more than Milton can
To justify God's ways to man.
Ale, man, ale's the stuff to drink
For fellows whom it hurts to think:
25 Look into the pewter pot
To see the world as the world's not.
And faith, 'tis pleasant till 'tis past:
The mischief is that 'twill not last.
Oh I have been to Ludlow fair
30 And left my necktie God knows where,
And carried half-way home, or near,
Pints and quarts of Ludlow beer:
Then the world seemed none so bad,
And I myself a sterling lad;
35 And down in lovely muck I've lain,

Happy till I woke again.
Then I saw the morning sky:
Heigho, the tale was all a lie;
The world, it was the old world yet,
40 I was I, my things were wet,
And nothing now remained to do
But begin the game anew.

Therefore, since the world has still
Much good, but much less good than ill,
45 And while the sun and moon endure
Luck's a chance, but trouble's sure,
I'd face it as a wise man would,
And train for ill and not for good.
'Tis true, the stuff I bring for sale
50 Is not so brisk a brew as ale:
Out of a stem that scored the hand
I wrung it in a weary land.
But take it: if the smack is sour,
The better for the embittered hour;
55 It should do good to heart and head
When your soul is in my soul's stead;
And I will friend you, if I may,
In the dark and cloudy day.

There was a king reigned in the East:
60 There, when kings will sit to feast,
They get their fill before they think
With poisoned meat and poisoned drink.
He gathered all that springs to birth
From the many venomed earth;
65 First a little, thence to more,
He sampled all her killing store;
And easy, smiling, seasoned sound,
Sate the king when healths went round.
They put arsenic in his meat
70 And stared aghast to watch him eat;
They poured strychnine in his cup
And shook to see him drink it up:
They shook, they stared as white's their shirt:
Them it was their poison hurt.
75 —I tell the tale that I heard told.
Mithridates, he died old.[4]

From "A Shropshire Lad"—Authorised Edition—from *The Collected Poems of A. E. Housman*. Copyright 1939, 1940 © 1959 by Holt, Rinehart and Winston, Inc. Copyright © 1967, 1968 by Robert E. Symons. Reprinted by permission of Holt, Rinehart and Winston, Inc., and The Society of Authors as the literary representative of the Estate of A. E. Housman, and Jonathan Cape Ltd., publishers.

1. *Terence*, the imagined character through whom Housman speaks in the poems in *A Shropshire Lad*.
2. *such tunes as killed the cow*, a reference to the traditional expression "the tune which the old cow died of," which refers to a boring or badly performed piece of music.
3. Burton-on-Trent is a famous English brewing town.

4. *Mithridates, he died old*. Mithridates VI, King of Pontus (120–63 B.C.) is reported to have taken the precautions against assasination by his enemies which are described here. It is said that after his country was defeated by Rome, Mithridates tried to commit suicide, but his body was so inured that poison had no effect. He finally had to command a soldier to kill him with a sword.

IS MY TEAM PLOUGHING

everything goes on after you die

"Is my team ploughing,
   That I was used to drive
And hear the harness jingle
   When I was man alive?"

5 Ay, the horses trample,
   The harness jingles now;
No change though you lie under
   The land you used to plough.

"Is football playing
10   Along the river shore,
With lads to chase the leather,
   Now I stand up no more?"

Ay, the ball is flying,
   The lads play heart and soul;
15 The goal stands up, the keeper
   Stands up to keep the goal.

"Is my girl happy,
   That I thought hard to leave,
And has she tired of weeping
20   As she lies down at eve?"

Ay, she lies down lightly,
   She lies not down to weep:
Your girl is well contented.
   Be still, my lad, and sleep.

25 "Is my friend hearty,
   Now I am thin and pine,
And has he found to sleep in
   A better bed than mine?"

Yes, lad, I lie easy,
30   I lie as lads would choose;
I cheer a dead man's sweetheart,
   Never ask me whose.

From "A Shropshire Lad"—Authorised Edition—from *The Collected Poems of A. E. Housman*. Copyright 1939, 1940 © 1959 by Holt, Rinehart and Winston, Inc. Copyright © 1967, 1968 by Robert E. Symons. Reprinted by permission of Holt, Rinehart and Winston, Inc., and The Society of Authors as the literary representative of the Estate of A. E. Housman, and Jonathan Cape Ltd., publishers.

DISCUSSION

1. (a) How old is the speaker in "Loveliest of Trees"?

(b) Are the mathematical computations about his age out of keeping with the general tone of the poem? Explain.

(c) Some critics claim that this brief lyric epitomizes springtime. Do you agree?

2. How seriously is the reader supposed to take the complaint of the speaker in "When I Was One-and-Twenty"? Justify your answer.

3. Several poems in this book concern a person who is dead and buried, among them "The Unquiet Grave" (page 108), "Ah, Are You Digging on My Grave," and "Is My Team Ploughing?" Compare these three poems with regard to the feelings of the survivors and the general tone of the poems. Does there appear to be any change across the centuries? Explain.

4. (a) What is the mood of the speaker in "To an Athlete Dying Young"?

(b) Are his words intended to relieve his own grief, to console the spirit of the dead athlete, to have an even wider application—or to do all of these? Explain.

(c) What is meant by the lines "And early though the laurel grows/ It withers quicker than the rose"?

5. (a) What contrasting qualities of poetry and ale are implied in "Terence, This Is Stupid Stuff"?

(b) What does the story of Mithridates have to do with Terence's view of the world? Which lines in stanza 3 best express the point Terence is making?

(c) What does this poem have in common with such poems in the *carpe diem* tradition as Marlowe's "The Passionate Shepherd to His Love" (page 143), Jonson's "Come, My Celia" (page 245), and "The Rubáiyát"? How is it different?

WRITING

1. Tennyson's poems express some measure of religious doubt and the disorientation that accompanied it. Reread the selections by Tennyson in this book (as well as others, if you wish); then write a short paper in which you compare his feelings about religious belief with your own or with those you have observed generally in your experience as representative of today.

2. Reread Robert Browning's "Summum Bonum," "Prospice," and the Sonnets of Elizabeth Barrett Browning and discuss the strength of their mutual love, as revealed in their poetry, in giving purpose to their lives.

3. Matthew Arnold seemed to concern himself with the feelings of alienation that resulted from the weakening of traditional faith. Discuss both "To Marguerite" and "Dover Beach" in the light of that alienation.

4. Write a short paper comparing your personal responses to Tennyson, Browning, and Arnold. You may wish to concentrate on which of the three appears most modern, which wrote what seems to you the most relevant poetry, which wrote the most universal poetry, or which you personally like best.

5. Using the poems of the "Other Victorians" as your basis, write a paper describing matters that seemed to be of prime concern to them—universals such as life, love, and death as well as the more particular problems of the age: loss of faith, concern over growing industrialization, disorientation as traditional values crumbled.

6. Imagine that "Loveliest of Trees," "When I Was One-and-Twenty," and "Is My Team Ploughing" all deal with the same young man, and write an account of what happened to him.

7. One critic has described Hopkins' faith as "ecstatically anguished."

Discuss the extent to which the poems included in this section bear out that evaluation.

8. Thomas Hardy is sometimes called "the artist of the ironic in both poetry and fiction." Write a short paper in which you discuss the irony in some of his poems, and, if you wish, also in his short story "The Three Strangers."

9. Consider the three early Victorians —Tennyson, Browning, and Arnold— and the three late Victorians—Housman, Hardy, and Hopkins—and write a paper in which you make a general comparison of the prominent early figures with the prominent late figures.

READERS' THEATER

Many of the poems in this section are dramatic monologues or poems for two voices. Select some of these and present an all-Victorian poetry reading program.

IV. SHORT FICTION

HORATIO SPARKINS

by Charles Dickens

INDEED, my love, he paid Teresa very great attention on the last assembly night," said Mrs. Malderton, addressing her spouse, who, after the fatigues of the day in the City, was sitting with a silk handkerchief over his head, and his feet on the fender, drinking his port;—"very great attention; and I say again, every possible encouragement ought to be given him. He positively must be asked down here to dine."

"Who must?" inquired Mr. Malderton.

"Why, you know whom I mean, my dear—the young man with the black whiskers and the white cravat, who has just come out at our assembly, and whom all the girls are talking about. Young—— dear me! what's his name?—Marianne, what *is* his name?" continued Mrs. Malderton, addressing her youngest daughter, who was engaged in netting a purse, and looking sentimental.

"Mr. Horatio Sparkins, ma," replied Miss Marianne, with a sigh.

"Oh! yes, to be sure—Horatio Sparkins," said Mrs. Malderton. "Decidedly the most gentleman-like young man I ever saw. I am sure in the beautifully-made coat he wore the other night, he looked like—like——"

"Like Prince Leopold, ma—so noble, so full of sentiment!" suggested Marianne, in a tone of enthusiastic admiration.

"You should recollect, my dear," resumed Mrs. Malderton, "that Teresa is now eight-and-twenty; and that it really is very important that something should be done."

Miss Teresa Malderton was a very little girl, rather fat, with vermilion cheeks, but good-humoured, and still disengaged, although, to do her justice, the misfortune arose from no lack of perseverance on her part. In vain had she flirted for ten years; in vain had Mr. and Mrs. Malderton assiduously kept up an extensive acquaintance among the young eligible bachelors of Camberwell, and even of Wandsworth and Brixton; to say nothing of those who "dropped in" from town. Miss Malderton was as well known as the lion on the top of Northumberland House, and had an equal chance of "going off."

"I am quite sure you'd like him," continued Mrs. Malderton, "he is so gentlemanly!"

"So clever!" said Miss Marianne.

"And has such a flow of language!" added Miss Teresa.

"He has a great respect for you, my dear," said Mrs. Malderton to her husband. Mr. Malderton coughed, and looked at the fire.

"Yes, I'm sure he's very much attached to pa's society," said Miss Marianne.

"No doubt of it," echoed Miss Teresa.

"Indeed, he said as much to me in confidence," observed Mrs. Malderton.

"Well, well," returned Mr. Malderton, somewhat flattered; "if I see him at the assembly to-morrow, perhaps I'll ask him down. I hope he knows we live at Oak Lodge, Camberwell, my dear?"

"Of course—and that you keep a one-horse carriage."

"I'll see about it," said Mr. Malderton, composing himself for a nap; "I'll see about it."

Mr. Malderton was a man whose whole scope of ideas was limited to Lloyd's, the Exchange, the India House, and the Bank. A few successful speculations had raised him from a situation of obscurity and comparative poverty, to a state of affluence. As frequently happens in such cases, the ideas of himself and his family became elevated to an extraordinary pitch as their means increased; they affected fashion, taste, and many other fooleries, in imitation of their betters, and had a very decided and becoming horror of anything which could, by possibility, be considered *low*. He was hospitable from ostentation, illiberal from ignorance, and prejudiced from conceit. Egotism and the love of display induced him to keep an excellent table: convenience, and a love of good things of this life, ensured him plenty of guests. He liked to have clever men, or what he considered such, at his table, because it was a great thing to talk about; but he never could endure what he called "sharp fellows." Probably, he cherished this feeling out of compliment to his two sons, who gave their respected parent no uneasiness in that particular. The family were ambitious of forming acquaintances and connexions in some sphere of society superior to that in which they themselves moved; and one of the necessary consequences of this desire, added to their utter ignorance of the world beyond their own small circle, was, that any one who could lay claim to an acquaintance with people of rank and title, had a sure passport to the table at Oak Lodge, Camberwell.

The appearance of Mr. Horatio Sparkins at the assembly, had excited no small degree of surprise and curiosity among its regular frequenters. Who could he be? He was evidently reserved, and apparently melancholy. Was he a clergyman?—He danced too well. A barrister?—He said he was not called. He used very fine words, and talked a great deal. Could he be a distinguished foreigner, come to England for the purpose of describing the country, its manners and customs; and frequenting public balls and public dinners, with the view of becoming acquainted with high life, polished etiquette, and English refinement?—No, he had not a foreign accent. Was he a surgeon, a contributor to the magazines, a writer of fashionable novels, or an artist?—No; to each and all of these surmises, there existed some valid objection.—"Then," said everybody, "he must be *somebody*."—"I should think he must be," reasoned Mr. Malderton, within himself, "because he perceives our superiority, and pays us so much attention."

The night succeeding the conversation we have just recorded, was "assembly night." The double-fly was ordered to be at the door of Oak Lodge at nine o'clock precisely. The Miss Maldertons were dressed in sky-blue satin trimmed with artificial flowers; and Mrs. M. (who was a little fat woman), in ditto ditto, looked like her eldest daughter multiplied by two. Mr. Frederick Malderton, the eldest son, in full-dress costume, was the very *beau idéal* of a smart waiter; and Mr. Thomas Malderton, the youngest, with his white dress-stock, blue coat, bright buttons, and red watch-ribbon, strongly resembled the portrait of that interesting, but rash young gentleman, George Barnwell. Every member of the party had made up his or her mind to cultivate

the acquaintance of Mr. Horatio Sparkins. Miss Teresa, of course, was to be as amiable and interesting as ladies of eight-and-twenty on the look-out for a husband, usually are. Mrs. Malderton would be all smiles and graces. Miss Marianne would request the favour of some verses for her album. Mr. Malderton would patronise the great unknown by asking him to dinner. Tom intended to ascertain the extent of his information on the interesting topics of snuff and cigars. Even Mr. Frederick Malderton himself, the family authority on all points of taste, dress, and fashionable arrangement; who had lodgings of his own in town; who had a free admission to Covent-garden theatre; who always dressed according to the fashions of the months; who went up the water twice a-week in the season; and who actually had an intimate friend who once knew a gentleman who formerly lived in the Albany,—even he had determined that Mr. Horatio Sparkins must be a devilish good fellow, and that he would do him the honour of challenging him to a game at billiards.

The first object that met the anxious eyes of the expectant family on their entrance into the ball-room, was the interesting Horatio, with his hair brushed off his forehead, and his eyes fixed on the ceiling, reclining in a contemplative attitude on one of the seats.

"There he is, my dear," whispered Mrs. Malderton to Mr. Malderton.

"How like Lord Byron!" murmured Miss Teresa.

"Or Montgomery!" whispered Miss Marianne.

"Or the portraits of Captain Cook!" suggested Tom.

"Tom—don't be an ass!" said his father, who checked him on all occasions, probably with a view to prevent his becoming "sharp"—which was very unnecessary.

The elegant Sparkins attitudinised with admirable effect, until the family had crossed the room. He then started up, with the most natural appearance of surprise and delight; accosted Mrs. Malderton with the utmost cordiality; saluted the young ladies in the most enchanting manner; bowed to, and shook hands with, Mr. Malderton, with a degree of respect amounting almost to veneration; and returned the greetings of the two young men in a half-gratified, half-patronising manner, which fully convinced them that he must be an important, and, at the same time, condescending personage.

"Miss Malderton," said Horatio, after the ordinary salutations, and bowing very low, "may I be permitted to presume to hope that you will allow me to have the pleasure——"

"I don't *think* I am engaged," said Miss Teresa, with a dreadful affectation of indifference—"but, really—so many——"

Horatio looked handsomely miserable.

"I shall be most happy," simpered the interesting Teresa, at last. Horatio's countenance brightened up, like an old hat in a shower of rain.

"A very genteel young man, certainly!" said the gratified Mr. Malderton, as the obsequious Sparkins and his partner joined the quadrille which was just forming.

"He has a remarkably good address," said Mr. Frederick.

"Yes, he is a prime fellow," interposed Tom, who always managed to put his foot in it—"he talks just like an auctioneer."

"Tom!" said his father solemnly, "I think I desired you, before, not to be a fool." Tom looked as happy as a cock on a drizzly morning.

"How delightful!" said the interesting Horatio to his partner, as they promenaded the room at the conclusion of the set—"how delightful, how refreshing it is, to retire from the cloudy storms, the vicissitudes, and the troubles, of life, even if it be but for a few short fleeting moments: and to spend those moments, fading and evanescent though they be, in the delightful, the blessed society of one individual—whose frowns would be death, whose coldness would be madness, whose falsehood would be ruin, whose constancy would be bliss; the possession of whose affection would be the brightest and best reward that Heaven could bestow on man?"

"What feeling! what sentiment!" thought Miss Teresa, as she leaned more heavily on her companion's arm.

"But enough—enough!" resumed the elegant Sparkins, with a theatrical air. "What have I said? what have I—I—to do with sentiments like these! Miss Malderton"—here he stopped short—"may I hope to be permitted to offer the humble tribute of ——"

"Really, Mr. Sparkins," returned the enraptured Teresa, blushing in the sweetest confusion, "I must refer you to papa. I never can, without his consent, venture to——"

"Surely he cannot object——"

"Oh, yes. Indeed, indeed, you know him not!" interrupted Miss Teresa, well knowing there was nothing to fear, but wishing to make the interview resemble a scene in some romantic novel.

"He cannot object to my offering you a glass of negus," returned the adorable Sparkins, with some surprise.

"Is that all?" thought the disappointed Teresa. "What a fuss about nothing!"

"It will give me the greatest pleasure, sir, to see you to dinner at Oak Lodge, Camberwell, on Sunday next at five o'clock, if you have no better engagement," said Mr. Malderton, at the conclusion of the evening, as he and his sons were standing in conversation with Mr. Horatio Sparkins.

Horatio bowed his acknowledgments, and accepted the flattering invitation.

"I must confess," continued the father, offering his snuff-box to his new acquaintance, "that I don't enjoy these assemblies half so much as the comfort—I had almost said' the luxury—of Oak Lodge. They have no great charms for an elderly man."

"And after all, sir, what is man?" said the metaphysical Sparkins. "I say, what is man?"

"Ah! very true," said Mr. Malderton; "very true."

"We know that we live and breath," continued Horatio; "that we have wants and wishes, desires and appetites——"

"Certainly," said Mr. Frederick Malderton, looking profound.

"I say, we know that we exist," repeated Horatio, raising his voice, "but there we stop; there, is an end to our knowledge; there, is the summit of our attainments; there, is the termination of our ends. What more do we know?"

"Nothing," replied Mr. Frederick—than whom no one was more capable of answering for himself in that particular. Tom was about to hazard something, but, fortunately for his reputation, he caught his father's angry eye, and slunk off like a puppy convicted of petty larceny.

"Upon my word," said Mr. Malderton the elder, as they were returning home in the fly, "that Mr. Sparkins is a wonderful young man. Such surprising knowledge! such extraordinary information! and such a splendid mode of expressing himself!"

"I think he must be somebody in disguise," said Miss Marianne. "How charmingly romantic!"

"He talks very loud and nicely," timidly observed Tom, "but I don't exactly understand what he means."

"I almost begin to despair of *your* understanding anything, Tom," said his father, who, of course, had been much enlightened by Mr. Horatio Sparkins's conversation.

"It strikes me, Tom," said Miss Teresa, "that you have made yourself very ridiculous this evening."

"No doubt of it," cried everybody—and the unfortunate Tom reduced himself into the least possible space. That night, Mr. and Mrs. Malderton had a long conversation respecting their daughter's prospects and future arrangements. Miss Teresa went to bed, considering whether, in the event of her marrying a title, she could conscientiously encourage the visits of her present associates; and dreamed, all night, of disguised noblemen, large routs, ostrich plumes, bridal favours, and Horatio Sparkins.

Various surmises were hazarded on the Sunday morning, as to the mode of conveyance which the anxiously-expected Horatio would adopt. Did he keep a gig?—was it possible he could come on horseback?—or would he patronize the stage? These, and other various conjectures of equal importance, engrossed the attention of Mrs. Malderton and her daughters during the whole morning after church.

"Upon my word, my dear, it's a most annoying thing that that vulgar brother of yours should have invited himself to dine here to-day," said Mr. Malderton to his wife. "On account of Mr. Sparkins's coming down, I purposely abstained from asking any one but Flamwell. And then to think of your brother—a trades-man—it's insufferable. I declare I wouldn't have him mention his shop, before our new guest—no, not for a thousand pounds! I wouldn't care if he had the good sense to conceal the disgrace he is to the family; but he's so fond of his horrible business, that he *will* let people know what he is."

Mr. Jacob Barton, the individual alluded to, was a large grocer; so vulgar, and so lost to all sense of feeling, that he actually never scrupled to avow that he wasn't above his business: "he'd made his money by it, and he didn't care who know'd it."

"Ah! Flamwell, my dear fellow, how d'ye do?" said Mr. Malderton, as a little spoffish man, with green spectacles, entered the room. "You got my note?"

"Yes, I did; and here I am in consequence."

"You don't happen to know this Mr. Sparkins by name? You know everybody?"

Mr. Flamwell was one of those gentlemen of remarkably extensive information whom one occasionally meets in society, who pretend to know everybody, but in reality know nobody. At Malderton's, where any stories about great people were received with a greedy ear, he was an especial favourite; and, knowing the kind of people he had to deal with, he carried his passion of claiming acquaintance with everybody, to the most immoderate length. He had rather a singular way of telling his greatest lies in a parenthesis, and with an air of self-denial, as if he feared being thought egotistical.

"Why, no, I don't know him by that name," returned Flamwell, in a low tone, and with an air of immense importance. "I have no doubt I know him, though. Is he tall?"

"Middle-sized," said Miss Teresa.

"With black hair?" inquired Flamwell, hazarding a bold guess.

"Yes," returned Miss Teresa, eagerly.

"Rather a snub nose?"

"No," said the disappointed Teresa, "he has a Roman nose."

"I said a Roman nose, didn't I?" inquired Flamwell. "He's an elegant young man?"

"Oh, certainly."

"With remarkably prepossessing manners?"

"Oh, yes!" said all the family together. "You must know him."

"Yes, I thought you knew him, if he was anybody," triumphantly exclaimed Mr. Malderton. "Who d'ye think he is?"

"Why, from your description," said Flamwell, ruminating, and sinking his voice, almost to a whisper, "he bears a strong resemblance to the Honourable Augustus Fitz-Edward Fitz-John Fitz-Osborne. He's a very talented young man, and rather eccentric. It's extremely probable he may have changed his name for some temporary purpose."

Teresa's heart beat high. Could he be the Honourable Augustus Fitz-Edward Fitz-John Fitz-Osborne! What a name to be elegantly engraved upon two glazed cards, tied together with a piece of white satin ribbon! "The Honourable Mrs. Augustus Fitz-Edward Fitz-John Fitz-Osborne!" The thought was transport.

"It's five minutes to five," said Mr. Malderton,

looking at his watch: "I hope he's not going to disappoint us."

"There he is!" exclaimed Miss Teresa, as a loud double-knock was heard at the door. Everybody endeavoured to look—as people when they particularly expect a visitor always do—as if they were perfectly unsuspicious of the approach of anybody.

The room-door opened—"Mr. Barton!" said the servant.

"Confound the man!" murmured Malderton. "Ah! my dear sir, d'ye do! Any news?"

"Why no," returned the grocer, in his usual bluff manner. "No, none partickler. None that I am much aware of. How d'ye do, gals and boys? Mr. Flamwell, sir—glad to see you."

"Here's Mr. Sparkins!" said Tom, who had been looking out at the window, "on *such* a black horse!" There was Horatio, sure enough, on a large black horse, curvetting and prancing along, like an Astley's supernumerary. After a great deal of reining in, and pulling up, with the accompaniments of snorting, rearing, and kicking, the animal consented to stop at about a hundred yards from the gate, where Mr. Sparkins dismounted, and confided him to the care of Mr. Malderton's groom. The ceremony of introduction was gone through, in all due form. Mr. Flamwell looked from behind his green spectacles at Horatio with an air of mysterious importance; and the gallant Horatio looked unutterable things at Teresa.

"Is he the Honourable Mr. Augustus What's-his-name?" whispered Mrs. Malderton to Flamwell, as he was escorting her to the dining-room.

"Why, no—at least not exactly," returned that great authority—"not exactly."

"Who *is* he then?"

"Hush!" said Flamwell, nodding his head with a grave air, importing that he knew very well; but was prevented, by some grave reasons of state, from disclosing the important secret. It might be one of the ministers making himself acquainted with the views of the people.

"Mr. Sparkins," said the delighted Mrs. Malderton, "pray divide the ladies. John, put a chair for the gentleman between Miss Teresa and Miss Marianne." This was addressed to a man who, on ordinary occasions, acted as half-groom, half-gardener; but who, as it was important to make an impression on Mr. Sparkins, had been forced into a white neckerchief and shoes, and touched up, and brushed, to look like a second footman.

The dinner was excellent; Horatio was most attentive to Miss Teresa, and every one felt in high spirits, except Mr. Malderton, who, knowing the propensity of his brother-in-law, Mr. Barton, endured that sort of agony which the newspapers inform us is experienced by the surrounding neighbourhood when a pot-boy hangs himself in a hay-loft, and which is "much easier to be imagined than described."

"Have you seen your friend, Sir Thomas Noland, lately, Flamwell?" inquired Mr. Malderton, casting a sidelong look at Horatio, to see what effect the mention of so great a man had upon him.

"Why, no—not very lately. I saw Lord Gubbleton the day before yesterday."

"Ah! I hope his lordship is very well?" said Malderton, in a tone of the greatest interest. It is scarcely necessary to say that, until that moment, he had been quite innocent of the existence of such a person.

"Why, yes; he was very well—very well indeed. He's a devilish good fellow. I met him in the City, and had a long chat with him. Indeed, I'm rather intimate with him. I couldn't stop to talk to him as long as I could wish, though, because I was on my way to a banker's, a very rich man, and a member of Parliament, with whom I am also rather, indeed I may say very, intimate."

"I know whom you mean," returned the host, consequentially—in reality knowing as much about the matter as Flamwell himself. "He has a capital business."

This was touching on a dangerous topic.

"Talking of business," interposed Mr. Barton, from the centre of the table. "A gentleman whom you knew very well, Malderton, before you made that first lucky spec of yours, called at our shop the other day, and——"

"Barton, may I trouble you for a potato?" interrupted the wretched master of the house, hoping to nip the story in the bud.

"Certainly," returned the grocer, quite insensible of his brother-in-law's object—"and he said in a very plain manner——"

"*Floury*, if you please," interrupted Malderton again; dreading the termination of the anecdote, and fearing a repetition of the word "shop."

"He said, says he," continued the culprit, after despatching the potato; "says he, how goes on your business? So I said, jokingly—you know my way—

says I, I'm never above my business, and I hope my business will never be above me. Ha, ha!"

"Mr. Sparkins," said the host, vainly endeavouring to conceal his dismay, "a glass of wine?"

"With the utmost pleasure, sir."

"Happy to see you."

"Thank you."

"We were talking the other evening," resumed the host, addressing Horatio, partly with the view of displaying the conversational powers of his new acquaintance, and partly in the hope of drowning the grocer's stories—"we were talking the other night about the nature of man. Your argument struck me very forcibly."

"And me," said Mr. Frederick. Horatio made a graceful inclination of the head.

"Pray, what is your opinion of woman, Mr. Sparkins?" inquired Mrs. Malderton. The young ladies simpered.

"Man," replied Horatio, "man, whether he ranged the bright, gay, flowery plains of a second Eden, or the more sterile, barren, and I may say, commonplace regions, to which we are compelled to accustom ourselves, in times such as these; man, under any circumstances, or in any place—whether he were bending beneath the withering blasts of the frigid zone, or scorching under the rays of a vertical sun—man, without woman, would be—alone."

"I am very happy to find you entertain such honourable opinions, Mr. Sparkins," said Mrs. Malderton.

"And I," added Miss Teresa. Horatio looked his delight, and the young lady blushed.

"Now, it's my opinion——" said Mr. Barton.

"I know what you're going to say," interposed Malderton, determined not to give his relation another opportunity, "and I don't agree with you."

"What!" inquired the astonished grocer.

"I am sorry to differ from you, Barton," said the host, in as positive a manner as if he really were contradicting a position which the other had laid down, "but I cannot give my assent to what I consider a very monstrous proposition."

"But I meant to say——"

"You never can convince me," said Malderton, with an air of obstinate determination. "Never."

"And I," said Mr. Frederick, following up his father's attack, "cannot entirely agree in Mr. Sparkins's argument."

"What!" said Horatio, who became more meta-physical, and more argumentative, as he saw the female part of the family listening in wondering delight—"what! Is effect the consequence of cause? Is cause the precursor of effect?"

"That's the point," said Flamwell.

"To be sure," said Mr. Malderton.

"Because, if effect is the consequence of cause, and if cause does precede effect, I apprehend you are wrong," added Horatio.

"Decidedly," said the toad-eating Flamwell.

"At least, I apprehend that to be the just and logical deduction?" said Sparkins, in a tone of interrogation.

"No doubt of it," chimed in Flamwell again. "It settles the point."

"Well, perhaps it does," said Mr. Frederick; "I didn't see it before."

"I don't exactly see it now," thought the grocer; "but I suppose it's all right."

"How wonderfully clever he is!" whispered Mrs. Malderton to her daughters, as they retired to the drawing-room.

"Oh, he's quite a love!" said both the young ladies together; "he talks like an oracle. He must have seen a great deal of life."

The gentlemen being left to themselves, a pause ensued, during which everybody looked very grave, as if they were quite overcome by the profound nature of the previous discussion. Flamwell, who had made up his mind to find out who and what Mr. Horatio Sparkins really was, first broke silence.

"Excuse me, sir," said that distinguished personage, "I presume you have studied for the bar? I thought of entering once, myself—indeed, I'm rather intimate with some of the highest ornaments of that distinguished profession."

"N—no!" said Horatio, with a little hesitation; "not exactly."

"But you have been much among the silk gowns, or I mistake?" inquired Flamwell, deferentially.

"Nearly all my life," returned Sparkins.

The question was thus pretty well settled in the mind of Mr. Flamwell. He was a young gentleman "about to be called."

"I shouldn't like to be a barrister," said Tom, speaking for the first time, and looking round the table to find somebody who would notice the remark.

No one made any reply.

"I shouldn't like to wear a wig," said Tom, hazarding another observation.

"Tom, I beg you will not make yourself ridiculous," said his father. "Pray listen, and improve yourself by the conversation you hear, and don't be constantly making these absurd remarks."

"Very well, father," replied the unfortunate Tom, who had not spoken a word since he had asked for another slice of beef at a quarter-past five o'clock, P.M., and it was then eight.

"Well, Tom," observed his good-natured uncle, "never mind! *I* think with you. *I* shouldn't like to wear a wig. I'd rather wear an apron."

Mr. Malderton coughed violently. Mr. Barton resumed—"For if a man's above his business——"

The cough returned with tenfold violence, and did not cease until the unfortunate cause of it, in his alarm, had quite forgotten what he intended to say.

"Mr. Sparkins," said Flamwell, returning to the charge, "do you happen to know Mr. Delafontaine, of Bedford-square?"

"I have exchanged cards with him; since which, indeed, I have had an opportunity of serving him considerably," replied Horatio, slightly colouring; no doubt, at having been betrayed into making the acknowledgment.

"You are very lucky, if you have had an opportunity of obliging that great man," observed Flamwell, with an air of profound respect.

"I don't know who he is," he whispered to Mr. Malderton, confidentially, as they followed Horatio up to the drawing-room. "It's quite clear, however, that he belongs to the law, and that he is somebody of great importance, and very highly connected."

"No doubt, no doubt," returned his companion.

The remainder of the evening passed away most delightfully. Mr. Malderton, relieved from his apprehensions by the circumstance of Mr. Barton's falling into a profound sleep, was as affable and gracious as possible. Miss Teresa played the "Fall of Paris," as Mr. Sparkins declared, in a most masterly manner, and both of them, assisted by Mr. Frederick, tried over glees and trios without number; they having made the pleasing discovery that their voices harmonised beautifully. To be sure, they all sang the first part; and Horatio, in addition to the slight drawback of having no ear, was perfectly innocent of knowing a note of music; still, they passed the time very agreeably, and it was past twelve o'clock before Mr. Sparkins ordered the

mourning-coach-looking steed to be brought out—an order which was only complied with, on the distinct understanding that he was to repeat his visit on the following Sunday.

"But, perhaps, Mr. Sparkins will form one of our party to-morrow evening?" suggested Mrs. M. "Mr. Malderton intends taking the girls to see the pantomime." Mr. Sparkins bowed, and promised to join the party in box 48, in the course of the evening.

"We will not tax you for the morning," said Miss Teresa, bewitchingly; "for ma is going to take us to all sorts of places, shopping. I know that gentlemen have a great horror of that employment." Mr. Sparkins bowed again, and declared that he should be delighted, but business of importance occupied him in the morning. Flamwell looked at Malderton significantly—"It's term time!" he whispered.

At twelve o'clock on the following morning, the "fly" was at the door of Oak Lodge, to convey Mrs. Malderton and her daughters on their expedition for the day. They were to dine and dress for the play at a friend's house. First, driving thither with their band-boxes, they departed on their first errand to make some purchases at Messrs. Jones, Spruggins, and Smith's, of Tottenham-court-road; after which, they were to go to Redmayne's in Bond-street; thence, to innumerable places that no one ever heard of. The young ladies beguiled the tediousness of the ride by eulogising Mr. Horatio Sparkins, scolding their mamma for taking them so far to save a shilling, and wondering whether they should ever reach their destination. At length, the vehicle stopped before a dirty-looking ticketed linen-draper's shop, with goods of all kinds, and labels of all sorts and sizes, in the window. There were dropsical figures of seven with a little three-farthings in the corner; "perfectly invisible to the naked eye"; three hundred and fifty thousand ladies' boas, *from* one shilling and a penny halfpenny; real French kid shoes, at two and ninepence per pair; green parasols, at an equally cheap rate; and "every description of goods," as the proprietors said—and they must know best—"fifty percent under cost price."

"Lor! ma, what a place you have brought us to!" said Miss Teresa; "what *would* Mr. Sparkins say if he could see us!"

"Ah! what, indeed!" said Miss Marianne, horrified at the idea.

"Pray be seated, ladies. What is the first article?" inquired the obsequious master of the ceremonies of the establishment, who, in his large white neck-cloth and formal tie, looked like a bad "portrait of a gentleman" in the Somerset-house exhibition.

"I want to see some silks," answered Mrs. Malderton.

"Directly, ma'am.—Mr. Smith! Where *is* Mr. Smith?"

"Here, sir," cried a voice at the back of the shop.

"Pray make haste, Mr. Smith," said the M.C. "You never are to be found when you're wanted, sir."

Mr. Smith, thus enjoined to use all possible despatch, leaped over the counter with great agility, and placed himself before the newly-arrived customers. Mrs. Malderton uttered a faint scream; Miss Teresa, who had been stooping down to talk to her sister, raised her head, and beheld—Horatio Sparkins!

"We will draw a veil," as novel-writers say, over the scene that ensued. The mysterious, philosophical, romantic, metaphysical Sparkins—he who, to the interesting Teresa, seemed like the embodied idea of the young dukes and poetical exquisites in blue silk dressing-gowns, and ditto ditto slippers, of whom she had read and dreamed, but had never expected to behold, was suddenly converted into Mr. Samuel Smith, the assistant at a "cheap shop"; the junior partner in a slippery firm of some three weeks' existence. The dignified evanishment of the hero of Oak Lodge, on this unexpected recognition, could only be equalled by that of a furtive dog with a considerable kettle at his tail. All the hopes of the Maldertons were destined at once to melt away, like the lemon ices at a Company's dinner; Almack's was still to them as distant as the North Pole; and Miss Teresa had as much chance of a husband as Captain Ross had of the north-west passage.

Years have elapsed since the occurrence of this dreadful morning. The daisies have thrice bloomed on Camberwell-green; the sparrows have thrice repeated their vernal chirps in Camberwell-grove; but the Miss Maldertons are still unmated. Miss Teresa's case is more desperate than ever; but Flamwell is yet in the zenith of his reputation; and the family have the same predilection for aristocratic personages, with an increased aversion to anything *low*. ☐

DISCUSSION

1. "Horatio Sparkins" is obviously an attack on social climbing and its concomitant vice, snobbery. How many different aspects of this snobbery can you identify in the story?

2. Are any characters portrayed favorably? Explain.

3. Although much of the humor of this story lies in its surprise ending, it does contain other humorous touches. Discuss some of these, including the use of stylistic devices such as far-flown similes.

THE THREE STRANGERS

by Thomas Hardy

AMONG the few features of agricultural England which retain an appearance but little modified by the lapse of centuries, may be reckoned the long, grassy and furzy downs, coombs, or ewe leases,[1] as

From *Wessex Tales* by Thomas Hardy. By permission of the Hardy Estate; Macmillan London & Basingstoke; The Macmillan Company of Canada Limited, and St. Martin's Press, Incorporated.
1. *furzy downs . . . ewe leases.* Furzy downs are rolling lands overgrown with furze, a low evergreen shrub with yellow flowers; coombs are small valleys or hollows; ewe leases are sheep pastures.

they are called according to their kind, that fill a large area of certain counties in the south and southwest. If any mark of human occupation is met with hereon, it usually takes the form of the solitary cottage of some shepherd.

Fifty years ago such a lonely cottage stood on such a down, and may possibly be standing there now. In spite of its loneliness, however, the spot, by actual measurement, was not more than five miles from a county-town. Yet that affected it little. Five miles of irregular upland, during the long inimical seasons, with their sleets, snows, rains, and mists, afford withdrawing space enough to isolate a Timon or a Nebuchadnezzar[2]; much less, in fair weather, to please that less repellent tribe, the poets, philosophers, artists and others who "conceive and meditate of pleasant things."

Some old earthen camp or barrow, some clump of trees, at least some starved fragment of ancient hedge is usually taken advantage of in the erection of these forlorn dwellings. But, in the present case, such a kind of shelter had been disregarded. Higher Crowstairs, as the house was called, stood quite detached and undefended. The only reason for its precise situation seemed to be the crossing of two footpaths at right angles hard by, which may have crossed there and thus for a good five hundred years. Hence the house was exposed to the elements on all sides. But, though the wind up here blew unmistakably when it did blow, and the rain hit hard whenever it fell, the various weathers of the winter season were not quite so formidable on the down as they were imagined to be by dwellers on low ground. The raw rimes were not so pernicious as in the hollows, and the frosts were scarcely so severe. When the shepherd and his family who tenanted the house were pitied for their sufferings from the exposure, they said that upon the whole they were less inconvenienced by "wuzzes and flames" (hoarses and phlegms) than when they had lived by the stream of a snug neighboring valley.

The night of March 28, 182–, was precisely one of the nights that were wont to call forth these expressions of commiseration. The level rainstorm smote walls, slopes and hedges like the clothyard shafts of Senlac and Crecy.[3] Such sheep and outdoor animals as had no shelter stood with their buttocks to the winds; while the tails of little birds trying to roost on some scraggy thorn were blown inside out like umbrellas. The gable end of the cottage was stained with wet, and the eavesdroppings flapped against the wall. Yet never was commiseration for the shepherd more misplaced. For that cheerful

rustic was entertaining a large party in glorification of the christening of his second girl.

The guests had arrived before the rain began to fall, and they were all now assembled in the chief or living room of the dwelling. A glance into the apartment at eight o'clock on this eventful evening would have resulted in the opinion that it was as cosy and comfortable a nook as could be wished for in boisterous weather. The calling of its inhabitant was proclaimed by a number of highly polished sheepcrooks without stems that were hung ornamentally over the fireplace, the curl of each shining crook varying from the antiquated type engraved in the patriarchal pictures of old family Bibles to the most approved fashion of the last local sheep fair. The room was lighted by half-a-dozen candles, having wicks only a trifle smaller than the grease which enveloped them, in candlesticks that were never used but at high days, holy days, and family feasts. The lights were scattered about the room, two of them standing on the chimney piece. This position of candles was in itself significant. Candles on the chimney piece always meant a party.

On the hearth, in front of a back brand to give substance, blazed a fire of thorns, that crackled "like the laughter of the fool."

Nineteen persons were gathered here. Of these, five women, wearing gowns of various bright hues, sat in chairs along the wall; girls shy and not shy filled the window bench; four men, including Charley Jake the hedge carpenter, Elijah New the parish clerk, and John Pitcher, a neighboring dairyman, the shepherd's father-in-law, lolled in the settle; a young man and maid, who were blushing over tentative *pourparlers*[4] on a life companionship, sat beneath the corner cupboard; and an elderly engaged man of fifty or upward moved restlessly about from spots where his betrothed was not to the spot where she was. Enjoyment was pretty general, and so much the more prevailed in being unhampered by conventional restrictions. Absolute confidence in each other's good opinion begat perfect ease, while the finishing stroke of manner, amounting to a truly princely serenity, was lent to the majority by the absence of any expression or trait denoting that they wished to get on in the world, enlarge their minds, or do any eclipsing thing whatever—which nowadays so generally

---

2. *Timon or a Nebuchadnezzar.* Timon, in Shakespéare's *Timon of Athens*, mistrusted his fellowmen and lived as a hermit. Nebuchadnezzar, ancient king of Babylon, spent four years alone in the wilderness living on grass.
3. *clothyard shafts of Senlac and Crecy,* yard-long arrows used in two famous battles.

4. *pourparlers* (pür′ pär′ lā′), discussions preliminary to negotiations (French).

nips the bloom and *bonhomie* of all except the two extremes of the social scale.

Shepherd Fennel had married well, his wife being a dairyman's daughter from a vale at a distance, who brought fifty guineas in her pocket—and kept them there, till they should be required for ministering to the needs of a coming family. This frugal woman had been somewhat exercised as to the character that should be given to the gathering. A sit-still party had its advantages; but an undisturbed position of ease in chairs and settles was apt to lead on the men to such an unconscionable deal of toping that they would sometimes fairly drink the house dry. A dancing party was the alternative; but this, while avoiding the foregoing objection on the score of good drink, had a counterbalancing disadvantage in the matter of good victuals, the ravenous appetites engendered by the exercise causing immense havoc in the buttery. Shepherdess Fennel fell back upon the intermediate plan of mingling short dances with short periods of talk and singing, so as to hinder any ungovernable rage in either. But this scheme was entirely confined to her own gentle mind: the shepherd himself was in the mood to exhibit the most reckless phases of hospitality.

The fiddler was a boy of those parts, about twelve years of age, who had a wonderful dexterity in jigs and reels, though his fingers were so small and short as to necessitate a constant shifting for the high notes, from which he scrambled back to the first position with sounds not of unmixed purity of tone. At seven the shrill tweedle-dee of this youngster had begun, accompanied by a booming ground bass from Elijah New, the parish clerk, who had thoughtfully brought with him his favorite musical instrument, the serpent.[5] Dancing was instantaneous, Mrs. Fennel privately enjoining the players on no account to let the dance exceed the length of a quarter of an hour.

But Elijah and the boy in the excitement of their position quite forgot the injunction. Moreover, Oliver Giles, a man of seventeen, one of the dancers, who was enamored of his partner, a fair girl of thirty-three rolling years, had recklessly handed a new crown piece to the musicians, as a bribe to keep going as long as they had muscle and wind. Mrs. Fennel, seeing the steam begin to generate on the countenances of her guests, crossed over and touched the fiddler's elbow and put her hand on the serpent's mouth. But they took no notice, and fearing she might lose her character of genial hostess if she were to interfere too markedly, she retired and sat down helpless. And so the dance whizzed on with cumulative fury, the performers moving in their planet-like courses, direct and retrograde, from apogee to perigee, till the hand of the well-kicked clock at the bottom of the room had traveled over the circumference of an hour.

While these cheerful events were in the course of enactment within Fennel's pastoral dwelling an incident having considerable bearing on the party had occurred in the gloomy night without. Mrs. Fennel's concern about the growing fierceness of the dance corresponded in point of time with the ascent of a human figure to the solitary hill of Higher Crowstairs from the direction of the distant town. This personage strode on through the rain without a pause, following the little-worn path which, further on its course, skirted the shepherd's cottage.

It was nearly the time of full moon, and on this account, though the sky was lined with a uniform sheet of dripping cloud, ordinary objects out of doors were readily visible. The sad wan light revealed the lonely pedestrian to be a man of supple frame; his gait suggested that he had somewhat passed the period of perfect and instinctive agility, though not so far as to be otherwise than rapid of motion when occasion required. At a rough guess, he might have been about forty years of age. He appeared tall, but a recruiting sergeant, or other person accustomed to the judging of men's heights by the eye, would have discerned that this was chiefly owing to his gauntness, and that he was not more than five-feet-eight or nine.

Notwithstanding the regularity of his tread there was caution in it, as in that of one who mentally feels his way; and despite the fact that it was not a black coat nor a dark garment of any sort that he wore, there was something about him which suggested that he naturally belonged to the black-coated tribes of men. His clothes were of fustian, and his boots hobnailed, yet in his progress he showed not the mud-accustomed bearing of hobnailed and fustianed peasantry.

By the time that he had arrived abreast of the shepherd's premises the rain came down, or rather came along, with yet more determined violence.

---

5. *serpent*, a low-toned wind instrument made of wood, now obsolete.

The outskirts of the little settlement partially broke the force of wind and rain, and this induced him to stand still. The most salient of the shepherd's domestic erections was an empty sty at the forward corner of his hedgeless garden, for in these latitudes the principle of masking the homelier features of your establishment by a conventional frontage was unknown. The traveler's eye was attracted to this small building by the pallid shine of the wet slates that covered it. He turned aside, and, finding it empty, stood under the pent roof for shelter.

While he stood the boom of the serpent within the adjacent house, and the lesser strains of the fiddler, reached the spot as an accompaniment to the surging hiss of the flying rain on the sod, its louder beating on the cabbage leaves of the garden, on the straw hackles of eight or ten beehives just discernible by the path, and its dripping from the eaves into a row of buckets and pans that had been placed under the walls of the cottage. For at Higher Crowstairs, as at all such elevated domiciles, the grand difficulty of housekeeping was an insufficiency of water; and a casual rainfall was utilized by turning out, as catchers, every utensil that the house contained. Some queer stories might be told of the contrivances for economy of suds and dishwaters that are absolutely necessitated in upland habitations during the droughts of summer. But at this season there were no such exigencies; a mere acceptance of what the skies bestowed was sufficient for an abundant store.

At last the notes of the serpent ceased and the house was silent. This cessation of activity aroused the solitary pedestrian from the reverie into which he had lapsed, and, emerging from the shed, with an apparently new intention, he walked up the path to the house door. Arrived here, his first act was to kneel down on a large stone beside the row of vessels, and to drink a copious draught from one of them. Having quenched his thirst he rose and lifted his hand to knock, but paused with his eye upon the panel. Since the dark surface of the wood revealed absolutely nothing, it was evident that he must be mentally looking through the door, as if he wished to measure thereby all the possibilities that a house of this sort might include, and how they might bear upon the question of his entry.

In his indecision he turned and surveyed the scene around. Not a soul was anywhere visible. The garden path stretched downward from his feet, gleaming like the track of a snail; the roof of the little well (mostly dry), the well cover, the top rail of the garden gate, were varnished with the same dull liquid glaze; while, far away in the vale, a faint whiteness of more than usual extent showed that the rivers were high in the meads. Beyond all this winked a few bleared lamplights through the beating drops—lights that denoted the situation of the county town from which he had appeared to come. The absence of all notes of life in that direction seemed to clinch his intentions, and he knocked at the door.

Within, a desultory chat had taken the place of movement and musical sound. The hedge carpenter was suggesting a song to the company, which nobody just then was inclined to undertake, so that the knock afforded a not unwelcome diversion.

"Walk in!" said the shepherd promptly.

The latch clicked upward, and out of the night our pedestrian appeared upon the doormat. The shepherd arose, snuffed two of the nearest candles, and turned to look at him.

Their light disclosed that the stranger was dark in complexion and not unprepossessing as to feature. His hat, which for a moment he did not remove, hung low over his eyes, without concealing that they were large, open, and determined, moving with a flash rather than a glance round the room. He seemed pleased with his survey, and, baring his shaggy head, said, in a rich deep voice, "The rain is so heavy, friends, that I ask leave to come in and rest awhile."

"To be sure, stranger," said the shepherd. "And faith, you've been lucky in choosing your time, for we are having a bit of a fling for a glad cause—though, to be sure, a man could hardly wish that glad cause to happen more than once a year."

"Nor less," spoke up a woman. "For 'tis best to get your family over and done with, as soon as you can, so as to be all the earlier out of the fag o't."

"And what may be this glad cause?" asked the stranger.

"A birth and christening," said the shepherd.

The stranger hoped his host might not be made unhappy either by too many or too few of such episodes, and being invited by a gesture to pull at the mug, he readily acquiesced. His manner, which, before entering, had been so dubious, was now altogether that of a careless and candid man.

"Late to be traipsing athwart this coomb—hey?" said the engaged man of fifty.

"Late it is, master, as you say. I'll take a seat in the chimney corner, if you have nothing to urge against it, ma'am; for I am a little moist on the side that was next the rain."

Mrs. Shepherd Fennel assented, and made room for the self-invited comer, who, having got completely inside the chimney corner, stretched out his legs and his arms with the expansiveness of a person quite at home.

"Yes, I am rather cracked in the vamp," he said freely, seeing that the eyes of the shepherd's wife fell upon his boots, "and I am not well fitted either. I have had some rough times lately, and have been forced to pick up what I can get in the way of wearing, but I must find a suit better fit for working days when I reach home."

"One of hereabouts?" she inquired.

"Not quite that—further up the country."

"I thought so. And so be I; and by your tongue you come from my neighborhood."

"But you would hardly have heard of me," he said quickly. "My time would be long before yours, ma'am, you see."

This testimony to the youthfulness of his hostess had the effect of stopping her cross-examination.

"There is only one thing more wanted to make me happy," continued the newcomer. "And that is a little baccy, which I am sorry to say I am out of."

"I'll fill your pipe," said the shepherd.

"I must ask you to lend me a pipe likewise."

"A smoker, and no pipe about 'ee?"

"I have dropped it somewhere on the road."

The shepherd filled and handed him a new clay pipe, saying, as he did so, "Hand me your baccy box—I'll fill that too, now I am about it."

The man went through the movement of searching his pockets.

"Lost that too?" said his entertainer, with some surprise.

"I am afraid so," said the man with some confusion. "Give it to me in a screw of paper." Lighting his pipe at the candle with a suction that drew the whole flame into the bowl, he resettled himself in the corner and bent his looks upon the faint steam from his damp legs, as if he wished to say no more.

Meanwhile the general body of guests had been taking little notice of this visitor by reason of an absorbing discussion in which they were engaged with the band about a tune for the next dance.

The matter being settled, they were about to stand up when an interruption came in the shape of another knock at the door.

At sound of the same the man in the chimney corner took up the poker and began stirring the brands as if doing it thoroughly were the one aim of his existence; and a second time the shepherd said, "Walk in!" In a moment another man stood upon the straw-woven doormat. He too was a stranger.

This individual was one of a type radically different from the first. There was more of the commonplace in his manner, and a certain jovial cosmopolitanism sat upon his features. He was several years older than the first arrival, his hair being slightly frosted, his eyebrows bristly, and his whiskers cut back from his cheeks. His face was rather full and flabby, and yet it was not altogether a face without power. A few grog blossoms marked the neighborhood of his nose. He flung back his long drab greatcoat, revealing that beneath it he wore a suit of cinder-gray shade throughout, large heavy seals, of some metal or other that would take a polish, dangling from his fob as his only personal ornament. Shaking the waterdrops from his low-crowned glazed hat, he said, "I must ask for a few minutes' shelter, comrades, or I shall be wetted to my skin before I get to Casterbridge."

"Make yourself at home, master," said the shepherd, perhaps a trifle less heartily than on the first occasion. Not that Fennel had the least tinge of niggardliness in his composition; but the room was far from large, spare chairs were not numerous, and damp companions were not altogether desirable at close quarters for the women and girls in their bright-colored gowns.

However, the second comer, after taking off his greatcoat, and hanging his hat on a nail in one of the ceiling beams as if he had been specially invited to put it there, advanced and sat down at the table. This had been pushed so closely into the chimney corner, to give all available room to the dancers, that its inner edge grazed the elbow of the man who had ensconced himself by the fire; and thus the two strangers were brought into close companionship. They nodded to each other by way of breaking the ice of unacquaintance, and the first stranger handed his neighbor the family mug—a huge vessel of brown ware, having its upper edge worn away like a threshold by the rub of whole generations of thirsty lips that had gone the way of all flesh, and bearing the following inscription burnt upon its rotund side in yellow letters:

THERE IS NO FUN
UNTiLL i CUM.

The other man, nothing loth, raised the mug to his lips, and drank on, and on, and on—till a curious blueness overspread the countenance of the shepherd's wife, who had regarded with no little surprise the first stranger's free offer to the second of what did not belong to him to dispense.

"I knew it!" said the toper to the shepherd with much satisfaction. "When I walked up your garden before coming in, and saw the hives all of a row, I said to myself, 'Where there's bees there's honey, and where there's honey there's mead.' But mead of such a truly comfortable sort as this I really didn't expect to meet in my older days." He took yet another pull at the mug, till it assumed an ominous elevation.

"Glad you enjoy it!" said the shepherd warmly.

"It is goodish mead," assented Mrs. Fennel, with an absence of enthusiasm which seemed to say that it was possible to buy praise for one's cellar at too heavy a price. "It is trouble enough to make—and really I hardly think we shall make any more. For honey sells well, and we ourselves make shift with a drop o' small mead and metheglin for common use from the comb washings."[6]

"O, but you'll never have the heart!" reproachfully cried the stranger in cinder gray, after taking up the mug a third time, and setting it down empty. "I love mead, when 'tis old like this, as I love to go to church o' Sundays, or to relieve the needy any day of the week."

"Ha, ha, ha!" said the man in the chimney corner, who, in spite of the taciturnity induced by the pipe of tobacco, could not or would not refrain from this slight testimony to his comrade's humor.

Now the old mead of those days, brewed of the purest first year or maiden honey, four pounds to the gallon—with its due complement of white of eggs, cinnamon, ginger, cloves, mace, rosemary, yeast, and processes of working, bottling, and cellaring—tasted remarkably strong; but it did not taste so strong as it actually was. Hence, presently, the stranger in cinder gray at the table, moved by

its creeping influence, unbuttoned his waistcoat, threw himself back in his chair, spread his legs, and made his presence felt in various ways.

"Well, well, as I say," he resumed, "I am going to Casterbridge, and to Casterbridge I must go. I should have been almost there by this time; but the rain drove me into your dwelling, and I'm not sorry for it."

"You don't live in Casterbridge?" said the shepherd.

"Not as yet; though I shortly mean to move there."

"Going to set up in trade, perhaps?"

"No, no," said the shepherd's wife. "It is easy to see that the gentleman is rich, and don't want to work at anything."

The cinder-gray stranger paused, as if to consider whether he would accept that definition of himself. He presently rejected it by answering, "Rich is not quite the word for me, dame. I do work, and I must work. And even if I only get to Casterbridge by midnight I must begin work there at eight tomorrow morning. Yes, het or wet, blow or snow, famine or sword, my day's work tomorrow must be done."

"Poor man! Then, in spite o' seeming, you be worse off than we?" replied the shepherd's wife.

"'Tis the nature of my trade, men and maidens. 'Tis the nature of my trade more than my poverty. . . . But really and truly I must up and off, or I shan't get a lodging in the town." However, the speaker did not move, and directly added, "There's time for one more draught of friendship before I go; and I'd perform it at once if the mug were not dry."

"Here's a mug o' small," said Mrs. Fennel. "Small, we call it, though to be sure 'tis only the first wash o' the combs."

"No," said the stranger disdainfully. "I won't spoil your first kindness by partaking o' your second."

"Certainly not," broke in Fennel. "We don't increase and multiply every day, and I'll fill the mug again." He went away to the dark place under the stairs where the barrel stood. The shepherdess followed him.

"Why should you do this?" she said reproachfully, as soon as they were alone. "He's emptied it once though it held enough for ten people; and now he's not contented wi' the small, but must

---

6. *small mead . . . comb washings,* drinks less potent than mead, made by pouring water over honeycomb after the salable honey has been removed.

needs call for more o' the strong! And a stranger unbeknown to any of us. For my part, I don't like the look o' the man at all."

"But he's in the house, my honey; and 'tis a wet night, and a christening. Daze it, what's a cup of mead more or less? There'll be plenty more next bee-burning."[7]

"Very well—this time, then," she answered, looking wistfully at the barrel. "But what is the man's calling, and where is he one of, that he should come in and join us like this?"

"I don't know. I'll ask him again."

The catastrophe of having the mug drained dry at one pull by the stranger in cinder gray was effectually guarded against this time by Mrs. Fennel. She poured out his allowance in a small cup, keeping the large one at a discreet distance from him. When he had tossed off his portion the shepherd renewed his inquiry about the stranger's occupation.

The latter did not immediately reply, and the man in the chimney corner, with sudden demonstrativeness, said, "Anybody may know my trade—I'm a wheelwright."

"A very good trade for these parts," said the shepherd.

"And anybody may know mine—if they've the sense to find it out," said the stranger in cinder gray.

"You may generally tell what a man is by his claws," observed the hedge carpenter, looking at his own hands. "My fingers be as full of thorns as an old pincushion is of pins."

The hands of the man in the chimney corner instinctively sought the shade, and he gazed into the fire as he resumed his pipe. The man at the table took up the hedge carpenter's remark, and added smartly, "True; but the oddity of my trade is that, instead of setting a mark upon me, it sets a mark upon my customers."

No observation being offered by anybody in elucidation of this enigma the shepherd's wife once more called for a song. The same obstacles presented themselves as at the former time—one had no voice, another had forgotten the first verse. The stranger at the table, whose soul had now risen to a good working temperature, relieved the difficulty by exclaiming that, to start the company, he would

sing himself. Thrusting one thumb into the armhole of his waistcoat, he waved the other hand in the air, and, with an extemporizing gaze at the shining sheepcrooks above the mantelpiece, began:

O my trade it is the rarest one, simple shepherds all—
    My trade is a sight to see;
For my customers I tie, and take them up on high,
    And waft 'em to a far countree!

The room was silent when he had finished the verse—with one exception, that of the man in the chimney corner, who, at the singer's word, "Chorus!" joined him in a deep bass voice of musical relish—

    And waft 'em to a far countree!

Oliver Giles, John Pitcher the dairyman, the parish clerk, the engaged man of fifty, the row of young women against the wall, seemed lost in thought not of the gayest kind. The shepherd looked meditatively on the ground, the shepherdess gazed keenly at the singer, and with some suspicion; she was doubting whether this stranger were merely singing an old song from recollection, or was composing one there and then for the occasion. All were as perplexed at the obscure revelation as the guests at Belshazzar's Feast,[8] except the man in the chimney corner, who quietly said, "Second verse, stranger," and smoked on.

The singer thoroughly moistened himself from his lips inwards, and went on with his next stanza as requested:

My tools are but common ones, simple shepherds all—
    My tools are no sight to see:
A little hempen string, and a post whereon to swing,
    Are implements enough for me!

Shepherd Fennel glanced round. There was no longer any doubt that the stranger was answering his question rhythmically. The guests one and all started back with suppressed exclamations. The young woman engaged to the man of fifty fainted halfway, and would have proceeded, but finding him wanting in alacrity for catching her she sat down trembling.

"O, he's the——!" whispered the people in the background, mentioning the name of an ominous public officer. "He's come to do it! 'Tis to

7. *bee-burning*. Bee keepers use smoke as protection while taking honey from the beehive.

8. *perplexed . . . Feast*. According to the Old Testament story, handwriting appeared on the wall at Belshazzar's Feast, forecasting doom (Daniel 5:1–24).

be at Casterbridge jail tomorrow—the man for sheep stealing—the poor clock-maker we heard of, who used to live away at Shottsford and had no work to do—Timothy Summers, whose family were astarving, and so he went out of Shottsford by the highroad, and took a sheep in open daylight, defying the farmer and the farmer's wife and the farmer's lad, and every man jack among 'em. He'' (and they nodded towards the stranger of the deadly trade) ''is come from up the country to do it because there's not enough to do in his own county town, and he's got the place here now our own county man's dead; he's going to live in the same cottage under the prison wall.''

The stranger in cinder gray took no notice of this whispered string of observations, but again wetted his lips. Seeing that his friend in the chimney corner was the only one who reciprocated his joviality in any way, he held out his cup towards that appreciative comrade, who also held out his own. They clinked together, the eyes of the rest of the room hanging upon the singer's actions. He parted his lips for the third verse; but at that moment another knock was audible upon the door. This time the knock was faint and hesitating.

The company seemed scared; the shepherd looked with consternation towards the entrance, and it was with some effort that he resisted his alarmed wife's deprecatory glance, and uttered for the third time the welcoming words, ''Walk in!''

The door was gently opened, and another man stood upon the mat. He, like those who had preceded him, was a stranger. This time it was a short, small personage, of fair complexion, and dressed in a decent suit of dark clothes.

''Can you tell me the way to——?'' he began: when, gazing round the room to observe the nature of the company amongst whom he had fallen, his eyes lighted on the stranger in cinder gray. It was just at the instant when the latter, who had thrown his mind into his song with such a will that he scarcely heeded the interruption, silenced all whispers and inquiries by bursting into his third verse:

Tomorrow is my working day, simple shepherds all—
   Tomorrow is a working day for me:
For the farmer's sheep is slain, and the lad who did it
    ta'en,
   And on his soul may God ha' merc-y!

The stranger in the chimney corner, waving cups with the singer so heartily that his mead splashed over on the hearth, repeated in his bass voice as before:

   And on his soul may God ha' merc-y!

All this time the third stranger had been standing in the doorway. Finding now that he did not come forward or go on speaking, the guests particularly regarded him. They noticed to their surprise that he stood before them the picture of abject terror— his knees trembling, his hand shaking so violently that the door latch by which he supported himself rattled audibly: his white lips were parted, and his eyes fixed on the merry officer of justice in the middle of the room. A moment more and he had turned, closed the door, and fled.

''What a man can it be?'' said the shepherd.

The rest, between the awfulness of their late discovery and the odd conduct of this third visitor, looked as if they knew not what to think, and said nothing. Instinctively they withdrew further and further from the grim gentleman in their midst, whom some of them seemed to take for the Prince of Darkness himself, till they formed a remote circle, an empty space of floor being left between them and him—''. . . circulus, cujus centrum diabolus.''[9] The room was so silent—though there were more than twenty people in it—that nothing could be heard but the patter of the rain against the window shutters, accompanied by the occasional hiss of a stray drop that fell down the chimney into the fire, and the steady puffing of the man in the corner, who had now resumed his pipe of long clay.

The stillness was unexpectedly broken. The distant sound of a gun reverberated through the air— apparently from the direction of the county town.

''Be jiggered!'' cried the stranger who had sung the song, jumping up.

''What does that mean?'' asked several.

''A prisoner escaped from the jail—that's what it means.''

All listened. The sound was repeated, and none of them spoke but the man in the chimney corner, who said quietly, ''I've often been told that in this county they fire a gun at such times; but I never heard it till now.''

''I wonder if it is *my* man?'' murmured the personage in cinder gray.

9. *circulus . . . diabolus,* a circle in the center of which was the devil (Latin).

"Surely it is!" said the shepherd involuntarily. "And surely we've zeed him! That little man who looked in at the door by now, and quivered like a leaf when he zeed ye and heard your song!"

"His teeth chattered, and the breath went out of his body," said the dairyman.

"And his heart seemed to sink within him like a stone," said Oliver Giles.

"And he bolted as if he'd been shot at," said the hedge carpenter.

"True—his teeth chattered, and his heart seemed to sink; and he bolted as if he'd been shot at," slowly summed up the man in the chimney corner.

"I didn't notice it," remarked the hangman.

"We were all a-wondering what made him run off in such a fright," faltered one of the women against the wall, "and now 'tis explained!"

The firing of the alarm gun went on at intervals, low and sullenly, and their suspicions became a certainty. The sinister gentleman in cinder gray roused himself. "Is there a constable here?" he asked, in thick tones. "If so, let him step forward."

The engaged man of fifty stepped quavering out from the wall, his betrothed beginning to sob on the back of the chair.

"You are a sworn constable?"

"I be, sir."

"Then pursue the criminal at once, with assistance, and bring him back here. He can't have gone far."

"I will, sir, I will—when I've got my staff. I'll go home and get it, and come sharp here, and start in a body."

"Staff! Never mind your staff; the man'll be gone!"

"But I can't do nothing without my staff—can I, William, and John, and Charles Jake? No; for there's the king's royal crown a painted on en in yaller and gold, and the lion and the unicorn, so as when I raise en up and hit my prisoner, 'tis made a lawful blow thereby. I wouldn't 'tempt to take up a man without my staff—no, not I. If I hadn't the law to gie me courage, why, instead o' my taking up him he might take up me!"

"Now, I'm a king's man myself, and can give you authority enough for this," said the formidable officer in gray. "Now then, all of ye, be ready. Have ye any lanterns?"

"Yes—have ye any lanterns? I demand it!" said the constable.

"And the rest of you able-bodied——"

"Able-bodied men—yes—the rest of ye!" said the constable.

"Have you some good stout staves and pitchforks——"

"Staves and pitchforks—in the name o' the law! And take 'em in yer hands and go in quest, and do as we in authority tell ye!"

Thus aroused, the men prepared to give chase. The evidence was, indeed, though circumstantial, so convincing, that but little argument was needed to show the shepherd's guests that after what they had seen it would look very much like connivance if they did not instantly pursue the unhappy third stranger, who could not as yet have gone more than a few hundred yards over such uneven country.

A shepherd is always well provided with lanterns; and, lighting these hastily, and with hurdle-staves in their hands, they poured out of the door, taking a direction along the crest of the hill, away from town, the rain having fortunately a little abated.

Disturbed by the noise, or possibly by unpleasant dreams of her baptism, the child who had been christened began to cry heartbrokenly in the room overhead. These notes of grief came down through the chinks of the floor to the ears of the women below, who jumped up one by one, and seemed glad of the excuse to ascend and comfort the baby, for the incidents of the last half-hour greatly oppressed them. Thus in the space of two or three minutes the room on the ground floor was deserted quite.

But it was not for long. Hardly had the sound of footsteps died away when a man returned round the corner of the house from the direction the pursuers had taken. Peeping in at the door, and seeing nobody there, he entered leisurely. It was the stranger of the chimney corner, who had gone out with the rest. The motive of his return was shown by his helping himself to a cut piece of skimmer cake that lay on a ledge beside where he had sat, and which he had apparently forgotten to take with him. He also poured out half a cup more mead from the quantity that remained, ravenously eating and drinking these as he stood. He had not finished when another figure came in just as quietly—his friend in cinder gray.

"O—you here?" said the latter, smiling. "I thought you had gone to help in the capture." And this speaker also revealed the object of his return by looking solicitously round for the fascinating mug of old mead.

"And I thought you had gone," said the other, continuing his skimmer cake with some effort.

"Well, on second thoughts, I felt there were enough without me," said the first confidentially, "and such a night as it is, too. Besides, 'tis the business o' the Government to take care of its criminals—not mine."

"True; so it is. And I felt as you did, that there were enough without me."

"I don't want to break my limbs running over the humps and hollows of this wild country."

"Nor I neither, between you and me."

"These shepherd people are used to it—simpleminded souls, you know, stirred up to anything in a moment. They'll have him ready for me before the morning, and no trouble to me at all."

"They'll have him, and we shall have saved ourselves all labor in the matter."

"True, true. Well, my way is to Casterbridge; and 'tis as much as my legs will do to take me that far. Going the same way?"

"No, I am sorry to say! I have to get home over there" (he nodded indefinitely to the right), "and I feel as you do, that it is quite enough for my legs to do before bedtime."

The other had by this time finished the mead in the mug, after which, shaking hands heartily at the door, and wishing each other well, they went their several ways.

In the meantime the company of pursuers had reached the end of the hog's-back elevation which dominated this part of the down. They had decided on no particular plan of action; and, finding that the man of the baleful trade was no longer in their company, they seemed quite unable to form any such plan now. They descended in all directions down the hill, and straightway several of the party fell into the snare set by nature for all misguided midnight ramblers over this part of the cretaceous formation. The "lanchets," or flint slopes, which belted the escarpment at intervals of a dozen yards, took the less cautious ones unawares, and losing their footing on the rubbly steep they slid sharply downwards, the lanterns rolling from their hands to the bottom, and there lying on their sides till the horn was scorched through.

When they had again gathered themselves together the shepherd, as the man who knew the country best, took the lead, and guided them round these treacherous inclines. The lanterns, which seemed rather to dazzle their eyes and warn the fugitive than to assist them in the exploration, were extinguished, due silence was observed; and in this more rational order they plunged into the vale. It was a grassy, briery, moist defile, affording some shelter to any person who had sought it; but the party perambulated it in vain, and ascended on the other side. Here they wandered apart, and after an interval closed together again to report progress. At the second time of closing in they found themselves near a lonely ash, the single tree on this part of the coomb, probably sown there by a passing bird some fifty years before. And here, standing a little to one side of the trunk, as motionless as the trunk itself, appeared the man they were in quest of, his outline being well defined against the sky beyond. The band noiselessly drew up and faced him.

"Your money or your life!" said the constable sternly to the still figure.

"No, no," whispered John Pitcher. "'Tisn't our side ought to say that. That's the doctrine of vagabonds like him, and we be on the side of the law."

"Well, well," replied the constable impatiently; "I must say something, mustn't I? And if you had all the weight o' this undertaking upon your mind, perhaps you'd say the wrong thing too! Prisoner at the bar, surrender, in the name of the Father—the Crown, I mane!"

The man under the tree seemed now to notice them for the first time, and, giving them no opportunity whatever for exhibiting their courage, he strolled slowly towards them. He was, indeed, the little man, the third stranger; but his trepidation had in a great measure gone.

"Well, travelers," he said, "did I hear ye speak to me?"

"You did: you've got to come and be our prisoner at once!" said the constable. "We arrest 'ee on the charge of not biding in Casterbridge jail in a decent proper manner to be hung tomorrow morning. Neighbors, do your duty, and seize the culpet!"

On hearing the charge the man seemed enlightened, and, saying not another word, resigned himself with preternatural civility to the search party, who, with their staves in their hands, surrounded him on all sides, and marched him back towards the shepherd's cottage.

It was eleven o'clock by the time they arrived.

The light shining from the open door, a sound of men's voices within, proclaimed to them as they approached the house that some new events had arisen in their absence. On entering they discovered the shepherd's living room to be invaded by two officers from Casterbridge jail, and a well-known magistrate who lived at the nearest country seat, intelligence of the escape having become generally circulated.

"Gentlemen," said the constable, "I have brought back your man—not without risk and danger; but every one must do his duty! He is inside this circle of able-bodied persons, who have lent me useful aid, considering their ignorance of Crown work. Men, bring forward your prisoner!" And the third stranger was led to the light.

"Who is this?" said one of the officials.

"The man," said the constable.

"Certainly not," said the turnkey; and the first corroborated his statement.

"But how can it be otherwise?" asked the constable. "Or why was he so terrified at sight o' the singing instrument of the law who sat there?" Here he related the strange behavior of the third stranger on entering the house during the hangman's song.

"Can't understand it," said the officer coolly. "All I know is that it is not the condemned man. He's quite a different character from this one; a gauntish fellow with dark hair and eyes, rather good-looking, and with a musical bass voice that if you heard once you'd never mistake as long as you lived."

"Why, souls—'twas the man in the chimney corner!"

"Hey—what?" said the magistrate, coming forward after inquiring particulars from the shepherd in the background. "Haven't you got the man after all?"

"Well, sir," said the constable, "he's the man we were in search of, that's true; and yet he's not the man we were in search of. For the man we were in search of was not the man we wanted, sir, if you understand my everyday way; for 'twas the man in the chimney corner!"

"A pretty kettle of fish altogether!" said the magistrate. "You had better start for the other man at once."

The prisoner now spoke for the first time. The mention of the man in the chimney corner seemed to have moved him as nothing else could do.

"Sir," he said, stepping forward to the magistrate, "take no more trouble about me. The time is come when I may as well speak. I have done nothing; my crime is that the condemned man is my brother. Early this afternoon I left home at Shottsford to tramp it all the way to Casterbridge jail to bid him farewell. I was benighted, and called here to rest and ask the way. When I opened the door I saw before me the very man, my brother, that I thought to see in the condemned cell at Casterbridge. He was in this chimney corner; and jammed close to him, so that he could not have got out if he had tried, was the executioner who'd come to take his life, singing a song about it and not knowing that it was his victim who was close by, joining in to save appearances. My brother threw a glance of agony at me, and I knew he meant, 'Don't reveal what you see; my life depends on it.' I was so terror-struck that I could hardly stand, and, not knowing what I did, I turned and hurried away."

The narrator's manner and tone had the stamp of truth, and his story made a great impression on all around. "And do you know where your brother is at the present time?" asked the magistrate.

"I do not. I have never seen him since I closed this door."

"I can testify to that, for we've been between ye ever since," said the constable.

"Where does he think to fly to? What is his occupation?"

"He's a watch-and-clock-maker, sir."

"'A said 'a was a wheelwright—a wicked rogue," said the constable.

"The wheels of clocks and watches he meant, no doubt," said Shepherd Fennel. "I thought his hands were palish for 's trade."

"Well, it appears to me that nothing can be gained by retaining this poor man in custody," said the magistrate; "your business lies with the other, unquestionably."

And so the little man was released offhand; but he looked nothing the less sad on that account, it being beyond the power of magistrate or constable to raze out the written troubles in his brain, for they concerned another whom he regarded with more solicitude than himself. When this was done, and the man had gone his way, the night was found to be so far advanced that it was deemed useless to renew the search before the next morning.

Next day, accordingly, the quest for the clever

sheep stealer became general and keen, to all appearance at least. But the intended punishment was cruelly disproportioned to the transgression, and the sympathy of a great many country folk in that district was strongly on the side of the fugitive. Moreover, his marvelous coolness and daring in hob-and-nobbing with the hangman, under the unprecedented circumstances of the shepherd's party, won their admiration. So that it may be questioned if all those who ostensibly made themselves so busy in exploring woods and fields and lanes were quite so thorough when it came to the private examination of their own lofts and outhouses. Stories were afloat of a mysterious figure being occasionally seen in some old over-grown trackway or other, remote from turnpike roads; but when a search was instituted in any of these suspected quarters nobody was found. Thus the days and weeks passed without tidings.

In brief, the bass-voiced man of the chimney corner was never recaptured. Some said that he went across the sea, others that he did not, but buried himself in the depths of a populous city. At any rate, the gentleman in cinder gray never did his morning's work at Casterbridge, nor met anywhere at all, for business purposes, the genial comrade with whom he had passed an hour of relaxation in the lonely house on the slope of the coomb.

The grass has long been green on the graves of Shepherd Fennel and his frugal wife, the guests who made up the christening party have mainly followed their entertainers to the tomb; the baby in whose honor they all had met is a matron in the sere and yellow leaf. But the arrival of the three strangers at the shepherd's that night, and the de-tails connected therewith, is a story as well known as ever in the country about Higher Crowstairs. □

DISCUSSION

1. Does any one person stand out clearly as the protagonist in this story? Explain.

2. Could the three strangers have arrived at Shepherd Fennel's in any different order?

3. Discuss the importance of the setting, especially the stormy night and the occasion (a christening party).

4. Characterize one of the following:
   (a) Timothy Summers
   (b) The hangman
   (c) Timothy's brother
   (d) Shepherd Fennel
   (e) Shepherdess Fennel

5. Discuss some of the humorous touches in this story. Are they fitting, or do they interfere with the suspense?

6. (a) Comment on the severity of the sentence meted out to Timothy Summers. Does he have anything of the criminal about him?

   (b) How do the local people feel about his sentence?

7. One reader has criticized this story for overuse of coincidence; another has praised it for its supreme irony. With which do you agree?

WRITING

1. One school of criticism feels that the real protagonist in Hardy's works is Egdon Heath—the country-side he describes in his fiction. Some critics have expanded this idea even further to say that in the pages of his works he has preserved a bygone way of life for future generations. Read one of his novels (perhaps *The Mayor of Casterbridge* or *Tess of the D'Urber-villes*), and write an essay commenting on these suggestions.

2. In a brief essay discuss the im-portance of the ending of "Horatio Sparkins" to the point that Dickens is attempting to make. Or, as an alter-native, write your own ending to the story.

3. The short stories in this unit de-scribe life in two different areas of Vic-torian England: "The Three Strangers" that of Hardy's Egdon Heath or Wes-sex, and "Horatio Sparkins" that of the environs of London. Write an essay in which you do either of the following:
   (a) Compare the two settings and their effect on the life of the charac-ters.
   (b) Explain which area you would prefer to live in, using the stories as the basis for your decision.

BACKGROUND

The Victorian Age

THE familiar stereotype of the Victorians as smug, prudish, and inflexibly formal is largely false. Far from exhibiting a single style, the time spanned by the reign of Queen Victoria (1837–1901) was one of the most varied and diverse periods in the history of English life and letters. More than any period which preceded, it was a time in which great issues—social, moral, scientific, and religious—were earnestly, often heatedly, debated. The fact that it was a time characterized by energetic change and a belief in progress made settlement of these issues urgent.

By the beginning of Victoria's reign, a rigid code of conduct had indeed come into vogue. Those who wished to be thought respectable (appearances were very important) observed the Sabbath with strict prohibitions against amusements, and spent the rest of the week in quiet and pious domesticity. Women were expected to be frail and sheltered creatures, silent, obedient, and decorative, mothers of children equally silent and obedient. The model male could and often did rule his household with an iron will; but gambling, swearing, intemperance, and sometimes even smoking were enough to remove him from the ranks of the respectable.

Yet respectability did not for long remain a static code. The feminist movement, already under way in the 1790's, had by the last part of the nineteenth century created a revolution in women's dress and deportment. Between 1870 and 1880 campaigners for women's rights formed societies in most large English towns and flooded Parliament with petitions containing nearly three million signatures, requesting that the right to vote be extended to women. Because of Queen Victoria's unexplained hostility toward the idea, and the widely held view that women were incapable of casting an intelligent vote, such motions were defeated. But by 1882, with the passage of the Married Women's Property Act, which gave married women the right to own property and to keep what they earned, large gains for women's rights had been won. Also, novelists like the Brontë sisters and Mary Ann Evans (George Eliot) presented love and marriage honestly from the woman's point of view, and probably persuaded many young women that the choice of a husband was theirs by right, even though marriages still were often arranged by ambitious parents.

By 1851, when Victoria opened the first world's fair at the gigantic Crystal Palace in London, the Industrial Revolution had come of age. Ushered in by improved textile manufacturing equipment in the late eighteenth century, the Industrial Revolution had quickly gathered momentum and by the mid-1800's had begun to work profound changes on the face of the land and the personalities of English people. By the late 1800's the quiet mood of much of rural England had given way to the frenetic pace of factory towns, and a new social phenomenon had arisen: the industrial working class. Probably the most pressing and apparently insoluble problem which confronted concerned Victorians was the condition of the workers, who frequently labored inhumanly long hours, for low wages, in filthy, dangerous factories, who lived in inadequate housing, and were subject to recurrent unemployment. Among the most horrifying of the abuses were the brutalities of child labor.

Responses to the problems of the Industrial Revolution were varied. Those who owned mines and factories supported a policy of *laissez-faire*, or no government regulation; those who sympathized with the workers, notably the Socialists, recommended not only government regulation but government ownership. The debate fluctuated between extremes but produced at least moderate results. Of the vast number of reform bills passed by Victorian parliaments, the two most significant were those of 1867 and 1884–1885, the first extending the franchise to urban workers, the second enfranchising workers in agricultural districts. (However, the franchise did not extend to women, who had to wait until 1928 to gain equal voting rights.) By 1911 the House of Lords had been deprived of all power except a delaying veto, and England was on its way to becoming a modern democracy in which the people, through their representatives in the House of Commons, were politically sovereign.

More sudden and dramatic were the changes in attitude wrought by the publication, in 1859, of Charles Darwin's *Origin of Species*, a book which proposed a theory of evolution that was to have far-reaching impact. When the book appeared, most people still accepted the Biblical account of creation as literal truth. To them Darwin's proposal gave a particular shock, for he theorized that the species now on earth had evolved over a period of hundreds of thousands of years through a harsh struggle for existence which only the hardiest survived. Many eventually came to see that there was no necessary conflict between the new biology and the interpretations of religion, but initially Darwin's theories cast many into doubt, even despair, about their traditional faith. Whether accepted or rejected, Darwin's ideas worked on the imagination of the age. Industrial owners and managers were not dismayed to hear that the key to evolutionary development was the "survival of the fittest," for they were able to interpret this as reason enough why some should be at the top of the heap and others on the bottom. Imperialists leaned on Darwin to explain why the British should dominate an empire five times the size of England itself. For others, particularly Marxians, Darwin's theories lent support to political views which emphasized the inevitability of class struggle. But the depersonalized view of life suggested by both Darwinian theory and the realities of industrialization tinged the essentially optimistic Victorian belief in progress with a pervasive unease.

Victorian literature reflects the mixture of opposites so characteristic of the age: hope and despair, faith and doubt, radical social theory and conservative social practice, the espousal of Christian love and gentleness combined with the ruthless use of power.

Queen Victoria herself was the calm and stable center in these times of change. Quiet, prudent, conservative in speech and behavior, she exemplified the domestic virtues of this thoroughly middle-class age. She bore her husband Prince Albert nine children, and preferred to leave most of the business of governing to her able ministers Gladstone and Disraeli. By the time she died after more than six decades as queen, England had entered a more complex and turbulent century, but it was still innocent of the horrors of global war and the dehumanization of a fully mechanized society. □

FEMININE FASHION. BY COURTESY OF THE VICTORIA AND ALBERT MUSEUM, LONDON, CROWN COPYRIGHT.

FEMINIST FASHION: RADIO TIMES HULTON PICTURE LIBRARY.

BIOGRAPHIES

Matthew Arnold   1822 / 1888

Matthew Arnold was not only a poet, but an educator, a classical scholar, and one of the most brilliant literary and social critics of the Victorian age. His interest in education came naturally, for his father, Thomas Arnold, was the renowned headmaster of Rugby School who in the first half of the 19th century did much to revolutionize secondary-school education in England.

Shortly after leaving Oxford, Arnold became a government inspector of schools, a post he held until two years before his death. He also made an extensive study of school systems in Europe for the government and wrote several books on continental education. In 1857 he was appointed to the Professorship of Poetry at Oxford (a part-time post) and lectured there for ten years.

Arnold was sharply critical of the materialism and narrow-mindedness of the Victorian middle classes (whom he called Philistines), and preached the gospel of culture as a corrective. He defined culture as a compound of "sweetness and light" consisting of a knowledge of "the best that has been thought and said in the world." He maintained that no work of art could be great that did not possess both artistic merit and moral power.

Emily Brontë   1818 / 1848

Novelist and poet Emily Brontë was the middle of the three famous Brontë sisters (the others were Charlotte and Anne, both novelists). Except for brief and unhappy periods in boarding schools, she was educated at home and spent her entire life in her father's parsonage.

The Brontë children, much on their own, created an imaginary country which they called "Gondal" and composed poems and legends about it. In 1845, Charlotte discovered Emily's carefully guarded poems (some of them "Gondal" poems) and published them with her own and Anne's as *Poems by Currer, Ellis, and Acton Bell*. Not until the publication and enormous success of Charlotte's novel *Jane Eyre* and Emily's *Wuthering Heights* (both in 1847) did the poems attract any attention. Emily died of tuberculosis the following year.

Elizabeth Barrett Browning 1806 / 1861

Up to her 41st year, Elizabeth Barrett was a semi-invalid, confined to her gloomy home by an overly possessive and tyrannical father. Her secluded life gave her time to study and write, and by the time she met her future husband, Robert Browning, she had become famous enough as a poet to be considered a rival to Tennyson.

Browning admired her poetry, and corresponded with her for several months before they met. When they did, they both fell deeply in love. A little over a year later they were secretly married and Browning swept her off to Italy.

In poems like "The Cry of the Children" she showed her deep social sympathy; her scholarship was displayed in translations of Aeschylus. Her long blank-verse romance *Aurora Leigh* was immensely popular with Victorian readers. But her works that are best known today are the *Sonnets from the Portuguese*, a set of love-poems addressed to her husband.

Robert Browning   1812 / 1889

During the years of his marriage, Robert Browning was sometimes referred to as "Mrs. Browning's husband," for his wife was more famous than he. Only in middle age did he win wide acclaim. To many of his contemporaries his poetry seemed crude, for he was one of the first to use the diction of ordinary speech. His work was condemned as difficult and obscure, probably because he assumed that the reading public shared his enormous erudition, acquired from private tutoring and intensive reading in his father's excellent library. Yet these qualities, along with the psychological insights he displayed, particularly in his dramatic monologues, are what make him seem almost modern to readers today.

Browning was the son of a well-to-do banker, and at the age of 22 made the "grand tour" of Europe, spending much time in Russia and Italy. His first important work, the dramatic poem *Paracelsus* (1835) is based on the life of a 15th-century magician and alchemist; in it he showed both the interest in the Renaissance and in men and their motives that became dominant strains in his work. Other volumes followed, but gained little attention.

His romantic love affair with the poet Elizabeth Barrett has been celebrated in story and drama. After their marriage in 1846, the Brownings moved to Italy, where they spent 15 years of idyllic happiness. After his wife's death in 1861, Browning returned to England with their son. He continued to publish major works of poetry, and his reputation steadily rose. His greatest single work, the novel-length *The Ring and the Book*, appeared in 1868. He spent the last years of his life in Venice, and died there. He is buried in the Poets' Corner at Westminster Abbey, not far from the tomb of Tennyson.

Arthur Hugh Clough   1819 / 1861

Clough was troubled all his life by the religious doubts which agitated so many thoughtful people of the time, and in 1848 he resigned his post as a fellow and tutor at Oriel College, Oxford, where he was expected to subscribe to the doctrines of the Church of England. The next few restless years were spent in Italy, in London, and in the United States in various educational posts. Later he worked in the Education Office in London, until ill health drove him to travel. He died in Italy of malarial fever.

Charles Dickens   1812 / 1870

When Charles Dickens was 12, his father was imprisoned for debt. Forced to live by himself, the boy found employment in a factory where, for a few shillings a week, he labeled blacking bottles. A sensitive child, he was deeply affected by the time he spent in the London underworld, and later modeled many of the descriptions, characters, and events in his novels on his childhood observations. This traumatic period ended when his father received a legacy which permitted him to pay his debts and go free. Charles was sent to school for three years and, at the age of 15, became a solicitor's clerk. He taught himself shorthand and became a newspaper reporter in the House of Commons.

His first sketches, which he signed "Boz," appeared in popular periodicals and then in book form in 1836. These were immediately followed by the *Pickwick Papers*, published in twenty monthly installments beginning in April 1836, and an immediate success. For the next 34 years Dickens wrote an uninterrupted stream of novels, most of which originally appeared in serial form. Among them

were *Oliver Twist, Nicholas Nickleby, A Christmas Carol, David Copperfield, Bleak House, A Tale of Two Cities*, and *Great Expectations*.

In 1842, Dickens traveled to America, where his disgust with the institution of slavery and his advocation of international copyright laws aroused much resentment. (His own books were widely pirated.) After a short stint at acting —a profession which had always fascinated him—he founded and edited a succession of popular periodicals.

Although in increasingly poor health, he began giving public readings in 1858, making a second visit to America in 1867–68. After his return to England, he began a novel, *Edwin Drood*, but died suddenly before it was completed. He was buried in Westminster Abbey.

Edward Fitzgerald   1809 / 1883

Fitzgerald is known today only for his "translation" of the Persian poem *The Rubáiyát*, but he made similar free translations of the plays of the 17th-century Spanish dramatist Calderon, and paraphrases of plays by Aeschylus and Sophocles which were remarkably successful in transferring the spirit of the originals into English.

After graduating from Trinity College, Cambridge, he settled down on his country estate in Suffolk where he studied Greek, Spanish, and Persian and lived the life of a country gentleman. After the publication of *The Rubáiyát*, he bought a yacht and spent much of the rest of his life cruising on the North Sea.

Thomas Hardy   1840 / 1928

Thomas Hardy was born in Dorsetshire, the county in southwest England which he used as the "Wessex" setting for his novels. At the age of 16 he was apprenticed to a church architect. While pursuing his architectural career in London, he wrote poetry in his spare time. After unsuccessfully trying to get his poetry published, he turned to writing fiction. Although his first novel was rejected by publishers, his second, *Desperate Remedies* (1871), was well received, and he gave up his architectural practice to devote himself to writing.

The best of his prose works are those he classified as "novels of environment and character": *Under the Greenwood Tree* (1872), *Far from the Madding Crowd* (1874), *The Return of the Native* (1878), *The Mayor of Casterbridge* (1886), *The Woodlanders* (1887), *Tess of the D'Urbervilles* (1891), and *Jude the Obscure* (1896). Hardy's realistic representation of people and his fatalistic, pessimistic view of life offended many of his contemporaries. When his last novel was denounced and referred to as *Jude the Obscene*, he turned from the writing of prose to his first love, poetry.

His most ambitious poetic work was *The Dynasts*, an epic-drama about the Napoleonic wars and their impact on England, published in three parts 1904–1908. He wrote and published a great deal of fine poetry until the end of his life.

When he died at the age of 88, his heart was buried in his native Dorset in accordance with his wishes, but his ashes were placed in Westminster Abbey.

Gerard Manley Hopkins   1844 / 1889

Gerard Manley Hopkins entered Oxford in 1863 with the intention of becoming a minister in the Anglican Church, but instead he was converted to Roman Catholicism and was ordained as a Jesuit priest in 1877. After serving in several parishes, including one in the working-class slums of Liverpool where he was distressed by the poverty and squalor, he was appointed Professor of Classics at University College, Dublin.

Hopkins was a sensitive and innovative poet who sometimes had difficulty reconciling his religious vocation with his poetic art. After his conversion, he burned all his early poems (though working copies survive) and did not write poetry again until 1875, when he composed his long poem "The Wreck of the Deutschland," a memorial to five German nuns who had drowned in the disaster.

When he died, Hopkins left his manuscripts to his friend and fellow poet Robert Bridges. Convinced that Hopkins' poetry would be ignored if introduced too early, Bridges held up its publication for 29 years. When Hopkins' collected *Poems* appeared in 1918, they caused a sensation, and the poet was hailed as a brilliant innovator whose spirit was closer to that of the 20th century than to his own age.

A(lfred) E(dward) Housman 1859 / 1936

Housman's best-known work, *A Shropshire Lad*, was written mostly in a burst of creativity in 1895 and published the next year. His next small collection of poems appeared in 1922, and a few additional poems were published after his death.

Housman began writing poetry while a student at Oxford,

and it has been suggested that his failure to pass his final examinations in classical studies—though he had been an excellent scholar—was due to his greater devotion to poetry.

For the next ten years he worked in the Royal Patent Office and pursued his classical studies alone. He gradually built up a reputation as a scholar on the strength of contributions to learned journals. In 1892 he became a professor of Latin at University College, London, and in 1911 became a professor at Cambridge. His most important scholarly work was a translation of the minor Latin poet Manilius.

Christina Georgina Rossetti 1830 / 1894

Christina Rossetti was the daughter of an Italian political exile and sister to the poet and painter Dante Gabriel Rossetti. She was content to live within the circle of her family and their friends, many of them artists and writers. She was a devout Anglican, and in her later years spent much of her time in religious devotions. Although she shunned publicity, she became well known for her poetry after the publication of *Goblin Market* (1862) and succeeding books of verse. She also wrote short stories and devotional books.

Robert Louis Stevenson   1850 / 1894

Although he was in poor health all his life, Scottish novelist, poet, and essayist Robert Louis Stevenson had a great love for the sea and for travel. He studied law and passed his bar exams, but found writing more to his taste. He first attracted attention with accounts of his travels: *An Inland Voyage* and *Travels with a Donkey*. While on the continent, he met an American woman whom he married in California in 1880. For the next seven years, his health rapidly declined, and he moved about the British Isles and the continent, seeking a healthful climate. His literary reputation was established at this time with the publication of *Treasure Island*, *A Child's Garden of Verses*, *The Strange Case of Dr. Jekyll and Mr. Hyde*, and *Kidnapped*.

After a brief stay at Saranac Lake in the Adirondacks, the Stevensons set sail for the South Seas, settling in 1890 in Samoa. He found both the climate and the character of the Samoans to his liking; he was called "Tusitala" (teller of tales) by the people. He died suddenly in 1894, not from his lung ailment, but from a cerebral hemorrhage.

Algernon Charles Swinburne
1837 / 1909

Algernon Charles Swinburne shocked Victorian England with his unconventional religious ideas (he was an atheist), his political views (he was a liberal republican dedicated to the overthrow of governments), and his frankly sensual poetry. He came from a distinguished family and attended Eton and Oxford. He already had some reputation as a poet when he came to the university, and continued to write while there, but indiscretions in conduct forced him to withdraw. He then traveled on the continent and was attracted to bohemian circles in Paris and London. His play *Atalanta in Calydon* (1865) won critical acclaim; his volume *Poems and Ballads* (1866) created a furor throughout England for its frank sensuousness and paganism. Older Victorians almost universally condemned him (Carlyle called his poetry "the miaulings of a delirious cat"), but he was almost a god to the young rebels of his day. In the years that followed, his increasingly dissipated life took its toll on his frail physique, and in 1879, when he was on the point of dying of delirium tremens, he put himself into the care of his friend Theodore Watts-Dunton, who kept him sober, subdued, and writing for the next thirty years.

Alfred, Lord Tennyson   1809 / 1892

Alfred Tennyson was the fourth of the twelve children of a village rector. His father, a talented but moody man, brought up his family in an atmosphere of high thinking and lofty aspirations. Even before Alfred entered Trinity College, Cambridge, in 1828, he had published a book of verse with his brothers. In 1829 he won the Cambridge Poetry Prize for his poem "Timbuctoo," and in the next few years published several collections of poems. His works won enough public favor to encourage him in pursuing a career in poetry.

At Cambridge, Tennyson had formed a close friendship with Arthur Hallam, who later became engaged to Alfred's sister Emily. In 1833, Hallam died unexpectedly in Vienna —a shattering blow to Tennyson. Under the influence of this loss, he began work on his long poem *In Memoriam*, in which he explored some of the questions that were troubling many thinkers of the age, in particular the conflict between orthodox religious faith and the doubts which followed on new scientific theories such as Darwin's theories of evolution. *In Memoriam* was not completed until 1850; in the meantime, Tennyson also worked on other poems, including his second major work, *The Idylls of the King*, a series of twelve narrative poems which retell the Arthurian tales collected centuries earlier by Thomas Malory.

The publication of *In Memoriam* brought Tennyson fame, and in the same year he was appointed poet laureate to succeed Wordsworth. His popularity was firmly established as he continued to publish major poetic works. He was raised to the peerage in 1884.

Tennyson's work was out of favor for a time, but today he is considered the greatest poet of the Victorian age, who dealt, in poetry of great technical variety and complexity, with the basic moral questions of his and every age: Who am I? What can I believe?

Oscar Wilde   1854 / 1900

Irish dramatist, novelist, and poet Oscar Wilde was as famous—or notorious—as a personality and a wit as he was as a writer. His brilliant conversation, eccentric dress (he often wore a velvet jacket and knee breeches) and his activities as leader of the "Aesthetic" movement ("Art for Art's sake") earned him much attention. His first dramatic success was *Lady Windemere's Fan* (1892); he appeared onstage after the opening performance to congratulate the audience on the intelligence of their appreciation. In the next three years, *A Woman of No Importance, Salome* (which was refused a license in England), and *The Importance of Being Earnest* were produced. His novel *The Picture of Dorian Gray* appeared in 1891.

In 1895 Wilde imprudently filed a libel suit against the Marquess of Queensberry, who had objected to Wilde's liaison with his son, Lord Alfred Douglas. Wilde lost the case and was himself condemned to prison. Upon his release he went to France, where he wrote *The Ballad of Reading Gaol*. He died two years later of cerebral meningitis.

Alice in Wonderland

by Lewis Carroll

IN the little more than a hundred years since *Alice in Wonderland* was first published it has received an amount of attention and critical acclaim far surpassing that accorded to any other "children's story." It has been translated into more than forty languages, and has brought delight to millions. Many of Alice's most devoted fans have, in fact, not been children at all. Bertrand Russell, the late British mathematician and philosopher, once suggested that the *Alice* stories were unfit for anyone under fifteen years of age.

What is behind Alice's almost universal appeal? That depends on who you are, what you are looking for, and what your "porpoise" is, as the Mock Turtle would say. The literary critics have linked Alice's experiences in Wonderland with the descent and return archetype, the picaresque novel, and the English pastoral tradition, among other things. Psychoanalysts have commented at length about Alice's "identity crises" and her maturing behavior and growing self-control as the story unfolds. Scientists have puzzled over the improbabilities of Alice's free fall down the rabbit hole; mathematicians have pondered the Einsteinian implications of the White Rabbit's unusual watch; historians and biographers have speculated on Wonderland's veiled references to the contemporary Victorian scene; and linguists have unearthed with evident glee Carroll's complicated word play and his sometimes outrageous puns.

There is something else about the Alice stories that every reader feels: beneath the gauzy surface of innocent fantasy—the Wonderland where animals argue and philosophize, where lobsters dance and turtles sing, where croquet balls are hedgehogs—there are other, more significant, levels, and the reader emerges from Alice's world with a peculiar feeling that perhaps events there are no more zany than events in the world of everyday reality. In the real world, as in Alice's, there are people whose unmodulated response to every unpleasant or complicated social situation is, like that of the Queen of Hearts, "Off with their heads!"

Perhaps the last word on *Alice in Wonderland* should go to its author. "The why of this book," Lewis Carroll wrote, "cannot, and need not, be put into words. Those for whom a child's mind is a sealed book, and who see no divinity in a child's smile, would read such words in vain; while for anyone who has ever loved one true child, no words are needed." Through the eyes of Alice, the world for all of us—eight to eighty—is still wild and full of marvels.

The following introductory verses refer to a boating trip taken by Lewis Carroll and his friend, the Reverend Robinson Duckworth, with the three Liddell sisters in 1862. They rowed up the Thames river from Oxford to a small village, had tea, and returned before evening. The gently mock-heroic poem refers to the Liddell sisters as the "cruel Three": Lorina Liddell, Prima, was the eldest; Alice, Secunda, was younger; and Edith, Tertia, was youngest. Their demands for a story inspired Alice in Wonderland.

All in the golden afternoon
    Full leisurely we glide;
For both our oars, with little skill,
    By little arms are plied.
While little hands make vain pretence
    Our wanderings to guide.

Ah, cruel Three! In such an hour,
    Beneath such dreamy weather,
To beg a tale of breath too weak
    To stir the tiniest feather!
Yet what can one poor voice avail
    Against three tongues together?

Imperious Prima flashes forth
    Her edict "to begin it"—
In gentler tone Secunda hopes
    "There will be nonsense in it!"—
While Tertia interrupts the tale
    Not *more* than once a minute.

Anon, to sudden silence won,
    In fancy they pursue
The dream-child moving through a land

Of wonders wild and new,
In friendly chat with bird or beast—
    And half believe it true.

And ever, as the story drained
    The wells of fancy dry,
And faintly strove that weary one
    To put the subject by,
"The rest next time—" "It *is* next time!"
    The happy voices cry.

Thus grew the tale of Wonderland:
    Thus slowly, one by one,
Its quaint events were hammered out—
    And now the tale is done,
And home we steer, a merry crew,
    Beneath the setting sun.

Alice! a childish story take,
    And with a gentle hand
Lay it where Childhood's dreams are twined
    In Memory's mystic band,
Like pilgrim's wither'd wreath of flowers
    Plucked in a far-off land.

1 DOWN THE RABBIT-HOLE

ALICE was beginning to get very tired of sitting by her sister on the bank, and of having nothing to do: once or twice she had peeped into the book her sister was reading, but it had no pictures or conversations in it, "and what is the use of a book," thought Alice, "without pictures or conversations?"

So she was considering in her own mind, (as well as she could, for the hot day made her feel very sleepy and stupid), whether the pleasure of making a daisy-chain would be worth the trouble of getting up and picking the daisies, when suddenly a white rabbit with pink eyes ran close by her.

There was nothing so *very* remarkable in that; nor did Alice think it so *very* much out of the way to hear the Rabbit say to itself, "Oh dear! Oh dear! I shall be too late!" (when she thought it over afterwards, it occurred to her that she ought to have wondered at this, but at the time it all seemed quite natural); but when the Rabbit actually *took a watch out of its waistcoat-pocket,* and looked at it, and then hurried on, Alice started to her feet, for it flashed across her mind that she had never before seen a rabbit with either a waistcoat-pocket or a watch to take out of it, and, burning with curiosity, she ran across the field after it, and was just in time to see it pop down a large rabbit-hole under the hedge.

In another moment down went Alice after it, never once considering how in the world she was to get out again.

The rabbit-hole went straight on like a tunnel for

some way, and then dipped suddenly down, so suddenly that Alice had not a moment to think about stopping herself before she found herself falling down what seemed to be a very deep well.

Either the well was very deep, or she fell very slowly, for she had plenty of time as she went down to look about her, and to wonder what was going to happen next. First, she tried to look down and make out what she was coming to, but it was too dark to see anything: then she looked at the sides of the well, and noticed that they were filled with cupboards and bookshelves: here and there she saw maps and pictures hung upon pegs. She took down a jar from one of the shelves as she passed; it was labelled "Orange Marmalade," but to her great disappointment it was empty: she did not like to drop the jar for fear of killing somebody underneath, so managed to put it into one of the cupboards as she fell past it.

"Well!" thought Alice to herself, "after such a fall as this, I shall think nothing of tumbling down stairs! How brave they'll all think me at home! Why, I wouldn't say anything about it, even if I fell off the top of the house!" (Which was very likely true.)

Down, down, down. Would the fall *never* come to an end? "I wonder how many miles I've fallen by this time?" she said aloud. "I must be getting somewhere near the centre of the earth. Let me see: that would be four thousand miles down, I think—" (for, you see, Alice had learnt several things of this sort in her lessons in the schoolroom, and though this was not a *very* good opportunity for showing off her knowledge, as there was no one to listen to her, still it was good practice to say it over) "—yes, that's about the right distance—but then I wonder what Latitude or Longitude I've got to?" (Alice had not the slightest idea what Latitude was, or Longitude either, but she thought they were nice grand words to say.)

Presently she began again. "I wonder if I shall fall right *through* the earth! How funny it'll seem to come out among the people that walk with their heads downwards! The Antipathies, I think—" (she was rather glad there *was* no one listening, this time, as it didn't sound at all the right word) "—but I shall have to ask them what the name of the country is, you know. Please, Ma'am, is this New Zealand or Australia?" (and she tried to curtsey as she spoke—fancy *curtseying* as you're falling through the air! Do you think you could manage it?) "And what an ignorant little girl she'll think me for asking! No, it'll

never do to ask: perhaps I shall see it written up somewhere."

Down, down, down. There was nothing else to do, so Alice soon began talking again. "Dinah'll miss me very much to-night, I should think!" (Dinah was the cat.) "I hope they'll remember her saucer of milk at teatime. Dinah, my dear! I wish you were down here with me! There are no mice in the air, I'm afraid, but you might catch a bat, and that's very like a mouse, you know. But do cats eat bats, I wonder?" And here Alice began to get rather sleepy, and went on saying to herself, in a dreamy sort of way, "Do cats eat bats? Do cats eat bats?" and sometimes, "Do bats eat cats?" for, you see, as she couldn't answer either question, it didn't much matter which way she put it. She felt that she was dozing off, and had just begun to dream that she was walking hand in hand with Dinah, and was saying to her very earnestly, "Now, Dinah, tell me the truth: did you ever eat a bat?" when suddenly, thump! thump! down she came upon a heap of sticks and dry leaves, and the fall was over.

Alice was not a bit hurt, and she jumped up on to her feet in a moment: she looked up, but it was all dark overhead; before her was another long passage, and the White Rabbit was still in sight, hurrying down it. There was not a moment to be lost: away went Alice like the wind, and was just in time to hear it say, as it turned a corner, "Oh my ears and whiskers, how late it's getting!" She was close behind it when she turned the corner, but the Rabbit was no longer to be seen: she found herself in a long, low hall, which was lit up by a row of lamps hanging from the roof.

There were doors all around the hall, but they were all locked, and when Alice had been all the way down one side and up the other, trying every door, she walked sadly down the middle, wondering how she was ever to get out again.

Suddenly she came upon a little three-legged table, all made of solid glass; there was nothing on it but a tiny golden key, and Alice's first idea was that this might belong to one of the doors of the hall; but, alas! either the locks were too large, or the key was too small, but at any rate it would not open any of them. However, on the second time round, she came upon a low curtain she had not noticed before, and behind it was a little door about fifteen inches high: she tried the little golden key in the lock, and to her great delight it fitted!

Alice opened the door and found that it led into a small passage, not much larger than a rathole: she knelt down and looked along the passage into the loveliest garden you ever saw. How she longed to get out of that dark hall, and wander about among those beds of bright flowers and those cool fountains, but she could not even get her head through the doorway; "and even if my head would go through," thought poor Alice, "it would be of very little use without my shoulders. Oh, how I wish I could shut up like a telescope! I think I could, if I only knew how to begin." For, you see, so many out-of-the-way things had happened lately that Alice had begun to think that very few things indeed were really impossible.

There seemed to be no use in waiting by the little door, so she went back to the table, half hoping she might find another key on it, or at any rate a book of rules for shutting people up like telescopes: this time she found a little bottle on it, ("which certainly was not here before," said Alice,) and tied round the neck of the bottle was a paper label with the words "DRINK ME" beautifully printed on it in large letters.

It was all very well to say "Drink me," but the wise little Alice was not going to do that in a hurry: "no, I'll look first," she said, "and see whether it's marked 'poison' or not": for she had read several nice little stories about children who had got burnt, and eaten up by wild beasts, and other unpleasant things, all because they would not remember the simple rules their friends had taught them, such as, that a red-hot poker will burn you if you hold it too long; and that if you cut your finger very deeply with a knife, it usually bleeds; and she had never forgotten that, if you drink much from a bottle marked "poison," it is almost certain to disagree with you, sooner or later.

However, this bottle was not marked "poison," so Alice ventured to taste it, and finding it very nice, (it had, in fact, a sort of mixed flavour of cherry-tart, custard, pineapple, roast turkey, toffy, and hot buttered toast), she very soon finished it off.

"What a curious feeling!" said Alice, "I must be shutting up like a telescope."

And so it was indeed: she was now only ten inches high, and her face brightened up at the thought that she was now the right size for going through the little door into that lovely garden. First, however, she waited for a few minutes to see if she was going to shrink any further: she felt a little nervous about this,

"for it might end, you know," said Alice to herself, "in my going out altogether, like a candle. I wonder what I should be like then?" And she tried to fancy what the flame of a candle looks like after the candle is blown out, for she could not remember ever having seen such a thing.

After a while, finding that nothing more happened, she decided on going into the garden at once, but, alas for poor Alice! when she got to the door, she found she had forgotten the little golden key, and when she went back to the table for it, she found she could not possibly reach it: she could see it quite plainly through the glass, and she tried her best to climb up one of the legs of the table, but it was too slippery, and when she had tired herself out with trying, the poor little thing sat down and cried.

"Come, there's no use in crying like that!" said Alice to herself, rather sharply, "I advise you to leave off this minute!" She generally gave herself very good advice, (though she very seldom followed it), and sometimes she scolded herself so severely as to bring tears into her eyes, and once she remembered trying to box her own ears for having cheated herself in a game of croquet she was playing against herself, for this curious child was very fond of pretending to be two people. "But it's no use now," thought poor Alice, "to pretend to be two people! Why, there's hardly enough of me left to make one respectable person!"

Soon her eye fell on a little glass box that was lying under the table: she opened it, and found in it a very small cake, on which the words "EAT ME" were beautifully marked in currants. "Well, I'll eat it," said Alice, "and if it makes me grow larger, I can reach the key; and if it makes me grow smaller, I can creep under the door; so either way I'll get into the garden, and I don't care which happens!"

She ate a little bit, and said anxiously to herself "Which way? Which way?" holding her hand on the top of her head to feel which way it was growing, and she was quite surprised to find that she remained the same size: to be sure, this is what generally happens when one eats cake, but Alice had got so much into the way of expecting nothing but out-of-the-way things to happen, that it seemed quite dull and stupid for life to go on in the common way.

So she set to work, and very soon finished off the cake.

2

THE POOL OF TEARS

"CURIOUSER and curiouser!" cried Alice (she was so much surprised, that for the moment she quite forgot how to speak good English): "now I'm opening out like the largest telescope that ever was! Good-bye feet!" (for when she looked down at her feet, they seemed to be almost out of sight, they were getting so far off). "Oh, my poor little feet, I wonder who will put on your shoes and stockings for you now, dears? I'm sure I shan't be able! I shall be a great deal too far off to trouble myself about you: you must manage the best way you can;—but I must be kind to them," thought Alice, "or perhaps they won't walk the way I want to go! Let me see: I'll give them a new pair of boots every Christmas."

And she went on planning to herself how she would manage it. "They must go by the carrier," she thought; "and how funny it'll seem, sending presents to one's own feet! And how odd the directions will look!

> "Alice's Right Foot Esq.,
>   Hearthrug, near the Fender[1]
>   (with Alice's love.)

"Oh dear, what nonsense I'm talking!"

Just at this moment her head struck against the roof of the hall: in fact she was now rather more than nine feet high, and she at once took up the little golden key and hurried off to the garden door.

Poor Alice! It was as much as she could do, lying down on one side, to look through into the garden with one eye; but to get through was more hopeless than ever: she sat down and began to cry again.

"You ought to be ashamed of yourself," said Alice, "a great girl like you," (she might well say this), "to go on crying in this way! Stop this moment, I tell you!" But she went on all the same, shedding gallons of tears, until there was a large pool round her, about four inches deep and reaching half down the hall.

---

1. *Fender,* a metal screen that separated the fireplace from the hearth, and kept live coals or sparks from spilling out onto the hearthrug.

After a time she heard a little pattering of feet in the distance, and she hastily dried her eyes to see what was coming. It was the White Rabbit returning, splendidly dressed, with a pair of white kid gloves in one hand and a large fan in the other: he came trotting along in a great hurry, muttering to himself as he came, "Oh! the Duchess, the Duchess! Oh! won't she be savage if I've kept her waiting!" Alice felt so desperate that she was ready to ask help of any one; so when the Rabbit came near her, she began, in a low, timid voice, "If you please, sir—" The Rabbit started violently, dropped the white kid gloves and the fan, and scurried away into the darkness as hard as he could go.

Alice took up the fan and gloves, and, as the hall was very hot, she kept fanning herself all the time she went on talking: "Dear, dear! How queer everything is to-day! And yesterday things went on just as usual. I wonder if I've been changed in the night? Let me think: was I the same when I got up this morning? I almost think I can remember feeling a little different. But if I'm not the same, the next question is, Who in the world am I? Ah, *that's* the great puzzle!" And she began thinking over all the children she knew, that were of the same age as herself, to see if she could have been changed for any of them.

"I'm sure I'm not Ada," she said, "for her hair goes in such long ringlets, and mine doesn't go in ringlets at all; and I'm sure I can't be Mabel, for I know all sorts of things, and she, oh! she knows such a very little! Besides, *she's* she, and *I'm* I, and—oh dear, how puzzling it all is! I'll try if I know all the things I used to know. Let me see: four times five is twelve, and four times six is thirteen, and four times seven is—oh dear! I shall never get to twenty at that rate! However, the Multiplication Table don't signify: let's try Geography. London is the capital of Paris, and Paris is the capital of Rome, and Rome —no, *that's* all wrong, I'm certain! I must have been changed for Mabel! I'll try and say 'How doth the little—'" and she crossed her hands on her lap, as if she were saying lessons, and began to repeat it, but her voice sounded hoarse and strange, and the words did not come the same as they used to do:—

"How doth the little crocodile[2]
Improve his shining tail,
And pour the waters of the Nile
On every golden scale!

How cheerfully he seems to grin,
How neatly spreads his claws,
And welcomes little fishes in
With gently smiling jaws!

"I'm sure those are not the right words," said poor Alice, and her eyes filled with tears again as she went on, "I must be Mabel after all, and I shall have to go and live in that poky little house, and have next to no toys to play with, and oh! ever so many lessons to learn! No, I've made up my mind about it: if I'm Mabel, I'll stay down here! It'll be no use their putting their heads down and saying, 'Come up again, dear!' I shall only look up and say, 'Who am I, then? Tell me that first, and then, if I like being that person, I'll come up: if not, I'll stay down here till I'm somebody else'—but, oh dear!" cried Alice with a sudden burst of tears, "I do wish they *would* put their heads down! I am so *very* tired of being all alone here!"

As she said this, she looked down at her hands, and was surprised to see that she had put on one of the Rabbit's little white kid gloves while she was talking. "How *can* I have done that?" she thought. "I must be growing small again." She got up and went to the table to measure herself by it, and found that, as nearly as she could guess, she was now about two feet high, and was going on shrinking rapidly: she soon found out that the cause of this was the fan she was holding, and she dropped it hastily, just in time to save herself from shrinking away altogether.

"That *was* a narrow excape!" said Alice, a good deal frightened at the sudden change, but very glad to find herself still in existence; "and now for the garden!" and she ran with all speed back to the little door: but alas! the little door was shut again, and the little golden key was lying on the glass table as before, "and things are worse than ever," thought the poor child, "for I never was so small as this before, never! And I declare it's too bad, that it is!"

As she said these words her foot slipped, and in another moment, splash! she was up to her chin in salt water. Her first idea was that she had somehow fallen into the sea, "and in that case I can go back by railway," she said to herself. (Alice had been to the seaside once in her life, and had come to the general conclusion, that wherever you go to on the English coast you find a number of bathing machines[3] in the sea, some children digging in the sand with wooden spades, then a row of lodging houses, and behind them a railway station.) However she soon made out that she was in the pool of tears which she had wept when she was nine feet high.

"I wish I hadn't cried so much!" said Alice, as she swam about, trying to find her way out. "I shall be punished for it now, I suppose, by being drowned in my own tears! That *will* be a queer thing, to be sure! However, everything is queer to-day."

Just then she heard something splashing about in the pool a little way off, and she swam nearer to make out what it was: at first she thought it must be a walrus or hippopotamus, but then she remembered how small she was now, and she soon made out that it was only a mouse, that had slipped in like herself.

"Would it be of any use, now," thought Alice, "to speak to this mouse? Everything is so out-of-the-way down here, that I should think very likely it can talk: at any rate there's no harm in trying." So she began: "O Mouse, do you know the way out of this pool? I am very tired of swimming about here, O Mouse!" (Alice thought this must be the right way of speaking to a mouse: she had never done such a thing before, but she remembered having seen in her brother's Latin Grammar, "A mouse—of a mouse—to a mouse—a mouse—O mouse!") The Mouse looked at her rather inquisitively, and seemed to her to wink with one of its little eyes, but it said nothing.

"Perhaps it doesn't understand English," thought Alice; "I daresay it's a French mouse, come over with William the Conqueror." (For, with all her knowledge of history, Alice had no very clear notion how long ago anything had happened.) So she began again: "Où est ma chatte?"[4] which was the first

---

2. This is the first of many parodies that appear in *Alice in Wonderland*. See page 482 for the original.

3. *Bathing machines,* typically Victorian inventions designed to give the bather (swimmer) privacy. They were small wooden locker rooms on wheels. The bather entered and changed into his bathing costume while the contraption was on the beach; it was then drawn by horses into the sea, where the occupant could emerge and bathe out of public view. .

4. *French:* "Where is my cat?"

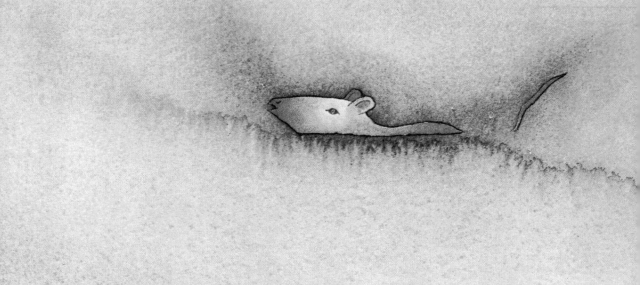
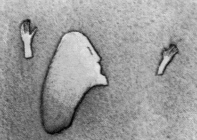

FOLON

sentence in her French lesson-book. The Mouse gave a sudden leap out of the water, and seemed to quiver all over with fright. "Oh, I beg your pardon!" cried Alice hastily, afraid that she had hurt the poor animal's feelings. "I quite forgot you didn't like cats."

"Not like cats!" cried the Mouse, in a shrill, passionate voice. "Would *you* like cats if you were me?"

"Well, perhaps not," said Alice in a soothing tone: "don't be angry about it. And yet I wish I could show you our cat Dinah: I think you'd take a fancy to cats if you could only see her. She is such a dear quiet thing," Alice went on, half to herself, as she swam lazily about in the pool, "and she sits purring so nicely by the fire, licking her paws and washing her face—and she is such a nice soft thing to nurse—and she's such a capital one for catching mice—oh, I beg your pardon!" cried Alice again, for this time the Mouse was bristling all over, and she felt certain it must be really offended. "We won't talk about her any more if you'd rather not."

"We, indeed!" cried the Mouse, who was trembling down to the end of his tail. "As if *I* would talk on such a subject! Our family always *hated* cats: nasty, low, vulgar things! Don't let me hear the name again!"

"I won't indeed!" said Alice, in a great hurry to change the subject of conversation. "Are you—are you fond—of—of dogs?" The mouse did not answer, so Alice went on eagerly: "There is such a nice little dog near our house I should like to show you! A little bright-eyed terrier, you know, with oh! such long curly brown hair! And it'll fetch things when you throw them, and it'll sit up and beg for its dinner, and all sorts of things—I can't remember half of them—and it belongs to a farmer, you know, and he says it's so useful, it's worth a hundred pounds! He says it kills all the rats and—oh dear!" cried Alice in a sorrowful tone. "I'm afraid I've offended it again!" For the Mouse was swimming away from her as hard as it could go, and making quite a commotion in the pool as it went.

So she called softly after it: "Mouse dear! Do come back again, and we won't talk about cats or dogs either, if you don't like them!" When the Mouse heard this, it turned round and swam slowly back to her: its face was quite pale (with passion, Alice thought), and it said in a low trembling voice, "Let us get to the shore, and then I'll tell you my history, and you'll understand why it is I hate cats and dogs."

It was high time to go, for the pool was getting quite crowded with the birds and animals that had fallen into it: there was a Duck and a Dodo, a Lory and an Eaglet,[5] and several other curious creatures. Alice led the way, and the whole party swam to the shore.

3

A CAUCUS RACE AND A LONG TALE

THEY were indeed a queer-looking party that assembled on the bank—the birds with draggled feathers, the animals with their fur clinging close to them, and all dripping wet, cross, and uncomfortable.

The first question of course was, how to get dry again: they had a consultation about this, and after a few minutes it seemed quite natural to Alice to find herself talking familiarly with them, as if she had known them all her life. Indeed, she had quite a long argument with the Lory, who at last turned sulky, and would only say, "I am older than you, and must know better"; and this Alice would not allow, without knowing how old it was, and as the Lory positively refused to tell its age, there was no more to be said.

At last the Mouse, who seemed to be a person of some authority among them, called out, "Sit down, all of you, and listen to me! *I'll* soon make you dry enough!" They all sat down at once, in a large ring, with the Mouse in the middle. Alice kept her eyes anxiously fixed on it, for she felt sure she would catch a bad cold if she did not get dry very soon.

"Ahem!" said the Mouse with an important air, "are you all ready? This is the driest thing I know. Silence all round, if you please! 'William the Conqueror, whose cause was favoured by the pope, was

---

5. The animals mentioned are thinly disguised representations of members of the party which boated on the Thames in 1862. The Duck is the Reverend Duckworth; the Dodo (a flightless bird already extinct by the 1860's) is Lewis Carroll (Charles Dodgson); the Lory (an Australian parrot) is Lorina Liddell; the Eaglet, Edith Liddell.

soon submitted to by the English, who wanted leaders, and had been of late much accustomed to usurpation and conquest. Edwin and Morcar, the earls of Mercia and Northumbria—'"[6]

"Ugh!" said the Lory, with a shiver.

"I beg your pardon?" said the Mouse, frowning, but very politely: "Did you speak?"

"Not I!" said the Lory, hastily.

"I thought you did," said the Mouse. "I proceed. 'Edwin and Morcar, the earls of Mercia and Northumbria, declared for him; and even Stigand, the patriotic archbishop of Canterbury, found it advisable—'"

"Found *what?*" said the Duck.

"Found *it*," the Mouse replied rather crossly: "of course you know what 'it' means."

"I know what 'it' means well enough, when *I* find a thing," said the Duck: "It's generally a frog or a worm. The question is, what did the archbishop find?"

The Mouse did not notice this question, but hurriedly went on, "'—found it advisable to go with Edgar Atheling to meet William and offer him the crown. William's conduct at first was moderate. But the insolence of his Normans—' How are you getting on now, my dear?" it continued, turning to Alice as it spoke.

"As wet as ever," said Alice in a melancholy tone: "it doesn't seem to dry me at all."

"In that case," said the Dodo solemnly, rising to its feet, "I move that the meeting adjourn, for the immediate adoption of more energetic remedies—"

"Speak English!" said the Eaglet. "I don't know the meaning of half those long words, and what's more, I don't believe you do either!" And the Eaglet bent down its head to hide a smile: some of the other birds tittered audibly.

"What I was going to say," said the Dodo in an offended tone, "was, that the best thing to get us dry would be a Caucus-race."[7]

"What *is* a Caucus-race?" said Alice; not that she much wanted to know, but the Dodo had paused as if it thought that *somebody* ought to speak, and no one else seemed inclined to say anything.

"Why," said the Dodo, "the best way to explain it is to do it." (And as you might like to try the thing yourself, some winter day, I will tell you how the Dodo managed it.)

First it marked out a race-course, in a sort of circle, ("the exact shape doesn't matter," it said,) and then all the party were placed along the course, here and there. There was no "One, two, three, and away," but they began running when they liked, and left off when they liked, so that it was not easy to know when the race was over. However, when they had been running half-an-hour or so, and were quite dry again, the Dodo suddenly called out, "The race is over!" and they all crowded round it, panting, and asking, "But who has won?"

This question the Dodo could not answer without a great deal of thought, and it sat for a long time with one finger pressed upon its forehead, (the position in which you usually see Shakespeare, in the pictures of him,) while the rest waited in silence. At last the Dodo said, "*Everybody* has won, and all must have prizes."

"But who is to give the prizes?" quite a chorus of voices asked.

"Why, *she*, of course," said the Dodo, pointing to Alice with one finger; and the whole party at once crowded round her, calling out in a confused way:

"Prizes! Prizes!"

Alice had no idea what to do, and in despair she put her hand into her pocket, and pulled out a box of comfits,[8] (luckily the salt water had not got into it,) and handed them round as prizes. There was exactly one a-piece, all round.

"But she must have a prize herself, you know," said the Mouse.

"Of course," the Dodo replied very gravely. "What else have you got in your pocket?" he went on, turning to Alice.

"Only a thimble," said Alice sadly.

"Hand it over here," said the Dodo.

Then they all crowded round her once more, while the Dodo solemnly presented the thimble, saying, "We beg your acceptance of this elegant thimble"; and, when it had finished this short speech, they all cheered.

Alice thought the whole thing very absurd, but they all looked so grave that she did not dare to laugh, and as she could not think of anything to say,

---

6. The passage that the mouse recites is probably from a contemporary English history textbook.

7. Although the term "caucus" originated in the United States and meant simply a gathering of political figures to select a candidate, the term, as it was used in Victorian England, carried harsher overtones of organizational confusion and political greed.

8. *Comfits*, a type of candy made by covering dried fruits or seeds with sugar.

she simply bowed, and took the thimble, looking as solemn as she could.

The next thing was to eat the comfits: this caused some noise and confusion, as the large birds complained that they could not taste theirs, and the small ones choked and had to be patted on the back. However it was over at last, and they sat down again in a ring, and begged the Mouse to tell them something more.

"You promised to tell me your history, you know," said Alice, "and why it is you hate—C and D," she added in a whisper, half afraid that it would be offended again.

"Mine is a long and sad tale!" said the Mouse, turning to Alice, and sighing.

"It *is* a long tail, certainly," said Alice, looking down with wonder at the Mouse's tail; "but why do you call it sad?" And she kept on puzzling about it while the Mouse was speaking, so that her idea of the tale was something like this:——"Fury

　　　　said to a mouse, That
　　　　　　he met in the house,
　　　　　　　　'Let us both go
　　　　　　　to law: *I* will prose-
　　　　　　cute *you*.—Come,
　　　　　I'll take no denial:
　　　　We must have the
　　　trial; for really
　　this morning I've
　　nothing to do.'
　　　Said the mouse
　　　　to the cur,
　　　　　'Such a trial,
　　　　　　dear sir,
　　　　　　　with no
　　　　　　　jury
　　　　　　or judge,
　　　　　would be
　　　　wasting our
　　breath.' 'I'll be
　　judge, I'll
　　be jury,'
　　　said cun-
　　　　ning old
　　　　　Fury: 'I'll
　　　　　try the
　　　　　whole
　　　　cause,
　　　　and
　　　con-
　　　demn
　　　　you
　　　　to death'."

"You are not attending!" said the Mouse to Alice, severely. "What are you thinking of?"

"I beg your pardon," said Alice very humbly: "you had got to the fifth bend, I think?"

"I had *not!*" cried the Mouse, sharply and very angrily.

"A knot!" said Alice, always ready to make herself useful, and looking anxiously about her. "Oh, do let me help to undo it!"

"I shall do nothing of the sort," said the Mouse, getting up and walking away. "You insult me by talking such nonsense!"

"I didn't mean it!" pleaded poor Alice. "But you're so easily offended, you know!"

The Mouse only growled in reply.

"Please come back, and finish your story!" Alice called after it; and the others all joined in chorus, "Yes, please do!" but the Mouse only shook its head impatiently, and walked a little quicker.

"What a pity it wouldn't stay!" sighed the Lory, as soon as it was quite out of sight; and an old crab took the opportunity of saying to her daughter, "Ah, my dear! Let this be a lesson to you never to lose *your* temper!"

"Hold your tongue, Ma!" said the young crab, a little snappishly. "You're enough to try the patience of an oyster!"

"I wish I had our Dinah here, I know I do!" said Alice aloud, addressing nobody in particular. "She'd soon fetch it back!"

"And who is Dinah, if I might venture to ask the question?" said the Lory.

Alice replied eagerly, for she was always ready to talk about her pet. "Dinah's our cat. And she's such a capital one for catching mice, you can't think! And oh, I wish you could see her after the birds! Why, she'll eat a little bird as soon as look at it!"

This speech caused a remarkable sensation among the party. Some of the birds hurried off at once: one old magpie began wrapping itself up very carefully, remarking, "I really must be getting home; the night-air doesn't suit my throat!" and a canary called out in a trembling voice to its children, "Come away, my dears! It's high time you were all in bed!" On various pretexts they all moved off, and Alice was soon left alone.

"I wish I hadn't mentioned Dinah!" she said to herself in a melancholy tone. "Nobody seems to like her, down here, and I'm sure she's the best cat in the world! Oh, my dear Dinah! I wonder if I shall ever see you any more!" And here poor Alice began to cry again, for she felt very lonely and low-spirited. In a little while, however, she again heard a little pattering of footsteps in the distance, and she looked up eagerly, half hoping that the Mouse had changed his mind, and was coming back to finish his story.

4

THE RABBIT SENDS IN A LITTLE BILL

IT was the White Rabbit, trotting slowly back again, and looking anxiously about as it went as if it had lost something; and she heard it muttering to itself, "The Duchess! The Duchess! Oh my dear paws! Oh my fur and whiskers! She'll get me executed, as sure as ferrets are ferrets! Where *can* I have dropped them, I wonder!" Alice guessed in a moment that it was looking for the fan and the pair of white kid gloves, and she very goodnaturedly began hunting about for them, but they were nowhere to be seen—everything seemed to have changed since her swim in the pool, and the great hall, with the glass table and the little door, had vanished completely.

Very soon the Rabbit noticed Alice, as she went hunting about, and called out to her in an angry tone, "Why, Mary Ann, what *are* you doing out here? Run home this moment, and fetch me a pair of gloves and a fan! Quick, now!" And Alice was so much frightened that she ran off at once in the direction it pointed to, without trying to explain the mistake that it had made.

"He took me for his housemaid," she said to herself as she ran. "How surprised he'll be when he finds out who I am! But I'd better take him his fan and gloves—that is, if I can find them." As she said this, she came upon a neat little house, on the door of which was a bright brass plate with the name "W. RABBIT," engraved upon it. She went in without knocking, and hurried upstairs, in great fear lest she should meet the real Mary Ann, and be turned out of the house before she had found the fan and gloves.

"How queer it seems," Alice said to herself, "to be going messages for a rabbit! I suppose Dinah'll be sending me on messages next!" And she began fancying the sort of thing that would happen: "'Miss Alice! Come here directly, and get ready for your walk!' 'Coming in a minute, nurse! But I've got to watch this mousehole till Dinah comes back, and see that the mouse doesn't get out.' Only I don't think," Alice went on, "that they'd let Dinah stop in the house if it began ordering people about like that!"

By this time she had found her way into a tidy little room with a table in the window, and on it (as she had hoped) a fan and two or three pairs of tiny white kid gloves: she took up the fan and a pair of the gloves, and was just going to leave the room, when her eye fell upon a little bottle that stood near the looking-glass. There was no label this time with the words "DRINK ME," but nevertheless she uncorked it and put it to her lips. "I know *something* interesting is sure to happen," she said to herself, "whenever I eat or drink anything; so I'll just see what this bottle does. I do hope it'll make me grow large again, for really I'm quite tired of being such a tiny little thing!"

It did so indeed, and much sooner than she had expected: before she had drunk half the bottle, she found her head pressing against the ceiling, and had to stoop to save her neck from being broken. She hastily put down the bottle, saying to herself, "That's quite enough—I hope I shan't grow any more—As it is, I can't get out at the door—I do wish I hadn't drunk quite so much!"

Alas! It was too late to wish that! She went on growing and growing, and very soon had to kneel down on the floor: in another minute there was not even room for this, and she tried the effect of lying down, with one elbow against the door, and the other arm curled round her head. Still she went on growing, and, as a last resource, she put one arm out of the window, and one foot up the chimney, and said to herself, "Now I can do no more, whatever happens. What *will* become of me?"

Luckily for Alice, the little magic bottle had now had its full effect, and she grew no larger: still it was very uncomfortable, and, as there seemed to be no sort of chance of her ever getting out of the room again, no wonder she felt unhappy.

"It was much pleasanter at home," thought poor Alice, "when one wasn't always growing larger and smaller, and being ordered about by mice and rab-

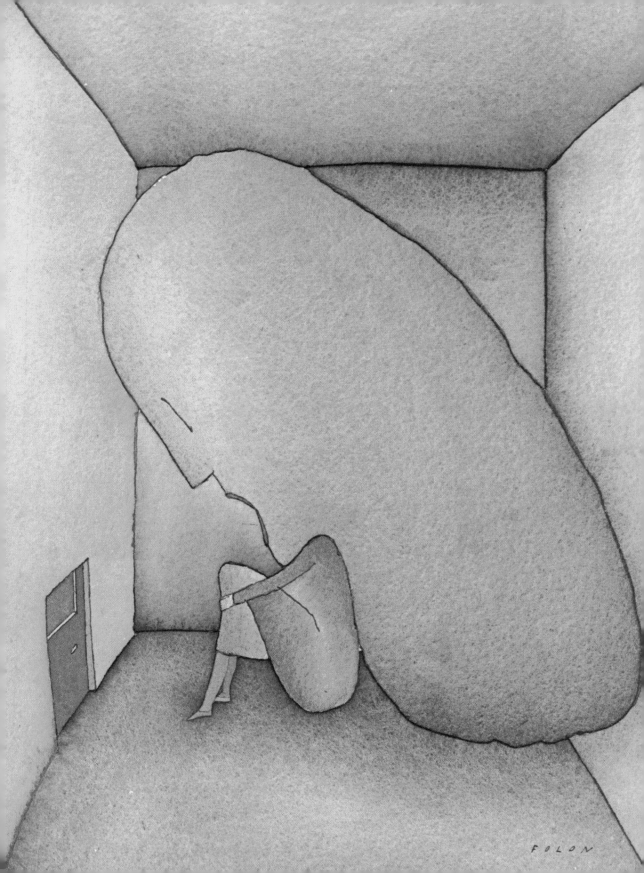

bits. I almost wish I hadn't gone down that rabbit-hole—and yet—and yet—it's rather curious, you know, this sort of life! I do wonder what *can* have happened to me! When I used to read fairy-tales, I fancied that kind of thing never happened, and now here I am in the middle of one! There ought to be a book written about me, that there ought! And when I grow up, I'll write one—but I'm grown up now," she added in a sorrowful tone, "at least there's no room to grow up any more *here*."

"But then," thought Alice, "shall I *never* get any older than I am now? That'll be a comfort, one way—never to be an old woman—but then—always to have lessons to learn! Oh, I shouldn't like *that*!"

"Oh, you foolish Alice!" she answered herself. "How can you learn lessons in here? Why, there's hardly room for you, and no room at all for any lesson-books!"

And so she went on, taking first one side and then the other, and making quite a conversation of it altogether, but after a few minutes she heard a voice outside, and stopped to listen.

"Mary Ann! Mary Ann!" said the voice, "fetch me my gloves this moment!" Then came a little pattering of feet on the stairs. Alice knew it was the Rabbit coming to look for her, and she trembled till she shook the house, quite forgetting that she was now about a thousand times as large as the Rabbit, and had no reason to be afraid of it.

Presently the Rabbit came up to the door, and tried to open it, but as the door opened inwards, and Alice's elbow was pressed hard against it, that attempt proved a failure. Alice heard it say to itself, "Then I'll go round and get in at the window."

"*That* you won't!" thought Alice, and, after waiting till she fancied she heard the Rabbit just under the window, she suddenly spread our her hand, and made a snatch in the air. She did not get hold of anything, but she heard a little shriek and a fall, and a crash of broken glass, from which she concluded that it was just possible it had fallen into a cucumber-frame,[9] or something of the sort.

Next came an angry voice—the Rabbit's—"Pat! Pat! Where are you?" And then a voice she had never heard before, "Sure then I'm here! Digging for apples, yer honour!"

"Digging for apples, indeed!" said the Rabbit

9, *cucumber-frame*, a sort of small hot-house or glass-enclosed structure for growing plants in cold weather.

angrily. "Here! Come and help me out of *this*!" (Sounds of more broken glass.)

"Now tell me, Pat, what's that in the window?"

"Sure, it's an arm, yer honour!" (He pronounced it "arrum.")

"An arm, you goose! Who ever saw one that size? Why, it fills the whole window!"

"Sure, it does, yer honour: but it's an arm for all that."

"Well, it's got no business there, at any rate: go and take it away!"

There was a long silence after this, and Alice could only hear whispers now and then, such as, "Sure, I don't like it, yer honour, at all at all!" "Do as I tell you, you coward!" and at last she spread out her hand again and made another snatch in the air. This time there were *two* little shrieks, and more sounds of broken glass. "What a number of cucumber-frames there must be!" thought Alice. "I wonder what they'll do next! As for pulling me out of the window, I only wish they *could*! I'm sure I don't want to stay in here any longer!"

She waited for some time without hearing anything more: at last came a rumbling of little cartwheels, and the sound of a good many voices all talking together: she made out the words, "Where's the other ladder?—Why, I hadn't to bring but one: Bill's got the other—Bill! fetch it here, lad!—Here, put 'em up at this corner—No, tie 'em together first—they don't reach half high enough yet—Oh! they'll do well enough; don't be particular—Here, Bill! catch hold of this rope—Will the roof bear? —Mind that loose slate—Oh, it's coming down! Heads below!" (a loud crash)—"Now, who did that?—It was Bill, I fancy—Who's to go down the chimney?—Nay, *I shan't! You* do it!—*That* I won't then! Bill's got to go down—Here, Bill! the master says you've got to go down the chimney!"

"Oh, so Bill's got to come down the chimney, has he?" said Alice to herself. "Why, they seem to put everything upon Bill! I wouldn't be in Bill's place for a good deal: this fireplace is narrow, to be sure, but I *think* I can kick a little!"

She drew her foot as far down the chimney as she could, and waited till she heard a little animal (she couldn't guess of what sort it was) scratching and scrambling about in the chimney close above her: then, saying to herself, "This is Bill," she gave one sharp kick and waited to see what would happen next. The first thing she heard was a general chorus of "there goes Bill!" then the Rabbit's voice alone: "catch him, you by the hedge!" —then silence, and then another confusion of voices—"Hold up his head—Brandy now—Don't choke him—How was it, old fellow? What happened to you? Tell us all about it!"

Last came a little feeble squeaking voice, ("That's Bill," thought Alice). "Well, I hardly know—No more, thank ye, I'm better now—but I'm a deal too flustered to tell you—all I know is, something comes at me like a Jack-in-the-box, and up I goes like a sky-rocket!"

"So you did, old fellow!" said the others.

"We must burn the house down!" said the Rabbit's voice, and Alice called out as loud as she could:

"If you do, I'll set Dinah at you!"

There was a dead silence instantly, and Alice thought to herself, "I wonder what they *will* do next! If they had any sense, they'd take the roof off." After a minute or two they began moving about again, and Alice heard the Rabbit say, "A barrowful will do, to begin with."

"A barrowful of *what?*" thought Alice; but she had not long to doubt, for the next moment a shower of little pebbles came rattling in at the window, and some of them hit her in the face. "I'll put a stop to this," she said to herself and shouted out:

"You'd better not do that again!" which produced another dead silence.

Alice noticed with some surprise that the pebbles were all turning into little cakes as they lay on the floor, and a bright idea came into her head.

"If I eat one of these cakes," she thought, "it's sure to make some change in my size: and as it can't possibly make me larger, it must make me smaller, I suppose."

So she swallowed one of the cakes, and was delighted to find that she began shrinking directly. As soon as she was small enough to get through the door, she ran out of the house, and found quite a crowd of little animals and birds waiting outside. The poor little Lizard, Bill, was in the middle, being held up by two guinea pigs, who were giving it something out of a bottle. They all made a rush at Alice the moment she appeared, but she ran off as hard as she could, and soon found herself safe in a thick wood.

"The first thing I've got to do," said Alice to herself, as she wandered about in the wood, "is to grow to my right size again; and the second thing is

to find my way into that lovely garden. I think that will be the best plan."

It sounded an excellent plan, no doubt, and very neatly and simply arranged; the only difficulty was, that she had not the smallest idea how to set about it; and while she was peering about anxiously among the trees, a little sharp bark just over her head made her look up in a great hurry.

An enormous puppy was looking down at her with large round eyes, and feebly stretching out one paw, trying to touch her. "Poor little thing!" said Alice in a coaxing tone, and she tried hard to whistle to it, but she was terribly frightened all the time at the thought that it might be hungry, in which case it would be very likely to eat her up in spite of all her coaxing.

Hardly knowing what she did, she picked up a little bit of stick, and held it out to the puppy; whereupon the puppy jumped into the air off all its feet at once, with a yelp of delight, and rushed at the stick, and made believe to worry it; then Alice dodged behind a great thistle, to keep herself from being run over, and, the moment she appeared on the other side, the puppy made another rush at the stick, and tumbled head over heels in its hurry to get hold of it; then Alice, thinking it was very like having a game of play with a cart-horse, and expecting every moment to be trampled under its feet, ran round the thistle again; then the puppy began a series of short charges at the stick, running a very little way forwards each time and a long way back, and barking hoarsely all the while, till at last it sat down a good way off, panting, with its tongue hanging out of its mouth, and its great eyes half shut.

This seemed to Alice a good opportunity for making her escape, so she set off at once, and ran till she was quite tired and out of breath, and till the puppy's bark sounded quite faint in the distance. "And yet what a dear little puppy it was!" said Alice, as she leant against a buttercup to rest herself, and fanned herself with one of the leaves; "I should have liked teaching it tricks very much, if—if I'd only been the right size to do it! Oh dear! I'd nearly forgotten that I've got to grow up again! Let me see—how *is* it to be managed? I suppose I ought to eat or drink something or other; but the great question is, what?"

The great question certainly was, what? Alice looked all round her at the flowers and the blades of grass, but she could not see anything that looked like the right thing to eat or drink under the circumstances. There was a large mushroom growing near her, about the same height as herself, and when she had looked under it, and on both sides of it, and behind it, it occurred to her that she might as well look and see what was on the top of it.

She stretched herself up on tiptoe, and peeped over the edge of the mushroom, and her eyes immediately met those of a large blue caterpillar, that was sitting on the top with its arms folded, quietly smoking a long hookah,[10] and taking not the smallest notice of her or of anything else.

5

ADVICE FROM A CATERPILLAR

THE Caterpillar and Alice looked at each other for some time in silence: at last the Caterpillar took the hookah out of its mouth, and addressed her in a languid, sleepy voice.

"Who are *you?*" said the Caterpillar.

This was not an encouraging opening for a conversation. Alice replied, rather shyly, "I—I hardly know, sir, just at present—at least I know who I *was* when I got up this morning, but I think I must have been changed several times since then."

"What do you mean by that?" said the Caterpillar sternly. "Explain yourself!"

"I can't explain *myself*, I'm afraid, sir," said Alice, "because I'm not myself, you see."

"I don't see," said the Caterpillar.

"I'm afraid I can't put it more clearly," Alice replied very politely, "for I can't understand it myself to begin with; and being so many different sizes in one day is very confusing."

"It isn't," said the Caterpillar.

"Well, perhaps you haven't found it so yet," said Alice; "but when you have to turn into a chrysalis—you will some day, you know—and then after that into a butterfly, I should think you'll feel it a little queer, won't you?"

"Not a bit," said the Caterpillar.

"Well, perhaps your feelings may be different," said Alice; "all I know is, it would feel very queer to *me*."

"You!" said the Caterpillar contemptuously. "Who are *you?*"

Which brought them back again to the beginning of the conversation. Alice felt a little irritated at the Caterpillar's making such *very* short remarks, and she drew herself up and said, very gravely, "I think you ought to tell me who *you* are, first."

"Why?" said the Caterpillar.

Here was another puzzling question; and, as Alice could not think of any good reason, and as the Caterpillar seemed to be in a *very* unpleasant state of mind, she turned away.

"Come back!" the Caterpillar called after her. "I've something important to say!"

This sounded promising, certainly: Alice turned and came back again.

"Keep your temper," said the Caterpillar.

"Is that all?" said Alice, swallowing down her anger as well as she could.

"No," said the Caterpillar.

Alice thought she might as well wait, as she had nothing else to do, and perhaps after all it might tell her something worth hearing. For some minutes it puffed away without speaking, but at last it unfolded its arms, took the hookah out of its mouth again, and said:

"So you think you're changed, do you?"

"I'm afraid I am, sir," said Alice; "I can't remember things as I used—and I don't keep the same size for ten minutes together!"

"Can't remember *what* things?" said the Caterpillar.

"Well, I've tried to say 'How doth the little busy bee,' but it all came different!" Alice replied in a very melancholy voice.

"Repeat *'You Are Old, Father William,'*"[11] said the Caterpillar.

Alice folded her hands, and began:—

---

10. *hookah*, a water pipe.

11. The poem being parodied is given on page 482.

"You are old, father William," the young man said,
    "And your hair has become very white;
And yet you incessantly stand on your head—
    Do you think, at your age, it is right?"

"In my youth," father William replied to his son,
    "I feared it might injure the brain;
But now that I'm perfectly sure I have none,
    Why, I do it again and again."

"You are old," said the youth, "as I mentioned
      before,
    And have grown most uncommonly fat;
"Yet you turned a back-somersault in at the door—
    Pray, what is the reason of that?"

"In my youth," said the sage, as he shook his grey
      locks,
    "I kept all my limbs very supple
By the use of this ointment—one shilling the box—
    Allow me to sell you a couple."

"You are old," said the youth, "and your jaws are
      too weak
    For anything tougher than suet;
Yet you finished the goose, with the bones and the
      beak—
    Pray, how did you manage to do it?"

"In my youth," said his father, "I took to the law,
    And argued each case with my wife;
And the muscular strength, which it gave to my jaw,
    Has lasted the rest of my life."

"You are old," said the youth; "one would hardly
      suppose
    That your eye was as steady as ever;
Yet you balanced an eel on the end of your nose—
    What made you so awfully clever?"

"I have answered three questions, and that is
      enough,"
    Said his father; "don't give yourself airs!
Do you think I can listen all day to such stuff?
    Be off, or I'll kick you downstairs!"

"That is not said right," said the Caterpillar.

"Not *quite* right, I'm afraid," said Alice timidly; "some of the words have got altered."

"It is wrong from beginning to end," said the Caterpillar decidedly, and there was silence for some minutes.

The Caterpillar was the first to speak.

"What size do you want to be?" it asked.

"Oh, I'm not particular as to size," Alice hastily replied; "only one doesn't like changing so often, you know."

"I *don't* know," said the Caterpillar.

Alice said nothing: she had never been so much contradicted in all her life before, and she felt that she was losing her temper.

"Are you content now?" said the Caterpillar.

"Well, I should like to be a *little* larger, sir, if you wouldn't mind," said Alice: "three inches is such a wretched height to be."

"It is a very good height indeed!" said the Caterpillar angrily, rearing itself upright as it spoke (it was exactly three inches high).

"But I'm not used to it!" pleaded poor Alice in a piteous tone. And she thought to herself, "I wish the creatures wouldn't be so easily offended!"

"You'll get used to it in time," said the Caterpillar; and it put the hookah into its mouth and began smoking again.

This time Alice waited patiently until it chose to speak again. In a minute or two the Caterpillar took the hookah out of its mouth, and yawned once or twice, and shook itself. Then it got down off the mushroom, and crawled away into the grass, merely remarking as it went, "One side will make you grow taller, and the other side will make you grow shorter."

"One side of *what?* The other side of *what?*" thought Alice to herself.

"Of the mushroom," said the Caterpillar, just as if she had asked it aloud; and in another moment it was out of sight.

Alice remained looking thoughtfully at the mushroom for a minute, trying to make out which were the two sides of it; and, as it was perfectly round, she found this a very difficult question. However, at last she stretched her arms round it as far as they would go, and broke off a bit of the edge with each hand.

"And now which is which?" she said to herself, and nibbled a little of the right-hand bit to try the effect: the next moment she felt a violent blow underneath her chin; it had struck her foot!

She was a good deal frightened by this very sudden change, but she felt that there was no time to be

lost, as she was shrinking rapidly; so she set to work at once to eat some of the other bit. Her chin was pressed so closely against her foot, that there was hardly room to open her mouth; but she did it at last, and managed to swallow a morsel of the left-hand bit.

"Come, my head's free at last!" said Alice in a tone of delight, which changed into alarm in another moment, when she found that her shoulders were nowhere to be found: all she could see, when she looked down, was an immense length of neck, which seemed to rise like a stalk out of a sea of green leaves that lay far below her.

"What *can* all that green stuff be?" said Alice. "And where *have* my shoulders got to? And oh, my poor hands, how is it I can't see you?" She was moving them about as she spoke, but no result seemed to follow, except a little shaking among the distant green leaves.

As there seemed to be no chance of getting her hands up to her head, she tried to get her head down to them, and she was delighted to find that her neck would bend about easily in any direction, like a serpent. She had just succeeded in curving it down into a graceful zig-zag, and was going to dive in among the leaves, which she found to be nothing but the tops of the trees under which she had been wandering, when a sharp hiss made her draw back in a hurry: a large pigeon had flown into her face, and was beating her violently with its wings.

"Serpent!" screamed the Pigeon.

"I'm *not* a serpent!" said Alice indignantly. "Let me alone!"

"Serpent, I say again!" repeated the Pigeon, but in a more subdued tone, and added with a kind of sob, "I've tried every way, and nothing seems to suit them!"

"I haven't the least idea what you're talking about," said Alice.

"I've tried the roots of trees, and I've tried banks, and I've tried hedges," the Pigeon went on, without attending to her; "but those serpents! There's no pleasing them!"

Alice was more and more puzzled, but she thought there was no use in saying anything more till the Pigeon had finished.

"As if it wasn't trouble enough hatching the eggs," said the Pigeon, "but I must be on the look-out for serpents night and day! Why, I haven't had a wink of sleep, these three weeks!"

"I'm very sorry you've been annoyed," said Alice, who was beginning to see its meaning.

"And just as I'd taken the highest tree in the wood," continued the Pigeon, raising its voice to a shriek, "and just as I was thinking I should be free of them at last, they must needs come wriggling down from the sky! Ugh! Serpent!"

"But I'm *not* a serpent, I tell you!" said Alice, "I'm —I'm a—"

"Well! *What* are you?" said the Pigeon. "I can see you're trying to invent something."

"I—I'm a little girl," said Alice, rather doubtfully, as she remembered the number of changes she had gone through that day.

"A likely story indeed!" said the Pigeon in a tone of the deepest contempt. "I've seen a good many little girls in my time, but never one with such a neck as that! No, no! You're a serpent; and there's no use denying it. I suppose you'll be telling me next that you've never tasted an egg!"

"I *have* tasted eggs, certainly," said Alice, who was a very truthful child; "but little girls eat eggs quite as much as serpents do, you know."

"I don't believe it," said the Pigeon; "but if they do, why then they're a kind of serpent, that's all I can say."

This was such a new idea to Alice, that she was quite silent for a minute or two, which gave the Pigeon the opportunity of adding, "You're looking for eggs, I know *that* well enough; and what does it matter to me whether you're a little girl or a serpent?"

"It matters a good deal to *me*," said Alice hastily; "but I'm not looking for eggs, as it happens; and if I was, I shouldn't want *yours:* I don't like them raw."

"Well, be off, then!" said the Pigeon in a sulky tone, as it settled down again into its nest. Alice crouched down among the trees as well as she could, for her neck kept getting entangled among the branches, and every now and then she had to stop and untwist it. After a while she remembered that she still held the pieces of mushroom in her hands, and she set to work very carefully, nibbling first at one and then at the other, and growing sometimes taller and sometimes shorter, until she had succeeded in bringing herself down to her usual height.

It was so long since she had been anything near the right size, that it felt quite strange at first, but she got used to it in a few minutes, and began talking to herself as usual. "Come, there's half my plan done now! How puzzling all these changes are! I'm never sure what I'm going to be, from one minute to another! However, I've got back to my right size: the next thing is, to get into that beautiful garden—how *is* that to be done, I wonder?" As she said this, she came suddenly upon an open place, with a little house in it about four feet high. "Whoever lives there," thought Alice, "it'll never do to come upon them *this* size: why, I should frighten them out of their wits!" So she began nibbling at the right-hand bit again, and did not venture to go near the house till she had brought herself down to nine inches high.

6

PIG AND PEPPER

FOR a minute or two she stood looking at the house, and wondering what to do next, when suddenly a footman in livery came running out of the wood—(she considered him to be a footman because he was in livery: otherwise, judging by his face only, she would have called him a fish)—and rapped loudly at the door with his knuckles. It was opened by another footman in livery, with a round face and large eyes like a frog; and both footmen, Alice noticed, had powdered hair that curled all over their heads. She felt very curious to know what it was all about, and crept a little way out of the wood to listen.

The Fish-Footman began by producing from under his arm a great letter, nearly as large as himself, and this he handed over to the other, saying in a solemn tone, "For the Duchess. An invitation from the Queen to play croquet." The Frog-Footman repeated, in the same solemn tone, only changing the order of the words a little, "From the Queen. An invitation for the Duchess to play croquet." Then they both bowed low, and their curls got entangled together.

Alice laughed so much at this that she had to run back into the wood for fear of their hearing her, and when she next peeped out the Fish-Footman was gone, and the other was sitting on the ground near the door, staring stupidly up into the sky.

Alice went timidly up to the door, and knocked.

"There's no sort of use in knocking," said the Footman, "and that for two reasons. First, because I'm on the same side of the door as you are; secondly, because they're making such a noise inside, no one could possibly hear you." And certainly there *was* a most extraordinary noise going on within—a constant howling and sneezing, and every now and then a great crash, as if a dish or kettle had been broken to pieces.

"Please, then," said Alice, "how am I to get in?"

"There might be some sense in your knocking," the Footman went on without attending to her, "if we had the door between us. For instance, if you were *inside*, you might knock, and I could let you out, you know." He was looking up into the sky all the time he was speaking, and this Alice thought decidedly uncivil. "But perhaps he can't help it," she said to herself; "his eyes are so *very* nearly at the top of his head. But at any rate he might answer questions—How am I to get in?" she repeated, aloud.

"I shall sit here," the Footman remarked, "till tomorrow—"

At this moment the door of the house opened, and a large plate came skimming out, straight at the Footman's head: it just grazed his nose, and broke to pieces against one of the trees behind him.

"—or next day, maybe," the Footman continued in the same tone, exactly as if nothing had happened.

"How am I to get in?" Alice asked again in a louder tone.

"*Are* you to get in at all?" said the Footman. "That's the first question, you know."

It *was*, no doubt: only Alice did not like to be told so. "It's really dreadful," she muttered to herself, "the way all the creatures argue. It's enough to drive one crazy!"

The Footman seemed to think this a good opportunity for repeating his remark, with variations. "I shall sit here," he said, "on and off, for days and days."

"But what am *I* to do?" said Alice.

"Anything you like," said the Footman, and began whistling.

"Oh, there's no use in talking to him," said Alice desperately: "he's perfectly idiotic!" And she opened the door and went in.

The door led right into a large kitchen, which was full of smoke from one end to the other: the Duchess was sitting on a three-legged stool in the middle, nursing a baby; the cook was leaning over the fire, stirring a large cauldron which seemed to be full of soup.

"There's certainly too much pepper in that soup!" Alice said to herself, as well as she could for sneezing.

There was certainly too much of it in the air. Even the Duchess sneezed occasionally; and as for the baby, it was sneezing and howling alternately without a moment's pause. The only two creatures in the kitchen that did not sneeze, were the cook, and a large cat which was sitting on the hearth and grinning from ear to ear.

"Please, would you tell me," said Alice, a little timidly, for she was not quite sure whether it was good manners for her to speak first, "why your cat grins like that?"

"It's a Cheshire Cat," said the Duchess, "and that's why. Pig!"

She said the last word with such sudden violence that Alice quite jumped; but she saw in another moment that it was addressed to the baby, and not to her, so she took courage, and went on again:—

"I didn't know that Cheshire Cats always grinned; in fact, I didn't know that cats *could* grin."

"They all can," said the Duchess; "and most of 'em do."

"I don't know of any that do," Alice said very politely, feeling quite pleased to have got into a conversation.

"You don't know much," said the Duchess; "and that's a fact."

Alice did not at all like the tone of this remark, and thought it would be as well to introduce some other subject of conversation. While she was trying to fix on one, the cook took the cauldron of soup off the fire, and at once set to work throwing everything within her reach at the Duchess and the baby— the fire-irons came first; then followed a shower of saucepans, plates, and dishes. The Duchess took no notice of them, even when they hit her; and the baby was howling so much already, that it was quite impossible to say whether the blows hurt it or not.

"Oh, *please* mind what you're doing!" cried Alice, jumping up and down in an agony of terror. "Oh, there goes his *precious* nose!" as an unusually large saucepan flew close by it, and very nearly carried it off.

"If everybody minded their own business," said the Duchess in a hoarse growl, "the world would go round a deal faster than it does."

"Which would *not* be an advantage," said Alice, who felt very glad to get an opportunity of showing off a little of her knowledge. "Just think what work it would make with the day and night! You see the earth takes twenty-four hours to turn round on its axis—"

"Talking of axes," said the Duchess, "chop off her head!"

Alice glanced rather anxiously at the cook, to see if she meant to take the hint; but the cook was busily stirring the soup, and seemed not to be listening, so she went on again: "Twenty-four hours, I *think*; or is it twelve? I—"

"Oh, don't bother *me*," said the Duchess; "I never could abide figures." And with that she began nursing her child again, singing a sort of lullaby to it as she did so, and giving it a violent shake at the end of every line:—

"*Speak roughly to your little boy*,[12]
And beat him when he sneezes;
He only does it to annoy,
Because he knows it teases."

CHORUS
(in which the cook and the baby joined)
"*Wow! wow! wow!*"

While the Duchess sang the second verse of the song, she kept tossing the baby violently up and down, and the poor little thing howled so, that Alice could hardly hear the words:—

"*I speak severely to my boy,*
I beat him when he sneezes;
For he can thoroughly enjoy
The pepper when he pleases!"

CHORUS
"*Wow! wow! wow!*"

"Here! you may nurse it a bit, if you like!" said the Duchess to Alice, flinging the baby at her as she spoke. "I must go and get ready to play croquet with the Queen," and she hurried out of the room. The

---

12. See page 482 for the poem which Carroll was parodying.

cook threw a fryingpan after her as she went, but it just missed her.

Alice caught the baby with some difficulty, as it was a queer-shaped little creature, and held out its arms and legs in all directions, "just like a star-fish," thought Alice. The poor little thing was snorting like a steam-engine when she caught it, and kept doubling itself up and straightening itself out again, so that altogether, for the first minute or two, it was as much as she could do to hold it.

As soon as she had made out the proper way of nursing it, (which was to twist it up into a sort of knot, and then keep tight hold of its right ear and left foot, so as to prevent its undoing itself,) she carried it out into the open air. "If I don't take this child away with me," thought Alice, "they're sure to kill it in a day or two: wouldn't it be murder to leave it behind?" She said the last words out loud, and the little thing grunted in reply (it had left off sneezing by this time). "Don't grunt," said Alice: "that's not at all a proper way of expressing yourself."

The baby grunted again, and Alice looked very anxiously into its face to see what was the matter with it.

There could be no doubt that it had a *very* turn-up nose, much more like a snout than a real nose; also its eyes were getting extremely small, for a baby: altogether Alice did not like the look of the thing at all, "—but perhaps it was only sobbing," she thought, and looked into its eyes again, to see if there were any tears.

No, there were no tears. "If you're going to turn into a pig, my dear," said Alice, seriously, "I'll have nothing more to do with you. Mind now!" The poor little thing sobbed again, (or grunted, it was impossible to say which,) and they went on for some while in silence.

Alice was just beginning to think to herself, "Now, what am I to do with this creature when I get it home?" when it grunted again, so violently, that she looked down into its face in some alarm. This time there could be *no* mistake about it: it was neither more nor less than a pig, and she felt that it would be quite absurd for her to carry it any further.

So she set the little creature down, and felt quite relieved to see it trot away quietly into the wood. "If it had grown up," she said to herself, "it would have been a dreadfully ugly child: but it makes rather a handsome pig, I think." And she began thinking over other children she knew, who might do very well as

pigs, and was just saying to herself, "if one only knew the right way to change them—" when she was a little startled by seeing the Cheshire Cat sitting on a bough of a tree a few yards off.

The Cat only grinned when it saw Alice. It looked goodnatured, she thought: still it had *very* long claws and a great many teeth, so she felt it ought to be treated with respect.

"Cheshire Puss," she began, rather timidly, as she did not at all know whether it would like the name: however, it only grinned a little wider. "Come, it's pleased so far," thought Alice, and she went on, "Would you tell me, please, which way I ought to walk from here?"

"That depends a good deal on where you want to get to," said the Cat.

"I don't care much where—" said Alice.

"Then it doesn't matter which way you walk," said the Cat.

"—so long as I get *somewhere*," Alice added as an explanation.

"Oh, you're sure to do that," said the Cat, "if you only walk long enough."

Alice felt that this could not be denied, so she tried another question. "What sort of people live about here?"

"In *that* direction," the Cat said, waving its right paw round, "lives a Hatter: and in *that* direction," waving the other paw, "lives a March Hare. Visit either you like: they're both mad."[13]

"But I don't want to go among mad people," Alice remarked.

"Oh, you can't help that," said the Cat: "we're all mad here. I'm mad. You're mad."

"How do you know I'm mad?" said Alice.

"You must be," said the Cat, "or you wouldn't have come here."

Alice didn't think that proved it at all; however, she went on: "and how do you know that you're mad?"

"To begin with," said the Cat, "a dog's not mad. You grant that?"

"I suppose so," said Alice.

"Well then," the Cat went on, "you see a dog

---

13. The March Hare is so named because of its crazy antics during its mating season, March. The phrase, "mad as a hatter," probably derives from the fact that nineteenth-century makers of hats used mercury for curing and shaping the felt from which gentlemen's hats were commonly made. Continuous contact with mercury caused tremors, hallucinations, and in some cases madness.

FOLO

growls when it's angry, and wags its tail when it's pleased. Now *I* growl when I'm pleased, and wag my tail when I'm angry. Therefore I'm mad."

"*I* call it purring, not growling," said Alice.

"Call it what you like," said the Cat. "Do you play croquet with the Queen to-day?"

"I should like it very much," said Alice, "but I haven't been invited yet."

"You'll see me there," said the Cat, and vanished. Alice was not much surprised at this, she was getting so well used to queer things happening. While she was still looking at the place where it had been, it suddenly appeared again.

"By-the-bye, what became of the baby?" said the Cat. "I'd nearly forgotten to ask."

"It turned into a pig," Alice answered very quietly, just as if the Cat had come back in a natural way.

"I thought it would," said the Cat, and vanished again.

Alice waited a little, half expecting to see it again, but it did not appear, and after a minute or two she walked on in the direction in which the March Hare was said to live. "I've seen hatters before," she said to herself: "the March Hare will be much the most interesting, and perhaps as this is May it won't be raving mad—at least not so mad as it was in March." As she said this, she looked up, and there was the Cat again, sitting on a branch of a tree.

"Did you say pig, or fig?" said the Cat.

"I said pig," replied Alice; "and I wish you wouldn't keep appearing and vanishing so suddenly: you make one quite giddy."

"All right," said the Cat; and this time it vanished quite slowly, beginning with the end of the tail, and ending with the grin, which remained some time after the rest of it had gone.

"Well! I've often seen a cat without a grin," thought Alice; "but a grin without a cat! It's the most curious thing I ever saw in all my life!"

She had not gone much farther before she came in sight of the house of the March Hare: she thought it must be the right house, because the chimneys were shaped like ears and the roof was thatched with fur. It was so large a house, that she did not like to go nearer till she had nibbled some more of the left-hand bit of mushroom, and raised herself to about two feet high: even then she walked up towards it rather timidly, saying to herself, "Suppose it should be raving mad after all! I almost wish I'd gone to see the Hatter instead!"

7

A MAD TEA-PARTY

THERE was a table set out under a tree in front of the house, and the March Hare and the Hatter were having tea at it: a Dormouse[14] was sitting between them, fast asleep, and the other two were using it as a cushion, resting their elbows on it, and talking over its head. "Very uncomfortable for the Dormouse," thought Alice; "only, as it's asleep, I suppose it doesn't mind."

The table was a large one, but the three were all crowded together at one corner of it. "No room! No room!" they cried out when they saw Alice coming. "There's *plenty* of room!" said Alice indignantly, and she sat down in a large arm-chair at one end of the table.

"Have some wine," the March Hare said in an encouraging tone.

Alice looked all round the table, but there was nothing on it but tea. "I don't see any wine," she remarked.

"There isn't any," said the March Hare.

"Then it wasn't very civil of you to offer it," said Alice angrily.

"It wasn't very civil of you to sit down without being invited," said the March Hare.

"I didn't know it was *your* table," said Alice; "it's laid for a great many more than three."

"Your hair wants cutting," said the Hatter. He had been looking at Alice for some time with great curiosity, and this was his first speech.

"You should learn not to make personal remarks," Alice said with some severity: "it's very rude."

The Hatter opened his eyes very wide on hearing this; but all he *said* was, "Why is a raven like a writing-desk?"

"Come, we shall have some fun now!" thought Alice. "I'm glad they've begun asking riddles—I believe I can guess that," she added aloud.

"Do you mean that you think you can find out the answer to it?" said the March Hare.

"Exactly so," said Alice.

"Then you should say what you mean," the March Hare went on.

---

14. The Dormouse is not a mouse but a kind of small squirrel.

"I do," Alice hastily replied; "at least—at least I mean what I say—that's the same thing, you know."

"Not the same thing a bit!" said the Hatter. "Why, you might just as well say that 'I see what I eat' is the same thing as 'I eat what I see'!"

"You might just as well say," added the March Hare, "that 'I like what I get' is the same thing as 'I get what I like'!"

"You might just as well say," added the Dormouse, who seemed to be talking in his sleep, "that 'I breathe when I sleep' is the same thing as 'I sleep when I breathe'!"

"It *is* the same thing with you," said the Hatter, and here the conversation dropped, and the party sat silent for a minute, while Alice thought over all she could remember about ravens and writing-desks, which wasn't much.

The Hatter was the first to break the silence. "What day of the month is it?" he said, turning to Alice: he had taken his watch out of his pocket, and was looking at it uneasily, shaking it every now and then, and holding it to his ear.

Alice considered a little, and said, "The fourth."

"Two days wrong!" sighed the Hatter. "I told you butter wouldn't suit the works!" he added, looking angrily at the March Hare.

"It was the *best* butter," the March Hare meekly replied.

"Yes, but some crumbs must have got in as well," the Hatter grumbled: "you shouldn't have put it in with the bread-knife."

The March Hare took the watch and looked at it gloomily: then he dipped it into his cup of tea, and looked at it again: but he could think of nothing better to say than his first remark, "It was the *best* butter, you know."

Alice had been looking over his shoulder with some curiosity. "What a funny watch!" she remarked. "It tells the day of the month, and doesn't tell what o'clock it is!"

"Why should it?" muttered the Hatter. "Does *your* watch tell you what year it is?"

"Of course not," Alice replied very readily: "but that's because it stays the same year for such a long time together."

"Which is just the case with *mine*," said the Hatter.

Alice felt dreadfully puzzled. The Hatter's remark seemed to her to have no sort of meaning in it, and yet it was certainly English. "I don't quite understand you," she said as politely as she could.

"The Dormouse is asleep again," said the Hatter, and he poured a little hot tea on to its nose.

The Dormouse shook its head impatiently, and said, without opening its eyes, "Of course, of course: just what I was going to remark myself."

"Have you guessed the riddle yet?" the Hatter said, turning to Alice again.

"No, I give it up," Alice replied: "what's the answer?"

"I haven't the slightest idea," said the Hatter. "Nor I," said the March Hare.

Alice sighed wearily. "I think you might do something better with the time," she said, "than wasting it in asking riddles that have no answers."[15]

"If you knew Time as well as I do," said the Hatter, "you wouldn't talk about wasting *it*. It's *him*."

"I don't know what you mean," said Alice.

"Of course you don't!" the Hatter said, tossing his head contemptuously. "I dare say you never even spoke to Time!"

"Perhaps not," Alice cautiously replied: "but I know I have to beat time when I learn music."

"Ah! that accounts for it," said the Hatter. "He won't stand beating. Now, if you only kept on good terms with him, he'd do almost anything you liked with the clock. For instance, suppose it were nine o'clock in the morning, just time to begin lessons: you'd only have to whisper a hint to Time, and round goes the clock in a twinkling! Half-past one, time for dinner!"

("I only wish it was," the March Hare said to itself in a whisper.)

"That would be grand, certainly," said Alice thoughtfully: "but then—I shouldn't be hungry for it, you know."

"Not at first, perhaps," said the Hatter: "but you could keep it to half-past one as long as you liked."

"Is that the way *you* manage?" Alice asked.

The Hatter shook his head mournfully. "Not I!" he replied. "We quarrelled last March—just before *he* went mad, you know—" (pointing with his teaspoon at the March Hare,) "—it was at the great concert given by the Queen of Hearts, and I had to sing

---

15. Although the answer to this riddle is not given in the Alice stories, Carroll later supplied this answer: "Because it can produce a few notes, tho they are *very* flat; and it is never put with the wrong end in front." Among other well-known suggestions are: (1) Because Poe wrote on them both. (2) Bills and tails are their features. (3) Because they both stand on legs, and should be made to shut up.

'Twinkle, twinkle, little bat!
How I wonder what you're at!'

You know the song, perhaps?''

"I've heard something like it," said Alice.

"It goes on, you know," the Hatter continued, "in this way:—

'Up above the world you fly,
Like a teatray in the sky.
Twinkle, twinkle—'''

Here the Dormouse shook itself, and began singing in its sleep *"Twinkle, twinkle, twinkle, twinkle—"* and went on so long that they had to pinch it to make it stop.

"Well, I'd hardly finished the first verse," said the Hatter, "when the Queen bawled out 'He's murdering the time! Off with his head!'"

"How dreadfully savage!" exclaimed Alice.

"And ever since that," the Hatter went on in a mournful tone, "he won't do a thing I ask! It's always six o'clock now."

A bright idea came into Alice's head. "Is that the reason so many tea-things are put out here?" she asked.

"Yes, that's it," said the Hatter with a sigh: "it's always tea-time, and we've no time to wash the things between whiles."

"Then you keep moving round, I suppose?" said Alice.

"Exactly so," said the Hatter: "as the things get used up."

"But when you come to the beginning again?" Alice ventured to ask.

"Suppose we change the subject," the March Hare interrupted, yawning. "I'm getting tired of this. I vote the young lady tells us a story."

"I'm afraid I don't know one," said Alice, rather alarmed at the proposal.

"Then the Dormouse shall!" they both cried. "Wake up, Dormouse!" And they pinched it on both sides at once.

The Dormouse slowly opened his eyes. "I wasn't asleep," he said in a hoarse, feeble voice: "I heard every word you fellows were saying."

"Tell us a story!" said the March Hare.

"Yes, please do!" pleaded Alice.

"And be quick about it," added the Hatter, "or you'll be asleep again before it's done."

"Once upon a time there were three little sisters," the Dormouse began in a great hurry; "and their names were Elsie, Lacie, and Tillie;[16] and they lived at the bottom of a well—"

"What did they live on?" said Alice, who always took a great interest in questions of eating and drinking.

"They lived on treacle,"[17] said the Dormouse, after thinking a minute or two.

"They couldn't have done that, you know," Alice gently remarked: "they'd have been ill."

"So they were," said the Dormouse; "*very* ill."

Alice tried a little to fancy to herself what such an extraordinary way of living would be like, but it puzzled her too much, so she went on: "But why did they live at the bottom of a well?"

"Take some more tea," the March Hare said to Alice, very earnestly.

"I've had nothing yet," Alice replied in an offended tone, "so I can't take more."

"You mean, you can't take *less*," said the Hatter: "it's very easy to take *more* than nothing."

"Nobody asked *your* opinion," said Alice.

"Who's making personal remarks now?" the Hatter asked triumphantly.

Alice did not quite know what to say to this: so she helped herself to some tea and bread-and-butter, and then turned to the Dormouse, and repeated her question.

"Why did they live at the bottom of a well?"

The Dormouse again took a minute or two to think about it, and then said, "It was a treacle-well."

"There's no such thing!" Alice was beginning very angrily, but the Hatter and the March Hare went "Sh! sh!" and the Dormouse sulkily remarked, "If you can't be civil, you'd better finish the story for yourself."

"No, please go on!" Alice said very humbly: "I won't interrupt you again. I dare say there may be *one*."

"One, indeed!" said the Dormouse indignantly. However, he consented to go on. "And so these three little sisters—they were learning to draw, you know—"

"What did they draw?" said Alice, quite forgetting her promise.

---

16. Another reference to the three Liddell sisters. Elsie stands for L. C. or Lorina C. Liddell; Lacie is an anagram for Alice; Tillie is a form of Matilda, Edith's nickname.

17. *treacle*, molasses.

"Treacle," said the Dormouse, without considering at all this time.

"I want a clean cup," interrupted the Hatter: "let's all move one place on."

He moved on as he spoke, and the Dormouse followed him: the March Hare moved into the Dormouse's place, and Alice rather unwillingly took the place of the March Hare. The Hatter was the only one who got any advantage from the change: and Alice was a good deal worse off than before, as the March Hare had just upset the milk-jug into his plate.

Alice did not wish to offend the Dormouse again, so she began very cautiously: "But I don't understand. Where did they draw the treacle from?"

"You can draw water out of a water-well," said the Hatter: "so I should think you could draw treacle out of a treacle-well—eh, stupid?"

"But they were *in* the well," Alice said to the Dormouse, not choosing to notice this last remark.

"Of course they were," said the Dormouse, "—well in." This answer so confused poor Alice, that she let the Dormouse go on for some time without interrupting it.

"They were learning to draw," the Dormouse went on, yawning and rubbing its eyes, for it was getting very sleepy; "and they drew all manner of things—everything that begins with an M—"

"Why with an M?" said Alice.

"Why not?" said the March Hare.

Alice was silent.

The Dormouse had closed its eyes by this time, and was going off into a doze, but on being pinched by the Hatter, it woke up again with a little shriek, and went on: "—that begins with an M, such as mousetraps, and the moon, and memory, and muchness—you know you say things are 'much of a muchness'[18]—did you ever see such a thing as a drawing of a muchness?"

"Really, now you ask me," said Alice, very much confused, "I don't think—"

"Then you shouldn't talk," said the Hatter.

This piece of rudeness was more than Alice could bear: she got up in great disgust, and walked off: the Dormouse fell asleep instantly, and neither of the others took the least notice of her going, though she looked back once or twice, half hoping that they would call after her: the last time she saw them, they were trying to put the Dormouse into the teapot.

"At any rate I'll never go *there* again!" said Alice as she picked her way through the wood. "It's the stupidest tea-party I ever was at in all my life!"

Just as she said this, she noticed that one of the trees had a door leading right into it. "That's very curious!" she thought. "But everything's curious to-day. I think I may as well go in at once." And in she went.

Once more she found herself in the long hall, and close to the little glass table. "Now, I'll manage better this time," she said to herself, and began by taking the little golden key, and unlocking the door that led into the garden. Then she set to work nibbling at the mushroom (she had kept a piece of it in her pocket) till she was about a foot high: then she walked down the little passage: and *then* she found herself at last in the beautiful garden, among the bright flowerbeds and the cool fountains.

8

THE QUEEN'S CROQUET-GROUND

A large rose-tree stood near the entrance of the garden: the roses growing on it were white, but there were three gardeners at it, busily painting them red. Alice thought this a very curious thing, and she went nearer to watch them, and just as she came up to them she heard one of them say, "Look out now, Five![19] Don't go splashing paint over me like that!"

"I couldn't help it," said Five in a sulky tone; "Seven jogged my elbow."

On which Seven looked up and said, "That's right, Five! Always lay the blame on others!"

"*You'd* better not talk!" said Five. "I heard the Queen say only yesterday you deserved to be beheaded!"

---

18. The British phrase "much of a muchness" means "things are pretty much the same."

19. The organization of various characters in this chapter, as well as in Chapter 12, is ingeniously modeled on a deck of playing cards. The gardeners, for instance, are the two, five, and seven of spades. The clubs are soldiers; the diamonds are courtiers; the hearts are the royal children. The royal cards are, of course, kings and queens, among them the King and Queen of Hearts. The Knave is the jack.

"What for?" said the one who had spoken first.

"That's none of *your* business, Two!" said Seven.

"Yes, it *is* his business!" said Five, "and I'll tell him—it was for bringing the cook tulip-roots instead of onions."

Seven flung down his brush, and had just begun, "Well, of all the unjust things—" when his eye chanced to fall upon Alice as she stood watching them, and he checked himself suddenly: the others looked round also, and all of them bowed low.

"Would you tell me, please," said Alice, a little timidly, "why you are painting those roses?"

Five and Seven said nothing, but looked at Two. Two began, in a low voice, "Why, the fact is, you see, Miss, this here ought to have been a *red* rose-tree, and we put a white one in by mistake, and if the Queen was to find it out, we should all have our heads cut off, you know. So you see, Miss, we're doing our best, afore she comes, to—" At this moment Five, who had been anxiously looking across the garden, called out "The Queen! The Queen!" and the three gardeners instantly threw themselves flat upon their faces. There was a sound of many footsteps, and Alice looked round, eager to see the Queen.

First came ten soldiers carrying clubs; these were all shaped like the three gardeners, oblong and flat, with their hands and feet at the corners; next the ten courtiers: these were ornamented all over with diamonds and walked two and two, as the soldiers did. After these came the royal children; there were ten of them, and the little dears came jumping merrily along hand in hand, in couples: they were all ornamented with hearts. Next came the guests, mostly Kings and Queens, and among them Alice recognized the White Rabbit: it was talking in a hurried nervous manner, smiling at everything that was said, and went by without noticing her. Then followed the Knave of Hearts, carrying the King's crown on a crimson velvet cushion; and, last of all this grand procession, came THE KING AND QUEEN OF HEARTS.

Alice was rather doubtful whether she ought not to lie down on her face like the three gardeners, but she could not remember ever having heard of such a rule at processions: "and besides, what would be the use of a procession," she thought, "if people had all to lie down on their faces, so that they couldn't see it?" So she stood where she was and waited.

When the procession came opposite to Alice, they all stopped and looked at her, and the Queen said severely, "Who is this?" She said it to the Knave of Hearts, who only bowed and smiled in reply.

"Idiot!" said the Queen, tossing her head impatiently; and turning to Alice, she went on, "What's your name, child?"

"My name is Alice, so please your Majesty," said Alice very politely; but she added, to herself, "Why, they're only a pack of cards, after all. I needn't be afraid of them!"

"And who are *these?*" said the Queen, pointing to the three gardeners who were lying round the rose-tree; for you see, as they were lying on their faces, and the pattern on their backs was the same as the rest of the pack, she could not tell whether they were gardeners, or soldiers, or courtiers, or three of her own children.

"How should *I* know?" said Alice, surprised at her own courage. "It's no business of *mine*." The Queen turned crimson with fury, and after glaring at her for a moment like a wild beast, began screaming, "Off with her head! Off—"

"Nonsense!" said Alice, very loudly and decidedly, and the Queen was silent.

The King laid his hand upon her arm, and timidly said, "Consider, my dear: she is only a child!"

The Queen turned angrily away from him, and said to the Knave, "Turn them over!"

The Knave did so, very carefully, with one foot.

"Get up!" said the Queen in a shrill, loud voice, and the three gardeners instantly jumped up, and began bowing to the King, the Queen, the royal children, and everybody else.

"Leave off that!" screamed the Queen. "You make me giddy." And then, turning to the rose-tree, she went on, "What *have* you been doing here?"

"May it please your Majesty," said Two, in a very humble tone, getting down on one knee as he spoke, "we were trying—"

"*I* see!" said the Queen, who had meanwhile been examining the roses. "Off with their heads!" and the procession moved on, three of the soldiers remaining behind to execute the unfortunate gardeners, who ran to Alice for protection.

"You shan't be beheaded!" said Alice, and she put them into a large flower-pot that stood near. The three soldiers wandered about for a minute or two, looking for them, and then quietly marched off after the others.

"Are their heads off?" shouted the Queen.

"Their heads are gone, if it please your Majesty!" the soldiers shouted in reply.

"That's right!" shouted the Queen. "Can you play croquet?"

The soldiers were silent, and looked at Alice, as the question was evidently meant for her.

"Yes!" shouted Alice.

"Come on then!" roared the Queen, and Alice joined the procession, wondering very much what would happen next.

"It's—it's a very fine day!" said a timid voice at her side. She was walking by the White Rabbit, who was peeping anxiously into her face.

"Very," said Alice: "where's the Duchess?"

"Hush! Hush!" said the Rabbit in a low, hurried tone. He looked anxiously over his shoulder as he spoke, and then raised himself upon tiptoe, put his mouth close to her ear, and whispered, "She's under sentence of execution."

"What for?" said Alice.

"Did you say 'What a pity?'" the Rabbit asked.

"No, I didn't," said Alice: "I don't think it's at all a pity. I said 'What for?'"

"She boxed the Queen's ears—" the Rabbit began. Alice gave a little scream of laughter. "Oh, hush!" the Rabbit whispered in a frightened tone. "The Queen will hear you! You see she came rather late, and the Queen said—"

"Get to your places!" shouted the Queen in a voice of thunder, and people began running about in all directions, tumbling up against each other: however, they got settled down in a minute or two, and the game began.

Alice thought she had never seen such a curious croquet-ground in her life: it was all ridges and furrows; the croquet-balls were live hedgehogs,[20] and the mallets live flamingoes, and the soldiers had to double themselves up and stand on their hands and feet to make the arches.

The chief difficulty Alice found at first was in managing her flamingo: she succeeded in getting its body tucked away, comfortably enough, under her arm, with its legs hanging down, but generally, just as she had got its neck nicely straightened out, and was going to give the hedgehog a blow with its head, it *would* twist itself round and look up into

her face, with such a puzzled expression that she could not help bursting out laughing: and when she had got its head down, and was going to begin again, it was very provoking to find that the hedgehog had unrolled itself, and was in the act of crawling away: besides all this, there was generally a ridge or a furrow in the way wherever she wanted to send the hedgehog to, and, as the doubled-up soldiers were always getting up and walking off to other parts of the ground, Alice soon came to the conclusion that it was a very difficult game indeed.

The players all played at once without waiting for turns, quarrelling all the while, and fighting for the hedgehogs; and in a very short time the Queen was in a furious passion, and went stamping about, and shouting, "Off with his head!" or "Off with her head!" about once in a minute.

Alice began to feel very uneasy: to be sure, she had not as yet had any dispute with the Queen, but she knew that it might happen any minute, "and then," thought she, "what would become of me? They're dreadfully fond of beheading people here: the great wonder is that there's any one left alive!"

She was looking about for some way of escape, and wondering whether she could get away without being seen, when she noticed a curious appearance in the air: it puzzled her very much at first, but after watching it a minute or two she made it out to be a grin, and she said to herself, "It's the Cheshire Cat: now I shall have somebody to talk to."

"How are you getting on?" said the Cat, as soon as there was mouth enough for it to speak with.

Alice waited till the eyes appeared, and then nodded. "It's no use speaking to it," she thought, "till its ears have come, or at least one of them." In another minute the whole head appeared, and then Alice put down her flamingo, and began an account of the game, feeling very glad she had some one to listen to her. The Cat seemed to think that there was enough of it now in sight, and no more of it appeared.

"I don't think they play at all fairly," Alice began, in rather a complaining tone, "and they all quarrel so dreadfully one can't hear one's self speak—and they don't seem to have any rules in particular; at least, if there are, nobody attends to them—and you've no idea how confusing it is all the things being alive; for instance, there's the arch I've got to go through next walking about at the other end of the ground—and I should have croqueted the

---

20. Hedgehogs are harmless, porcupine-like animals which roll themselves into a tight ball when alarmed, hence their rôle here as croquet balls.

Queen's hedgehog just now, only it ran away when it saw mine coming!"

"How do you like the Queen?" said the Cat in a low voice.

"Not at all," said Alice: "she's so extremely—" Just then she noticed that the Queen was close behind her, listening: so she went on "—likely to win, that it's hardly worth while finishing the game."

The Queen smiled and passed on.

"Who *are* you talking to?" said the King, coming up to Alice, and looking at the Cat's head with great curiosity.

"It's a friend of mine—a Cheshire Cat," said Alice: "allow me to introduce it."

"I don't like the look of it at all," said the King: "however, it may kiss my hand if it likes."

"I'd rather not," the Cat remarked.

"Don't be impertinent," said the King, "and don't look at me like that!" He got behind Alice as he spoke.

"A cat may look at a king," said Alice. "I've read that in some book, but I don't remember where."

"Well, it must be removed," said the King very decidedly, and he called to the Queen, who was passing at the moment, "My dear! I wish you would have this cat removed!"

The Queen had only one way of settling all difficulties, great or small. "Off with his head!" she said without even looking round.

"I'll fetch the executioner myself," said the King eagerly, and he hurried off.

Alice thought she might as well go back and see how the game was going on, as she heard the Queen's voice in the distance, screaming with passion. She had already heard her sentence three of the players to be executed for having missed their turns, and she did not like the look of things at all, as the game was in such confusion that she never knew whether it was her turn or not. So she went off in search of her hedgehog.

The hedgehog was engaged in a fight with another hedgehog, which seemed to Alice an excellent opportunity for croqueting one of them with the other; the only difficulty was, that her flamingo was gone across to the other side of the garden, where Alice could see it trying in a helpless sort of way to fly up into a tree.

By the time she had caught the flamingo and brought it back, the fight was over, and both the hedgehogs were out of sight: "but it doesn't matter much," thought Alice, "as all the arches are gone from this side of the ground." So she tucked it away under her arm, that it might not escape again, and went back to have a little more conversation with her friend.

When she got back to the Cheshire Cat, she was surprised to find quite a large crowd collected round it: there was a dispute going on between the executioner, the King, and the Queen, who were all talking at once, while all the rest were quite silent, and looked very uncomfortable.

The moment Alice appeared, she was appealed to by all three to settle the question and they repeated their arguments to her, though, as they all spoke at once, she found it very hard to make out exactly what they said. The executioner's argument was, that you couldn't cut off a head unless there was a body to cut it off from: that he had never had to do such a thing before, and he wasn't going to begin at *his* time of life.

The King's argument was, that anything that had a head could be beheaded, and that you weren't to talk nonsense.

The Queen's argument was, that if something wasn't done about it in less than no time, she'd have everybody executed, all round. (It was this last remark that had made the whole party look so grave and anxious.)

Alice could think of nothing else to say but "It belongs to the Duchess: you'd better ask *her* about it."

"She's in prison," the Queen said to the executioner: "fetch her here." And the executioner went off like an arrow.

The Cat's head began fading away the moment he was gone, and, by the time he had come back with the Duchess, it had entirely disappeared: so the King and the executioner ran wildly up and down looking for it, while the rest of the party went back to the game.

9

THE MOCK TURTLE'S STORY

Y OU can't think how glad I am to see you again, you dear old thing!" said the Duchess, as she tucked her arm affectionately into Alice's, and they walked off together.

Alice was very glad to find her in such a pleasant temper, and thought to herself that perhaps it was only the pepper that had made her so savage when they met in the kitchen. "When *I'm* a Duchess," she said to herself (not in a very hopeful tone though,) "I won't have any pepper in my kitchen *at all.* Soup does very well without. —Maybe it's always pepper that makes people hot-tempered," she went on, very much pleased at having found out a new kind of rule, "and vinegar that makes them sour—and camomile[21] that makes them bitter—and—and barley-sugar and such things that make children sweet-tempered. I only wish people knew *that:* then they wouldn't be so stingy about it, you know—"

She had quite forgotten the Duchess by this time, and was a little startled when she heard her voice close to her ear. "You're thinking about something, my dear, and that makes you forget to talk. I can't tell you just now what the moral of that is, but I shall remember it in a bit."

"Perhaps it hasn't one," Alice ventured to remark.

"Tut, tut, child!" said the Duchess. "Everything's got a moral, if only you can find it." And she squeezed herself up closer to Alice's side as she spoke.

Alice did not much like her keeping so close to her: first, because the Duchess was *very* ugly; and secondly, because she was exactly the right height to rest her chin on Alice's shoulder, and it was an uncomfortably sharp chin. However, she did not like to be rude, so she bore it as well as she could.

"The game's going on rather better now," she said, by way of keeping up the conversation a little.

"'Tis so," said the Duchess: "and the moral of that is—'Oh, 'tis love, 'tis love, that makes the world go round!'"

"Somebody said," Alice whispered, "that it's

done by everybody minding their own business!"

"Ah well! It means much the same thing," said the Duchess, digging her sharp little chin into Alice's shoulder as she added, "and the moral of *that* is— 'Take care of the sense, and the sounds will take care of themselves.'"[22]

"How fond she is of finding morals in things!" Alice thought to herself.

"I dare say you're wondering why I don't put my arm round your waist," said the Duchess after a pause: "the reason is, that I'm doubtful about the temper of your flamingo. Shall I try the experiment?"

"He might bite," Alice cautiously replied, not feeling at all anxious to have the experiment tried.

"Very true," said the Duchess: "flamingoes and mustard both bite. And the moral of that is—'Birds of a feather flock together.'"

"Only mustard isn't a bird," Alice remarked.

"Right as usual," said the Duchess: "what a clear way you have of putting things!"

"It's a mineral, I *think,*" said Alice.

"Of course it is," said the Duchess, who seemed ready to agree to everything that Alice said; "there's a large mustard-mine near here. And the moral of that is—'The more there is of mine, the less there is of yours.'"

"Oh, I know!" exclaimed Alice, who had not attended to this last remark, "it's a vegetable. It doesn't look like one, but it is."

"I quite agree with you," said the Duchess, "and the moral of that is—'Be what you would seem to be' —or, if you'd like it put more simply—'Never imagine yourself not to be otherwise than what it might appear to others that what you were or might have been was not otherwise than what you had been would have appeared to them to be otherwise.'"

"I think I should understand that better," Alice said very politely, "if I had it written down: but I can't quite follow it as you say it."

"That's nothing to what I could say if I chose," the Duchess replied in a pleased tone.

"Pray don't trouble yourself to say it any longer than that," said Alice.

"Oh, don't talk about trouble!" said the Duchess. "I make you a present of everything I've said as yet."

"A cheap sort of present!" thought Alice. "I'm

---

21. *camomile,* a bitter medicine used in Victorian times, extracted from a flower of the same name.

22. The Duchess' maxim is a pun on the English proverb, "Take care of the pence, and the pounds will take care of themselves."

glad they don't give birthday presents like that!" But she did not venture to say it out loud.

"Thinking again?" the Duchess asked, with another dig of her sharp little chin.

"I've a right to think," said Alice sharply, for she was beginning to feel a little worried.

"Just about as much right," said the Duchess, "as pigs have to fly: and the m—"

But here, to Alice's great surprise, the Duchess' voice died away, even in the middle of her favourite word "moral," and the arm that was linked into hers began to tremble. Alice looked up, and there stood the Queen in front of them, with her arms folded, frowning like a thunderstorm.

"A fine day, your Majesty!" the Duchess began in a low, weak voice.

"Now, I give you fair warning," shouted the Queen, stamping on the ground as she spoke; "either you or your head must be off, and that in about half no time! Take your choice!"

The Duchess took her choice, and was gone in a moment.

"Let's go on with the game," the Queen said to Alice, and Alice was too much frightened to say a word, but slowly followed her back to the croquet-ground.

The other guests had taken advantage of the Queen's absence, and were resting in the shade: however, the moment they saw her, they hurried back to the game, the Queen merely remarking that a moment's delay would cost them their lives.

All the time they were playing the Queen never left off quarrelling with the other players, and shouting "Off with his head!" or "Off with her head!" Those whom she sentenced were taken into custody by the soldiers, who of course had to leave off being arches to do this, so that by the end of half an hour or so there were no arches left, and all the players, except the King, the Queen, and Alice, were in custody, and under sentence of execution.

Then the Queen left off, quite out of breath, and said to Alice, "Have you seen the Mock Turtle yet?"

"No," said Alice. "I don't even know what a Mock Turtle is."

"It's the thing Mock Turtle Soup[23] is made from," said the Queen.

"I never saw one, or heard of one," said Alice.

"Come on, then," said the Queen, "and he shall tell you his history."

As they walked off together, Alice heard the King say in a low voice, to the company generally, "You are all pardoned." "Come, *that's* a good thing!" she said to herself, for she had felt quite unhappy at the number of executions the Queen had ordered.

They very soon came upon a Gryphon,[24] lying fast asleep in the sun. "Up, lazy thing!" said the Queen, "and take this young lady to see the Mock Turtle, and to hear his history. I must go back and see after some executions I have ordered"; and she walked off, leaving Alice alone with the Gryphon. Alice did not quite like the look of the creature, but on the whole she thought it would be quite as safe to stay with it as to go after that savage Queen: so she waited.

The Gryphon sat up and rubbed its eyes: then it watched the Queen till she was out of sight: then it chuckled. "What fun!" said the Gryphon, half to itself, half to Alice.

"What *is* the fun?" said Alice.

"Why, *she*," said the Gryphon. "It's all her fancy, that: they never executes nobody, you know. Come on!"

"Everybody says 'come on!' here," thought Alice, as she went slowly after it: "I never was so ordered about before in all my life, never!"

They had not gone far before they saw the Mock Turtle in the distance, sitting sad and lonely on a little ledge of rock, and, as they came nearer, Alice could hear him sighing as if his heart would break. She pitied him deeply.

"What is his sorrow?" she asked the Gryphon, and the Gryphon answered, very nearly in the same words as before, "It's all his fancy, that: he hasn't got no sorrow, you know. Come on!"

So they went up to the Mock Turtle, who looked at them with large eyes full of tears, but said nothing.

"This here young lady," said the Gryphon, "She wants for to know your history, she do."

"I'll tell it her," said the Mock Turtle in a deep, hollow tone: "sit down both of you, and don't speak a word till I've finished."

So they sat down, and nobody spoke for some minutes. Alice thought to herself, "I don't see how he can

---

23. Mock turtle soup is made from veal. One of Tenniel's original illustrations for *Alice in Wonderland* shows the Mock Turtle with the head, tail, and hooves of a calf, along with a sea-turtle's shell and flippers.

24. The Gryphon is a mythical beast, half lion and half eagle.

ever finish, if he doesn't begin." But she waited patiently.

"Once," said the Mock Turtle at last, with a deep sigh, "I was a real Turtle."

These words were followed by a very long silence, broken only by an occasional exclamation of "Hjckrrh!" from the Gryphon, and the constant heavy sobbing of the Mock Turtle. Alice was very nearly getting up and saying, "Thank you, sir, for your interesting story," but she could not help thinking there *must* be more to come, so she sat still and said nothing.

"When we were little," the Mock Turtle went on at last, more calmly, though still sobbing a little now and then, "we went to school in the sea. The master was an old Turtle—we used to call him Tortoise—"

"Why did you call him Tortoise, if he wasn't one?" Alice asked.

"We called him Tortoise because he taught us," said the Mock Turtle angrily; "really you are very dull!"

"You ought to be ashamed of yourself for asking such a simple question," added the Gryphon; and then they both sat silent and looked at poor Alice, who felt ready to sink into the earth. At last the Gryphon said to the Mock Turtle, "Drive on, old fellow! Don't be all day about it!" and he went on in these words: "Yes, we went to school in the sea, though you mayn't believe it—"

"I never said I didn't!" interrupted Alice.

"You did," said the Mock Turtle.

"Hold your tongue!" added the Gryphon, before Alice could speak again. The Mock Turtle went on.

"We had the best of educations—in fact, we went to school every day—"

"*I've* been to a day-school too," said Alice; "you needn't be so proud as all that."

"With extras?" asked the Mock Turtle a little anxiously.

"Yes," said Alice, "we learned French and music."

"And washing?" said the Mock Turtle.

"Certainly not!" said Alice indignantly.

"Ah! Then yours wasn't a really good school," said the Mock Turtle in a tone of great relief. "Now at *ours* they had at the end of the bill, 'French, music, *and washing*—extra.' "[25]

---

25. English boarding schools frequently charged extra for courses not in the normal curriculum, such as music and French, as well as for laundry done at the school.

"You couldn't have wanted it much," said Alice; "living at the bottom of the sea."

"I couldn't afford to learn it," said the Mock Turtle with a sigh. "I only took the regular course."

"What was that?" enquired Alice.

"Reeling and Writhing, of course, to begin with," the Mock Turtle replied: "and then the different branches of Arithmetic—Ambition, Distraction, Uglification, and Derision."

"I never heard of 'Uglification,' " Alice ventured to say. "What is it?"

The Gryphon lifted up both its paws in surprise. "Never heard of uglifying!" it exclaimed. "You know what to beautify is, I suppose?"

"Yes," said Alice, doubtfully: "it means—to—make—anything—prettier."

"Well then," the Gryphon went on, "if you don't know what to uglify is, you *are* a simpleton.' "

Alice did not feel encouraged to ask any more questions about it, so she turned to the Mock Turtle, and said, "What else had you to learn?"

"Well, there was Mystery," the Mock Turtle replied, counting off the subjects on his flappers,— "Mystery, ancient and modern, with Seography,— then Drawling—the Drawling-master was an old conger-eel, that used to come once a week: *he* taught us Drawling, Stretching, and Fainting in Coils."

"What was *that* like?" said Alice.

"Well, I can't show it to you, myself," the Mock Turtle said: "I'm too stiff. And the Gryphon never learnt it."

"Hadn't time," said the Gryphon: "I went to the Classical master, though. He was an old crab, *he* was."

"I never went to him," the Mock Turtle said with a sigh: "he taught Laughing and Grief, they used to say."

"So he did, so he did," said the Gryphon, sighing in his turn, and both creatures hid their faces in their paws.

"And how many hours a day did you do lessons?" said Alice, in a hurry to change the subject.

"Ten hours the first day," said the Mock Turtle: "nine the next, and so on."

"What a curious plan!" exclaimed Alice.

"That's the reason they're called lessons," the Gryphon remarked: "because they lessen from day to day."

This was quite a new idea to Alice, and she

thought it over a little before she made her next remark. "Then the eleventh day must have been a holiday?"

"Of course it was," said the Mock Turtle.

"And how did you manage on the twelfth?" Alice went on eagerly.

"That's enough about lessons," the Gryphon interrupted in a very decided tone: "tell her something about the games now."

10

THE LOBSTER QUADRILLE

THE Mock Turtle sighed deeply, and drew the back of one flapper across his eyes. He looked at Alice and tried to speak, but for a minute or two sobs choked his voice. "Same as if he had a bone in his throat," said the Gryphon, and it set to work shaking him and punching him in the back. At last the Mock Turtle recovered his voice, and, with tears running down his cheeks, he went on again:—

"You may not have lived much under the sea—" ("I haven't," said Alice)—"and perhaps you were never introduced to a lobster—" (Alice began to say "I once tasted—" but checked herself hastily, and said, "No, never")—"so you can have no idea what a delightful thing a Lobster-Quadrille[26] is!"

"No, indeed," said Alice. "What sort of a dance is it?"

"Why," said the Gryphon, "you first form into a line along the seashore—"

"Two lines!" cried the Mock Turtle. "Seals, turtles, salmon, and so on: then, when you've cleared all the jelly-fish out of the way—"

"That generally takes some time," interrupted the Gryphon.

"—you advance twice—"

"Each with a lobster as a partner!" cried the Gryphon.

"Of course," the Mock Turtle said: "advance twice, set to partners—"

"—change lobsters, and retire in same order," continued the Gryphon.

"Then, you know," the Mock Turtle went on, "you throw the—"

"The Lobsters!" shouted the Gryphon, with a bound into the air.

"—as far out to sea as you can—"

"Swim after them!" screamed the Gryphon.

"Turn a somersault in the sea!" cried the Mock Turtle, capering wildly about.

"Change lobsters again!" yelled the Gryphon at the top of its voice.

"Back to land again, and—that's all the first figure," said the Mock Turtle, suddenly dropping his voice, and the two creatures, who had been jumping about like mad things all this time, sat down again very sadly and quietly, and looked at Alice.

"It must be a very pretty dance," said Alice timidly.

"Would you like to see a little of it?" said the Mock Turtle.

"Very much indeed," said Alice.

"Come, let's try the first figure!" said the Mock Turtle to the Gryphon. "We can do it without lobsters, you know. Which shall sing?"

"Oh, you sing," said the Gryphon. "I've forgotten the words." So they began solemnly dancing round and round Alice, every now and then treading on her toes when they passed too close, and waving their fore-paws to mark the time, while the Mock Turtle sang this, very slowly and sadly:—

"Will you walk a little faster?" said a whiting to
        a snail,[27]
"There's a porpoise close behind us, and he's
        treading on my tail.
    See how eagerly the lobsters and the turtles all
        advance!
    They are waiting on the shingle—will you come
        and join the dance?
Will you, won't you, will you, won't you, will you
        join the dance?
Will you, won't you, will you, won't you, won't you
        join the dance?

---

26. The quadrille was a kind of square dance fashionable in Victorian England.

27. See page 482.

"You can really have no notion how delightful it
  will be
When they take us up and throw us, with the
  lobsters, out to sea!"
But the snail replied "Too far, too far!" and gave
  a look askance—
Said he thanked the whiting kindly, but he would
  not join the dance.
Would not, could not, would not, could not, would
  not join the dance.
Would not, could not, would not, could not, could
  not join the dance.

"What matters it how far we go?" his scaly friend
  replied,
"There is another shore, you know, upon the other
  side.
The further off from England the nearer is to
  France—
Then turn not pale, beloved snail, but come and
  join the dance.
Will you, won't you, will you, won't you, will you
  join the dance?
Will you, won't you, will you, won't you, won't you
  join the dance?"

"Thank you, it's a very interesting dance to watch," said Alice, feeling very glad that it was over at last; "and I do so like that curious song about the whiting!"

"Oh, as to the whiting," said the Mock Turtle, "they—you've seen them, of course?"

"Yes," said Alice, "I've often seen them at dinn—" she checked herself hastily.

"I don't know where Dinn may be," said the Mock Turtle, "but if you've seen them so often, of course you know what they're like."

"I believe so," Alice replied thoughtfully. "They have their tails in their mouths;—and they're all over crumbs."[28]

"You're wrong about the crumbs," said the Mock Turtle: "crumbs would all wash off in the sea. But they *have* their tails in their mouths; and the reason is—" here the Mock Turtle yawned and shut his eyes.—"Tell her about the reason and all that," he said to the Gryphon.

---

28. Whiting, a fish related to cod, was displayed for sale by Victorian fish-vendors with its tail inserted through its eye socket. Whiting is often cooked in bread crumbs. Hence Alice's observations.

"The reason is," said the Gryphon, "that they *would* go with the lobsters to the dance. So they got thrown out to sea. So they had to fall a long way. So they got their tails fast in their mouths. So they couldn't get them out again. That's all."

"Thank you," said Alice, "it's very interesting. I never knew so much about a whiting before."

"I can tell you more than that, if you like," said the Gryphon. "Do you know why it's called a whiting?"

"I never thought about it," said Alice. "Why?"

"It does the boots and shoes," the Gryphon replied very solemnly.

Alice was thoroughly puzzled. "Does the boots and shoes!" she repeated in a wondering tone.

"Why, what are *your* shoes done with?" said the Gryphon. "I mean, what makes them so shiny?"

Alice looked down at them, and considered a little before she gave her answer. "They're done with blacking, I believe."

"Boots and shoes under the sea," the Gryphon went on in a deep voice, "are done with whiting. Now you know."

"And what are they made of?" Alice asked in a tone of great curiosity.

"Soles and eels, of course," the Gryphon replied rather impatiently: "any shrimp could have told you that."

"If I'd been the whiting," said Alice, whose thoughts were still running on the song, "I'd have said to the porpoise, 'Keep back, please: we don't want *you* with us!'"

"They were obliged to have him with them," the Mock Turtle said: "no wise fish would go anywhere without a porpoise."

"Wouldn't it really?" said Alice in a tone of great surprise.

"Of course not," said the Mock Turtle: "why, if a fish came to *me*, and told me he was going a journey, I should say 'With what porpoise?'"

"Don't you mean 'purpose?'" said Alice.

"I mean what I say," the Mock Turtle replied in an offended tone. And the Gryphon added "Come, let's hear some of *your* adventures."

"I could tell you my adventures—beginning from this morning," said Alice a little timidly: "but it's no use going back to yesterday, because I was a different person then."

"Explain all that," said the Mock Turtle.

"No, no! the adventures first," said the Gryphon in

an impatient tone: "explanations take such a dreadful time."

So Alice began telling them her adventures from the time when she first saw the White Rabbit: she was a little nervous about it just at first, the two creatures got so close to her, one on each side, and opened their eyes and mouths so *very* wide, but she gained courage as she went on. Her listeners were perfectly quiet till she got to the part about her repeating "*You are old, Father William,*" to the Caterpillar, and the words all coming different, and then the Mock Turtle drew a long breath, and said, "That's very curious."

"It's all about as curious as it can be," said the Gryphon.

"It all came different!" the Mock Turtle repeated thoughtfully. "I should like to hear her try and repeat something now. Tell her to begin." He looked at the Gryphon as if he thought it had some kind of authority over Alice.

"Stand up and repeat ' *'Tis the voice of the sluggard,*'" said the Gryphon.

"How the creatures order one about, and make one repeat lessons!" thought Alice, "I might just as well be at school at once." However, she got up, and began to repeat it, but her head was so full of the Lobster-Quadrille, that she hardly knew what she was saying, and the words came very queer indeed:—

"'Tis the voice of the lobster; I heard him declare,[29]
*'You have baked me too brown, I must sugar my
      hair.'*
As a duck with its eyelids, so he with his nose
*Trims his belt and his buttons, and turns out his
      toes.*
When the sands are all dry, he is gay as a lark,
And will talk in contemptuous tones of the Shark:
But, when the tide rises and sharks are around,
His voice has a timid and tremulous sound."

"That's different from what *I* used to say when I was a child," said the Gryphon.

"Well, I never heard it before," said the Mock Turtle; "but it sounds uncommon nonsense."

Alice said nothing: she had sat down again with her face in her hands, wondering if anything would *ever* happen in a natural way again.

"I should like to have it explained," said the Mock Turtle.

"She can't explain it," said the Gryphon hastily. "Go on with the next verse."

"But about his toes?" the Mock Turtle persisted. "How *could* he turn them out with his nose, you know?"

"It's the first position in dancing," Alice said; but she was dreadfully puzzled by the whole thing, and longed to change the subject.

"Go on with the next verse," the Gryphon repeated impatiently: "it begins '*I passed by his garden.*'"

Alice did not dare to disobey, though she felt sure it would all come wrong, and she went on in a trembling voice:—

"I passed by his garden, and marked, with one eye,
How the Owl and the Panther were sharing a pie:
The Panther took pie-crust, and gravy, and meat,
While the Owl had the dish as its share of the treat.
When the pie was all finished, the Owl, as a boon,
Was kindly permitted to pocket the spoon:
*While the Panther received knife and fork with a
      growl,*
And concluded the banquet by—"

"What *is* the use of repeating all that stuff," the Mock Turtle interrupted, "if you don't explain it as you go on? It's by far the most confusing thing *I* ever heard!"

"Yes, I think you'd better leave off," said the Gryphon, and Alice was only too glad to do so.

"Shall we try another figure of the Lobster-Quadrille?" the Gryphon went on. "Or would you like the Mock Turtle to sing you a song?"

"Oh, a song please, if the Mock Turtle would be so kind," Alice replied, so eagerly that the Gryphon said, in a rather offended tone, "Hm! No accounting for tastes! Sing her '*Turtle Soup,*' will you, old fellow?"

The Mock Turtle sighed deeply, and began, in a voice sometimes choked with sobs, to sing this:—

"Beautiful Soup, so rich and green,[30]
Waiting in a hot tureen!
Who for such dainties would not stoop?
Soup of the evening, beautiful Soup!

---

29. See page 482.

30. See page 484.

Soup of the evening, beautiful Soup!
Beau—ootiful Soo—oop!
Beau—ootiful Soo—oop!
Soo—oop of the e—e—evening,
Beautiful, beautiful Soup!

"Beautiful Soup! Who cares for fish,
Game, or any other dish?
Who would not give all else for two p
ennyworth only of beautiful Soup?
Pennyworth only of beautiful Soup?
Beau—ootiful Soo—oop!
Beau—ootiful Soo—oop!
Soo—oop of the e—e—evening,
*Beautiful, beauti—*FUL SOUP!*"*

"Chorus again!" cried the Gryphon, and the Mock Turtle had just begun to repeat it, when a cry of "The trial's beginning!" was heard in the distance.

"Come on!" cried the Gryphon, and, taking Alice by the hand, it hurried off, without waiting for the end of the song.

"What trial is it?" Alice panted as she ran, but the Gryphon only answered "Come on!" and ran the faster while more and more faintly came, carried on the breeze that followed them, the melancholy words:—

"Soo—oop of the e—e—evening,
Beautiful, beautiful Soup!"

11

WHO STOLE THE TARTS?

THE King and Queen of Hearts were seated on their throne when they arrived, with a great crowd assembled about them—all sorts of little birds and beasts, as well as the whole pack of cards: the Knave was standing before them, in chains, with a soldier on each side to guard him; and near the King was the White Rabbit, with a trumpet in one hand, and a scroll of parchment in the other. In the very middle of the court was a table, with a large dish of tarts upon it: they looked so good, that it made Alice quite hungry to look at them—"I wish they'd get the trial done," she thought, "and hand round the refreshments!" But there seemed to be no chance of this, so she began looking at everything about her to pass away the time.

Alice had never been in a court of justice before, but she had read about them in books, and she was quite pleased to find that she knew the name of nearly everything there. "That's the judge," she said to herself, "because of his great wig."

The judge, by the way, was the King, and as he wore his crown over the wig, he did not look at all comfortable, and it was certainly not becoming.

"And that's the jury-box," thought Alice, "and those twelve creatures," (she was obliged to say "creatures," you see, because some of them were animals, and some were birds,) "I suppose they are the jurors." She said this last word two or three times over to herself, being rather proud of it: for she thought, and rightly too, that very few little girls of her age knew the meaning of it at all. However, "jurymen" would have done just as well.

The twelve jurors were all writing very busily on slates. "What are they doing?" Alice whispered to the Gryphon. "They can't have anything to put down yet, before the trial's begun."

"They're putting down their names," the Gryphon whispered in reply, "for fear they should forget them before the end of the trial."

"Stupid things!" Alice began in a loud indignant voice, but she stopped herself hastily, for the White Rabbit cried out, "Silence in the court!" and the King put on his spectacles and looked anxiously round, to make out who was talking.

Alice could see, as well as if she were looking over their shoulders, that all the jurors were writing down "stupid things!" on their slates, and she could even make out that one of them didn't know how to spell "stupid," and that he had to ask his neighbour to tell him. "A nice muddle their slates'll be in before the trial's over!" thought Alice.

One of the jurors had a pencil that squeaked. This, of course, Alice could *not stand*, and she went round the court and got behind him, and very soon found an opportunity of taking it away. She did it so quickly that the poor little juror (it was Bill, the Lizard) could not make out at all what had become of it; so, after hunting all about for it, he was obliged to write with one finger for the rest of the day; and this was of very little use, as it left no mark on the slate.

"Herald, read the accusation!" said the King.

On this the White Rabbit blew three blasts on the trumpet, and then unrolled the parchment scroll, and read as follows:—

"*The Queen of Hearts, she made some tarts,*
  All on a summer day:
The Knave of Hearts, he stole those tarts,
  And took them quite away!"

"Consider your verdict," the King said to the jury.

"Not yet, not yet!" the Rabbit hastily interrupted. "There's a great deal to come before that!"

"Call the first witness," said the King; and the White Rabbit blew three blasts on the trumpet, and called out, "First witness!"

The first witness was the Hatter. He came in with a teacup in one hand, and a piece of bread-and-butter in the other. "I beg pardon, your Majesty," he began, "for bringing these in: but I hadn't quite finished my tea when I was sent for."

"You ought to have finished," said the King. "When did you begin?"

The Hatter looked at the March Hare, who had followed him into the court, arm-in-arm with the Dormouse. "Fourteenth of March, I *think* it was," he said.

"Fifteenth," said the March Hare.

"Sixteenth," added the Dormouse.

"Write that down," the King said to the jury, and the jury eagerly wrote down all three dates on their slates, and then added them up, and reduced the answer to shillings and pence.

"Take off your hat," the King said to the Hatter.

"It isn't mine," said the Hatter.

"*Stolen!*" the King exclaimed, turning to the jury, who instantly made a memorandum of the fact.

"I keep them to sell," the Hatter added as an explanation: "I've none of my own. I'm a hatter."

Here the Queen put on her spectacles, and began staring hard at the Hatter, who turned pale and fidgeted.

"Give your evidence," said the King; "and don't be nervous, or I'll have you executed on the spot."

This did not seem to encourage the witness at all: he kept shifting from one foot to the other, look-ing uneasily at the Queen, and in his confusion he bit a large piece out of his teacup instead of the bread-and-butter.

Just at this moment Alice felt a very curious sensation, which puzzled her a good deal until she made out what it was: she was beginning to grow larger again, and she thought at first she would get up and leave the court; but on second thoughts she decided to remain where she was as long as there was room for her.

"I wish you wouldn't squeeze so," said the Dormouse, who was sitting next to her. "I can hardly breathe."

"I can't help it," said Alice very meekly: "I'm growing."

"You've no right to grow *here*," said the Dormouse.

"Don't talk nonsense," said Alice more boldly: "you know you're growing too."

"Yes, but *I* grow at a reasonable pace," said the Dormouse: "not in that ridiculous fashion." And he got up very sulkily and crossed over to the other side of the court.

All this time the Queen had never left off staring at the Hatter, and, just as the Dormouse crossed the court, she said to one of the officers at the court, "Bring me the list of the singers in the last concert!" on which the wretched Hatter trembled so, that he shook both his shoes off.[31]

"Give your evidence," the King repeated angrily, "or I'll have you executed, whether you're nervous or not."

"I'm a poor man, your Majesty," the Hatter began in a trembling voice, "and I hadn't but just begun my tea—not above a week or so—and what with the bread-and-butter getting so thin—and the twinkling of the tea—"

"The twinkling of *what?*" said the King.

"It *began* with the tea," the Hatter replied.

"Of course twinkling begins with a T!" said the King sharply. "Do you take me for a dunce? Go on!"

"I'm a poor man," the Hatter went on, "and most things twinkled after that—only the March Hare said—"

"I didn't!" the March Hare interrupted in a great hurry.

"You did!" said the Hatter.

---

31. The Hatter trembles because he "murdered the time" (i.e. forgot the meter) when he sang before the Queen. (See his report of the affair in Chapter 7.)

"I deny it!" said the March Hare.

"He denies it," said the King: "leave out that part."

"Well, at any rate, the Dormouse said—" the Hatter went on, looking anxiously round to see if he would deny it too: but the Dormouse denied nothing, being fast asleep.

"After that," continued the Hatter, "I cut some more bread-and-butter—"

"But what did the Dormouse say?" one of the jury asked.

"That I can't remember," said the Hatter.

"You *must* remember," remarked the King, "or I'll have you executed."

The miserable Hatter dropped his teacup and bread-and-butter, and went down on one knee. "I'm a poor man, your Majesty," he began.

"You're a *very* poor *speaker*," said the King.

Here one of the guinea-pigs cheered, and was immediately suppressed by the officers of the court.

(As that is rather a hard word, I will just explain to you how it was done. They had a large canvas bag, which tied up at the mouth with strings: into this they slipped the guinea-pig, head first, and then sat upon it.)

"I'm glad I've seen that done," thought Alice. "I've so often read in the newspapers, at the end of trials, 'There was some attempt at applause, which was immediately suppressed by the officers of the court,' and I never understood what it meant till now."

"It that's all you know about it, you may stand down," continued the King.

"I can't go no lower," said the Hatter: "I'm on the floor as it is."

"Then you may *sit* down," the King replied.

Here the other guinea-pig cheered, and was suppressed.

"Come, that finishes the guinea-pigs!" thought Alice. "Now we shall get on better."

"I'd rather finish my tea," said the Hatter with an anxious look at the Queen, who was reading the list of singers.

"You may go," said the King, and the Hatter hurriedly left the court, without even waiting to put his shoes on.

"—and just take his head off outside," the Queen added to one of the officers; but the Hatter was out of sight before the officer could get to the door.

"Call the next witness!" said the King.

The next witness was the Duchess' cook. She carried the pepper-box in her hand, and Alice guessed who it was, even before she got into the court, by the way the people near the door began sneezing all at once.

"Give your evidence," said the King.

"Shan't," said the cook.

The King looked anxiously at the White Rabbit, who said in a low voice, "Your Majesty must cross-examine *this* witness."

"Well, if I must, I must," the King said with a melancholy air, and, after folding his arms and frowning at the cook till his eyes were nearly out of sight, he said in a deep voice, "What are tarts made of?"

"Pepper, mostly," said the cook.

"Treacle," said a sleepy voice behind her.

"Collar that Dormouse!" the Queen shrieked out. "Behead that Dormouse! Turn that Dormouse out of court! Suppress him! Pinch him! Off with his whiskers!"

For some minutes the whole court was in confusion, getting the Dormouse turned out, and, by the time they had settled down again, the cook had disappeared.

"Never mind!" said the King, with an air of great relief. "Call the next witness." And he added in an under-tone to the Queen, "Really my dear, *you* must cross-examine the next witness. It quite makes my forehead ache!"

Alice watched the White Rabbit as he fumbled over the list, feeling very curious to see what the next witness would be like, "—for they haven't got much evidence *yet*," she said to herself. Imagine her surprise, when the White Rabbit read out, at the top of his shrill little voice, the name "Alice!"

12

"HERE!" cried Alice, quite forgetting in the flurry of the moment how large she had grown in the last few minutes, and she jumped up in such a hurry that she tipped over the jury-box with the edge of her skirt, upsetting all the jurymen onto the heads of the crowd below, and there they lay sprawling about, reminding her very much of a globe of goldfish she had accidentally upset the week before.

"Oh, I *beg* your pardon!" she exclaimed in a tone of great dismay, and began picking them up again as quickly as she could, for the accident of the goldfish kept running in her head, and she had a vague sort of idea that they must be collected at once and put back into the jury-box, or they would die.

"The trial cannot proceed," said the King in a very grave voice, "until all the jurymen are back in their proper places—*all*," he repeated with great emphasis, looking hard at Alice as he said so.

Alice looked at the jury-box, and saw that, in her haste, she had put the Lizard in head downwards, and the poor little thing was waving its tail about in a melancholy way, being quite unable to move. She soon got it out again, and put it right; "not that it signifies much," she said to herself; "I should think it would be *quite* as much use in the trial one way up as the other."

As soon as the jury had a little recovered from the shock of being upset, and their slates and pencils had been found and handed back to them, they set to work very diligently to write out a history of the accident, all except the Lizard, who seemed too much overcome to do anything but sit with its mouth open, gazing up into the roof of the court.

"What do you know about this business?" the King said to Alice.

"Nothing," said Alice.

"Nothing *whatever?*" persisted the King.

"Nothing whatever," said Alice.

"That's very important," the King said, turning to the jury. They were just beginning to write this down on their slates, when the White Rabbit interrupted: "*Un*important, your Majesty means, of course," he said in a very respectful tone, but frowning and making faces at him as he spoke.

"*Un*important, of course, I meant," the King hastily said, and went on to himself in an undertone, "important—unimportant—unimportant—important—" as if he were trying which word sounded best.

Some of the jury wrote it down "important," and some "unimportant." Alice could see this, as she was near enough to look over their slates; "but it doesn't matter a bit," she thought to herself.

At this moment the King, who had been for some time busily writing in his note-book, called out "Silence!" and read out from his book, "Rule Forty-two. *All persons more than a mile high to leave the court.*"

Everybody looked at Alice.

"*I'm* not a mile high," said Alice.

"You are," said the King.

"Nearly two miles high," added the Queen.

"Well, I shan't go at any rate," said Alice; "besides, that's not a regular rule: you invented it just now."

"It's the oldest rule in the book," said the King.

"Then it ought to be Number One," said Alice.

The King turned pale, and shut his notebook hastily. "Consider your verdict," he said to the jury, in a low trembling voice.

"There's more evidence to come yet, please your Majesty," said the White Rabbit, jumping up in a great hurry; "this paper has just been picked up."

"What's in it?" said the Queen.

"I haven't opened it yet," said the White Rabbit, "but it seems to be a letter, written by the prisoner to—to somebody."

"It must have been that," said the King, "unless it was written to nobody, which isn't usual, you know."

"Who is it directed to?" said one of the jurymen.

"It isn't directed at all," said the White Rabbit; "in fact, there's nothing written on the *outside*." He unfolded the paper as he spoke, and added, "it isn't a letter after all: it's a set of verses."

"Are they in the prisoner's handwriting?" asked another of the jurymen.

"No, they're not," said the White Rabbit, "and that's the queerest thing about it." (The jury all looked puzzled.)

"He must have imitated somebody else's hand," said the King. (The jury all brightened up again.)

"Please your Majesty," said the Knave: "I didn't

write it, and they can't prove I did: there's no name signed at the end."

"If you didn't sign it," said the King, "that only makes the matter worse. You *must* have meant some mischief, or else you'd have signed your name like an honest man."

There was a general clapping of hands at this: it was the first really clever thing the King had said that day.

"That *proves* his guilt," said the Queen.

"It proves nothing of the sort!" said Alice. "Why, you don't even know what they're about!"

"Read them," said the King.

The White Rabbit put on his spectacles. "Where shall I begin, please your Majesty?" he asked.

"Begin at the beginning," the King said, gravely, "and go on till you come to the end: then stop."

These were the verses the White Rabbit read:—

> "They told me you had been to her,
> And mentioned me to him:
> She gave me a good character,
> But said I could not swim.
>
> He sent them word I had not gone
> (We know it to be true):
> If she should push the matter on,
> What would become of you?
>
> I gave her one, they gave him two,
> You gave us three or more;
> They all returned from him to you,
> Though they were mine before.
>
> If I or she should chance to be
> Involved in this affair,
> He trusts to you to set them free,
> Exactly as we were.
>
> My notion was that you had been
> (Before she had this fit)
> An obstacle that came between
> Him, and ourselves, and it.
>
> Don't let him know she liked them best,
> For this must ever be
> A secret, kept from all the rest,
> Between yourself and me."

"That's the most important piece of evidence we've heard yet," said the King, rubbing his hands; "so now let the jury—"

"If any one of them can explain it," said Alice, (she had grown so large in the last few minutes that she wasn't a bit afraid of interrupting him,) "I'll give him sixpence. *I* don't believe there's an atom of meaning in it."

The jury all wrote down on their slates, "*She* doesn't believe there's an atom of meaning in it," but none of them attempted to explain the paper.

"If there's no meaning in it," said the King, "that saves a world of trouble, you know, as we needn't try to find any. And yet I don't know," he went on, spreading out the verses on his knee, and looking at them with one eye; "I seem to see some meaning in them, after all. '—*said I could not swim—*' you can't swim, can you?" he added, turning to the Knave.

The Knave shook his head sadly. "Do I look like it?" he said (which he certainly did *not*, being made entirely of cardboard).

"All right, so far," said the King, and he went on muttering over the verses to himself: "'*We know it to be true—*' that's the jury of course—'*I gave her one, they gave him two—*' why, that must be what he did with the tarts, you know—"

"But it goes on '*they all returned from him to you,*'" said Alice.

"Why, there they are!" said the King triumphantly, pointing to the tarts on the table. "Nothing can be clearer than that. Then again—'*before she had this fit—*' you never had fits, my dear, I think?" he said to the Queen.

"Never!" said the Queen furiously, throwing an inkstand at the Lizard as she spoke.

(The unfortunate little Bill had left off writing on his slate with one finger, as he found it made no mark; but he now hastily began again, using the ink, that was trickling down his face, as long as it lasted.)

"Then the words don't *fit* you," said the King, looking round the court with a smile. There was a dead silence.

"It's a pun!" the King added in an angry tone, and everybody laughed. "Let the jury consider their verdict," the King said, for about the twentieth time that day.

"No, no!" said the Queen. "Sentence first—verdict afterwards."

"Stuff and nonsense!" said Alice loudly. "The idea of having the sentence first!"

"Hold your tongue!" said the Queen, turning purple.

"I won't!" said Alice.

"Off with her head!" the Queen shouted at the top of her voice. Nobody moved.

"Who cares for you?" said Alice, (she had grown to her full size by this time). "You're nothing but a pack of cards!"

At this the whole pack rose up into the air, and came flying down upon her; she gave a little scream, half of fright and half of anger, and tried to beat them off, and found herself lying on the bank, with her head in the lap of her sister, who was gently brushing away some dead leaves that had fluttered down from the trees on to her face.

"Wake up, Alice dear!" said her sister; "why, what a long sleep you've had!"

"Oh, I've had such a curious dream!" said Alice, and she told her sister, as well as she could remember, all these strange Adventures of hers that you have just been reading about; and when she had finished, her sister kissed her, and said, "It *was* a curious dream, dear, certainly: but now run in to your tea; it's getting late." So Alice got up and ran off, thinking while she ran, as well she might, what a wonderful dream it had been.

But her sister sat still just as she left her, leaning her head on her hand, watching the setting sun, and thinking of little Alice and all her wonderful Adventures, till she too began dreaming after a fashion, and this was her dream:—

First, she dreamed of little Alice herself:—once again the tiny hands were clasped upon her knee, and the bright eager eyes were looking up into hers —she could hear the very tones of her voice, and see that queer little toss of her head, to keep back the wandering hair that *would* always get into her eyes—and still as she listened, or seemed to listen, the whole place around her became alive with the strange creatures of her little sister's dream.

The long grass rustled at her feet as the White Rabbit hurried by—the frightened Mouse splashed his way through the neighbouring pool—she could hear the rattle of the teacups as the March Hare and his friends shared their never-ending meal, and the shrill voice of the Queen ordering off her unfortunate guests to execution—once more the pig-baby was sneezing on the Duchess' knee, while plates and dishes crashed around it—once more the shriek of the Gryphon, the squeaking of the Lizard's slate-pencil, and the choking of the suppressed guinea-pigs, filled the air, mixed up with the distant sob of the miserable Mock Turtle.

So she sat on, with closed eyes, and half believed herself in Wonderland, though she knew she had but to open them again and all would change to dull reality—the grass would be only rustling in the wind, and the pool rippling to the waving of the reeds— the rattling teacups would change to tinkling sheep-bells, and the Queen's shrill cries to the voice of the shepherd boy—and the sneeze of the baby, the shriek of the Gryphon, and all the other queer noises, would change (she knew) to the confused clamour of the busy farm-yard—while the lowing of the cattle in the distance would take the place of the Mock Turtle's heavy sobs.

Lastly, she pictured to herself how this same little sister of hers would, in the aftertime, be herself a grown woman; and how she would keep, through all her riper years, the simple and loving heart of her childhood: and how she would gather about her other little children, and make *their* eyes bright and eager with many a strange tale, perhaps even with the dream of Wonderland of long-ago: and how she would feel with all their simple sorrows, and find a pleasure in all their simple joys, remembering her own child-life, and the happy summer days.

THE END

NOTES

2. The poems and songs parodied by Carroll were well known to his contemporary readers. Victorian children were often required to memorize them as part of their lessons. The original of the parody on page 444 is a moralistic poem by Isaac Watts (1674–1748), titled "Against Idleness and Mischief." It runs as follows:

> How doth the little busy bee
> Improve each shining hour
> And gather honey all the day
> From every opening flower!
>
> How skillfully she builds her cell!
> How neat she spreads her wax!
> And labours hard to store it well
> With the sweet food she makes.
>
> In works of labour or of skill,
> I would be busy too;
> For Satan finds some mischief still
> For idle hands to do.
>
> In books, or work, or healthful play
> Let my first years be passed,
> That I may give for every day
> Some good account at last.

11. The verses on page 454 are a parody of Robert Southey's (1774–1843) didactic poem, "The Old Man's Comforts and How He Gained Them."

> "You are old, father William," the young man cried,
> "The few locks which are left you are grey;
> You are hale, father William, a hearty old man;
> Now tell me the reason, I pray."
>
> "In the days of my youth," father William replied,
> "I remember'd that youth would fly fast,
> And abus'd not my health and my vigour at first,
> That I never might need them at last."
>
> "You are old, father William," the young man cried,
> "And pleasures with youth pass away.
> And yet you lament not the days that are gone;
> Now tell me the reason, I pray."
>
> "In the days of my youth," father William replied,
> "I remember'd that youth could not last;
> I thought of the future, whatever I did,
> That I never might grieve for the past."
>
> "You are old, father William," the young man cried,
> "And life must be hast'ning away;

> You are cheerful and love to converse upon death;
> Now tell me the reason, I pray."
>
> "I am cheerful, young man," father William replied,
> "Let the cause thy attention engage;
> In the days of my youth I remember'd my God!
> And He hath not forgotten my age."

12. The verses on page 458 are a parody of a poem attributed to David Bates, a nineteenth-century versifier from Philadelphia. The original was titled "Speak Gently." Below are several stanzas selected from it:

> Speak gently! It is better far
> To rule by love than fear;
> Speak gently; let no harsh words mar
> The good we might do here!
>
> Speak gently! Love doth whisper low
> The vows that true hearts bind;
> And gently Friendship's accents flow;
> Affection's voice is kind.
>
> Speak gently to the little child!
> Its love be sure to gain;
> Teach it in accents soft and mild;
> It may not long remain.
>
> Speak gently to the young, for they
> Will have enough to bear;
> Pass through this life as best they may,
> 'Tis full of anxious care!

27. The song of the Mock Turtle is patterned on, and parodies the first line of a poem by Mary Howitt, "The Spider and the Fly." The first stanza of the original reads:

> "Will you walk into my parlour?" said the spider to the fly.
> "'Tis the prettiest little parlour that ever you did spy.
> The way into my parlour is up a winding stair,
> And I've got many curious things to show when you are
> there."
> "Oh, no, no," said the little fly, "to ask me is in vain.
> For who goes up your winding stair can ne'er come down
> again."

29. Alice's poem is a parody of a moralistic poem by Isaac Watts, "The Sluggard," which reads in part as follows:

> 'Tis the voice of the sluggard; I heard him complain,
> "You have wak'd me too soon, I must slumber again."
> As the door on its hinges, so he on his bed,

On this page are a few of the original illustrations for *Alice in Wonderland,* drawn by John Tenniel, a cartoonist on the staff of the British humor magazine *Punch*. He worked closely with Lewis Carroll, and his interpretations of the characters have defined the way most readers visualize them. Since then, however, many other artists—including Arthur Rackham, N. C. Wyeth, and Salvador Dali—have pictured the characters in a variety of styles.

The illustrations in this volume were painted especially for it by the young Belgian artist Jean Michel Folon.

Turns his sides and his shoulders and his heavy head.

"A little more sleep, and a little more slumber,"
Thus he wastes half his days, and his hours without number,
And when he gets up, he sits folding his hands,
Or walks about sauntering, or trifling he stands.

I pass'd by his garden, and saw the wild brier,
The thorn and the thistle grow broader and higher;
The clothes that hang on him are turning to rags;
And his money still wastes till he starves or he begs.

30.   The Mock Turtle's paean to real turtle soup is a parody of a popular contemporary song, "Star of the Evening," with words and music by James Sayles. The first verse of the original runs as follows:

> Beautiful star in heav'n so bright,
> Softly falls thy silv'ry light,
> As thou movest from earth afar,
> Star of the evening, beautiful star.
>
> CHORUS:
> Beautiful star,
> Beautiful star,
> Star of the evening, beautiful star.

DISCUSSION

1. Various critics of *Alice in Wonderland* have interpreted Alice's troubles with her variations in size, her confusion and forgetfulness, her slips of the tongue, etc., as representative of the "problems of growing up." Argue for or against such an interpretation, using the following questions as guidelines:

(a) Specifically, what types of problems in communication and self-control does she experience?

(b) Do any aspects of these problems have symbolic overtones? (For example, what do Alice's troubles with the golden key, her struggles to get through the small door into the beautiful garden, suggest?)

(c) In what instances does she muse over or struggle with questions about her identity? How are these questions answered?

(d) Does Alice seem to gain in self-control as the story progresses? (Is she, for instance, more sure of herself, more socially adept, in her second encounter with the Duchess on the croquet field than when she first met her in the kitchen?)

(e) Would you go so far as to say that *Alice* is primarily a story of "growing up"? Would you deny such a statement altogether?

2. Wonderland is full of improbabilities: the hierarchy of men and animals is reversed; the rules of time, space, orderly sequence, and cause and effect are broken; events and conversations sometimes have little pattern or sense. This state of affairs has led more than one interpreter to suggest that Alice's dream is actually a "nightmare" vision of a purposeless and chaotic universe which threatens and contradicts the conscious and seemingly logical assumptions we live by. Does *Alice in Wonderland* have this darker aspect, or is it merely a story of a child's innocent travels through a whimsical but harmless realm? Can you identify any points in the story where the chaos of Wonderland actually threatens Alice?

3. How might the White Rabbit, the Frog-Footman, the Pigeon, the Caterpillar, and the Mock Turtle be satirical reflections of certain human characteristics or tendencies?

4. Which of all the remarkable characters in Wonderland does Alice feel most comfortable with? Why?

5. (a) *Alice in Wonderland* has been called a view of the incomprehensible adult world as seen through the eyes of a child. To what extent is Alice childlike? Is there anything in her behavior that seems precocious?

(b) To what extent is Alice the obedient, polite, prim and proper model of Victorian girlhood? Does she ever break the rules of proper behavior? Does Carroll at any point reveal a critical attitude toward contemporary standards of child-rearing? How?

6. What aspects of the trial scene in the last two chapters seem most pointed as social satire? Are the satirical elements increased or decreased by Alice's naivete?

7. Psychoanalytic critics are fond of remarking that the male characters in Wonderland are generally weak and timid, dominated by the female characters. Which would you list among the "weakest" and "strongest" characters? Does your listing bear out such an interpretation? Into which category do you put Alice? Who dominates her? Whom does she dominate? Do these roles shift?

8. Is the Queen of Hearts merely a harmless blusterer, or do her actions and words hint at something more ominous?

9. A parody is defined as a composition imitating another, usually serious, work with intent to ridicule or criticize. The success of a parody depends largely on the cleverness with which the imitator has used a form similar to the original to convey an entirely different (and often irreverent) meaning. Using this definition as a point of departure, choose the one parody in *Alice* which you think is most successful, and explain why.

10. "You're nothing but a pack of cards!" Alice exclaims at the end of the story, and up to this point the reader has perhaps forgotten that most of the characters in the last four chapters are really nothing but animated playing cards. What devices has Carroll used to give them such successful animation? What is there about their actions and speech that makes them convincing? Which among them is the most fully characterized?

11. Compare the poem recited by the White Rabbit in Chapter 12 with "Jabberwocky," which appears in *Through the Looking Glass.* Does either poem finally make any kind of sense? Why might one poem make some sort of sense and the other none at all? What linguistic elements contribute to the sense or nonsense of each?

JABBERWOCKY

'T was brillig, and the slithy toves
  Did gyre and gimble in the wabe:
All mimsy were the borogoves,
  And the mome raths outgrabe.

"Beware the Jabberwock, my son!
  The jaws that bite, the claws that catch!
Beware the Jubjub bird, and shun
  The frumious Bandersnatch!"

He took his vorpal sword in hand:
  Long time the manxome foe he sought—
So rested he by the Tumtum tree,
  And stood awhile in thought.

And, as in uffish thought he stood,
  The Jabberwock, with eyes of flame,
Came whiffling through the tulgey wood,
  And burbled as it came!

One, two! One, two! And through and through
  The vorpal blade went snicker-snack!
He left it dead, and with its head
  He went galumphing back.

"And hast thou slain the Jabberwock?
  Come to my arms, my beamish boy!
O frabjous day! Callooh! Callay!"
  He chortled in his joy.

'T was brillig, and the slithy toves
  Did gyre and gimble in the wabe:
All mimsy were the borogoves,
  And the mome raths outgrabe.

12. Alice's dream and all the elements of her fantasy world are "framed" by scenes from the real world. In the beginning Alice grows drowsy and falls asleep by the river bank; in the end she is awakened by some dead leaves that have fluttered down onto her face. What relationships are there between these elements of the real world and Alice's dream world? How does Carroll explain one in terms of the other, and what devices does he use to submerge his heroine into the realm of dreams and then extract her? Do you find his transition effective? Is it at all like the experience of sleeping and waking?

13. If there is anything that can be called plot in *Alice in Wonderland* it concerns Alice's attempts to enter the beautiful garden. How does the garden look to her when she first looks at it longingly through the small door? What is it like when she finally comes to inspect it closely? What might the garden symbolize?

EXTENSIONS (1)

Puns and other forms of word-play

A professor of English is once supposed to have boasted to friends (during a five-course dinner) that he had a most unusual collection of literature. He had, he said, Burns in the kitchen, Dryden in the laundry, Lamb in the pantry, Frost in the refrigerator, and De la Mare in the barn. Whereupon one of his guests rose from the table, remarking that he had had enough and "was groaning board" as well as suffering from "authoritis." "Wait!" cried the professor, "We have not Donne!" Thereupon everybody got in his Wordsworth, and the remainder of the evening, as afterwards described by one survivor of it, was "cruel and unusual punishment."

The same verdict might be given to Chapters 9 and 10 of *Alice in Wonderland,* which contain as prickly a thicket of puns as one could hope to find anywhere in English literature.

Puns have been called the lowest form of wit. Yet among the dabblers in this form of word-play are Shakespeare and James Joyce. The tradition of the pun, in fact, has its roots in the earliest English literature (notably the Anglo-Saxon riddles), and continues to the present—John Lennon, the Liverpool musician and wit, being one of the most visible modern practitioners.

Puns are a form of word-play made technically possible by the abundance of homonyms in the English language—words which sound alike but have variant meanings (and sometimes spellings). Puns are not restricted to established vocabulary, and often make use of nonsense verbiage, portmanteau (blend) words, dialect, and other vagaries of speech. Anything is fair game in punning, so long as there is a recognizable sound (some would say unsound) connection between the double or multiple meanings. Here is an example that runs the whole gamut:

NICELY NICELY CLIVE

by John Lennon

To Clive Barrow it was just an ordinary day nothing unusual or strange about it, everything quite novel, nothing outstanley just another day but to Roger it was something special, a day amongst days . . . a red lettuce day . . . because Roger was getting married and as he dressed that morning he thought about the gay batchelor soups he'd had with all his pals. And Clive said nothing. To Roger everything was different, wasn't this the day his Mother had told him about, in his best suit and all that, grimming and shakeing hands, people tying boots and ricebudda on his car.

To have and to harm . . . till death duty part . . . he knew it all off by hertz. Clive Barrow seemed oblivious. Roger could visualise Anne in her flowing weddy drag, being wheeled up the aisle, smiling a blessing. He had butterfield in his stomarce as he fastened his bough tie and brushed his hairs. "I hope I'm doing the right thing" he thought looking in the mirror, "Am I good enough for her?" Roger need not have worried because he was. "Should I have flowers all round the spokes?" said Anne polishing her foot rest. "Or should I keep it syble?" she continued looking down on her grain haired Mother.

"Does it really matter?" repaid her Mother wearily wiping her sign. "He won't be looking at your spokes anyway." Anne smiled the smile of someone who's seen a few laughs.

Then luckily Anne's father came home from sea and cancelled the husband.

From In His Own Write by John Lennon. Copyright © 1964, 1965 by John Lennon. Reprinted by permission of Simon and Schuster, Inc., and Jonathan Cape Limited.

First cousin to the pun is the malapropism—the use of an inappropriate word which bears some similarity to the correct one. Malapropisms also have a long history; Shakespeare, for instance, delighted in making his comic characters abuse language. The prime practitioner of this form of tongue-tied derangement, and the source of its name, is Mrs. Malaprop in Richard Sheridan's play The Rivals (1775). She describes one character as being "as headstrong as an allegory on the banks of the Nile," and calls another "the pineapple of politeness." When Lewis Carroll wrote the scene in which the Mock Turtle and the Gryphon discuss their school-ing, perhaps he had this monologue by Mrs. Malaprop in mind:

MRS. MALAPROP. Observe me, Sir Anthony. I would by no means wish a daughter of mine to be a progeny of learning; I don't think so much learning becomes a young woman; for instance, I would never let her meddle with Greek, or Hebrew, or Algebra, or simony, or fluxions, or paradoxes, or such inflammatory branches of learning—neither would it be necessary for her to handle any of your mathematical, astronomical, diabolical instruments.—But, Sir Anthony, I would send her, at nine years old, to a boarding-school, in order to learn a little ingenuity and artifice. Then, sir, she should have a supercilious knowledge in accounts;—and as she grew up, I would have her instructed in geometry, that she might know something of the contagious countries;—but above all, Sir Anthony, she should be mistress of orthodoxy, that she might not misspell, and mispronounce words so shamefully as girls usually do; and likewise that she might reprehend the true meaning of what she is saying. This, Sir Anthony, is what I would have a woman know;—and I don't think there is a superstitious article in it. □

EXTENSIONS (2)

Alice and Gulliver

The scene in which Alice grows to Gargantuan proportions and finds herself wedged inside the White Rabbit's house calls to mind the scene from Jonathan Swift's *Gulliver's Travels*, when Gulliver wakes up in Lilliput. The abnormal size of both Alice and Gulliver is not the only similarity. Gulliver, like Alice, is trapped and almost totally immobilized; both are pelted with missiles, both bellow and send their captors flying; both scenes are suffused in confused action and noise.

. . . When I awaked, it was just daylight. I attempted to rise, but was not able to stir: for, as I happened to lie on my back, I found my arms and legs were strongly fastened on each side to the ground; and my hair, which was long and thick, tied down in the same manner. I likewise felt several slender ligatures across my body, from my armpits to my thighs. I could only look upwards; the sun began to grow hot, and the light offended mine eyes. I heard a confused noise about me, but in the posture I lay, could see nothing except the sky.

In a little time I felt something alive moving on my left leg, which advancing gently forward over my breast, came almost up to my chin; when bending eyes downwards as much as I could, I perceived it to be a human creature not six inches high, with a bow and arrow in his hands, and a quiver at his back. In the meantime, I felt at least forty more of the same kind (as I conjectured) following the first.

I was in the utmost astonishment, and roared so loud, that they all run back in a fright; and some of them, as I was afterwards told, were hurt with the falls they got by leaping from my sides upon the ground. However, they soon returned; and one of them, who ventured so far as to get a full sight of my face, lifting up his hands and eyes by way of admiration, cried out in a shrill, but distinct voice, "Hekina degul"; the others repeated the same words several times, but I then knew not what they meant.

I lay all this while, as the reader may believe, in great uneasiness; at length, struggling to get loose, I had the fortune to break the strings, and wrench out the pegs that fastened my left arm to the ground: for by lifting it up to my face, I discovered the methods they had taken to bind me; and, at the same time, with a violent pull, which gave me excessive pain, I a little loosened the strings that tied down my hair on the left side; so that I was just able to turn my head about two inches. But the creatures ran off a second time, before I could seize them; whereupon there was a great shout in a very shrill accent; and after it ceased, I heard one of them cry aloud, "Tolgo Phonac"; when in an instant, I felt above an hundred arrows discharged on my left hand, which pricked me like so many needles. . . . □

EXTENSIONS (3)

From REMINISCENCES OF CHILDHOOD

by Dylan Thomas

The memories of childhood have no order, and so I remember that never was there such a dame school as ours, so firm and kind and smelling of galoshes, with the sweet and fumbled music of the piano lessons drifting down from upstairs to the lonely schoolroom, where only the sometimes tearful wicked sat over undone sums, or to repeat a little crime—the pulling of a little girl's hair during geography, the sly shin kick under the table during English literature. Behind the school was a narrow lane where only the oldest and boldest threw pebbles at windows, scuffled and boasted, fibbed about their relations—

"My father's got a chauffeur."

"What's he want a chauffeur for? He hasn't got a car."

"My father's the richest man in town."

"My father's the richest man in Wales."

"My father owns the world."

And swapped gob-stoppers for slings, old knives for marbles, kite strings for foreign stamps.

The lane was always the place to tell your secrets; if you did not have any, you invented them. Occasionally now I dream that I am turning out of school into the lane of confidences when I say to the boys of my class, "At last, I have a real secret."

"What is it—what is it?"

"I can fly."

And when they do not believe me, I flap my arms and slowly leave the ground only a few inches at first, then gaining air until I fly waving my cap level with the upper windows of the school, peering in until the mistress at the piano screams and the metronome falls to the ground and stops, and there is no more time.

And I fly over the trees and chimneys of my town, over the dockyards skimming the masts and funnels, over Inkerman Street, Sebastopol Street, and the street where all the women wear men's caps, over the trees of the everlasting park, where a brass band shakes the leaves and sends them showering down on to the nurses and the children, the cripples and the idlers, and the gardeners, and the shouting boys: over the yellow seashore, and the stone-chasing dogs, and the old men, and the singing sea.

The memories of childhood have no order, and no end. □

From *Quite Early One Morning.* Copyright 1954 by New Directions Publishing Corporation. Reprinted by permission of New Directions Publishing Corporation, J. M. Dent & Sons Ltd., and the Trustees for the Copyrights of the late Dylan Thomas.

BETTMANN ARCHIVE, INC.

BIOGRAPHY

Charles Lutwidge Dodgson
1832 / 1898

While he is known today primarily as Lewis Carroll, the author of *Alice in Wonderland, Through the Looking-Glass,* and *The Hunting of the Snark,* Charles Lutwidge Dodgson was for the greater part of his life a Lecturer in Mathematics at Christ Church, one of the colleges of Oxford University. He was also a member of the Anglican clergy, though he never served a parish. He was the author of abstruse works on mathematics and logic, booklets of games and puzzles, some light poetry, and a variety of witty pamphlets on contemporary affairs at Oxford.

Shortly after the first publication of *Alice in Wonderland* in 1865, so the anecdote runs, Queen Victoria, who was delighted with the story, graciously suggested that the author might dedicate his next book to her. He did, but it was a mathematical work titled *An Elementary Treatise on Determinants.* The anecdote is challenged by at least one Carroll biographer, but it underscores the fact that Dodgson's life was almost wholly academic.

Yet there were other facets to Dodgson's donnish existence. He was an expert photographer who took exceptional portraits of children and adults at a time when photography was a new art. He was personally acquainted with Tennyson, Rossetti, Thackeray, Ruskin, and other notables of the day. He regularly walked a dozen miles before retiring. But his favorite pastime was the entertainment of young children, particularly young girls, towards whom he demonstrated strong and intensely idealistic affection. Retiring academic though he was, there was in him a vein of childlike playfulness, as on one occasion when he was invited to tea with some of his young friends. Punctual as always, attired in clerical black, he mistakenly entered the house next door where a group of elderly ladies were taking afternoon tea. He flung open the door and entered on all fours, growling, hoping to surprise the children. Realizing his mistake, he rose, bowed to the astonished ladies, and departed without a word of apology.

Alice in Wonderland grew out of Dodgson's affection for one little girl, Alice Liddell, daughter of the Dean of Christ Church. On July 4, 1862, Dodgson and a friend, the Reverend Duckworth, took three of the Liddell girls, Alice among them, boating on the river Thames. As they rowed along, Dodgson began to tell extemporaneous stories of Alice's adventures underground; at the end of the day, Alice Liddell asked him to write out the adventures for her. By the end of 1863 he had finished a hand-written copy with his own illustrations, which he presented to her. Two years later, at the urging of friends, he revised and polished the original, added several chapters, commissioned illustrations by John Tenniel, and published the story under the pen name of Lewis Carroll.

Early reviews of *Alice in Wonderland* were mixed, but it soon became popular and has not been out of print since. It represented a remarkable departure from the generally sober and moralistic children's literature of the time. Throughout the rest of his life Dodgson only grudgingly admitted his link with Lewis Carroll, writer of whimsical stories, although he continued to publish other works under that name. Alice, of course, grew up and married (she became Mrs. Hargreaves, and raised three sons), but the memory of that sunny afternoon on the river Thames remained with Dodgson to give purpose and poignancy to his stories, which he doubtless considered only a minor part of his life's work.